U

Public Policy Toward Pensions

Public Policy Toward Pensions

edited by Sylvester J. Schieber
and John B. Shoven

A Twentieth Century Fund Book

The MIT Press
Cambridge, Massachusetts
London, England

This book was set in Palatino on the Monotype "Prism Plus" PostScript Imagesetter by Asco Trade Typesetting Ltd., Hong Kong.

Printed and bound in the United States of America.

Library of Congress Cataloging-in-Publication Data

Public policy toward pensions / edited by Sylvester J. Schieber and
  John B. Shoven.
      p.   cm.
  Includes bibliographical references and index.
  ISBN 0-262-19387-6 (alk. paper)
  1. Old age pensions—United States. 2. Retirement income—United
States. 3. Baby boom generation—United States. I. Schieber,
Sylvester J. II. Shoven, John B.
HD7105.35.U6P83   1997
331.25'2'0973—dc21   97-34285
                                                    CIP

Contents

Foreword

The aging of the enormous generation known as baby boomers has set off a scramble, in both the popular press and among scholars, to assess the effects of their movement from the workforce to retirement. Most of the attention centers on political questions concerning key federal support programs for the elderly, especially Social Security, Medicare, and Medicaid. While this focus overlooks a number of vital aspects of the change in American demographics, it is likely to remain very much in the news.

The American people have been treated to a steady diet of alarming "news" about the state of their most basic pension program, the Social Security Trust Fund. But, like the rhetoric about employment, most of the concern is overblown. Social Security is currently running a surplus, and even when that runs out in about thirty years, the program would still be able to continue at 75 percent of current benefits, indefinitely. Compounding the confusion is the persistence of perhaps an even greater misunderstanding about private pensions. Although the assets of these plans have grown enormously, now totaling over $5 trillion, they still are available to less than half of American workers. Private pensions, like Social Security and Medicare, pose important public policy problems—problems that are largely ignored.

The most salient trend related to private pensions in recent years has been the shift from traditional defined benefit plans to defined contribution plans. Instead of receiving pension payments based primarily on years of service and past earnings, tomorrow's retirees will be much more dependent on accounts whose value will turn on the size of past worker contributions and investment performance. In the process, the responsibility for ensuring the security of workers' retirement also has shifted from employer (backed ultimately by government guarantees) to employee.

Inevitably this change means that workers bear more market risk, something few of them are able to either understand or manage. Interestingly, in the public sector, those who argue for privatization of Social Security are, in effect, endorsing a similar migration of the responsibility for basic social insurance from government to employees.

As discussed in this volume, the long-term consequences of the boom in defined contribution plans are far from clear. Many workers still do not have access to any sort of pension plan (about 60 percent of all workers are without plans). Those who have only a defined contribution plan as an option often lack any investment experience. At the lower end of the income scale, contributions may be less than the level required to provide for a decent retirement. Importantly, most American workers simply lack financial assets—85 percent of such assets are in the hands of the richest 10 percent of the population. In other words, the changes in retirement patterns are likely to add to the already high inequality in the United States.

The Twentieth Century Fund is pursuing a variety of projects designed to enhance understanding of various aspects of the aging of the population. Dr. Robert Butler is bringing together a group of scholars to look at life in an older America, Joseph White is examining the prospects for entitlement reform, and Theda Skocpol is exploring the issues raised by both old and young for social policy. In this volume, John B. Shoven and Sylvester J. Schieber have assembled a wide variety of essay authors to discuss pension issues. The editors' own contributions show that private pension funds face some of the same demographic stresses as the Social Security system.

The authors of these essays explore many current topics in the pension arena, including the issues raised by present governmental guarantees for private pensions and the debate about incentives for today's workers to increase their pension savings. The volume places a special emphasis on how to structure government guarantees of pensions through the Pension Benefit Guarantee Corporation and the growing significance of the rapid spread of 401(k) plans. And at the heart of all discussions about the growth of the retirement population are issues involving increased saving and increased real economic growth. Only real changes in these areas can truly affect the overall "burden" of a larger retired population.

Public Policy Toward Pensions addresses one of the most important public policy questions facing America. It will help keep public and media attention focused on the vast, unresolved set of scholarly and practical problems about the consequences of the aging of America. On behalf of the Trustees of the Twentieth Century Fund/Century Foundation, I thank all those who contributed to this ongoing debate.

Richard C. Leone, President
The Twentieth Century Fund
June 1997

Acknowledgments

We would like to express our thanks for the help of several individuals and organizations for making this volume possible. First, the authors as a group distinguished themselves, not only for producing high-quality research, but also for meeting the various deadlines that we gave them as editors. The research was conducted within the Finance Program of Stanford University's *Center for Economic Policy Research*. The staff of that organization, particularly Deborah Carvahlo, have provided superb support for this whole enterprise. Clearly, the entire research program would not have been possible without the financial and creative support of the Twentieth Century Fund. They were generous, flexible, and responsive. Similarly, Melissa Vaughn of the MIT Press has been patient, helpful, and supportive throughout the creation of this volume. Several organizations and individuals provided financial support for this effort, including the Smith Richardson Foundation, the Association of Private Pension and Welfare Plans, the U.S. Department of Labor, the Dean Witter Foundation, Barclays Global Investors, Gordon Cain, and Charles Schwab. We owe a special debt of gratitude to Rossannah Reeves of the West Coast office of the National Bureau of Economic Research and Nina Droubay of Watson Wyatt Worldwide, our administrators, who put in long hours of work into this project and prodded us to do out share.

Sylvester J. Schieber
John B. Shoven

1

The Economics of U.S. Retirement Policy: Current Status and Future Directions

Sylvester J. Schieber and John B. Shoven

It seems sensible to start a book such as this with a question: Why should you be interested in this subject? Why would someone who tries to follow the important public policy issues of the times care to become knowledgeable about pensions? Fortunately, there are fairly compelling answers to this question. One obvious reason to learn something about public and private pensions is that they control almost a quarter of the nation's tangible wealth—approximately $5.5 trillion at the end of 1995. To put that number in some perspective, it is of the same order of magnitude as the value of all the residential real estate in the country. To paraphrase Willie Sutton, the infamous New York state bank robber, you should be interested in pensions "because that's where the money is."

It is not only that pensions control a tremendous amount of money that makes them interesting and important right now. They also are the source of most of the current saving in the United States, are a crucial component of household retirement resources, and significantly affect labor market mobility and efficiency. The tax treatment of pensions has been changed frequently in recent years, and this treatment is still considered by the federal government as the biggest tax preference of them all.

We think pension policy will emerge as one of the next decade's key issues simply because of the pressures the retirement of the post–World War II baby boomers will put on our society. This tremendously large cohort stressed the K–12 education systems in the 1950s, higher education in the 1960s, and labor and housing markets in the 1970s. It takes no great forecasting ability to predict that this same cohort will similarly affect markets in the first three or four decades of the next century. In retirement, we can reliably predict that they will be decumulating pension assets (rather than accumulating them) and will also probably be gradually divesting themselves of housing. The Social Security system will be under pressure as never before, and it is already clear it will require major changes to remain solvent.

In this brief preamble, we cannot provide all the motivations for reading the volume. However, we hope the system's enormous financial size, the complexity of existing government regulations involving pensions, and the importance of pensions for national saving and investment are reason enough to want more information about this subject.

Historical Growth of Private Pensions

Although pensions have existed in the United States almost as long as the country itself (pensions were offered to disabled Revolutionary War veterans), they have emerged as important institutions covering a nontrivial proportion of the population only since World War II. Veterans of each major war were offered pensions, and gradually military pensions were extended to those who had long careers in the service regardless of whether they were war veterans. In 1907 Andrew Carnegie set up a fund to provide retirement income for college and university professors in the United States. When it became clear that even Carnegie's resources were going to be insufficient for the job, the Teachers Insurance Annuity Association (TIAA) was established in 1921. At about the same time (1920), the federal government established the Civil Service Retirement System. Private pension funds' tax advantages were established in the 1920s, but private pensions did not begin to grow noticeably until the late 1940s: Perhaps people didn't have the luxury of worrying about retirement during the Great Depression and the war, although, of course, Social Security was established in 1935.

The growth of pensions in the last 50 years or so has been nothing short of spectacular: 659 pension plans qualified for tax-preferred status with the IRS in 1939; by 1975 the number of plans had grown to 311,000; and there are more than 700,000 plans today. The portion of the workforce participating in pension plans grew from a very small percentage in the 1940s to roughly 50% by the early 1970s. Over the last 15 years, however, participation rates have remained relatively stable. Perhaps most dramatic of all has been the growth of the financial assets in pension funds. As figure 1.1 shows, pension assets accounted for approximately 2% of national wealth in 1950, in contrast to 24% in 1993. Pension assets have grown more rapidly than any other form of wealth, including home values, corporate net worth, life insurance reserves, and the like. Pension assets in 1994 approximated the value of the entire New York Stock

Percent

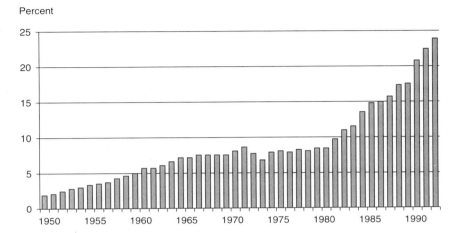

Figure 1.1
Pension assets as a percentage of national wealth
Source: Authors' calculations based on Federal Reserve Flow of Funds Balance Sheets.

Exchange. Because pensions hold a diversified portfolio of assets (stocks, bonds, and real estate, for instance), they do not own all the common stock on the NYSE. However, collectively they have tremendously large positions and assume considerable responsibility for governing American corporations. Even individually, pensions are often the largest shareholder of some of the country's biggest companies. The largest pension fund, Teachers Insurance and Annuity Association College Retirement Equities Fund (TIAA-CREF), holds an extremely diversified stock portfolio and as a result owns about 1.5% of the stock of each of the largest 1,000 or so companies in the economy. Any way you look at it, pension funds are now enormous institutions. Perhaps partly for that reason they are one of the country's most highly regulated entities.

Pension Plan Regulation

Prior to 1974, no single law or group of laws regulated the operations of private pensions in the United States. In 1974, the passage of the Employee Retirement Income Security Act (ERISA) significantly changed that situation. While 1974 changed the regulation of employer-sponsored plans significantly, a variety of regulatory provisions date back to much earlier times. In 1921, the Revenue Act eliminated the taxation of income at the time it was earned from employer-sponsored stock bonus and profit-sharing plans established by employers for their workers. By administrative ruling, pension trusts were also accorded preferential tax treatment, and the 1926 Revenue Act permitted reasonable deductions in excess of contemporaneously accruing liabilities. The 1926 act made past service credits employers provided to workers participating in their plans tax-deductible. Until 1938, retirement plans set up by employers were revocable, which allowed plan sponsors to set up and fund their retirement plans during profitable periods and revoke them during unprofitable ones. The 1938 Revenue Act required that retirement trusts exclusively benefit employees covered under the plans until all plan obligations were met.

Pension regulations until the early 1940s allowed plan sponsors to offer benefits selectively to their workers. The 1942 Revenue Act and amendments to it in the 1954 Internal Revenue Code precluded plan sponsors from discriminating in favor of shareholders, officers, supervisors, and highly compensated individuals with respect to coverage, benefits, and financing of plan operations. At this time the tax code also began to address concerns about these plans' tax revenue implications and to limit the deductibility of contributions. Between the passage of these two significant pieces of legislation, the Internal Revenue Service developed a substantial body of regulations and rulings to accomplish the goals of the 1942 act. In many regards, this initial body of regulations and rulings was the precursor to the far more voluminous body of regulations the IRS has promulgated in the modern environment with which plans must now comply.

In 1958 Congress passed the Federal Welfare and Pension Plans Disclosure Act to provide participants with sufficient information to detect instances of improprieties in plan administration. It also allowed participants certain legal rights to seek protection under the plan in accordance with state and federal laws. Mainly, however, this act and amendments to it in 1962 aimed to protect plan assets rather than employee rights.

ERISA significantly changed both the scope and nature of the regulatory environment surrounding pension plan operations. ERISA was adopted to assure retirement assets' widespread and equitable delivery through employer-sponsored retirement plans. It established participation and vesting requirements to assure that workers would be included in the plans, funding requirements to make sure money was laid aside to provide for the benefits being offered, disclosure requirements to keep participants informed of the state of plans' operations, and fiduciary requirements to make sure the plans were properly administered with the participants' interests being properly represented. ERISA also amended the requirements for plans to be "tax qualified." It set minimum and maximum funding standards for plan sponsors to meet. It laid out standards and qualifications for actuaries who perform the necessary valuations of plan liabilities and assets. These actuaries determine the periodic contributions made to plans to keep them in compliance with the law and certify the appropriateness of the underlying assumptions used in developing the disclosure reports submitted to the government. ERISA also established the Pension Benefit Guaranty Corporation (PBGC) to provide pension benefit insurance for plan participants when plan sponsors go bankrupt or can no longer maintain their plans because of financial considerations.

The regulatory environment controlling pensions over the decades leading up to ERISA's passage had evolved steadily. For example, the regulatory environment that developed out of the 1942 Revenue Act took more than a decade to evolve. Likewise, the development of ERISA itself took place over a full decade with widespread input from virtually all groups with an interest in the legislation. After ERISA's passage, many plan sponsors felt somewhat burdened by the new requirements resulting from the law, but with the exception of some of the smaller plans affected, the overwhelming majority of workers covered by the new pension requirements continued their coverage under their pre-ERISA plans. Though some plans terminated during ERISA's phase-in, by the end of the decade the number of both defined-benefit and defined-contribution plans was again increasing.

Although most people would point to ERISA as the piece of legislation passed in 1974 that most significantly changed the pension world, it was not the only significant development for pensions that year, which also marked the passage of the Congressional Budget and Impoundment Control Act of 1974. Between them, these acts radically changed the deliberative process by which pension legislation was developed. The budget act was important because it heightened government policy makers' sensitivity to the value of the tax incentives accorded pensions. ERISA was particularly important because it resulted in congressional tax committees wresting control of retirement policy development away from the labor committees, which previously had much greater jurisdictional control over retirement policy deliberations, including the development of ERISA itself.

The forces that were to combine these two laws into a powerful driver of retirement policy reached critical mass in the early 1980s shortly after the passage of the Economic Recovery Tax Act of 1981. In slightly more

than a decade we saw the passage of the Tax Equity and Fiscal Responsibility Act (TEFRA) of 1982; the Social Security Amendments of 1983;
the Deficit Reduction Act (DEFRA) and Retirement Equity Act (REA)
of 1984; the Tax Reform Act (TRA), the Single-Employer Pension Plan
Amendments Act, and the Amendments to the Age Discrimination in
Employment Act in 1986; the Omnibus Budget Reconciliation Act of
1987 (OBRA87); the Technical and Miscellaneous Revenue Act of 1988
(TAMRA); the Omnibus Budget Reconciliation Act of 1989 (OBRA89);
the Omnibus Budget Reconciliation Act of 1990 (OBRA90) and the Older
Workers' Benefit Protection Act of 1990; the Unemployment Compensation Amendments (UCA) of 1992; and the Omnibus Budget Reconciliation Act of 1993 (OBRA93) and the Family and Medical Leave Act
(FMLA) of 1993. Virtually all these measures contained provisions that
affected employer-sponsored retirement plans in some way.

Most of the legislation affecting pensions that evolved during the 1980s
and early 1990s was developed in a much shorter time than previous legislation. In many cases the plan sponsor or participant community had
little input in the deliberations about the legislative changes. These legislative measures still pursued traditional retirement policy goals, benefit
security and equitable benefit distribution, but these goals often took a
back seat to heightened concerns about increasing tax revenues and eliminating tax abuses perceived to exist under many plans. All this legislation
and the voluminous administrative regulations accompanying it naturally
increased the complexity of the requirements for establishing and maintaining plans significantly. As sponsorship of plans became more complex,
the cost of establishing and maintaining them rose accordingly.

In 1975 there were 103,000 private-sector tax-qualified defined-benefit
plans in operation. Year by year this number increased to 175,000 plans
in 1982. In 1983 the number of private-sector defined-benefit plans held
steady at the 1982 level, but it began to decline thereafter until only
132,000 remained in 1989. From 1983 to 1989, the number of participants
whose primary plan was a private-sector defined-benefit plan declined
from 30 to 27 million workers. Defined-contribution plans fared differently. The number of those plans grew from 208,000 in 1975 to 419,000
in 1982. Between 1982 and 1989, however, the number of plans kept on
growing, reaching 599,000 in the latter year. Overall participation in
these plans grew from 25 to 36 million between 1982 and 1989, but the
number of participants whose defined-contribution plan was their primary
retirement plan grew from 8 million in 1982 to 15 million in 1989. In

chapter 5, James Poterba points out that the difference in the overall growth of participation in defined-contribution plans and the growth in defined-contribution plans as the primary retirement plan resulted from the creation and expansion of 401(k) plans as secondary plans.

Smaller and middle-sized firms accounted for the majority of the decline in the number of defined-benefit plans and participation in them, a decline largely caused by the change in the administration cost. Ippolito (1990) has shown that the difference in the costs of administering a defined-benefit versus a defined-contribution plan is heavily skewed toward the smaller plans. For example, he found that a defined-benefit plan with 10,000 active participants in 1986 would have cost the employer $30.46 per capita more to administer than a defined-contribution plan. The difference in administering these two types of plans for a firm covering 15 employees would have been $463.07 per capita. These plans' administrative costs in 1986 were about one-and-a-half times what they were in 1981 for the larger plan and more than four times what they were for the smaller, with most of the difference attributable to the increased costs of plan administration related to regulatory compliance. Although the increased costs of regulatory compliance were a significant factor in the relative desirability of one type of plan over the other for many employers, the overall costs of compliance undoubtedly limited some employers' willingness to set up any plan at all. The tax legislation and regulations that came out of the 1980s and early 1990s resulted in a limiting of the availability of certain kinds of benefits for some workers and elimination of the availability of benefits altogether for others. This was a far different result than the outcomes related to the earlier pension initiatives leading up to and including the passage of ERISA, whose impetus had mostly been to encourage ever-expanding coverage. The motivation for this change in legislative approach can be traced back to the passage of ERISA and the budget act in 1974 and the accumulation of unprecedented federal deficits during the 1980s.

Preferential Tax Treatment of Employer-Sponsored Plans

In market economies throughout the world, governments wishing to encourage employers to establish voluntary retirement programs generally offer preferential tax treatment for their plans or the participants in them. In the United States, employer contributions to retirement programs are deductible expenses at the time the contributions are made as long as the plans meet tax-qualifying criteria regarding their operations and the contributions are within specified limits. Although the contributions are deductible to the employer, neither the contributions nor the investment earnings on the accumulated assets are taxable to the plan participants until benefits are paid. The net effect is that contributions to the plans are made with pre-tax dollars that then accumulate returns that are not taxed on a year-to-year basis until benefits are distributed. Although this is the "American way" of encouraging employers to establish a pension program for their workers, Dilnot (1994) points out that other governments around the world offer somewhat different tax incentives encouraging the establishment of pension plans that ultimately have the same effect as those implemented in the United States.

Since 1913, the federal government has depended on the personal income tax for a significant portion of its revenues. In the administration of the income tax, regular income is taxed in the year earned. If a worker saves some of his or her regular income outside of a tax-qualified retirement plan, such saving can be accomplished only with post-tax dollars. The returns on many forms of savings are taxed in the year in which they are earned. In chapter 2, Robert Clark and Elisa Wolper demonstrate the economic value the preferential tax treatment of employer-sponsored retirement plans renders to their participants. The extent to which pension plans are accorded preferential tax treatment is the measure of the government's significant commitment to these endeavors, which has become somewhat controversial in recent years.

For the past 40 years, discussion has been ongoing in the United States about tax preferences in the federal income tax system and the implied loss in federal income tax revenues that arises because of them. The actual budgetary measures of the value of the resulting lost federal revenues have come to be called "tax expenditures." In the parlance of federal budgeteers, tax expenditures are revenues the government does not collect because the tax code does not treat certain forms of income as regular income or because certain consumption expenditures are treated as deductible expenses in calculating income tax liabilities.

A series of federal deficits in fiscal 1982 through 1994 higher than over any comparable time in U.S. history has highlighted the losses in federal tax revenues attributed to tax preferences in recent years. Tax expenditures attributed to employer-sponsored retirement plans are the largest of all tax expenditure categories, at an estimated $54 billion in fiscal 1994. As federal deficits have mounted there has been a growing clamor to cut back on a variety of government expenditure programs or to raise federal income tax rates. Advocates of specific spending programs argue there is no inherent difference between a program that requires direct government outlays to certain segments of society and one that allows other segments of society to avoid the application of the statutory tax rates on regular income. Advocates of low tax rates argue that preferences in the tax code distort taxpayer economic behavior and that tax rates higher than they would otherwise be if the tax preferences did not exist at all magnify these distortions. These concerns in some analysts' minds suggest the elimination of the tax preferences afforded employer-sponsored retirement plans. For example, Munnell (1989, 49) argued: "In an era of large budget deficits and a future that includes the rising costs of an aging society, it is difficult to understand why such a large source of potential revenue is allowed to go untapped."

Munnell's argument, although directed toward eliminating the federal tax preferences currently afforded employer-sponsored retirement plans, also contains the seed of the argument for extending these tax incentives and possibly even expanding them. In the statement's initial clause, she focuses on the large budget deficits we are now incurring. The arguments for curtailing retirement plan tax preference have been built for the most part around this short-term focus.

Later in the same clause, Munnell focuses on the "rising costs of an aging society." The die has already been cast on the demographics of our baby boom generation and the demands it will place on our retirement income security system. We might be able to change the baby boomers' retirement plans somewhat at the margins by increasing retirement ages or reducing their retirement benefit expectations slightly. It is unlikely, however, that we might be able to or even want to generate revolutionary new attitudes completely curtailing workers' desires to retire prior to the onset of significant physical or mental limitations that often accompany older ages. If we cannot eliminate workers' desire to retire and if we are facing a particularly heavy demand on our retirement system beginning in approximately 15 years and lasting as much as 40 or 50 years beyond that, we must not lose sight of our longer-term horizons.

Since the early 1980s, public policy affecting employer-sponsored retirement plans has been largely based on short-term considerations of the tax incentives they enjoy and the tax expenditures attributed to them. However, as Clark and Wolper point out, several fundamental criticisms can be directed at the basic concept of tax expenditures as it applies to employer-sponsored retirement plans. In addition, the ways of measuring tax expenditures that arise because of the preferences accorded retirement programs have come to be questioned. More important than the issues surrounding the tax expenditures accorded pensions, however, are a host of other longer-term policy considerations that largely have been ignored over the last 10 to 15 years.

Fundamentally, the federal government's historical commitment to retirement plans has emanated from a concern about its older citizens' retirement income security. Though the fiscal implications of the early tax incentives for employer plans might not have been fully appreciated, there is no evidence that the government did not hope to encourage the broad distribution of retirement benefits with their establishment. Early in the history of tax preferences for pensions, the government exercised its regulatory control in assuring that benefits arising under employer plans be distributed to more than officers and directors of the sponsoring organizations. If there was any confusion about the government's wish to provide for retiree economic security prior to 1935, the passage of the Social Security Act in that year eliminated it.

In 1965, the Older Americans Act was passed, which specified as its first goal that the nations' older citizens should be able to enjoy "an adequate income in retirement in accordance with the American standard of living." Although it did not specify what resources might be required to assure such a standard of living, the passage of this law closely corresponded to the development of governmental measures of minimal adequacy in 1965 that came to be adopted as the official poverty line in the United States in 1969. The act ultimately led the President's Commission on Pension Policy in 1981 to suggest that above minimal needs, the adequacy of retirement income should be judged against preretirement disposable-income levels.

In 1974, with ERISA's passage, the government again clarified its commitment to retirement security of workers covered by employer-sponsored plans. As previously noted, ERISA imposed new participation and vesting standards on plans, required that promised benefits be funded as they accrued, and established the PBGC to assure that promised benefits would be paid up to the guaranteed levels. Even as late as 1978, with the establishment of the section 401(k) provisions in the tax code, Congress was expanding the availability of plan options.

In 1981 Congress passed President Ronald Reagan's proposed tax cuts as part of the Economic Recovery Act. The first year of the three-year tax cut made it clear that it had thrown the relationship between federal revenues and expenditures badly out of balance. The Reagan administration responded by proposing a number of expenditure program reductions, including reductions to Social Security's disability and early retirement programs. The general public and Congress were quite hostile to the Reagan proposals, with the Social Security proposals being voted down 99 to 0 in the Senate. Although the Reagan proposals were not popular, Congress felt compelled to address the fiscal imbalances wrought by the reduction in tax rates begun in 1981.

In hearings before the House Ways and Means Committee, Representative Charles Rangel (D-NY) argued that if we needed to reduce retirement program expenditures to bring the federal budget back into balance, we should be willing to look toward the tax expenditures accorded highly compensated individuals if we were willing to consider cutbacks in Social Security. These and similar hearings in the Senate ultimately led in 1982 to TEFRA, the first in a series of legislative measures passed over the next 11 years aimed at restricting tax benefits accorded employer-sponsored retirement plans. The deliberations on virtually every one of these measures focused much more intensely on the budgetary implications of the laws affecting pensions than on the proposals' long-term retirement policy implications.

Although tax policy considerations took the upper hand in the development of pension policy during the 1980s, other considerations did not disappear completely. As the decade began to unfold, it became increasingly clear that participation in employer-sponsored plans had plateaued and possibly was beginning to fall. The legislative and regulatory response was to implement new coverage and discrimination requirements that compelled employers offering plans to make the benefits more widely available within their workforces. As the measures to limit the tax expenditures flowing to pension plans increasingly limited what employers could put into their retirement plans, the PBGC became increasingly aware that inadequate funding of defined-benefit plans was exposing the federal government to large unfunded liabilities in a subset of the pension universe.

As we have moved into the 1990s it is becoming increasingly clear that our commitments to our major retirement vehicles are insufficient to guarantee today's workers the benefits that current generations of retirees have come to enjoy and that current workers expect will be available to them. This imbalance between workers' expectations and program ability to deliver on those expectations suggests it is time to step back and balance the short-term budgetary considerations raised by our retirement system against the longer-term claims that must be met. The sooner such rebalancing takes place, the longer the baby boom generation will have to adjust to the more realistic retirement options they will face.

Coverage under Employer-Sponsored Retirement Plans

Pension participation rates have been a major concern of policy makers for more than 15 years. In some regards, the concerns about pension participation are merely an extension of the policy conflicts discussed in the previous section between the short-term desires to minimize tax preferences accorded pensions and the long-term desires to effectively provide for the retirement security of current and future generations of workers. For nearly 25 years after the end of World War II, pension participation climbed steadily. Then in the early 1970s, participation rates in employer-sponsored retirement plans generally stabilized. Between 1972 and 1979, participation rates for all nonagricultural wage and salary workers grew from about 48% to 50% according to *Current Population Surveys* of pension participation periodically conducted by the Bureau of the Census for the Department of Labor. By 1983, pension participation rates had fallen back to the 1972 level. They remained at 48% when measured in 1988 and had climbed slightly to 50% again in 1993.

Tax equity considerations raise concerns among some policy analysts about the participation rates. They criticize the tax preferences accorded pensions on the grounds that the income tax system does not treat all workers the same. Workers who participate in pension plans and ultimately qualify for benefits pay less taxes during their lives than workers with similar earnings patterns who do not qualify for benefits. Furthermore, analysis of pension program participation indicates lower-wage workers are far less likely to partake of the tax benefits accorded employer-sponsored plans than are higher-wage workers. The extent to which similarly situated individuals do not benefit similarly from the tax preferences raises horizontal-equity issues. The extent to which higher-wage workers get greater tax incentives from participating in pensions than lower-wage workers raises vertical-equity issues.

Other policy analysts are concerned about levels of participation in employer-sponsored plans because of the implications for future generations of retirees' retirement security prospects. Retirees depend on three major sources of income to meet their consumption needs: Social Security, personal saving, and employer-sponsored retirement plans. Social Security is the fundamental underpinning of most workers' retirement system, but it was not designed and has never been considered sufficient to meet reasonable standards of income adequacy for the overwhelming majority of workers in the economy. For lifetime, low-wage workers, Social Security provides relatively high replacement of preretirement earnings. But even with high replacement rates, Social Security is inadequate for low-wage workers because it leaves them in a permanent state of poverty in their retirement years. For workers with higher lifetime wages, Social Security replaces a relatively small proportion of their preretirement earnings. Such workers might receive Social Security benefits that exceed minimalist measures of need—for example, poverty-level income—but the benefits by themselves are not nearly large enough to maintain their preretirement standards of living.

Although Social Security was never intended to provide sufficient benefits to meet most retirees' income needs, Schieber and Shoven's chapter 7 analysis of financing projections from the Social Security Administration suggests that the program will not meet even the benefit promises implied by current law for many future retirees now working their way through their careers. If Social Security as it is currently configured is inadequate to meet the retirement needs of most if not all workers across the income spectrum, and if even the current benefit promises are in some doubt of being delivered, then personal saving and employer-sponsored retirement plans take on heightened importance.

The problem with personal saving in American society is that it is simply insufficient. Between the end of World War II and the early 1980s, the U.S. saving rate averaged around 7% of gross domestic product (GDP). In the early 1980s, the saving rate plummeted. In the early 1990s, it averaged less than 1% per year. Part of this decline has resulted from the federal deficit's growth since 1980, but the decline in personal saving by consumers has played an equally important role. If Social Security benefits cannot alone assure adequate retirement incomes, and personal saving rates have been falling, employer-sponsored retirement programs take on an increasingly important role. In this context, the stabilization of the pension coverage rates over the past two decades has been most disconcerting.

Given the stable levels of pension participation at around 50% of the workforce, it is easy to jump to the conclusion that half the population will never get a pension. Such a conclusion would be wrong, because pension accruals are earned over time, and the measures of 50% participation are taken at various discrete points in time. For example, these cross-sectional pictures of pension participation catch young workers still in school working part-time without pension protection and lead to the conclusion that such workers are not benefiting adequately from the system. Such conclusions fail to consider that these young workers will mature and take on regular career employment that will ordinarily carry with it pension protection. Cross-sectional analyses catch other workers who regularly work part-time to supplement the primary breadwinner's income and lead to the conclusion that such workers also do not benefit from the pension system. In this case, the conclusions fail to consider that such part-time workers' incomes generally supplement those of someone working full-time and earning a pension. Cross-sectional analyses catch individuals still working after retirement from their main career at short-term or part-time jobs that provide no retirement plan coverage. In this case, the conclusions fail to consider that such "shadow career" workers are already getting pensions from their main career jobs. Cross-sectional analyses catch individuals in low-wage jobs that generally provide no coverage but often fail to consider that such low-wage workers cannot afford the luxury of deferring consumption (in the form of pension savings) from the current time into the future because the necessities of life fully consume current wages. Virtually every analysis of employer-based retirement plans indicates that the low levels of participation are concentrated among younger, part-time, and low-wage workers.

An alternative way to consider the pension system's effectiveness in providing protection to workers is to examine the group clearly beginning to focus on retirement. For example, in 1990 approximately 36.4 million people in the United States fell between the ages of 45 and 59. Slightly more than one-fourth of the group, 27.1 percent, were single. Considering everyone within this age bracket, 22.3 million of the 36.4 million total, or 61.3 percent, were participating in an employer-sponsored retirement plan in some way. Some were already receiving benefits; others were still participating in a plan but had not yet retired; still others were not participating directly in a plan themselves but were married to someone who was; and finally some were doing more than one of these—that is, receiving a benefit from one plan while participating in another, both participating in a plan and having a spouse participating in a plan, or some other combination of options. If the base population was narrowed to include only those already retired or those who had some record of employment over the prior year, 70.1% were included in an employer-sponsored retirement program in some fashion (Goodfellow and Schieber 1993).

Even if pension participation rates are inherently higher than critics claim they are, however, there is still reason to be concerned that they are not higher yet. Pensions themselves are a critical contributor to private and national savings, and greater participation in the plans would lead to increased national saving rates. Higher participation and greater saving would also significantly enhance the retirement income security of future generations of retirees who may dearly need such enhanced security. Although there is a great deal to feel positive about concerning employer-based retirement plans, over the past 15 years discontent has been growing about the evolution of these plans' role in our general economy and within the retirement income security system.

Impact of Pensions on National and Personal Savings

One of the fundamental problems facing the U.S. economy is its low national saving rate. The concept of national saving may not be widely understood, but fundamentally it is no different from that of household saving. A household's saving is income not consumed but rather set aside and invested. Saving is the only reliable way to add to one's wealth. At the national level, the idea is the same. National saving is national income not used for consumption. Again, the nation's saving is the only reliable way for the country's wealth to grow. The country's saving is nothing more or less than the sum of the saving of all the households plus those of businesses (which take the form of retained earnings) and those of the federal, state and local governments (i.e., their surpluses). Figure 1.2 illustrates the rate of net national saving in the United States between 1951 and 1993 relative to GDP. The figure refers to "net" saving because it is saving over and above what is necessary to offset depreciation due to the wear, tear, and obsolescence of the existing capital stock. The bars in the figure show personal saving, business saving, and government saving, while the line shows total net national saving relative to GDP. The story is both dramatic and familiar. The net national saving rate in this economy was very stable from 1951 to 1980 at approximately 7% of GDP, but it has collapsed since 1980 and in the most recent period was less than 1% of GDP. Personal saving, which includes pension accumulations, fell, as did business saving, and the government became a much larger dissaver than previously.

The actual performance of U.S. saving is even more alarming than these figures would indicate, because the appropriate saving rate is probably the amount of saving relative to national wealth or the capital stock rather than relative to one year's output. Since saving changes wealth, the ratio of saving to wealth is the sustainable rate of growth of the domestically owned capital stock. One constant economists learn early in their study of the U.S. economy is that the value of tangible assets in the United States (i.e., total national wealth) is about three times either annual national income or GDP. A national saving rate of 3% of GDP therefore translates

Savings rates (percent)

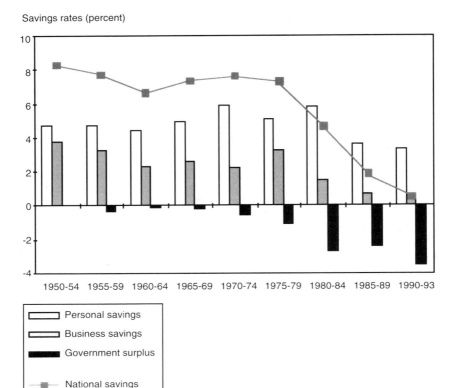

Personal savings

Business savings

Government surplus

National savings

Figure 1.2
Sectoral saving and U.S. net national saving as a percentage of gross domestic product, 1951–93
Source: Authors' calculations from the National Income and Product Accounts.

to a saving rate relative to wealth of only 1%. Even the country's population has been growing that rapidly; therefore, our saving performance has been consistent with complete stagnation in per capita wealth. Although plenty of other factors determine the growth of real wages, the very low rate of national saving almost certainly explains, at least partly, the slow rate of improvement in worker productivity and real wages in this country. Pension accumulations are a very important source of national saving as figure 1.1, which showed how pension wealth has grown to almost 25% of the nation's wealth, would suggest. In fact, one way to measure saving is simply to calculate the change in real wealth. Figure 1.3 looks at the change in the nation's real wealth and also in real pension fund assets,

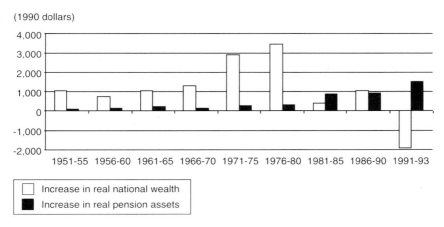

Figure 1.3
Real change in wealth deflated by gross domestic product deflator
Source: Authors' calculations from National Balance Sheets, Federal Reserve System.

both based on estimates by the Flow of Funds Division of the Federal Reserve Board. Here it appears that pension fund saving was the one type that did not collapse after 1980. In fact, most amazingly, the data show that since 1980 the growth in pension fund real wealth has been greater than the growth in the country's real wealth. In this sense, pensions have accounted for all the saving in the United States.

Even pension saving has shown some signs of weakness since 1980. Although assets have grown remarkably rapidly, much of that growth has been due to the extraordinarily high real rates of return realized on pension funds' previously accumulated financial assets. Stock and bond returns have been at historically high levels since 1982, far higher than the pension fund managers themselves had assumed. Real employer contributions to pensions, on the other hand, have fallen markedly since 1980. Figure 1.4 shows that the benefits paid from pension funds first exceeded employer contributions in 1983; by the late 1980s, benefit payments amounted to more than double employer contributions. The fact is that real employer contributions to pensions fell precisely in tandem with the other components of national saving.

Two reasons employer pension contributions fell can be immediately identified. First, more than half the assets in private pension funds back the commitments made by employers with defined-benefit plans. With this type of plan, employers promise their employees retirement annuities, with the size of the annuity payments typically determined by years of

Billions of dollars

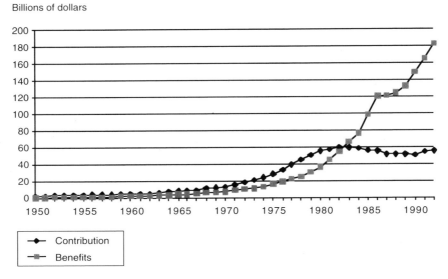

Figure 1.4
Employer contributions and benefits paid by private pension and profit-sharing plans,
1950–92
Source: National Income and Product Accounts.

service to the firm and final pay. The higher-than-expected rates of return
on plan assets realized over the last dozen or so years translates quite
directly into lower contributions. The firm is in the position of a target
saver, the target being full funding of promises made. The higher the earnings on assets, the less the firm has to put aside to reach the target. The
magnitude of this effect can be quite large. Second, a large shift has been
occurring from defined-benefit to defined-contribution and 401(k) plans,
perhaps partly triggered by the regulatory environment facing defined-
benefit plans, but the point here is that defined-benefit plans usually do
not involve employee contributions whereas defined-contribution plans
most commonly do.

The national income account measures of saving do not include gains
from stock market revaluations; rather, the measures reflect corporate
retained earnings. At least for those measures, the decline in employer
pension contributions may account for part of the depression in personal
saving rates since 1980. In an earlier study, Bernheim and Shoven (1988)
tested the target saving model of pension contributors against the data.
To a first approximation, the target saving theory says that a 1% increase
in the rate of return on assets, holding future wage trajectories constant,

decreases the necessary contribution by 35% if the average time between funding and payout is 35 years. The point here is that pension obligations are often very far in the future, and therefore their present value is very sensitive to the assumed rate of return on assets in the plan. This assumed rate of return is used as the interest rate in the discounting process to determine the present value of future annuity obligations.

The Bernheim and Shoven study performed an econometric evaluation of the determinants of pension contributions using aggregate data from 1952–82 to see whether the pension contribution evidence would confirm the target saving model's negative elasticity with respect to real interest rates. The answer was a resounding yes, with the data closely ratifying the model's predictions. In preparing this chapter, we conducted very similar econometric regressions for the 40-year period 1953–92. The real interest rate continues to be a significant and important determinant of contributions, albeit in a negative way. That is, higher real interest rates depress contributions. The effect's magnitude is large and roughly consistent with the target saving theory.

The nature of pensions has shifted since 1980 with a massive swing toward personal retirement accounts—that is, IRAs, 401(k)s, and Keogh plans—and away from traditional employer-provided defined-benefit and defined-contribution plans. In chapter 3, Steven Venti and David Wise examine this shift and consider its effect on the assets of recent retirees and those approaching retirement. The question is whether personal retirement accounts' increased availability and popularity have added to household savings and retirement resources or whether changes in other forms of personal savings have offset the enhanced contributions to these accounts.

There can be little doubt about the growth of personal retirement accounts. In 1980, contributions to these plans amounted to 7.6% of total pension contributions; by 1989, they accounted for more than half. Similarly, the balance sheets of families with heads between ages 65 and 69 show a dramatic shift. In 1984, personal retirement accounts amounted to only 6.6% of total personal financial assets; seven years later, in 1991, they amounted to 20.6% of the total.

Venti and Wise use data from the Survey of Income and Program Participation (SIPP) to examine the wealth accumulation of different age cohorts in the 1980s. Because the availability of IRAs and 401(k)s changed dramatically in the 1980s, they are able to compare younger and older cohorts which had different lengths of exposure to personal retirement savings programs. They find that the younger cohorts have accumulated much more in these vehicles than the older cohorts did at the same age mostly because of differences in the plans' availability, and that to date the extra saving that has gone into these accounts has not been significantly offset. The authors examined all possible avenues for such an offset—changes in other personal saving, accumulation of home equity and employer-provided pension plans—but none was evident in the data. The results of the Venti and Wise cohort analysis indicate that the personal retirement saving accounts will cause important increases in the elderly's overall wealth. In particular, their projections imply that the personal financial assets of the cohort that will reach age 76 in 28 years will be almost twice as large as those assets of the cohort that reached age 76 in 1991. Personal retirement account saving is clearly the one bright spot in an overall weak personal and national saving economy.

One must be cautious in generalizing results about household and pension saving to similar conclusions regarding national saving, and vice versa. Although we can document that pension saving has been crucial for aggregate saving and that aggregate saving has fallen to modern historical lows in recent years, this does not necessarily mean that private pension saving has fallen too low from the viewpoint of workers now participating in plans. To demonstrate this point, assume that workers save while working at a rate such that on the day they retire they have sufficient assets to maintain the standard of living they had achieved while working. Further assume they decumulate these assets during retirement at such a rate that on the day they die, they have fully expended all their retirement savings. Given these assumptions, it is possible to construct a variety of hypothetical cases in which net pension saving might be positive or negative, thus contributing or subtracting from net national savings in an economy, but the level of saving from the perspective of participants in pension plans is always appropriate. The key links between household saving and national saving are the population's demographic structure and the productivity growth rate.

First, consider the case of a stable society in which the distribution of retirees relative to workers is constant over time and in which the real standard of living is fixed. Because the accumulation of retirement assets by the population's working portion exactly matches the decumulation of retirement assets by its retired portion, retirement saving will have no effect over time on national saving in this economy. If there were a sudden, one-time increase in the number of workers such that the worker population's size increased relative to that of the retiree population, we would expect workers' pension asset accumulation to exceed retirees' decumulation until a new equilibrium was reasserted when the relative ratio of workers to retirees came back into balance. In this case, while the working population's relative size was surging, the pension system would be a net contributor to the national saving rate. Of course, the opposite situation could develop as well. In this case, the retiree population's size would increase relative to that of the active work force, and we might expect a net decumulation of pension assets, thus reducing national savings, while a new equilibrium between the working and retiree population evolved. In none of these cases, however, would the level of retirement savings have been inappropriate.

Within the U.S. context, some pension plans clearly may have reached the point where they are naturally net dissavers. Given the age of pension plans in many of our older, more established industries, and given the industrial reorganization occurring in segments of our economy, the number of retirees under some pension plans relative to the number of active participants has increased significantly in recent years. Although this may be occurring in selected firms, or even across some industries, it is not the case across the whole economy. Since the late 1970s, while pension contributions have been declining, the baby boom generation has been fully employed, and the number of retirement plans and the number of workers covered by them has steadily grown. In other words, although some employers' retirement plans may have matured such that they are experiencing net outflows, the whole system should not currently be at that stage given the plan age and the baby boom generation's relative size.

Indeed, in chapter 7 Schieber and Shoven document that much of the slowdown in private-employer contributions to their defined-benefit plan has been in response to federal legislation adopted over the last decade regulating pension plan funding. The pension funding laws adopted during the 1980s largely changed the perspective private employers could take in funding their pension programs. ERISA's initial provisions limited employers' tax-deductible funding of their plans based on projected benefits for workers, anticipating the future growth in their wages between the annual valuation dates and their anticipated retirement. Under the tax provisions that exist today, employers can no longer deduct contributions that anticipate future wage growth. Once the new funding rules were adopted, we moved from only about 10% of larger defined-benefit plans' being fully funded under the tax law to nearly half exceeding the reduced limits.

Employers used to be able to fund their pension plans from the perspective that they intended to operate them in perpetuity, or at least through all current workers' expected retirement. Under the new funding perspective, the plans can be funded with full deductibility only on the basis of actual contractual obligations accrued, as though the plan was going to be terminated relatively soon. This shift and the slowdown in pension funding that has resulted from it imply existing plans will become much more expensive as the baby boom participants in the plans age. Schieber and Shoven estimate contribution rates to private-employer pension plans will have to increase an average of 60% if existing plans are to deliver retirement benefits to baby boom workers that correspond to those provided to individuals eligible to retire under these plans today.

Even though pension funding has slowed in recent years, this still does not mean that private pension saving has fallen too low from the viewpoint of workers now participating in plans. The nature of the defined-benefit promise is such that actual pension funding patterns do not necessarily correspond directly to workers' perceptions about their accruing benefit rights. There has been a well-developed discussion in the economic literature on how workers value their pension rights under defined-benefit plans (see Bulow 1982; Gustman and Steinmeier 1989 and 1993; Gustman, Mitchell, and Steinmeier 1994; Mitchell and Pozzebon 1987; and Montgomery, Shaw, and Benedict 1992). Many workers likely value their accruing pensions under the assumption that their plans will be in operation throughout their remaining period of service under the plans—that is, that the plans' operations will be ongoing. In this regard, the slowdown in pension funding because of changes in the regulatory environment should have little effect on workers' perceptions about their plans' accruing value. Potentially, however, some employers may ultimately truncate or terminate their defined-benefit plans because they are unable to meet the higher future costs they will face because they have slowed their funding in recent years. Should that happen, workers who personally have been saving at a rate to augment anticipated benefits from an ongoing defined-benefit plan would find that their aggregate retirement saving will fall short of their anticipated targets because their pension benefits turn out smaller than anticipated.

The Schieber and Shoven discussion in chapter 7 pursues the issue of how demographics determine pension saving and national saving. Pensions have been contributing a great deal to national saving partly because many more individuals are in the accumulation phase of their participation than the annuity phase. The baby boom generation, which constitutes an enormous demographic bulge, is only now entering its peak earning years. It is not surprising that Social Security is running a cash flow surplus and pension assets are mounting rapidly. All this will change in another 20 to 25 years. The nation's demographics will change rapidly as the ranks of the retired swell. Public and private pension systems cannot expect to be a source of surpluses or saving at that time; in fact, just the opposite is likely to be the case. As chapter 7 describes in much greater detail, the pension system by that time could become a massive seller of assets. In this scenario, pensions would still be a major determinant of national saving; but the nature of the contribution would switch from highly positive today to negative then. It is our viewpoint that national saving should be of great concern to those interested in the U.S. economy's future and that public policy toward pensions inevitably plays an important part in any national saving program.

The Pension Benefit Guaranty Corporation

Another area of concern for public policy makers is the ongoing operation of the PBGC's pension guaranty program. ERISA established the PBGC as one of its cornerstones, an insurance program to assure that workers would not lose their accumulated pension promises if they worked for a company that went bankrupt or could no longer support its pension program. Today, the PBGC program's operation often is likened pejoratively to that of the deposit insurance program that bailed out the savings and loan industry during the late 1980s and early 1990s. Although we believe likening the PBGC situation to the savings and loan bailout is misleading and inappropriate, the PBGC program is clearly under considerable stress.

Assessment of that stress depends on a variety of factors, including whether the program is viewed from a short-term or longer-term perspective and how it is perceived as an insurance program. One view is that the PBGC is meant to insure individual defined-benefit plans against the contingencies of the plan sponsor's inability to continue to support the retirement plan. Alternatively, it is perceived as a social insurance program through which the collective body of defined-benefit plan sponsors insure against the contingency that some individual sponsors will be unable to carry on their plans. Under the latter interpretation, the need for social insurance arose because private insurance markets were unwilling, when ERISA was passed in 1974, to issue individual insurance policies to plan sponsors against the contingency of default in meeting plan obligations. In chapter 4, Carolyn Weaver of the American Enterprise Institute analyzes the current problems with the PBGC program and suggests solutions.

From the perspective of its government operators, the PBGC program's long-term viability is threatened because it is financed by a stream of premiums levied against defined-benefit plan sponsors, but the combination of current cash on hand and the expected flow of premiums is expected to be insufficient to meet the stream of future benefit obligations under the program. In setting up the PBGC, Congress did not give the agency any claim to the U.S. Treasury, so to whatever extent premiums collected to date or current premiums have fallen short of accumulated obligations, future participants in the plan will have to make up these shortfalls. As Weaver and a number of other policy analysts see the problem, this added claim on future participants in defined-benefit plans may ignite an employer exodus from this type of program.

One problem with operating the pension insurance program as a social insurance program is that employers offer defined-benefit plans voluntarily. Although large employers have shown a strong disposition toward offering defined-benefit plans, the defined-contribution plan may prove a viable substitute for many. Indeed, with the declining prevalence of defined-benefit plans among smaller employers, there clearly has already been a great shift from defined-benefit to defined-contribution plans. In an environment in which employers who have well-funded pension plans subsidize those with significantly underfunded plans, the premiums well-funded employers pay exceed the value of the insurance benefit they are receiving. Well-funded employers may derive some added company value from the incentives in defined-benefit plans that exceed the value of the incentives in having only a defined-contribution plan. In such cases, they will continue to support the defined-benefit plan as long as the extra value derived from keeping it exceeds the extra PBGC premium they have to pay. If the PBGC premium exceeds the value of the derivative benefits accruing from the defined-benefit plan, employers will likely abandon it for a defined-contribution plan.

The minimal premiums charged for the pension insurance program when first established likely put the cost of the program below the value of what even well-funded plans were receiving. But these low premiums have built up the unfunded liabilities for the PBGC and portend much higher premiums. Currently the PBGC estimates that it has accumulated unfunded liabilities of nearly $3 billion, liabilities it faces for plans it has already taken over and for which there are insufficient assets to pay all the obligations assumed. Examining assets likely to be available when potential future claims are made, the PBGC estimates its more likely exposure to unfunded obligations is in the $40–$60 billion range.

The higher premiums required to make up for past underfunding in combination with the subsidizing of unfunded plans by well-funded ones increase the likelihood some well-funded employers will shift to defined-contribution plans. Weaver points out that such a shift would likely begin a death spiral as good firms withdrew from the program because the remaining risk pool would require higher premiums, which would cause yet more well-funded firms to withdraw, which would require even higher premiums, and so on, until no plans were left in the program but badly underfunded ones. This analytical track leads many policy analysts to conclude that the pension insurance program ought to be run like a true casualty-risk insurance plan with premiums being set in accordance with the risk each plan presents to the insurer.

Opponents of financing the PBGC through risk-based premiums argue that current assets in hand are sufficient to pay benefit claims for at least the next 20 to 30 years, that the current accumulated deficit of $2.9 billion is relatively immaterial in comparison to the $2 trillion in assets that lie behind the private defined-benefit system, and the potential liabilities of $40–$60 billion are based on prognostications about several of the most prominent U.S. companies going bankrupt. Companies sponsoring underfunded retirement plans have reasonable concerns that they have obeyed all the funding and other compliance rules and that moving to a premium-based system on a short-term basis would drive them to or over the brink of financial ruin. But that does not mean the concerns about the potential for the death spiral under the program's current structure can be ignored.

Weaver points out that the abnormally low premiums the PBGC has charged up until now merely push off to the future the obligations that will have to be met if current promises are going to be delivered. Figure 4.2 shows that public policies adopted in recent years have not reduced the extent of underfunding and may actually be increasing it among those plans posing the greatest risks to the PBGC. In addition, these policies have reduced the amount of overfunding among well-funded plans. One can tie her analysis to the earlier discussion about the conflicts between federal policies focused on minimizing these retirement plans' cost in a short-term fiscal context while attempting to maximize their effectiveness in providing retirement income security in a long-term sense. The short- and long-term strategies being pursued by the government in the case of the PBGC and other facets of retirement policy are simply incompatible.

Weaver advocates separating the PBGC's current insurance function from its transfer function. She argues that it does not make economic sense to have back-door industrial policy being made through a scheme of penalties and subsidies established and operated as a pension insurance program in which only some companies participate and in which companies are often forced to subsidize their own competitors. Weaver would shift the transfer function now handled through PBGC premiums to transfers funded through general-revenue financing. The governmental financing for badly funded plans, though, would come at a cost of some restrictions on the plans' sponsors, including strict standards on funding, asset allocation, increases in insured benefits, and reporting and monitoring.

Weaver would move PBGC's insurance function to private insurance markets. She acknowledges that the private markets were not willing to take on this risk when ERISA was passed in 1974 but argues that a number of things have changed over the intervening 20 years. Since that time, she argues, we have a record of claims experience that did not exist then, the insured event is no longer under the plan sponsors' exclusive control, and we now have large, sophisticated financial markets that could take on the risks involved with well-developed secondary insurance markets to support that role.

Weaver's prescription for improving the insurance of private pensions, though clearly worthy of careful consideration and further research, does not seem to solve all the problems, and many details would have to be attended to before implementing the plan. Determining the boundary between which plans general revenues would subsidize and which would be forced to purchase private risk-based insurance would undoubtedly be complicated, and almost certainly some plan providers would face unfortunate incentives in the process. For example, one can easily imagine a situation where it is in a company's interest to underfund its plan sufficiently to be classified as one needing a government transfer. Weaver asserts that private insurers would find insuring the bulk of private pension plans an attractive market, but this cannot be known with certainty. The whole concept of funding guaranteed benefits with risky investments, then insuring the entire operation to make it safe to the participant, is highly dubious. The failed experiment with private portfolio insurance in the October 1987 stock market crash is enough to give one pause regarding the feasibility of private insurance guaranteeing pension plans' portfolio adequacy. This raises the question of who insures the insurers. If the country experienced catastrophic financial-market returns similar to those in the Great Depression, either workers would find their private insurance failed, or the government would find it was still guaranteeing benefits after all. Finally, once employers face realistic risk-based premiums on their defined-benefit pension funds, they may decide to drop such plans in favor of simpler, safer and cheaper (from their point of view) defined-contribution plans. The move toward defined-contribution plans would likely continue and perhaps even accelerate. We raise these cautions not to reject Weaver's plan, but only to highlight that much work needs to be done before it can be seriously considered for implementation.

One aspect of Weaver's analysis and conclusions parallels those in the other chapters of this volume. It seems clear that legislation developed over the last 20 years intended to improve workers' retirement income security has increased the cost of operating plans for most plan sponsors, especially defined-benefit plans. The net result has been a marked decrease in the likelihood of defined-benefit plans' being offered. Some people may prefer the defined-contribution plans that already have been substituted for defined-benefit plans or that will be if the trends of the last 15 years continue. But many do not. To the extent that government policy rather than workers' and employers' tastes is driving these trends, it has not contributed to the efficient operation of the employer-based retirement system.

The Impact of 401(k) Plans

One type of pension plan—known by its section of the tax code, 401(k) —has enjoyed explosive growth in the past decade or so. These plans first became available in 1978, but their use did not become widespread until the Treasury Department issued some clarifying regulations in late 1981. In 1983 there were 1,700 such plans in the country with 4.4 million participants, whereas by 1989 there were more than 83,000 plans and 17.3 million participants. The number of plans and participants in conventional defined-benefit and defined-contribution programs was either flat or declining at the same time. Most impressively of all, by 1989 the dollar level of contributions to 401(k) plans ($46.1 billion) exceeded the contributions to either defined-benefit plans ($29.9 billion) or conventional defined-contribution plans ($34.0 billion). Because of the new prominence of 401(k) plans among retirement income vehicles, two chapters in this book deal with them.

Chapter 5, by James Poterba of MIT, describes the structure of the 401(k) plans, documents their phenomenal growth, and examines the determinants of workers' choice whether to participate if their employer offers a plan. Finally, and perhaps most importantly, it asks whether 401(k) plans have displaced other pension plans and whether the contributions added to 401(k) accounts amount to new saving or whether they have displaced saving in other forms.

Section 401(k) plans are similar to other defined-contribution plans, with several attractive and key differences. Typically, with a 401(k) plan, employees make tax-deductible contributions to one or more funds—a money market fund, a bond fund, and a common stock fund are usually offered. Frequently, but not universally, employers offer to match employee contributions to some degree. Some employers contribute one dollar for every four contributed by employees; others match dollar for dollar or even more. Section 401(k) plans offer hardship withdrawals before retirement, and many offer loan provisions to allow participants to borrow some fraction of their accumulated assets, again before retirement.

The available evidence shows that employees are more likely to participate if the employers match their contributions, but that the participation rate is not very sensitive to the match's generosity, although this does influence the size of employee contributions. By 1991, the overall participation rate among employees who had the option to have a 401(k) plan was 71%. Given that roughly 35% of the wage and salary workforce had 401(k) plans at their workplace, this means that about 25% of all workers between the ages of 25 and 65 who are not self-employed have a 401(k) plan. Another important finding regarding 401(k) participation is that contributions show a remarkable persistence. Among those who stay at the same firm, more than 99% of those who contribute in one year contribute the following year.

Poterba's findings, buttressed by considerable previous research, on whether 401(k) contributions represent a net addition to personal saving are of central importance. Poterba reaches two basic conclusions. First, the growth of 401(k) plans is not responsible for the weak growth or even shrinkage of other forms of retirement plans. That is, 401(k) plans did not crowd out other pension plans. Second, thee is no evidence of substitution between 401(k) contributions and other forms of saving. Poterba concludes that 401(k) pension contributions represent new, incremental household saving. The immaturity of the 401(k) plans means there are very few retirement withdrawals from these plans, and therefore they contribute significantly to aggregate personal saving. It should be noted that other studies reach the opposite conclusion (see Engen, Gale, and Scholz 1996).

Considerable concern has been expressed about those eligible to participate in 401(k) plans who do not sign up for them. Are they making a big mistake, and are they likely to be impoverished in their old age? How do their financial profiles compare to those of participants? How do their financial circumstances compare to those who work for organizations that do not offer 401(k) plans? And what would be the impact of mandating a minimum level of participation for those workers whose employers offer 401(k) plans? Andrew Samwick and Jonathan Skinner answer these questions in detail in chapter 6, but we summarize their findings here. First, almost half of today's workers currently have no pension plan other than Social Security; at least within the context of their current jobs, they have no option of an employment-based pension plan. Those who could have a 401(k) plan but choose not to participate amount to slightly less than 10% of the workforce, but more than three-fourths of these participate in a conventional pension plan. All told, then, less than 2% of the workforce choose not to participate in a 401(k) and as a result have no pension plan at all. Samwick and Skinner conclude that it probably makes more sense to worry about the portion of the workforce that is offered no pension plan than about the 2% of the workforce offered a 401(k) who decline it.

Samwick and Skinner also find that those who decline 401(k) participation and have no basic pension plan are better off financially than those whose jobs offer no plan at all. Not surprisingly, those who have the most financial assets have both a primary pension plan and a supplemental 401(k) plan. The authors find that mandating participation with minimum contribution rates of 3 or 5% would make a difference only for those at the bottom of the distribution of pension benefits, and the difference it would make is fairly small. Once again, our conclusion from their work is that mandated, pension participation should be required for all full-time workers, not just those whose jobs currently offer pension benefits.

Samwick and Skinner also examine how 401(k) participants use the lump sum distributions they often receive when they switch jobs. They estimate that only about half the lump sum distributions are rolled over into tax-sheltered retirement accounts such as IRAs. The other half finance a huge variety of consumption and investment expenditures ranging from vacations and home improvement projects to college educations and automobile purchases. The failure of half the recipients to reinvest the money distributed may concern those interested in retirement income security or national saving. Samwick and Skinner examine the potential impact on retirement resources of a mandatory minimum 50 percent rollover of distributions into other pension vehicles. Their simulations find that such a policy has substantially more potential for increasing retirement resources than requiring those currently offered 401(k) plans to participate. The larger pensions resulting from mandatory partial rollovers would be spread throughout the distribution of pension annuities, rather than just concentrated at the tail as in the case of mandatory participation.

The two chapters on 401(k) plans lead us to conclude that they are a wildly popular innovation among retirement plans. Further consideration should be given to restricting the use of distributions made when workers terminate their jobs. Similarly, a review of policies on loan provisions and the use of hardship withdrawals might be appropriate. Although neither chapter discusses this issue, the public appears poorly informed and educated regarding the asset allocation choices 401(k) plans offer, and public policy may have a role in addressing this problem. If anything, participants seem to err on the side of excess conservatism in their frequent choices of money market instruments and Guaranteed Investment Contracts (GICs) in preference to stocks. Historical experience suggests stocks have almost always been the better retirement investment (see MaCurdy and Shoven 1992).

The 75-Year Outlook for Private Pensions

It is widely accepted that the retirement of the baby boom generation will strain Social Security's finances tremendously. In fact, Social Security is the only government spending program that annually examines its financial outlook 75 years into the future. In the early 1980s, Social Security's retirement trust fund was almost depleted. The system was amended comprehensively in 1983, including changes in immediate and future increases in the payroll tax rate and delayed increases in the age of normal retirement. One practical result of the 1983 reforms was that the baby boom generation's Social Security benefits would be partially prefunded if things worked out as planned, thereby reducing the pressure on the system during their retirement period. After the 1983 Social Security amendments, system actuaries projected that the retirement and disability trust fund would grow from $27.5 billion at that time to a staggering $20.7 trillion in 2045. Even more reassuring was the finding that these trust funds would remain solvent until 2063 when the trailing edge of the baby boomers would be 99. It certainly sounded like the system had been fixed for the long run.

As figure 1.5 shows, the future doesn't look so promising in 1996. In the latest forecast, the trust fund will peak at $2.5 trillion in roughly 2020, rather than $21 trillion around 2045. The retirement and disability trust funds are now projected, if the program is not modified, to be exhausted in 2029, when the youngest baby boomers will be turning 65 and just beginning their retirements. The assumptions of the 1983 long-run forecast were clearly far too optimistic, and another round of significant pro-

Billions of dollars

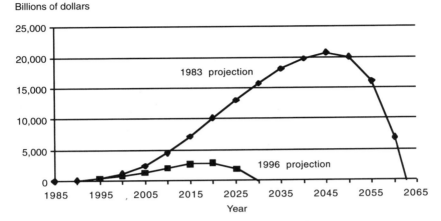

Figure 1.5
Projected OASDI trust fund accumulations (in current dollars by year of estimate)
Source: Harry C. Ballantyne, "Long-Range Projections of Social Security Trust Fund Operations in Dollars," Social Security Administration, *Actuarial Notes* (October 1983), no. 117, p. 2, and *1996 Annual Report of the Board of Trustees of the Federal Old-Age and Survivors Insurance and Disability Insurance Trust Funds* (June 1996), p. 180.

gram changes will obviously be required. The sooner the program is put in long-run fiscal balance, the less drastic the modifications will have to be. It now appears, however, that the program is so far out of balance that correcting the situation will necessarily involve major changes.

In chapter 7, Schieber and Shoven examine the 75-year outlook for the funded pension system in much the same way that Social Security is often evaluated, using the same economic and demographic forecasts, and raise some questions. First, if firms and workers continue their recent contribution rates to pensions and if the benefit structure of defined-benefit plans is left unchanged, how will pension fund assets evolve? Further, will pension funds continue to be the major source of saving in the economy and, if not, what consequences are likely? Second, what sort of adjustment in the pension contribution of firms with defined-benefit plans would achieve adequate long-run funding of their aggregate promises?

The results of chapter 7 are briefly summarized here. First, as is fairly obvious, the same demographic forces that strain Social Security exert themselves on the funded pension plans as well—that is, the private plans and those of state and local governments. The ramification is that if pension contribution behavior and pension benefit formulae remain unchanged, real pension assets will peak in 2023 and then begin to fall. As has already been mentioned, the pension system has been a major source of national saving in recent decades, perhaps the major source. The saving contribution of pensions is forecast to gradually decline but remain significant over the next 10 years or so and then take a far more precipitous downward turn. By 2024, pensions are forecast to become negative savers, that is, net sellers of assets. Even more alarmingly, defined-benefit pension plans in aggregate face the same kind of fund exhaustion as Social Security, although our simulations project the date of that exhaustion as roughly 2040.

The chapter's second finding concerns employers' actions to bring their defined-benefit plans into approximate long-run equilibrium. If adjustments are made by increasing contributions rather than cutting benefits, we find that employers would need to increase their pension funding fairly rapidly by 60% and then maintain that higher level indefinitely. This may not be as burdensome as it first appears, as employer contributions in the late 1970s and early 1980s were closer to this higher level than to the relatively low levels that have prevailed in the last decade or so. An increase in pension funding in this manner would dramatically alter the forecast for pension fund assets and saving. The saving rate would actually increase over the next decade or so as employers raised their funding. Thereafter, pension saving would gradually fall, until it was slightly less than half its current level, but would always remain positive. Correspondingly, pension assets would continue to grow, albeit at a rate which would slow after about 2005.

The striking thing in looking at the long-run outlook of private pensions and the options we face is that the situation is very analogous to that faced by Social Security. The economic and demographic trends are such that the saving and surpluses the programs are realizing today cannot be sustained without modifying either benefits or contributions. Both the funded defined-benefit pensions and Social Security require significant adjustments to benefits, contributions, or both, and the sooner these changes are made, the less dramatic they will have to be.

Public-Sector Plan Issues

Chapter 8, by Ping-Lung Hsin and Olivia Mitchell, deals with public-sector pensions. Though public-employee retirement plans show some similarities to private-employee plans, they nonetheless differ from them substantially. The overwhelming majority of public-employer retirement programs are defined-benefit plans, although the 401(k) supplemental plan phenomenon that has swept the private sector in the last decade has a counterpart in the public sector's Section 427 plans. However, public-sector plans, unlike those sponsored by private-sector employers, are not subject to ERISA's funding and disclosure requirements.

At the state and local level, the lack of regulatory oversight means considerable variability in the plans' operation. Some jurisdictions prefund their pension plans and provide information to participants in a manner comparable to ERISA requirements for private plans. Other jurisdictions fund on a pay-as-you-go basis and provide relatively little information to workers and retirees depending on the plans. It is sometimes argued that public retirement programs need not be subjected to the same funding standards as those imposed on private employers because public entities enjoy taxing power and will be able to raise the resources needed over time to meet the pension obligations to former workers. Private employers do not enjoy such taxing authority, so logic suggests that for benefits to be secure they should be funded as they are being earned over the lifetime of the covered workers.

Although public employers historically have been able to raise taxes as needed to meet current budget obligations, it is increasingly questionable whether such ability will prevail universally, or at all widely, in the future, rendering the argument against funding requirements for public retirement programs questionable. Tax revolts have spread across the land from the smallest school districts to the largest states to the federal government itself. In essence, taxpayers have become increasingly unwilling to let their elected representatives raise taxes for many purposes. Often constraints on taxes relate to school financing, supporting public welfare, and the like, but evidence is growing that in some jurisdictions taxpayers are not willing to pay for pensions earned in prior periods but not funded.

Even to the extent that taxpayers might be willing to support public pensions on a pay-as-you-go basis, doing so raises both efficiency and equity considerations. Public pension programs are subject to exactly the same demographic pressures as private plans and Social Security. Efficiency issues arise to the extent a public employer with an aging workforce defers contributions for pensions until the worker retires. By doing so, the employer reduces the cost of government while workers are younger and providing services and raises the cost of government while they are retired and no longer providing services. It is difficult to appropriately allocate resources to various governmental activities in both periods because the costs of those resources are inappropriately priced in both periods. Equity issues arise because the taxpayers who belatedly have to pay, in the form of pensions, the deferred governmental costs for services may not have received any of the services when they were provided.

The nature of the funding problem in public pensions takes on increasing importance in inverse proportion to the size of the jurisdiction under consideration. A good example of this can be drawn from the situation Washington, D.C., finds itself in currently. District employees were covered under the federal government's retirement programs until 1976 but became the District's responsibility when Congress ceded home rule responsibility to local government. At the same time the retirement plans were split off, assets and liabilities were assigned in accordance with the current funding status. The federal plans in which the affected workers were participating were quite generous, providing relatively early retirement benefits for most workers, benefits that were fully indexed by increases in the consumer price index (CPI). The District government continued those benefits after it took over full responsibility for the programs.

Throughout the 1970s and 1980s the population in the District declined, going from 757,000 in 1970 to 638,000 in 1980 and then to 589,000 in 1992. Yet the pension obligations based on the extremely generous plan characteristics continued to mount, partly driven by an aging police force expanded significantly after the racial unrest the city experienced toward the end of the 1960s. By the end of the 1980s, those police personnel were approaching retirement eligibility having served in the police department for 20 years. By early 1994, the District's retirement programs' unfunded liabilities had reached $5 billion, and budgetary pressures were driving the mayor to attempt to suspend statutory contributions to the plans. The District government now faces the prospect of having current residents, many of whom did not live in the area during the 1970s or 1980s, belatedly pay for police services. The cost of the pensions is so great and the budgetary situation so tight that funding the pensions will likely jeopardize some contemporary services current residents might desire.

The smaller the political jurisdiction, the easier it is for citizens to shift the true cost of their government services to subsequent residents by failing to fund public pension plans. In a larger jurisdiction, it becomes more difficult to shift the obligation totally to new citizens because it becomes increasingly difficult to move away from the tax-levying body that pays the bill. It is possible for any resident in the District of Columbia to move to another taxing jurisdiction by moving as little as five miles. Indeed much of the District's population decline in the 1980s occurred because residents moved to the Maryland and Virginia suburbs. In larger jurisdictions it is harder for residents to move away. In the case of the obligations that the U.S. government has amassed for its workers and retirees, it would be impractical for even a small minority of its citizens to move to foreign countries to escape the pension obligations left by the largely pay-as-you-go systems.

Running federal pensions predominantly on the basis of pay-as-you-go funding poses a slightly different but related set of problems than running local government pension plans on that basis. Today, the federal government has approximately $1.3 trillion in combined unfunded pension obligations for its civilian employee and military retirement plans. Although it may be more difficult in this case for citizens to move away and leave somebody else holding the bag, as they could more easily do in small jurisdictions, they can certainly shift these obligations substantially across generations. In addition, these plans' lack of funding could ultimately put the beneficiaries in jeopardy of not receiving the benefits they have been led to expect. Congressional concerns about the persistent federal deficits led to the creation of a Commission on Entitlements in early 1994 to look into ways to curtail explosive government spending on a variety of entitlement programs including pensions for government retirees. Public plans not fully funded as obligations accrue generally run a much greater political risk of benefits' being cut than funded programs.

Although the funding of public pensions tends to make them more equitable for taxpayers and more secure for participants, the public commitment to fund these plans does not free them completely from being subject to political manipulation. Hsin and Mitchell's analysis of the management of public-sector plans suggests the assumptions used for calculating public funding of plan obligations and the actual contributions to plans vary significantly depending on the sponsoring jurisdiction's fiscal status, who is involved in making the actuarial and funding decisions related to the plans, and the flexibility the jurisdiction has in deficit financing of other aspects of its fiscal operations.

Future Prospects for Retirement Income Adequacy

In chapter 9, Schieber examines alternative approaches to narrowing the funding gaps in both employer-based pensions and Social Security. His analysis begins with the development of measures of retirement income adequacy that assess retirement program effectiveness. Although he discusses both absolute and relative measures of adequacy, he develops the analysis in the context of relative-needs standards. Maintaining retirees at poverty-level incomes might be the minimum standard applied to future generations, but the overwhelming majority of today's workers themselves undoubtedly aspire to a retirement standard of living comparable to what they have achieved during their working careers. Schieber looks at options that would reduce current benefit promises from both pensions and Social Security, but he also considers options that would increase the funding of these programs.

The general framework for Schieber's analysis is the extent to which retirement income will allow workers to maintain preretirement disposable-income levels. This is the familiar replacement rate framework often used to assess retirement system adequacy. This particular analysis is unique in that it estimates the personal saving workers at various points on the economic spectrum would have to generate as a supplement to existing formal retirement programs to finance sufficient annuities to maintain their preretirement disposable-income levels. Within this framework, the analysis focuses on changes to Social Security and pensions and the implications such changes would have for both required savings levels and retirement income levels.

Schieber's analysis shows that benefit reductions under Social Security would require workers to increase saving if they wished to reestablish an equilibrium where their postretirement disposable-income levels matched that attained while working. It also shows that maintaining current benefit promises by increasing the payroll tax would likely result in reduced personal savings. Both the benefit reduction and the tax increase options considered, however, would result in lower standards of living before and after retirement in comparison to the level of benefits Social Security currently offers. The problem with the current program, though, is that benefits promised under current law cannot be delivered under currently legislated payroll tax rates. This dilemma leads Schieber to conclude that if the policy concern is attempting to find solutions to the Social Security financing shortfall for baby boomers that would lead to increased savings, benefit reductions would be preferable to tax increases. Because he finds that across-the-board benefit cuts would hit low-wage workers harder than high-wage workers, he concludes that if the policy concern is that benefit reductions might disproportionately affect lower-wage workers retirement security, a shift to a flatter benefit structure would protect those most vulnerable to the potential benefit cuts.

ERISA will ultimately force employers and their workers to reconcile the financial imbalances in their pension plans largely brought on by public policies adopted over the last 15 years. Analyzing potential curtailments of the defined-benefit system shows a symmetry between potential reductions in workers' retirement benefits, which they would attempt to make up by saving more personally, and reductions in their preretirement disposable-wage levels. Schieber argues that as employers face the prospects of higher funding costs in their defined-benefit plans, they might be able to convince workers they should consider a slowing of the growth rates in their cash wages to sustain the benefits currently offered by the defined-benefit system. The alternative of letting cash wages continue to grow while curtailing pensions would likely result in some myopic workers not adjusting their personal savings rates sufficiently to make up for pension curtailments, with the ultimate result that such workers would end up with a reduced standard of living in retirement.

The overall conclusion of this analysis is that if today's workers cannot be convinced to reduce their current consumption levels, they will have no choice but to work much longer than current retirement patterns suggest they will be disposed to do. The only alternative is they will end up with significantly lower standards of living in retirement than they achieved while working. This means workers should begin to save more now. Schieber argues the incentives encouraging retirement savings curtailed over the last 15 years should once again be expanded. If the expansion in savings incentives must be financed by offsetting policies, then it may be time to limit tax provisions that encourage specific kinds of consumption, notably housing and health care.

Policy Directions for Pensions

In the final chapter, we attempt to pull together the recurring themes from the remainder of the chapters. Essentially, we argue that federal policy should become more oriented toward encouraging savings, which are taking on ever-increasing importance in both macroeconomic and microeconomic contexts.

In the macroeconomic context, our economy is starved for savings, which are crucial to continued growth. Our anemic national savings rates have partly been caused by the ongoing stream of federal government deficits that trail back to the early 1980s. These deficits should be curtailed with policies that encourage savings, such as moving toward consumption-type taxes. Policies that discourage savings, such as those that curtailed the funding of employer-based pensions adopted during the 1980s, are counterproductive from both national savings and retirement income security perspectives.

On the microeconomic front, the lack of personal savings portends an unusually large elderly population that has not adequately provided for its retirement needs. This group, the baby boom generation, has made its needs felt in virtually every other aspect of our social fabric as it has progressed from birth through school and into the labor and consumer markets. If the baby boomers reach retirement without adequately providing for their own retirement needs, they will likely exact a high price from the remainder of society as they attempt to maintain a level of consumption in retirement that they really could not afford even when they were working.

References

Bernheim, B. Douglas, and John B. Shoven. 1988. "Pension Funding and Saving," in Zvi Bodie, John B. Shoven, and David A. Wise, eds., *Pensions in the U.S. Economy* (Chicago: The University of Chicago Press), pp. 85–111.

Bulow, Jeremy I. 1982. "What Are Corporate Pension Liabilities?" *Quarterly Journal of Economics* (August), vol. 97, no. 3, pp. 435–52.

Bulow, Gustman, and Steinmeier, 1989. 1993. "The Impact of the 1985 Budget on the Household Sector," *Fiscal Studies*, vol. 5, no. 2, 57–62.

Dilnot, Andrew, 1994. "The Taxation of Private Pensions," presented at conference, "Securing Employer Based Pensions: An International Perspective," sponsored by The Pension Research Council, The Wharton School, The University of Pennsylvania, May 5 and 6.

Engen, Eric M., William G. Gale, and John Karl Scholz. 1996. "The Illusory Effects of Saving Incentives on Savings," *Journal of Economic Perspectives*, vol. 10, no. 4, 113–38.

Goodfellow, Gordon P., and Sylvester J. Schieber. 1993. "Death and Taxes: Can We Fund for Retirement Between Them?" in Ray Schmitt, ed., *The Future of Pensions in the United States* (Philadelphia: The University of Pennsylvania Press), pp. 126–79.

Gustman, Alan L., and Thomas L. Steinmeier. 1993. "Pension Portability and Labor Mobility: Evidence from the Survey of Income and Program Participation," *Journal of Public Economics*, vol. 50, no. 1, pp. 299–323.

Gustman, Alan L., and Thomas L. Steinmeier. 1989. "An Analysis of Pension Benefit Formulas, Pension Wealth, and Incentives from Pensions," in Ronald Ehrenberg, ed., *Research in Labor Economics*, vol. 1 (Greenwich, CT.: JAI Press), 53–106.

Gustman, Alan L., Olivia S. Mitchell, and Thomas L. Steinmeier. 1994. "The Role of Pensions in the Labor Market: A Survey of the Literature," *Industrial and Labor Relations Review* (April), vol. 47, no. 3, 417–38.

Ippolito, Richard. 1990. *Pension Plan Choice* (Washington, DC: Pension Benefit Guaranty Corporation).

MaCurdy, Thomas E., and John B. Shoven. 1992. "Stocks, Bonds, and Pension Wealth," in David A. Wise, ed., *Topics in the Economics of Aging* (Chicago: The University of Chicago Press), pp. 61–75.

Mitchell, Olivia S., and Silvana Pozzebon. 1987. Unpublished paper, "Wages, Pensions and the Wage-Pension Tradeoff," Department of Labor Economics, New York State School of Industrial and Labor Relations, Cornell University, July.

Montgomery, Edward, Kathryn Shaw, and Mary Ellen Benedict. 1992. "Pensions and Wages: An Hedonic Price Theory Approach," *International Economic Review* (February), vol. 33, no. 1, pp. 111–28.

Munnell, Alicia H. 1989. "It's Time to Tax Employee Benefits," *New England Economic Review* (Boston: Federal Reserve Bank of Boston, July/August), pp. 49–63.

Silverman, Celia. 1993. "Pension Evolution in a Changing Economy," *EBRI Issue Brief* (Washington, DC: The Employee Benefit Research Institute, September), no. 141.

2

Pension Tax Expenditures: Magnitude, Distribution, and Economic Effects

Robert L. Clark and
Elisa Wolper

During the 20th century, employer pension plans have become a significant component of labor compensation for many workers in the United States.[1] Employer-provided pensions were very rare at the beginning of the century, with only about 1% of the civilian nonfarm labor force participating in retirement plans. The proportion of the labor force covered by employer pensions and ultimately the proportion of retirees receiving benefits grew rapidly until the 1970s. That proportion has remained around 50% during the past decade (Silverman and Yakoboski 1994).[2]

Government tax policy establishing a preferential tax status for pension contributions and the earnings of pension funds stimulated, in part, the growth of coverage during the first three quarters of this century (Ippolito 1986; Bloom and Freeman 1992; Craig and White 1993). Shortly after the enactment of income tax legislation in 1913, federal tax policy made direct employer payments of pension benefits to retirees and employer contributions into pension trust funds tax-deductible expenses for the firm.[3]

Under current law, neither employer contributions nor pension fund earnings count as current, taxable income to workers. Pension benefits paid to retirees are included in the retiree's taxable income. This deferment of tax liability on implied pension compensation or the increases in pension wealth with continued employment differs from the normal tax treatment of income under the current income tax structure.[4] The preferential tax treatment accorded to pension compensation lowers the implied price of a dollar of pension compensation to workers relative to an additional dollar of cash earnings. The resulting lower price of pension compensation increases employee demand for pension coverage as well as more generous pension benefits.

In general, the deferment of tax payments on pension contributions or accruals and pension fund earnings until benefits are actually received in retirement reduces net aggregate tax revenues in a particular year. Such reductions are often referred to as tax expenditures. Estimates of the total tax expenditure for employer-provided pensions have exceeded $50 billion per year in the 1990s. These expenditures represent the largest recorded in the federal budget (U.S. Congress, Joint Committee on Taxation 1993).[5] Measured in this manner, the estimates of tax expenditures pertain only to the decline in income tax revenues and do not address any reduction in payroll tax revenues.

Because of the size of these tax expenditures, some policy analysts have questioned the desirability of pensions' preferential tax status (Munnell 1989, 1991, 1992; Gravelle 1994). This chapter examines the magnitude of the tax expenditure for employer pensions and its impact on the nation's income and wealth distributions. In addition, it explores likely responses to further changes in their tax treatment.

What Are Tax Expenditures?

The Congressional Budget and Impoundment Control Act of 1974 defines tax expenditures as "those revenue losses attributable to provisions of the federal tax laws which allow a special exclusion, exemption or deduction from gross income or which provide a special credit, a preferential rate of tax or a deferral of tax liability." The tax code classifies a special provision for a particular type of income as a tax expenditure when that provision deviates from the general tax treatment of income.[6]

Tax expenditures are measured by calculating the difference between tax liability under current law and tax liability that would accrue to individuals and firms without the tax expenditure provision, holding constant taxpayer economic behavior. Thus, it is important not to equate an estimate of a tax expenditure to the additional revenue that eliminating the tax expenditure provision would raise. Taxpayers' responses to increases in marginal and average tax rates should be expected so that eliminating the tax preferences typically results in an actual gain in tax revenues lower than the calculated tax expenditure.

The Joint Committee on Taxation calculates tax expenditures for retirement plans on a per year, cash flow basis. The calculation assumes tax policy is changed so that all employer and employee contributions into the pension fund become taxable as current income to workers. In addition, the pension fund's estimated investment earnings are added to taxable wages. This estimates "pension compensation" or "pension income" not being taxed at the time earned and hence deviates from the general tax treatment of income. Next, the tax payments on pension benefits currently received by retirees are determined. If contributions and fund earnings were taxed during the work life, pension benefits would not be subject to taxation since they would represent withdrawal from pension savings accounts that had already been fully taxed. Thus, taxes paid on current benefits are subtracted from the tax liability calculated from the changed tax status of contributions and plan earnings. The difference in these values is the implied tax expenditure for pensions.

This measurement of pension tax expenditures is based on an annual, aggregate cash flow of pension accounts. It does not consider the implied accumulation in the wealth value of pension benefits promised to workers through their pension plan, and it does not measure the lifetime value of deferred taxation of benefits to pension participants. Instead it is based on the mechanical calculation associated with contributions to, earnings of, and payments out of the pension funds. This concept is more appropriate for defined-contribution plans; however, it has serious shortcomings as a measure of pension compensation under defined-benefit plans.

A defined-contribution plan bases future retirement benefits solely on annual contributions and the accumulated return on the fund over the participant's work life. Calculating pension tax expenditure on annual contributions and estimated fund earnings is a reasonable proxy for the growth in any one participant's pension wealth. Aggregating these items across participants also yields a good estimate of total pension compensation throughout the economy.

A similar conclusion is not consistent with defined-benefit plan structure. Pension compensation is a function of the benefit formula, expected age of retirement, interest rate assumptions, and mortality and turnover expectations. In general, pension compensation based on projected growth in earnings and the probability of remaining with the firm exceeds the value based on work experience to date.[7]

Individual and aggregate pension compensation is not directly linked to actual contributions to pension funds or plan earnings during any one year. Basing estimates of tax expenditures on actual contributions and earnings may give a misleading picture about the size of an individual taxpayer's pension compensation. Furthermore, changing tax policy to count contributions and plan earnings instead of pension compensation would provide firms and workers with incentives to reduce the funding in defined-benefit plans.[8]

Table 2.1
Five-year projections of pension tax expenditures (in billions of dollars)

First year of projection[a]	Tax expenditure in year one	1	Out-year projections 2	3	4
1977	6.5	7.1	7.8	8.6	9.5
1978	9.9	11.3	12.9	14.7	16.8
1979	11.3	12.9	14.7	16.8	19.2
1980	12.9	14.7	16.8	19.2	21.9
1981	14.7	16.8	19.2	21.9	24.9
1982	27.9	32.9	38.8	45.9	54.1
1983	27.5	30.5	35.6	42.1	48.5
1984	56.6	66.4	78.3	92.4	109.0
1985	52.7	59.0	66.1	74.0	82.9
1986	55.1	61.7	69.1	77.4	86.7
1987	58.9	64.3	70.3	76.8	83.9
1988	49.3	51.7	56.5	61.8	67.5
1989	45.6	48.2	51.1	54.5	57.2
1990	48.5	51.3	54.4	57.6	61.1
1991	52.2	54.3	56.5	58.8	61.3
1992	54.0	57.0	59.0	61.0	64.0
1993	56.5	58.8	61.3	63.8	66.0
1994	55.3	58.5	62.0	65.7	69.6

Source: U.S. Congress, Joint Committee on Taxation, "Estimates of Federal Tax Expenditures," Washington, D.C.: USGPO, annual reports for years 1976 through 1993
a. Projections are for fiscal years as made in spring of preceding calendar year. Between 1976 and 1984, estimates were presented for current fiscal year. These numbers are not shown in the table.

What Is the Magnitude of Tax Expenditures for Pensions?

The Joint Committee on Taxation estimates tax expenditures annually as part of the congressional budget process. Table 2.1 presents a history of these projections from 1977 to 1994. The table indicates the first fiscal year of the projection along with the projected pension tax expenditure for that year and the next four fiscal years.[9]

Changes in tax expenditures over time depend on changes in tax provisions concerning pension funding, changes in tax rates, changes in pension coverage among both workers and retirees, and pension fund investment performance. To illustrate these changes, examine each year's estimates for the tax expenditure in the following fiscal year (column 1 of table 2.1). Pension tax expenditures were estimated to be $6.5 billion for fiscal 1977.

Table 2.2
Pension tax expenditures (in billions of dollars)

Plan type	1993	1994	1995	1996	1997
Private employer	27.5	28.6	29.9	31.1	32.2
Defined-benefit	8.2	8.5	8.9	9.3	9.6
Defined-contribution	19.3	20.1	21.0	21.8	22.5
Public employer	29.0	30.1	31.5	32.7	33.9
Defined-benefit	27.9	29.0	30.3	31.5	32.6
Defined-contribution	1.1	1.1	1.2	1.2	1.3
Total	56.5	58.8	61.3	63.8	66.0
Percent public	51.3	51.2	51.4	51.3	51.4

Source: The values for total tax expenditures are reported in U.S. Congress, Joint Committee on Taxation, *Estimates of Federal Tax Expenditures for Fiscal Years 1993–97*, Washington: USGPO, 1992. Data on the tax expenditure for public and private plans are from Employee Benefit Research Institute, "Pension Tax Expenditures: Are They Worth the Cost?" *Issue Brief*, February 1993, p. 8.

The estimates increased gradually to $14.7 billion in 1981. The projections then indicate a sharp increase to $27.9 billion for 1982. Despite TEFRA's passage in 1982 and that of DEFRA and REA in 1984, which limited some preferential tax treatment accorded pension plans, the projected tax expenditure for pensions rose sharply to more than $50 billion between 1984 and 1987.[10]

Since the mid-1980s, projections of pension tax expenditures have ranged from a high of $58.9 billion in 1987 to a low of $45.6 billion in 1989. The estimated pension tax expenditure for fiscal 1994 was $55.3 billion. As a proportion of total personal income tax revenues collected, the pension tax expenditure fell from 17% in 1985 to 11% in 1993. Thus, pension tax expenditures have considerably less relative importance in the 1990s than they had in the mid-1980s.

Tax Expenditures for Public Pensions

Much of the early discussion concerning tax expenditures associated with employer pensions implied that the total tax expenditure was due to private-sector pensions. This assumption clearly is not true. Table 2.2 estimates the total pension tax expenditure for fiscal 1993 through fiscal 1997 (U.S. Congress, Joint Committee on Taxation 1992) and includes estimates for private pension plans, government civilian plans, and military plans made by Employee Benefit Research Institute (1993). Slightly more than half the tax expenditures for pensions in each of these years is attributable to public pension plans. Thus, analysts reviewing the value of pension tax expenditures must consider that the tax expenditure for private firms in 1993 was less than $30 billion and not the entire $56.5 billion the Joint Committee on Taxation reported. Changes in pension tax laws that affect public plans have substantially different effects on government budgets than changes that affect only private plans.

Another interesting observation from these data is that defined-benefit plans account for less than one-third of the tax expenditure for private plans but virtually all of that for public plans. These magnitudes reflect the distribution of pensions by plan type and recent investment performance of pension funds that may have limited the amount of deductible contributions private employers could make for their defined-benefit plans given full funding limits.

The size of the tax expenditure per participant also differs greatly by type of pension plan. In 1991, federal civilian and military pensions made an estimated tax expenditure of approximately $1,900 per active participant; state and local plans expended an estimated $1,150. In comparison, the per-participant tax expenditure in private plans was only $292 for defined-benefit plans and $665 for defined-contribution plans (Employee Benefit Research Institute 1993). Thus, the average public employee participating in a pension receives a much higher imputed value from the pension's tax status than does the average participant in a private plan.

Together these data indicate more than half the aggregate tax expenditure is attributable to public pensions, and the per-participant tax expenditure is much larger in the public sector. These data raise an interesting question: What impact would eliminating the preferential tax status for federal plans have on the federal budget and the current deficit?

Public-sector pensions are one factor that entices individuals to seek career government employment. Any systematic reduction in the value of working in the public sector relative to the private sector because of changes in pension tax treatment would make attracting and retaining quality workers more difficult. A decline in the value of pensions from the elimination of their preferential tax treatment would require governments to increase cash compensation to attract workers of the same quality. Alternatively, the government could simply "pay" the pension tax for public workers. With complete adjustments in compensation, either response would increase government expenditures, offsetting any increase in tax revenues due to pension compensation's changed tax status.

This analysis suggests that depending on government responses, the added revenue from changes in the tax code regarding pensions might yield less than half the projected pension tax expenditures. Alternatively, governments might not adjust compensation and therefore allow the quality of government workers to decline.

An additional issue to consider in relation to the tax expenditure for public plans is that federal civilian and military plans are considerably underfunded. Annual contributions are substantially less than those that would be required in the private sector under ERISA. The U.S. government would have needed an additional $62 billion in annual contributions to meet ERISA standards of funding in 1991.[11] This would have resulted in tax expenditures for public plans being $14.6 billion higher than reported in table 2.2 (Employee Benefit Research Institute 1993).[12] If this value is added to estimated tax expenditures for 1991, the implied proportion of the total pension tax expenditure attributable to public plans would have been 62.5% (Employee Benefit Research Institute 1993). Thus, private plans would have accounted for only 37.5% of the total.[13]

Tax Expenditures for IRAs and Keogh Plans

Preferential tax status has also been granted to some other types of retirement savings plans. Tax expenditures for individual retirement accounts (IRAs) and Keogh plans totaled $9.2 billion in 1993 and are projected to rise to about $12 billion in 1998.[14] Tax expenditures for IRAs have changed dramatically with shifts in tax policy while tax expenditures for Keogh plans have remained relatively stable.

IRAs were first established in 1974 for workers not enrolled in an employer pension plan. The same tax status afforded to employer-provided pensions was extended to IRAs—current contributions and returns to IRA investments were not included as current income.[15] Providing tax-deferred IRA investments with these restrictions was not very successful in extending retirement income coverage to uncovered workers. Only 13% of workers not covered by an employer-provided pension in 1983 contributed to an IRA (U.S. Congressional Budget Office 1987).

Beginning in 1982, tax-deferred contributions to a qualified IRA were also allowed as supplemental plans for workers participating in a company pension plan. In response to this expansion in eligibility and perhaps the national publicity accompanying the change in the tax code, IRA contributions increased substantially. The percentage of wage-and-salary taxpayers claiming a deduction for IRA contributions increased from 4.1% in 1981 to 15.1% in 1986. Total contributions rose from $3 billion in 1981 to more than $37 billion in 1986 (U.S. Congressional Budget Office 1987; Venti and Wise 1993).

Effective in 1987, the tax code was altered to deny tax deductibility of contributions to workers participating in an employer-provided pension or having income above a specified level.[16] Although this change affected only 27% of taxpayers (Poterba, Venti, and Wise 1993), participation rates fell sharply, even at income levels where contributions were still deductible. In one year contribution amounts fell by 63% to $14.1 billion. By 1990, contribution amounts had fallen further to $10 billion (Venti and Wise 1993).

These large fluctuations in IRA contributions driven by tax code changes obviously produced large swings in IRA tax expenditures. The Joint Committee on Taxation first reported tax expenditures for IRAs in 1982, when the IRA tax expenditure for fiscal 1983 was projected at $2.7 billion. The estimates for fiscal 1985 and 1987 were $9.8 billion and $15.9 billion respectively. Following the 1986 changes in the tax code, the estimated tax expenditure for 1988 declined sharply to $8.5 billion. The magnitude of the tax expenditure for IRAs has declined further in recent years, reaching $6.2 billion in fiscal 1994. The tax expenditure for IRAs is projected to grow slightly from $7.1 billion in 1993 to $8.2 billion in 1997 (Salisbury 1994; U.S. Congress, Joint Committee on Taxation 1992).

Keogh plans for the self-employed and noncorporate employees were established in 1962 with fairly stringent restrictions on contribution and benefit amounts (Hubbard 1994). These rules were relaxed in 1982, bringing Keogh rules in line with those for employer-provided pensions. In 1983, fewer than a half million taxpayers, or about 5% of the unincorporated self-employed, had established Keogh accounts (U.S. Congressional Budget Office 1987). Though amendments to the tax code should have increased participation and tax expenditures, the tax expenditures associated with Keogh accounts remained relatively small and stable at around $2–$3 billion per year. Current projections forecast that tax expenditures for Keogh accounts will rise from $2.7 billion in 1993 to $3.4 billion in 1997 (Salisbury 1994).

Most discussions of pension tax expenditures have ignored these plans. However, one would expect changes in the tax code affecting their tax status would also apply to these types of retirement savings plans.

Factors Influencing the Trend in Tax Expenditures

Private tax expenditures are estimated using a cash flow methodology and represent annual reductions in tax revenues. As a result, their annual magnitude depends on several economic and demographic factors including (1) changes in the proportion of the labor force covered by a pension, (2) changes in the population's age structure, (3) changes in pension generosity, (4) funding requirements and strategies, and (5) tax policy toward other forms of income. These issues are briefly discussed below.

Changes in Pension Coverage Rates

In a maturing pension system, coverage rates among workers are increasing, that is, the proportion of pension plan participants who are currently workers exceeds the proportion who are retirees receiving benefits. The latter proportion increases as successive cohorts of workers retire. In a pension system's early development, relatively few workers have spent their working careers covered by pensions. Therefore, employer pensions cover a relatively small proportion of retirees, and the added revenue associated with taxing pension benefits is relatively small.[17]

As a pension system develops and matures there will be an increasing and relatively large tax expenditure. Thus, using the current methodology for estimating tax expenditures, the spread of pension coverage influences the measured annual tax expenditure for pensions. The tax expenditure stabilizes when the pension coverage rate attains a long-run equilibrium.

A simple example illustrates this point. Consider a country that has a stable population with an unchanging age structure. Assume that everyone lives for two periods. Each person works one period, is retired for one period, and then dies. Let each cohort be composed of 100 people and assume a market interest rate of 6%. Each individual earns $1,000 during the period employed. To save for retirement, some workers join firms that offer a qualified pension plan. These firms pay cash wages of $700 and make contributions of $300 per worker into the pension fund at the beginning of the working period. When they retire, these covered workers receive a pension of $318.[18] Assume the prevailing tax structure has a tax rate of 28% for income in excess of $500 and a 15% bracket for incomes below.

During a six-year period, the pension coverage rate among workers increases from 0 to 50%. In period two, the coverage rate for workers

Table 2.3
Impact of pension system growth on tax expenditures

Year	1	2	3	4	5	6	7
Number of workers	100	100	100	100	100	100	100
Number of retirees	0	100	100	100	100	100	100
Coverage rate (%)	0	15	30	40	50	50	45
Number of participants	0	15	30	40	50	50	45
Number of beneficiaries	0	0	15	30	40	50	50
Tax expenditure ($) per participant	0	89.04	89.04	89.04	89.04	89.04	89.04
Tax paid ($) per beneficiary	0	0	47.70	47.70	47.70	47.70	47.70
Total ($) tax expenditure	0	1,336	1,956	2,131	2,544	2,067	1,622

increases to 15% and in subsequent periods rises to 30%, 40% and finally 50%.[19] The proportion of retirees receiving benefits follows these increases in coverage with a lag of one period.

Table 2.3 indicates that tax liabilities for each pension participant are reduced by $89.04 per year—$84.00 due to pension contributions and $5.04 associated with interest earnings on these contributions. Because the pension plan and wages remain constant throughout the period, this reduction in tax liability per participant remains unchanged over time. Each retiree with a pension pays an additional $47.70 in taxes per year, and this remains unchanged in the example. The reduction in the present value of total lifetime taxes is equal to $44.04.[20] Despite the unchanging values per participant and per retiree, the measured tax expenditure increases sharply while the pension system is maturing. The trend in tax expenditures shown in table 2.3 results from changes in the coverage rate for workers and with a one period lag, in the retiree coverage rate.

The measured aggregate tax expenditure rises as the pension system matures, nearly doubling from $1,336 in period 2 to $2,544 in period 5. When the system reaches a stable coverage rate in period 6, the tax expenditure falls to $2,067. If the coverage rate were to remain at this level, measured tax expenditures would not change further. However, if coverage among workers were to decline, the tax expenditure would begin to fall and would take at least two periods to reestablish a new equilibrium level. Period 7 shows the impact of declining coverage.

Table 2.4
Impact of changing demographics on tax expenditure

Year	1980	1990	2000	2020	2040	2060
Ratio of workers to retirees	5.1	4.8	4.6	3.5	2.6	2.5
Number of workers	100	100	100	100	100	100
Number of retirees	20	21	22	29	38	40
Coverage rate (%)	50	50	50	50	50	50
Number of participants	50	50	50	50	50	50
Number of beneficiaries	10	10	11	14	19	20
Total tax expenditure	$3,975	$3,951	$3,927	$3,784	$3,546	$3,498

This exercise indicates that, holding pension characteristics constant, the size of the pension tax expenditure varies with the pension system's stage of development. Relative to the actual experience of the United States, this model suggests that increases in the coverage rate have been one factor influencing the growth of pension tax expenditures and that this factor has probably exerted its maximum effect. In the future, the net effect of changes in coverage might be to reduce the overall tax expenditure.[21]

Aging of the Population

The population's changing age structure also affects the measured pension tax expenditure. The simple model economy used above can also illustrate an aging population's impact on estimated pension tax expenditures. To examine this impact, we hold constant the pension coverage rate and assume half of all current workers are covered by a pension and half of current retirees are receiving benefits. As in the case above, pension compensation to participants is $300 and the benefit to retirees is $318. Tax rates are 28% for workers and 15% for retirees.

The ratio of workers to retirees in the U.S. economy has fallen steadily in recent decades, from 8.85 in 1940 to 4.79 in 1990, and is projected to fall even further, to 2.48 by 2060.[22] Table 2.4 shows the effect of these population changes on pension tax expenditures. To illustrate demographic changes, the working population is held constant at 100 while the number of retirees grows from 20 in 1980 to 40 in the year 2060.

With stable pension coverage rates of 50% among workers, half of retirees will be pension recipients. Marginal tax rates, earnings, pension compensation for participants and the interest rate are the same as above. Net tax expenditures fall steadily with the population's aging because the number of retirees paying tax on pension benefits increases while the number of workers participating in pensions and thus deferring taxation remains constant.

This example indicates that given the population's 1980 age structure, the pension tax expenditure in this example would have been $3,975. This magnitude is projected to decline in the future by about 12% as the aging of the population and the decline in the participant-to-beneficiary ratio influences the measured tax expenditure.

Increasing Generosity of Pensions

Changes in pension plan provisions that increase the pension's lifetime value to current plan participants necessitate increases in contributions and ultimately increases in the pension fund's size. Therefore, plan improvements increase the absolute size of the pension fund's earnings. Significant plan improvements over the past three decades have included lowering the normal and early retirement ages, increasing benefit formulas, and lowering vesting requirements (Mitchell 1992).

Each change increases the pension's value to current workers and hence the current funding requirements. Only when these workers begin to retire are the higher benefits in retirement subject to taxation. Thus, trends in plan characteristics that increase future retirement benefits increase the calculated tax expenditure above its new equilibrium level. A new equilibrium level is established only when improvements have leveled off and workers and retirees are under the same plans.

The development of employer pensions has now reached a mature stage. Further, significant improvements in existing pensions are less likely in the coming decades. Increased government regulation also threatens to limit continued increases in pension plan generosity. In fact, the most important trend in pensions today is the shift away from defined-benefit plans toward defined-contribution plans, often less generous than the previous plans. Thus, future plan changes may well reduce tax expenditures instead of increasing them as they were during the past 30 years.

Funding Strategies

Systematic changes in funding strategies alter the size of the measured tax expenditure even though they do not alter the plan sponsor's pension liabilities or the individual's pension wealth. Consider funding policies in a completely unregulated pension environment. (That is, what funding level would prevail if neither government regulation nor standard accounting practices required firms to prefund plans?) Now consider the impact of legislation requiring full funding of accrued liabilities and the amortization of existing unfunded liabilities over 30 years.

In this example, annual contributions to pension funds would be expected to rise after the new regulations were imposed. Thus, with no change in the pension promise, the measured tax expenditure would increase. Similarly if standard accounting practices mandated a reduction in the amortization period for unfunded liabilities, funding would increase and hence, tax expenditures would rise. Clearly, using the current method of calculating tax expenditures, funding strategies alter measured tax expenditures even though they do not affect the real pension liabilities and accrued income.[23]

During the past decade, federal tax policy has attempted to reduce pension tax expenditures through a series of initiatives limiting the annual amount of qualified contributions into pension funds. During recent years, these policies have lowered pension contributions and hence pension tax expenditures. However, these policies ultimately make pension plans more risky and increase the likelihood that the government may have to cover greater unfunded liabilities associated with lower funding levels. Have these public policies been good pension policies?

Tax Policies

Trends in nonpension tax policies indirectly influence the size of the tax expenditures, most obviously through tax rate changes. Increases in the tax rates or in the degree of progressivity increase the value of the preferential tax status accorded pensions. Thus, trends in the overall tax structure alter measured tax expenditures. The effect of tax policy changes in the 1980s was to lower measured tax expenditures, but future tax increases are likely to increase measured pension tax expenditures, in the 1990s.

A second effect relates to the taxation of specific types of income. For example, full taxation of Social Security benefits would reduce the measured pension tax expenditure, because adding these benefits to retirees' taxable income would push more retirees into higher income tax brackets. Therefore, they would pay more tax on their pension benefits and thus reduce the measured tax expenditure.

Tax Expenditures for Pensions: The Distributional Issues

Tax expenditures' distributional effects depend on how coverage rates, the generosity of benefits, and work histories vary by individual characteristics and over the course of one's work life. To examine the implications of pension tax expenditures on income and wealth distributions, we first present a simple model of changes in accrued pension wealth with age and tenure. Next, cross-sectional patterns of pension coverage along with changes in coverage rates between 1979 and 1988 are examined using three Current Population Surveys (CPSs). Third, a point-in-time analysis of personal income and the effects of pension tax expenditures is presented. Finally, we examine pension contribution to household net worth and discuss how adding pension wealth alters the wealth distribution.

Models of Pension Compensation and Pension Wealth

The concept of tax expenditure for pensions has as its basic premise that workers are earning compensation through pension accruals and they receive increases in pension wealth because returns on the pension funds are not taxed when earned. To understand these issues, it is important to have a clear picture of pension compensation and changes in pension wealth that can be assigned to individual workers. These concepts must be addressed separately for defined-contribution and defined-benefit plans. In the analysis that follows, we assume workers pay the full cost of pension compensation in the form of lower cash earnings.[24]

Defined-Contribution Plans

In defined-contribution plans, the size of the individual's pension account at retirement directly determines retirement benefits. The account's wealth value is known at each point. The account value increases because of the employer's or employee's periodic contributions and the annual earnings on plan investments.

For participants in defined-contribution plans, employer contributions are equivalent to pension compensation based on continued employment. These contributions represent a component of total compensation not currently taxed and accurately estimate the nontaxable earnings that should be included in calculating the tax expenditure. Similarly, the pension fund's earnings accurately estimate the gain in pension wealth associated with the investment of the existing pension fund.

The methodology used to calculate the pension tax expenditure is consistent with the basic concepts of defined-contribution plans. Assuming workers bear the full incidence of employer contributions in the form of lower wages and are fully vested in their pension, eliminating the pension tax expenditure by directly taxing the pension participant or by taxing the pension fund itself produces equivalent reductions in their pension wealth.[25]

Defined-Benefit Plans

Pension compensation and changes in pension wealth are much more complex in defined-benefit plans. Sponsors of defined-benefit plans promise workers a benefit in retirement dependent on tenure at retirement, salary, and time of retirement. It is the employer's responsibility to ensure sufficient funds are invested to pay all promised benefits. Employer contributions are based on firm and plan experiences and are only loosely tied to any particular employee's work history. The link between earnings on plan investments and a particular worker's pension wealth is even more tenuous.[26]

In recent years, the benefit literature has clearly identified pension accruals' value to workers. Accruals can be valued at their legal or termination value or on expected or projected benefits at retirement. Pension wealth's legal value is the expected present value of retirement benefits if the worker were to leave the firm on a given day or the firm were to terminate the pension plan. The PBGC insures this benefit. The projected benefit is what workers will receive if they remain with the firm until retirement.

Because most plans provide benefits based on final average salary, legal or termination pension wealth tends to rise rapidly with advancing age and increased job tenure. Thus, pension compensation or the change in pension wealth associated with continued employment increases as a proportion of total compensation later in the work life.

Table 2.5 shows these relationships for a worker hired at age 25 with total compensation (earnings plus pension compensation) equal to $20,000. In this exercise, total compensation grows at 5.5% per year (1.5% real growth with a 4.0% rate of inflation), and the worker is covered by a pension with a normal retirement age of 65 and no early retirement option. The benefit formula is 0.015 times average earnings in the last five years times years of service. Age-specific mortality rates are those shown in the 1981 U.S. life table for white men (U.S. Department of Commerce 1984). The market interest rate is assumed to be 6%.

Table 2.5
Employee compensation and pension wealth: termination benefits

Age	Tenure	Earnings	Pension compensation	Pension compensation / Total compensation	Nominal pension wealth
25	0	$ 19,959	$ 45	0.21	$ 0
30	5	25,737	402	1.54	1,530
35	10	33,318	845	2.47	5,340
40	15	42,946	1,704	3.82	13,945
45	20	55,016	3,339	5.72	32,325
50	25	69,873	6,395	8.39	70,301
55	30	87,684	11,995	12.03	147,571
60	35	108,267	22,010	16.89	302,288
64	39	126,191	35,199	21.81	532,487
65	40	164,680	5,586	3.28	613,518

Note: The numerical values are based on a simulation of compensation for a male worker who remains with a firm throughout his work life. He is assumed to have been hired at age 25 with total annual compensation equal to $20,000. Total compensation is composed of earnings plus pension compensation. The worker is assumed to pay for pension compensation in the form of lower cash earnings. Total compensation grows at 5.5% per year based on 1.5% real growth and 4.0% inflation. The worker is covered by a pension with a normal retirement age of 65 and a benefit formula of 0.015 times average earnings in the last five years times years of service. The market interest rate is 6.0%. All values are based on the pension benefits that the worker would receive if he left the firm and its pension plan today.

Although the exact numerical values are sensitive to the assumptions, the simulation's basic findings are robust to particular values of the parameters. Pension compensation is shown to grow rapidly as a proportion of total compensation, increasing from 1.5% at age 30 to 8% at age 50 and 22% just prior to reaching the normal retirement age. Pension wealth increases with age because of annual pension compensation and the worker's approaching the age at which benefits can begin—65 in this example. This latter form of wealth gain is due both to the increased likelihood that the worker will survive to retirement and to a discounting effect associated with retirement age being one year closer.

This pattern of pension compensation raises several questions concerning proposals to eliminate the tax expenditure for pensions. If tax liability were assigned to specific pension participants based on their pension compensation, adding pension earnings to cash income would increase taxable income sharply with age and tenure. Thus, holding cash income constant, workers would pay a progressively higher proportion of their cash income in taxes with age and tenure.

Using the projected method of determining pension wealth and hence pension compensation, pension accruals are higher earlier in the work life and rise less rapidly. This method of estimating pension wealth assumes the worker will remain with the firm and in the present pension plan until retirement. If workers pay for this projected pension in the form of reduced wages, they face a loss in lifetime wealth through their pension if they leave prior to retirement (Allen, Clark, and McDermed 1993). Workers who leave the firm, whose firm goes bankrupt, or whose firm terminates the pension plan lose some pension wealth.

If workers were individually taxed on projected pension wealth and pension compensation, the increase in their tax liability would be more uniform across their lifetime; however, taxing projected pension wealth implies that workers pay tax on some wealth that may be lost depending on future events. Thus, the tax code would need to enable workers to recover these taxes if they suffered pension losses.

Using the same assumptions as noted above but basing pension compensation on the projected pension benefit, table 2.6 illustrates the lifetime pension compensation using the projected method. In this example, pension compensation is a higher proportion of total compensation from the outset (6.8% at age 30 compared to 1.5% using the termination method) and rises much more slowly, so that pension compensation is only 8% at age 50 and 10% at age 64.

Table 2.6
Employee compensation and pension wealth: projected benefits

Age	Tenure	Earnings	Pension compensation	Pension compensation / Total compensation	Nominal pension wealth	Capital loss[a]
25	0	$ 18,670	$ 1,330	6.65	$ 1,330	$ 1,330
30	5	24,353	1,786	6.83	10,717	9,272
35	10	31,762	2,401	7.03	26,414	21,346
40	15	41,415	3,234	7.24	51,752	38,399
45	20	53,982	4,373	7.49	91,835	60,452
50	25	70,303	5,964	7.82	155,076	85,357
55	30	91,432	8,247	8.27	255,654	105,082
60	35	118,664	11,612	8.91	418,048	96,610
64	39	145,802	15,587	9.66	623,494	31,700
65	40	173,397	-3,130	-1.84	690,677	0

Note: The numerical values are based on a simulation of compensation for a male worker who remains with a firm throughout his work life. He is assumed to have been hired at age 25 with total annual compensation equal to $20,000. Total compensation is composed of earnings plus pension compensation. The worker is assumed to pay for pension compensation in the form of lower cash earnings. Total compensation grows at 5.5% per year based on 1.5% real growth and 4.0% inflation. The worker is covered by a pension with a normal retirement age of 65 and a benefit formula of 0.015 times average earnings in the last five years times years of service. The market interest rate is 6.0%. All values are based on a projected pension benefit assuming that the worker remains with the firm until age 65.
a. Loss in pension wealth if worker were to leave the firm.

Table 2.6 also indicates the potential for loss in pension wealth if the worker leaves the pension plan. The magnitude of pension loss rises with age and tenure until reaching $105,000, or more than one year's earnings, at age 55. As the worker approaches the normal retirement age, the pension loss declines relative to earnings and also in absolute value. This loss in pension wealth reduces the probability that pension participants change employers (Allen, Clark, and McDermed 1988, 1993).

For a variety of reasons associated with the measurement and lifetime patterns of pension wealth, assigning specific individual tax liability to participants in defined-benefit plans seems cumbersome and unlikely to be implemented. Operational concerns include (1) What is the correct measurement of pension accruals to workers? (2) If taxed on projected benefits, will workers be able to recover taxes paid on pension losses if they separate from the pension prior to retirement? and (3) Given that payment of future benefits is still somewhat risky, are pension accruals an accurate measure of pension compensation to the worker?[27]

In the case of defined-benefit plans, the only practical option for eliminating the pension tax expenditure would be to tax the pension fund or the plan sponsor as proposed by Munnell (1991, 1992). We would expect firms to pass this tax on to workers in the form of lower benefits for a given reduction in wages.[28] Workers would then be expected to respond to this higher price of pension benefits by reducing their demand for pensions.

Pension Coverage Rates

The pattern of pension coverage that prevails in the U.S. economy raises issues of horizontal and vertical equity concerning the distributional effects of the pension tax expenditures. Critics of existing tax policy on pensions frequently point out that its benefits are regressive, accruing disproportionately to higher-income taxpayers. Since coverage rates and marginal tax rates increase with income, the value of the tax deferment for pension benefits is usually greater for households with higher incomes up to some level. A key to understanding pension tax expenditures' effect on vertical equity is knowing lifetime pension coverage rates. It is also important to recognize the variation in pension coverage holding income constant—the horizontal equity consideration.

Table 2.7 reports coverage rates for a sample of full-time, private-sector workers 16 and older from the May CPSs for 1979, 1983, and 1988. These data indicate that in 1988 only about one-sixth of workers earning less than $4.00 per hour (in 1983 dollars) were covered by an employer

Table 2.7
Pension coverage rates by firm and worker characteristic

	1979	1983	1988
Overall	56.5%	53.2%	52.4%
Union status			
Union	82.9	81.8	80.9
Nonunion	46..2	45.0	46.5
Firm size (number of employees)			
Less than 25	17.8	17.7	16.7
25–100	39.0	35.1	37.4
100–250			50.1
100–500	58.0	54.7	
250 or more			72.0
500–999	68.0	62.9	
1,000 or more	81.0	80.0	
Job tenure			
Less than 1 year	29.7	18.2	21.6
1–5 years	46.4	42.0	41.3
5–10	64.7	62.8	65.4
10–20	80.6	77.1	76.8
20–30	86.6	85.2	85.4
30 or more	84.6	82.8	84.4
Education			
High school graduate	58.4	54.9	54.9
Nongraduate	49.3	44.6	37.9
College graduate	64.1	61.6	61.4
Wage (1983 dollars)			
Less than $4	18.8	14.0	15.4
4–6	34.2	33.0	35.9
6–8	51.8	51.7	50.2
8–10	64.0	64.0	60.4
10–15	77.8	73.8	72.9
15 or more	80.1	79.3	76.4
Age			
16–24	33.5	27.6	26.0
25–34	57.7	51.5	50.0
35–44	63.6	62.6	60.7
45–54	68.4	63.8	63.7
55–64	66.8	64.8	63.2
64 or more	32.6	35.7	39.1

Table 2.7 (continued)

	1979	1983	1988
Occupation			
Manager/professional	67.5	61.9	60.9
Technical	63.9	61.1	64.2
Sales	45.6	43.0	45.2
Administrative	57.2	56.4	55.5
Service	30.7	27.8	26.6
Production	60.6	56.8	54.3
Farm	13.1	11.4	15.4
Industry			
Agriculture/forest	16.0	10.4	13.7
Mining	75.9	71.4	68.7
Construction	44.4	36.4	35.9
Manufacturing			
Durable	74.5	72.6	69.1
Nondurable	68.6	64.8	64.8
Transportation/communications	70.9	71.6	64.6
Wholesale trade	56.5	52.9	53.6
Retail trade	35.2	32.9	34.8
Finance/insurance	59.4	59.9	62.1
Services	27.0	25.3	29.1
Professional services	49.5	49.7	50.1

Source: Analysis of May 1979, 1983 and 1988 Current Population Surveys of private-sector, full-time workers over age 15.

pension. The coverage rate rose sharply with increases in wages, reaching 76.4% for workers earning over $15.00 per hour. Viewing coverage only from a point-in-time perspective indicates the likelihood of receiving benefits from pension tax expenditures increases with earnings.

Pension coverage also increases sharply with age as workers sort themselves into career jobs and attempt to meet minimum-service requirements. Lifetime patterns of earnings indicate a direct relationship between age and earnings. Thus, workers with low wages early in their careers gradually move up the earnings distribution, and many workers who did not have pension coverage early in their careers participate in pension plans later in their work life. As a result, lifetime coverage rates are likely to be considerably higher than those indicated by cross-sectional data. Thus, any adverse effects on tax expenditure vertical equity are reduced when viewed from a lifetime perspective.

Pension coverage also varies by individual and job characteristics, thus raising some concerns about the horizontal equity related to pension tax expenditures. Pension coverage is greater among workers in large firms, under union contract, with greater education, in certain industries, and in managerial, technical, and production occupations.[29]

The relationship between wage and pension coverage can also be estimated in a pension coverage equation that holds constant worker characteristics such as age, job tenure, race, sex, marital status, union status, occupation, and education along with firm characteristics like size, industry, and region. Estimating a probit coverage equation using data from the 1988 CPS, we find that every dollar increase in the hourly wage rate increases the predicted probability of being covered by a pension 2.2%.

The implication of this estimate is shown by examining changes in the probability of workers being covered by a pension, holding other personal and job characteristics constant. Workers in the 1988 CPS had an average hourly wage of $10.11 or approximately $20,000 per year. Workers at this income level had a 52.4% probability of being covered by a pension; for workers earning one dollar less per hour or about $18,000 per year, the predicted probability was 50.2%; and the comparable rate for workers earning $22,000 was 54.6%.[30] The magnitude of this "wage effect" on pension coverage increased from .0147 to .0222 between 1979 and 1988.

These observations are based on a single point-in-time observation and do not measure individual experiences over full working lives. As table 2.7 shows, pension coverage rises steadily with age until it reaches its highest level for the 45–54 age group. This suggests the use of cross-sectional data to determine pension coverage rates does not accurately predict the proportion of a cohort of workers who will ultimately receive pension benefits in retirement.

The lower wage categories include many young workers who can expect both wage levels and pension coverage rates to increase with their age and job tenure. In 1988, workers under age 35 constituted 50% of the full-time private-sector labor force. However, these young workers represented 66% of workers with an hourly wage less than $4.75 and 61% of those with hourly wages between $4.75 and $6.15. In contrast, young workers accounted for only 35% of workers with hourly wages between $11.75 and $17.75. Those under age 35 constituted 58% of workers with less than a year of job tenure and 65% of those with between one and five years' experience on their current job. This relationship between age and wage or job tenure occurs as young workers gradually settle into career jobs characterized by implicit long-term contracts, including upward-sloping wage profiles and pension plans.

Younger workers employed by firms offering pension plans are also more likely than their older counterparts to be nonparticipants. The CPS contains information concerning why workers whose employer sponsors a pension plan are not included in that plan. In 1979, 74% of workers who had not worked long enough on their current job to be eligible to partic-ipate in the pension plan were under 35. This proportion fell slightly to 67% by 1988. Of this group, 61% had less than a year of job tenure in 1979. In 1988, 57% of young nonparticipants had been employed less than one year at their current job. Of respondents in the survey who said they were too young to participate in their company pension, 93% were under age 25 in 1979. This proportion had declined to 75% by 1988.

To measure these lifetime effects of pension coverage associated with developing careers, consider the aging of a single cohort of workers. For this example, we focus on the baby boom cohort born between 1946 and 1964. Table 2.8 shows how pension coverage rates and job tenure increased as this cohort aged from between 15 and 33 in 1979 to between 24 and 42 in 1988. The cohort's experience is then compared to that of the entire private-sector labor force.

Table 2.8
Changing pension coverage of baby boom cohort

	1979	1988
Baby boomers		
Pension coverage	.468	.529
Average wage (1983 dollars)	$7.79	$8.54
Years' tenure	4.08	5.14
Total labor force		
Pension coverage	.565	.524
Average wage	$8.77	$8.40
Years' tenure	8.91	6.73
Boomers/labor force		
Pension coverage	.83	1.01
Average wage	.89	1.02
Years' tenure	.46	.76

Source: Analysis of May 1979, 1983, and 1988 Current Population Surveys of private-sector full-time workers over age 15.

As their wage and experience grew relative to those of the total full-time workforce, so did their pension coverage. In 1979, 46.8% of the baby boom cohort was covered by an employer pension. The coverage rate increased to 52.9% in 1988. As a result, their "share" of the pension tax expenditure increased over time. Looking solely at 1979 data, one might conclude that pensions' preferential tax treatment did not substantially benefit this low income/low pension participation cohort. However, as this group aged and continued to increase their relative wages and pension coverage rates, their gain from pension tax expenditures increased.

Dividing this cohort into two groups further supports the growth in coverage among young workers. First, consider the younger members of the baby boom cohort—those born between 1956 and 1964. Their average hourly wage in 1979 was $6.19 (in 1983 dollars) compared to $8.74 for older members of the cohort (those born between 1946 and 1955) and $8.83 for the entire labor force. In 1979, only 31.4% of the younger baby boomers were covered by a pension while the coverage rate for the older baby boomers was 55.3%. The coverage rate for the entire labor force was 56.5%.

By 1988, the average wage of those born between 1956 and 1964 had risen to $7.92 (in 1983 dollars) while the wage of the older members of the cohort had increased to $9.30. In comparison, the average wage for the entire labor force decreased to $8.51. Because of these changes, the wage of the cohort's younger members increased from 70% to 93% of the entire labor force's wage. During the same time, the youngest baby boomers' coverage rate rose from 56% to 91% of that of the entire labor force. Similar but less pronounced trends are observed for the older baby boomers.[31] The coverage rate for these cohorts of workers is expected to continue to grow as they age and further develop their careers.

These data indicate that the relationship between wages and coverage should not be examined using a single cross-sectional data set. Lifetime coverage rates exceed point-in-time coverage rates. Those with low income and no coverage early in life often secure coverage later in their careers. Thus, the proportion of retirees receiving benefits should continue to rise. In a mature pension system, the proportion of retirees receiving benefits exceeds the proportion of workers covered by a pension in any particular year.

Recent experience supports the continued growth in the proportion of retirees receiving pension income. Pension income as a proportion of income for households aged 65 to 74 increased from 14.6% in 1980 to 18.4% in 1990. Income attributable to employer pensions for households

75 and older increased from 12.5% to 16.7% during the same period. Much of this increase resulted from an increase in the proportion of older households with pension income. Households 65 to 74 with some pension income increased from 35% of all households in 1980 to 47% in 1990. The corresponding increase for households 75 and older was from 29% to 40% (Hitschler 1993).

Incidence of Pension Tax Expenditures and Personal Income

The value of pension tax expenditures accrues to current participants in pension plans. Cross-sectional and lifetime pension coverage rates described above illustrate the characteristics of those receiving benefits from pension tax expenditures. The value to individual households depends on the pension plan generosity, workers' age and years of tenure in current job, and the marginal tax rates the household faces.

Several estimates of the distribution of pension tax expenditures in a single year have been presented (Schieber and Goodfellow 1994; Employee Benefit Research Institute 1993). These estimates indicate that most benefits from pension tax expenditures accrue to households with annual incomes from $20,000 to $100,000. For example, Schieber and Goodfellow (1994) report that 45% of the pension tax expenditure goes to households with annual incomes of $30,000 to $49,999 (see table 2.9). These households paid 22% of the nation's total personal income tax. Thus, they had a tax expenditure to income tax paid ratio of 2.0. Households with more than

Table 2.9
Federal taxes and pension tax expenditures

Household income	Share of income tax	Share of tax preference	Tax expenditure/ income tax ratio
Less than $5,000	0.15%	0.01%	0.04
$5,000–9,999	0.98	0.06	0.06
$10,000–14,999	2.31	0.52	0.23
$15,000–19,999	3.76	3.52	0.94
$20,000–29,999	9.74	10.09	1.04
$30,000–49,999	22.10	44.72	2.02
$50,000 or more	60.96	41.09	0.67

Source: Sylvester J. Schieber and Gordon Goodfellow, "Fat Cats, Bureaucrats, and Common Workers: Distributing The Pieces of the Pension Tax Preference Pie," in Dallas Salisbury and Nora Super Jones (eds.), *Pension Funding and Taxation: Implications for Tomorrow*, Washington, D.C.: Employee Benefit Research Institute, 1994, p. 111.

$50,000 of annual income received 41% of the pension tax expenditures while paying 61% of the income tax, for a tax expenditure to income tax ratio of 0.67.

Using somewhat different income categories, the Employee Benefit Research Institute (1993) reports that most tax expenditures going to upper-income households accrue to those with incomes between $50,000 and $99,999. Only households with incomes between $20,000 and $99,999 have a tax expenditure to income tax ratio exceeding one.

These two studies indicate that on an annual basis most pension tax expenditures benefit middle-income households, as shown by examining the distribution of tax expenditures across income groups and calculating the ratio of tax expenditures to income taxes paid for households. Households at the bottom of the income distribution do not benefit substantially from pension tax expenditures because they are less likely to be covered by a pension; if covered, they generally have lower pension benefits and hence a lower accrued tax expenditure, and they are in lower income tax brackets, so that for the same pension benefit they would receive a smaller implied tax expenditure.

These studies do not address the issue of lifetime distribution of pension tax expenditures. Just as lifetime incomes are more equally distributed than incomes for a single year (Lillard 1977), we would expect the lifetime distribution of pension tax expenditures to be more equally distributed than they are in a single year.

A final issue concerning pension tax expenditure impact on vertical equity relates to the permanent exclusion of pension compensation from the payroll tax. Including payroll taxes in the analysis reduces the seemingly adverse effect of pensions' preferential tax status. Workers with 1994 earnings in excess of $60,600 paid marginal payroll taxes of only 2.9% associated with health insurance. By contrast, workers with earnings below $60,600 paid marginal rates of 15.3% for Social Security retirement, disability and health programs.[32]

If pension compensation became taxable income subject to both income and payroll taxes, lower-income workers would face lower income tax rates but much higher payroll taxes on their newly taxable compensation. Combining the two tax effects indicates workers across the earnings distribution would face roughly the same total marginal tax rates on pension compensation.[33] For example, a worker making $25,000 per year is paying a marginal income tax of 15% and a marginal payroll tax of 15.3%. Thus, this low-wage worker would pay a combined tax rate of 30.3% on imputed pension compensation. In contrast, a high-wage earner making

$75,000 per year pays a marginal income tax of 28% and a marginal payroll tax of 2.9%. Thus, the high-wage worker would pay a combined marginal tax rate of 30.9 percent, or 0.6 percent higher, on the imputed pension income than the low-wage worker.

Pensions and the Distribution of Wealth

Most discussion concerning pension tax expenditure distributional effects has focused on the analysis of pension coverage rates by income and the distribution of implied tax expenditures across income groups in a given year. Missing in this discussion is pensions' effect on the distribution of wealth and how changes in the pension tax laws might alter that distribution.

McDermed, Clark, and Allen (1989) analyze pensions' impact on wealth distribution using the 1983 Survey of Consumer Finances. Employing information on survey respondents' pension plans, they calculated pension wealth and added this value to the estimates of nonpension wealth calculated by researchers at the Federal Reserve Board.[34] Table 2.10 presents the distribution of nonpension and pension wealth by age of head of household.

The table bases pension wealth on termination value and hence represents actual pension wealth if the worker were to leave his or her plan.[35] Calculating pension wealth using termination benefits produces a jump in

Table 2.10
Distribution of Wealth: 1983 Survey of Consumer Finances

Age	Mean nonpension wealth	Pension wealth: households with pension	Total wealth	Pension wealth / Total wealth	Percentage with pension wealth
<25	$ 6,342	$ 1,951	$ 6,879	7.8	27.5
25–34	31,735	6,899	35,612	11.1	57.2
35–44	82,181	20,383	98,924	16.9	66.0
45–54	188,503	70,764	230,128	20.0	65.0
55–64	196,492	121,183	270,380	27.3	61.0
65–74	222,514	55,060	247,411	10.1	45.2
75>	119,639	25,522	126,958	5.8	28.7
All	118,419	47,541	143,837	18.1	54.8

Source: Ann McDermed, Robert Clark, and Steven Allen, "Pension Wealth, Age-Wealth Profiles, and the Distribution of Net Worth," in Robert Lipsey and Helen Stone Tice, *The Measurement of Saving, Investment, and Wealth*, NBER studies in Income and Wealth, vol. 52, Chicago: University of Chicago Press, 1989, pp. 698–731.

pension wealth at vesting as the worker goes from having zero pension wealth to a value based on five or so years of work. More than half of all households had some pension wealth, as did more than 60% of those with heads aged 35 to 64. Pension wealth represented 18% of total wealth for all households. The proportion of wealth from pensions ranged from 11.1% for households whose head was 25 to 34 to 27.3% for households with heads 55 to 64.[36]

Opponents of pensions' preferential tax treatment have expressed concern over pension tax expenditure distributional effects. The preceding analysis of annual tax liability indicated how current expenditures are distributed relative to household income. We can now review pensions' impact on the distribution of household wealth and infer the impact of eliminating pensions' preferred tax status.

Including pension wealth in the analysis of the distribution of household wealth substantially reduces overall inequity as measured by the proportion of wealth held by the top 5% or top 1% of the income distribution or as measured by the Gini coefficient. Table 2.11 shows the top 5% of households hold 57.5% of nonpension wealth. This declines to 52.5% when pension wealth is included. The Gini coefficient declines from .806 to .777 when pension wealth is included.[37]

Including pension wealth in the analysis of total wealth reduces income inequality of the total population and within each of the age groups

Table 2.11
Impact of pensions on the distribution of wealth

Age	Nonpension wealth			Nonpension wealth		
	Percentage of wealth		Gini	Percentage of wealth		Gini
	Top 5%	Top 1%	ratio	Top 5%	Top 1%	ratio
<25	55.5	25.4	0.891	53.3	23.6	0.875
25–34	47.8	22.5	0.799	43.5	20.2	0.769
35–44	41.9	20.3	0.706	37.7	18.8	0.688
45–54	62.2	40.3	0.800	54.6	34.3	0.739
55–64	50.7	27.2	0.745	43.6	23.3	0.686
65–74	56.1	35.0	0.782	52.5	32.6	0.749
>75	50.9	35.7	0.763	49.3	34.0	0.750
All	57.5	35.5	0.806	52.5	31.1	0.777

Source: Ann McDermed, Robert Clark, and Steven Allen, "Pension Wealth, Age-Wealth Profiles, and the Distribution of Net Worth," in Robert Lipsey and Helen Stone Tice, *The Measurement of Saving, Investment, and Wealth*, NBER Studies in Income and Wealth, vol. 52, Chicago: University of Chicago Press, 1989, pp. 689–731.

shown in table 2.11. These data clearly indicate workers in the middle of the income distribution own most pension wealth. As a result, the elimination or significant reduction of pension wealth would exacerbate the variance in the distribution of wealth by increasing the relative size of the wealth holdings of the very wealthiest households in the United States.

Full Taxation of Pensions

Tax expenditures for pensions could be reduced or eliminated by various tax code changes, including: (1) the continued reduction in pension plan funding levels, (2) full taxation of pension contributions and plan earnings, and (3) taxation of plan assets. After briefly describing these policies, we examine possible implications of tax policy changes based on the current economic literature.[38]

Tax Policy Changes

Prior to the 1980s, government pension policies primarily aimed to encourage firms through preferential tax treatment to offer retirement plans, insure through discrimination tests that plans were not established exclusively for high-income workers, and increase through vesting and funding requirements the likelihood that pension participants would receive retirement benefits. Adequate funding of pension plans was an ongoing concern of government policy lest firms renege on the pension promise. During this period, most pension legislation originated in congressional labor committees.

Pension regulation based on the concerns for an optimal public policy for pensions reached its zenith in 1974 with the passage of ERISA, which established detailed regulations for funding, vesting, and participation. ERISA's clear objectives were to insure that workers covered by a pension would receive their promised benefits in retirement and to encourage increased pension coverage throughout the economy.

Since 1980, periodic, almost annual, tax code amendments have altered the tax status of pension contributions for qualified plans. These bills' principal objectives have been not to develop the best retirement policies but instead to increase federal tax revenues by reducing pension tax expenditures. Little or no concern has been shown for general pension policy aimed at providing adequate retirement benefits. Concern for adequate funding of pension plans has given way to the desire to limit contributions so as to limit associated foregone tax revenues. Most legislation during this period has originated in Congress's various tax committees.

This flurry of pension legislation has substantially altered the demand for employer-provided retirement plans. Government policy since 1980 has stimulated the dramatic shift away from defined-benefit pension plans toward defined-contribution plans (Clark and McDermed 1990; Chang 1991) while also altering the demand for any pension whatsoever.

One possible public policy for the rest of the decade would be to continue periodically enacting legislation limiting deductible contributions to pension plans, which could gradually reduce or eliminate pension tax expenditures. Another would be to eliminate the deferral of taxation on new contributions and to tax the value of plan earnings. Munnell (1992) advocates a 15% tax on annual contributions and pension earnings at the plan level. Alternatively, the assets of pension funds could be taxed directly. Munnell (1991) argues for a tax of 2.5% on plan assets.[39]

Each of these alternatives raises the cost of providing a dollar of retirement benefits. Holding constant employer contributions as a proportion of salary, the promised retirement benefit must be reduced. However, the change in tax treatment would provide incentives that would alter the demand for employer-provided retirement plans. In addition, each proposed policy contains incentives for plan sponsors to reduce pension plan funding to some minimum level.

Implications of Tax Policy Changes

Changes in the tax code to eliminate or significantly reduce pension tax expenditure would provoke responses by firms and workers. To assess the importance of these changes, we review the economic literature for evidence concerning response direction and magnitude. Economic theory suggests eliminating the preferential tax treatment for pensions would increase the implied price to workers of receiving this benefit. This would reduce the demand for pension coverage and reduce pension participants' total compensation. Most studies also indicate that as a result, national savings would decline somewhat.

Reductions in the Demand for Pensions

Workers bear the cost of employee benefits as reductions in cash wages. In general, when the firm contributes a dollar more to employee benefits, workers can expect a dollar less in cash wages. Workers willingly purchase benefits from their employers when the benefit effectively costs less bought through the employer than in the market. Lower prices are attributable to quantity discounts, risk pooling, and most importantly, some benefits' preferential tax status.[40]

Eliminating the preferential tax status for employer-provided pension plans would, in effect, raise the price of retirement benefits to workers. Each dollar of employer contributions would result in fewer dollars of retirement benefits. As a result, fewer pension plans would be demanded and for those plans remaining, lower retirement benefits would be purchased. In an often-cited study, Woodbury (1983) finds wages are easily substituted for benefits. He estimates a price elasticity of employee benefits of −1.7. Sloan and Adamache (1986) report the tax elasticity for pension contributions exceeds −1. Other studies finding significant substitution of cash for benefits include Rice 1966; Long and Scott 1982; Smith 1981; and Gunderson, Hyatt, and Pesando 1992.

Given these findings, eliminating the preferential tax status of pensions would be expected to substantially reduce the demand for employer-provided retirement plans. For example, if tax policies required current taxation of pension contributions and earnings of pension funds, the current price of a dollar of retirement income for a pension participant would increase sharply. The increased cost of one dollar of retirement benefit due to changes in pension taxation would depend on the interest rate, current and future tax rates, and the length of time until retirement.[41]

If the cost of providing a dollar in pension benefits increased, the demand for pensions as employee compensation would decline. Woodbury and Huang (1991) confirmed this decline in simulations that illustrate the effect of change in tax policy. For the period 1969 to 1982, they estimated that if the government had adopted a policy making it fully taxable, pension compensation would have decreased 64%. Although such a policy was not instituted, 1986 tax code amendments did modify pensions' tax status. Woodbury and Huang predicted that these changes would reduce future pension compensation by 50%. Thus, eliminating the preferential tax status of employer-provided pensions would clearly predict a substantial decline in the number of such plans and the generosity of those that remained.[42]

Decline in National Savings
Reducing or eliminating the preferential tax policy for employer-sponsored pensions would reduce demand for such pensions. The impact of reduced employer pensions on total aggregate savings would depend

on several factors. Pensions are only one form of retirement savings, and retirement savings only one component of total household savings. The ultimate impact on national savings of a decline in employer pensions would depend on (1) how sensitive pensions were to tax policy, (2) how closely other forms of retirement savings substituted for pensions, and (3) how total savings responded to changes in rates of return and lifetime wealth.[43]

Lifetime income and the rate of return on savings determine the desired size of retirement income. A change in tax policy that lowered the implied rate of return on pension savings would raise the cost of achieving a particular retirement income. This could decrease the target savings amount so that as the amount of pension savings fell, other savings would increase but by a smaller amount. As a result, total savings would decline (Venti and Wise 1992).[44]

Another effect of pensions on aggregate savings occurs through changes in retirement age. The growth in pension coverage over the postwar period has contributed to the trend toward lower retirement ages. Workers respond to a decline in working years relative to retirement years by increasing savings rates during the shorter working period. This latter effect suggests that a drop in pension coverage might cause an even larger drop in total savings.

Since the combined effects of these theoretical results are ambiguous, empirical research is required to determine the direction of change in aggregate savings as pension savings decline. Using various data sources, economists have generally found that a one dollar increase in pension savings is only partly offset by smaller decreases in other forms of savings. Ippolito (1986) estimates roughly a quarter to a half of pension savings are new savings, and the Employee Benefit Research Institute (1993, p. 127) notes estimates of this pension offset effect in the economics literature range between 32% and 84%.[45] Munnell and Yohn (1992) conclude that "all that can reasonably be said is that some offsetting behavior occurs and that it is less than dollar-for-dollar."

The dramatic rise in contributions into IRAs followed by a sharp decline after changes in their tax status presents a specific opportunity to assess retirement savings' impact on total savings.[46] Although IRAs are not identical savings vehicles to pensions (primarily because of limits on eligibility and contribution amounts), they are targeted to retirement savings, and prior to 1986 had almost identical tax treatment. Empirical estimates of IRA effects on aggregate savings have been divided between those that found IRA contributions to be primarily net new savings and those that found them to be a reallocation of existing savings or new borrowing. For example, Venti and Wise (1992) have estimated net new savings proportions as high as 66%. They summarize the empirical evidence and reject the assertion that no IRA saving was net new saving. Their conclusions are disputed by Gravelle (1991) and others.

The IRA experience indicates that allocating savings among different forms is sensitive to tax policy; however, it does not unambiguously reveal the sensitivity of the total level of savings to changes in tax policies concerning specific types of retirement savings. It is not surprising that it has been difficult to pinpoint the impact of changes in retirement savings on aggregate saving. General theoretical and empirical ambiguity continues about the impact of rates of return on savings. Pension savings can be viewed as an opportunity to save at a higher net rate of return than other forms of personal savings. Most recent empirical estimates of saving's elasticity with respect to the interest rate have found very low individual responses to changes in market rates of return. Though some researchers believe the true value may be somewhat higher, econometric obstacles have prevented accurate measurement of saving elasticity (Bovenberg 1989).

Given these ambiguities, predicting the impact of tax policy changes on aggregate saving is risky. Based on the consensus that some, but not all, of pension savings is net new savings, a decline in pension coverage should result in a decline in aggregate savings.

Conclusions

Until the last decade, public policy toward pensions had three primary objectives: to encourage the spread of employer-provided retirement programs through preferential tax treatment, to prevent employers from establishing plans that benefited only highly paid employees by instituting discrimination standards, and to ensure that promised benefits were paid by setting standards for funding, vesting, and participation and by establishing the PBGC. Over the last ten years, the focus of government policy has shifted toward concern for the lost tax revenue associated with the preferential tax status accorded employer pension plans.

The recent debate concerning the merits of maintaining pensions' current tax status has focused on the normative question of what the optimal federal pension policy is. The primary concern for the lost tax revenues versus recognizing the value of the existing pension system in providing retirement income has characterized the two sides of the argument. These positions are clearly expressed by two prominent advocates in this debate:

First, Munnell (1989, p. 49) states that "in an era of large budget deficits and a future that includes the rising costs of an aging society, it is difficult to understand why such a large source of potential revenue is allowed to go untapped. Moreover, the failure to tax nonwage compensation creates serious inequities between those workers who receive all their earnings in taxable cash wages and those who receive a substantial portion in nontaxable fringe benefits."

Second, Schieber (1990, p. 3) writes, "Congress is in a position of considering an option that may jeopardize the retirement income security of three-fourths of the baby boom generation so it can solve 2% of the federal tax shortfall without 'raising taxes.'"

Although these positions define the framework of the debate concerning the desirability of taxing pension compensation, public policy decisions should be based on a clear assessment of the impact of any tax code changes. In this chapter, we have attempted to focus on the positive economic questions concerning employee and employer responses to tax code changes relating to pension compensation and pension fund earnings. These points are summarized below.

1. Tax expenditures for pensions are relatively large and are estimated to have averaged around $55 billion during the past 10 years. However, since the mid-1980s, these tax expenditures have represented a declining proportion of the revenues from personal income taxes.

2. The current method of calculating the pension tax expenditure yields a point-in-time measure of foregone tax revenues. This calculation is affected by trends in pension coverage, population aging, benefit trends, and funding level changes. Each factor has generally increased the measured tax expenditure in the past but should reduce it in the future. Tax rate changes and other tax policy changes directly affect pension tax expenditures. Recent tax rate increases are likely to increase tax expenditures associated with employer pensions.

3. Pension tax policies provide relatively few benefits to low-wage workers in a given year. The seemingly adverse effect of pension tax expenditures on the tax system's vertical equity is reduced considerably when the frame of reference is individual lifetimes instead of a single year. Earnings and pension coverage rates rise with age, and lifetime pension coverage rates are substantially higher than those that prevail in a single year. Thus, many young, low-wage workers currently not covered by a pension who

do not benefit from the pension tax expenditure in a given year will ultimately obtain pension coverage and benefit from these tax policies later.

4. If implied pension compensation becomes subject to payroll as well as income taxes, low-wage pension participants will pay approximately the same combined (payroll plus income) marginal tax rates on this newly taxable income as high-wage workers. This implies that the full value in reduced taxes paid by pension participants does not increase significantly with increases in income since eliminating the payroll tax offsets much of the increase in higher marginal income tax rates.

5. Changing the tax laws so that pension compensation becomes taxable would be expected to result in a considerable decline in the demand for employer-provided pensions. Studies of pension elasticity indicate they are very responsive to changes in the implied price (in the form of reduced cash earnings). Thus, workers would shift away from employer-provided retirement plans toward more cash earnings. This change's impact on income in retirement would depend on these workers' future savings behavior.

6. Reductions in pension savings are expected to reduce total savings for retirement and total national saving. Estimates of pension impact on total saving indicate that when pension savings decline, other forms of savings increase but not at a dollar-for-dollar rate. An average of these studies might suggest that national saving would decline by around $0.50 for each dollar of decline in pension savings.

7. Pensions reduce the inequality of the distribution of wealth as measured by the Gini coefficient or by the proportion of wealth held by the top 5% of the population. Thus, declines in pension wealth would be expected to increase wealth inequality.

8. Pensions provide a significant component of income to retirees. If this form of retirement income were substantially reduced, it is uncertain what type of long-run savings would take its place. With the aging of the population, fiscal pressure will increase on national programs for the elderly. Concern is now being expressed for the baby boom cohort's future retirement income. Anticipated declines in the value of Social Security relative to lifetime earnings will increase the need for additional private retirement income. Any decline in these future retirees' pension income will exacerbate this problem.

9. A more appropriate measure of pension tax expenditures would be based on a life cycle concept and not the current point-in-time analysis

employed to estimate this loss in tax revenues. Such a measure would provide a better link between current pension compensation and the value of deferred income taxes.

10. Tax revenues would be expected to increase if the tax status of employer pensions were changed, but the increase in revenues would depend on employer and employee responses to the taxation of pension compensation. Especially important to this calculation would be government employer response and whether they increased cash compensation to offset the decline in value of the job to their workers.

Eliminating pension compensation's preferred tax treatment would surely increase government tax revenues; however, the net increase would certainly be less than the value of the calculated pension tax expenditure. Such an action would greatly change the pension system that has become an important source of income to many Americans and the development of which Congress has strongly encouraged for more than 75 years. Fewer people would be covered, and those covered would have lower retirement income. For the most part, middle-class families with incomes between $20,000 and $100,000 would be adversely affected, and total national wealth would become more unequally distributed unless private saving increased to match the decline in pension saving.

The evidence suggests Congress should not move quickly to alter pension tax status. Significant implications of the last decade's incremental changes are being observed. These changes have limited pension tax expenditures' growth as they have played a role in reducing the growth of pension coverage and ending the trend toward more generous benefits. Policy makers must decide if they are willing to impose on society the adverse effects of ending pensions' special tax treatment in exchange for the increase in tax revenues.

Notes

Robert Clark is Professor, College of Management, North Carolina State University, and Visiting Professor, Fuqua School of Business, Duke University. Elisa Wolper is a Ph.D. candidate, Department of Economics, North Carolina State University. From 1990 to 1993, she was a National Institute on Aging predoctoral fellow.

1. Kotlikoff and Smith (1983) report that pension contributions increased from 1.7% of wage and salary compensation in 1950 to 5.1% in 1975. Chen (1981) traces the growth in the proportion of earnings attributable to employee benefits from 1950 to 1980 and makes projections for future growth. He emphasizes the impact of the growth in the proportion of compensation devoted to employee benefits on the payroll tax revenues.

2. Craig and White (1993) review in detail employer pension development between 1913 and 1950. For more recent trends in pension coverage, see Andrews 1985; Woods 1989; Bloom and Freeman 1992; and Turner and Beller 1992. In comparing coverage rates across studies, one must carefully consider the definition of the labor force being examined.

3. Employee Benefit Research Institute 1988 and Schieber 1990 review the development of tax treatment of employer-provided retirement plans.

4. Pensions' current tax status is more consistent with the principles of a consumption tax than those of an income tax. Under a consumption tax, income is taxed not when earned but when used to purchase goods and services. See Mieszkowski 1978 and Ippolito 1994 for a discussion of the relative merits of a consumption-based versus an income-based tax system.

5. Given the current rapid growth in the cost of health insurance for employees, the tax expenditure associated with nontaxation of employer-provided health insurance may exceed the pension tax expenditure within the next five years (Employee Benefit Research Institute 1993). Extending health insurance coverage to all workers by mandating it would substantially increase the tax expenditure for employer-provided health insurance. Of course, tax policy could be changed so that employer contributions for health insurance also became taxable income.

6. U.S. Congress, Joint Committee on Taxation 1993 discusses in more detail the concept of tax expenditures.

7. The differences between termination pension wealth and pension wealth based on projected final earnings are discussed below.

8. For a given promise of retirement benefits, minimizing annual contributions and fund size minimizes taxes paid by the firm.

9. Projections for specific years made at different times can be compared. For example, in 1990 projected tax expenditures for 1991 were $52.2 billion, and projections for 1994 (out year 3) were $58.8 billion. In 1991, projections for 1994 (out year 2) were $59.0 billion, and projections for fiscal 1994 made in 1993 were $55.3 billion.

10. Schieber (1990) attributes some of this increase to a revision in the method used to estimate tax expenditures.

11. If workers consider their total compensation to be cash earnings plus the gain in pension wealth associated with continued employment, this $62 billion is part of their assessment of their compensation's value. If pensions were eliminated, governments would have to pay pension compensation in the form of cash—both funded and unfunded pension compensation would have to be included to hold the worker at the same level of pay. Thus, eliminating pensions could actually increase the government's net outlays because it was required to "fund" the unfunded component of pension compensation.

12. Federal pension plans' funding status is complex. These plans' assets typically are held in U.S. Treasury bonds. Because the liabilities are real and the assets merely another form of government liability, is there any difference between full funding with the entire fund composed of government bonds and no funding of these plans? This issue can be compared to the recent debate concerning Social Security funding and the buildup of the trust funds.

13. This example clearly indicates how plan sponsors' funding policies influence the size of the tax expenditure estimates. An extension of this relationship is that altering tax policy to one that mirrors the tax-expenditure concept would result in adverse incentives for funding

pension plans as plan sponsors attempted to provide benefits with the lowest possible tax liability. If tax laws were changed so that pension funds or employer contributions were subject to current taxation, tax liabilities would be minimized when plan sponsors satisfied the minimum legal funding requirements. Thus, plan sponsors would have a new incentive to minimize pension funding.

14. Estimates of tax expenditures for 1993 were $6.2 billion for IRAs and $3.0 billion for Keogh plans.

15. Since 1981, annual contributions to IRAs have been limited to $2,000 per worker or $2,250 per couple. Withdrawals prior to age 59.5 carry substantial penalties.

16. For single taxpayers, full deductibility for those with a company pension is limited to those with income below $25,000. The deductibility is phased out for those with incomes between $25,000 and $35,000. For couples filing joint returns, the comparable limits are $40,000 and $50,000.

17. In 1988, 52% of full-time private-sector workers were participating in a pension plan but only 29% of elderly households were receiving income from a private pension plan (Reno 1993).

18. Assuming an interest rate of 6%, the $300 of employer contributions is invested to yield sufficient funds to pay a benefit of $318 in retirement.

19. This growth in coverage rates roughly mirrors increases in coverage rates in the U.S. economy from 1940 to 1985.

20. These values are derived as follows: (1) tax reduction for pension participant during work life is ($300 × 0.28) = $84; (2) tax reduction on plan earnings is ($18 × 0.28) = $5.04; (3) tax increase during retirement is ($318 × 0.15) = $47.70; and (4) change in present value of lifetime taxes paid is ($89.04 − $47.70/1.06) = $44.04.

21. A similar concept can be applied to young versus more mature pension plans. Newly started pension plans obviously have relatively fewer assets than older, more mature plans. In addition, new plan sponsors can make only relatively small tax-deductible contributions because of the full-funding limits concerning termination liabilities. As a result, newly established plans account for relatively small pension tax expenditures even though they may be accruing substantial projected pension liabilities. In contrast, mature plans may be making substantial qualified contributions. Thus, eliminating pensions' tax-deferred status would affect them very differently depending on their stage of development.

22. Population age structure data are based on data and projections (alternative II) in U.S. Social Security Administration 1984, 1992.

23. An interesting parallel to the tax expenditure for pensions is the concept of retiree health insurance. Companies accrue liabilities as workers earn credit toward a promise for the provision of health insurance after they retire. Changes in generally accepted accounting practices now require firms to recognize these liabilities. Since these plans are often not funded, no tax expenditure is assessed; however, real liabilities exist. Would society, firms, and workers be better off if these plans were funded? Conversely, would society be better off if pensions were not funded and thus, pension tax expenditures were zero?

24. In general, workers are expected to bear the full costs of employee benefits in the form of reduced wages. Firms are assumed to be neutral sellers of these benefits and to make them available to their workers at cost. Workers desire to purchase benefits through their

employer because they can do so at a lower net price because of group discounts, risk pooling, and tax advantages (Smith 1979). In some cases, firms may use benefits to modify worker behavior and reduce other personnel costs. In these circumstances, the firm may not require a dollar-for-dollar reduction in wages (Allen and Clark 1987).

25. It is generally believed that defined-contribution pensions are direct compensation to workers. Therefore, workers receive a dollar of employer contribution into their pension account at the cost of a dollar in cash wages.

26. Defined-benefit plans may be part of long-term, implicit labor contracts used to alter worker behavior (Ippolito 1987; Allen and Clark 1987). As such, their existence may provide cost reductions to the firm due to lower turnover or more efficient retirement patterns. Thus, the firm may provide one dollar of benefits through a defined-benefit pension plan at less than the cost of one dollar in wage reduction.

27. Smith (1981) explores the issue of whether workers fully pay for benefits in the form of wage reductions in underfunded plans. Feldstein and Seligman (1981) make a similar point concerning underfunded pensions and their impact on savings.

28. Munnell's proposal specifically anticipates this type of employer response. She argues for taxing pension funds but allowing plan sponsors to reduce promised benefits accordingly (Munnell 1991, 1992).

29. Lazear and Rosen (1987) conclude that pension plans contribute to black-white inequality but do not affect male-female income differences among whites.

30. These values are based on a probit model estimated on the May 1988 CPS with major industry categories included in the probit equation along with the worker and firm characteristics listed in the text.

31. The older baby boomers' average wage increased from 99% to 109% of that for the entire labor force, and their pension coverage rate increased from 98% to 113% of that for the entire labor force.

32. These tax rates represent combined employer and employee taxes and thus assume that workers bear the incidence of the employer portion of the tax.

33. This discussion ignores any increase in future retirement benefits attributable to these payroll taxes.

34. This process involved examining all pension plans for each respondent. Information concerning the pension plans was then used to calculate pension benefits using both the termination and projected methods. See McDermed, Clark, and Allen 1989 for a detailed discussion of this methodology.

35. McDermed, Clark, and Allen (1989) used two methods to calculate termination pension wealth. The first was similar to that shown in table 2.5, and the second estimated each respondent's lifetime earnings profile, prepared by researchers at the Federal Reserve Board. In the case of termination pension wealth, these two measures of earnings growth yielded very similar estimates of pension wealth. Estimates of pension wealth were also made using the projected method. The two assumptions produce more varying results when earnings are projected years into the future.

36. Other measures of the distribution of pension wealth are found in Quinn 1985 and Cartwright and Friedland 1985.

37. Using the projected final earnings method for calculating pension wealth, 31.4% of total household wealth was in pension promises. Incorporating this measure of pension wealth into the analysis lowers the proportion of total wealth held by the top 5% to 55.0% and the Gini ratio to .783.

38. Gravelle (1994) assesses in detail the issues associated with taxing implied pension compensation. For a different assessment of the evidence, see Schieber 1990.

39. In her argument for taxing pensions, Munnell (1992) cites recent changes in pension tax status in Sweden, Australia, and New Zealand. For a discussion of taxing pensions in Japan, see Clark 1991.

40. The economics literature has regularly studied compensating wage differentials or the trade-off of cash wages for employee benefits. Examples include Rosen 1974; Smith 1979; Brown 1980; and Woodbury 1983. For a detailed study of the incidence of the payroll tax for Social Security, see Brittain 1972.

41. For many workers, the increase in the cost of a dollar of retirement benefits would be between 20% and 30%.

42. Another piece of evidence supporting a sharp decline in pension contributions in response to proposed elimination of pensions' preferential tax status is the substantial decline in contributions to IRAs when TRA altered their deductibility. Although the net impact on total savings has been debated (Gravelle 1991; Venti and Wise 1990), there is no doubt that use of IRAs as a savings instrument declined significantly after 1986.

43. In economic analysis, these factors would determine savings' price and income elasticities.

44. Pension saving may also have a psychological or recognition effect. Because their employer provides information on pensions, younger workers may plan more for retirement and thereby increase nonpension saving along with their pensions. Empirical work by Munnell (1982) and others indicates this effect is not very important in determining total saving.

45. Hubbard (1986) finds a much smaller offset. He estimates only a 16% decline in nonpension wealth for every dollar increase in pension wealth.

46. Gravelle (1994) presents a thorough overview of the empirical literature on IRA contributions' impact on aggregate savings.

References

Allen, Steven, and Robert Clark. 1987. "Pensions and Firm Performance." In *Human Resources and the Performance of the Firm*, ed. Morris Kleiner, Richard Block, Myron Roomkin, and Sidney Salsburg, 195–243. Madison, WI: Industrial Relations Research Association.

Allen, Steven, Robert Clark, and Ann McDermed. 1993. "Pensions, Bonding, and Lifetime Jobs." *Journal of Human Resources* 28:463–81.

Allen, Steven, Robert Clark, and Ann McDermed. 1988. "The Pension Cost of Changing Jobs." *Research on Aging* 10:459–71.

Andrews, Emily. 1985. *The Changing Profile of Pensions in America*. Washington, D.C.: Employee Benefit Research Institute.

Bloom, David, and Richard Freeman. 1992. "The Fall in Private Pension Coverage in the U.S." *American Economic Review* 82:539—45.

Bovenberg, Lans. 1989. "Tax Policy and National Saving in the U.S.: A Survey." *National Tax Journal* 42:123—28.

Brittain, John. 1972. *The Payroll Tax for Social Security*. Washington, D.C.: The Brookings Institution.

Brown, Charles. 1980. "Equalizing Differences in the Labor Market." *Quarterly Journal of Economics* 95:112—34.

Cartwright, William, and Robert Friedland. 1985. "The President's Commission on Pension Policy Household Survey 1979: Net Wealth Distributions by Type and Age for the United States." *Review of Income and Wealth* 31:285—308.

Chang, Angela. 1991. "Explanations for the Trend Away from Defined Benefit Pension Plans." Washington, D.C.: Congressional Research Service Report for Congress.

Chen, Yung-Ping. 1981. "The Growth of Fringe Benefits: Implications for Social Security." *Monthly Labor Review* 104(11):3—10.

Clark, Robert. 1991. *Retirement Systems in Japan*, Homewood, IL: Irwin for the Pension Research Council.

Clark, Robert, and Ann McDermed. 1990. *The Choice of Pension Plans in a Changing Regulatory Environment*. Washington, D.C.: American Enterprise Institute.

Craig, Lee, and Michelle White. 1993. "Federal Regulation and the Growth of Private-Sector Pensions, 1913—1950." Working paper, North Carolina State University, Raleigh.

Employee Benefit Research Institute. 1988. "The Tax Treatment of Pension and Capital Accumulation Plans." *Issue Brief* (September).

Employee Benefit Research Institute. 1993. "Pension Tax Expenditures: Are They Worth the Cost?" *Issue Brief* (February).

Feldstein, Martin, and Stephanie Seligman. 1981. "Pension Funding, Share Prices, and National Savings." *Journal of Finance* 36:801—24.

Gravelle, Jane. 1994. *Economic Effects of Taxing Capital Income*, Cambridge, MA: MIT Press.

Gravelle, Jane. 1991. "Do Individual Retirement Accounts Increase Savings?" *Journal of Economic Perspectives* 5:133—48.

Gunderson, Morley, Douglas Hyatt, and James Pesando. 1992. "Wage-Pension Trade-offs in Collective Agreements." *Industrial and Labor Relations Review* 46:146—60.

Hitschler, Pamela. 1993. "Spending by Older Consumers: 1980 and 1990 Compared." *Monthly Labor Review* 116 (May): 3—13.

Hubbard, Glenn. 1986. "Pension Wealth and Individual Saving." *Journal of Money, Credit and Banking* 18:167—78.

Hubbard, Richard. 1994. "The Tax Treatment of Pensions." In *Pension Funding and Taxation: Implications for Tomorrow*, ed. Dallas Salisbury and Nora Super Jones. Washington, D.C.: Employee Benefit Research Institute.

Ippolito, Richard. 1994. "Implementing Basic Tax Changes: Income versus Consumption Tax Treatment." In *Pension Funding and Taxation: Implications for Tomorrow*, ed. Dallas Salisbury and Nora Super Jones. Washington, D.C.: Employee Benefit Research Institute.

Ippolito, Richard. 1987. "The Implicit Contract: Developments and New Directions." *Journal of Human Resources* 22:441–67.

Ippolito, Richard. 1986. *Pensions, Economics, and Public Policy*. Homewood, IL.: Dow Jones-Irwin.

Kotlikoff, Laurence, and Daniel Smith. 1983. *Pensions in the American Economy*. Chicago: University of Chicago Press.

Lazear, Edward, and Sherwin Rosen. 1987. "Pension Inequality." In *Issues in Pension Economics*, ed. Zvi Bodie, John Shoven, and David Wise, 341–59. Chicago: University of Chicago Press.

Lillard, Lee. 1977. "Inequality: Earnings vs. Human Wealth." *American Economic Review* 67:42–53.

Long, James, and Frank Scott. 1982. "The Income Tax and Nonwage Compensation." *Review of Economics and Statistics* 64:211–19.

McDermed, Ann, Robert Clark, and Steven Allen. 1989. "Pension Wealth, Age-Wealth Profiles, and the Distribution of Net Worth." In *The Measurement of Saving, Investment, and Wealth*, ed. Robert Lipsey and Helen Stone Tice, 689–731. NBER Studies in Income and Wealth, vol. 52. Chicago: University of Chicago Press.

Mieszkowski, Peter. 1978. "Choice of the Tax Base: Consumption Versus Income Taxation." In *Federal Tax Reform: Myths and Realities*, ed. Michael Boskin. San Francisco: Institute for Contemporary Analysis.

Mitchell, Olivia. 1992. "Trends in Pension Benefit Formulas and Retirement Provisions." In *Trends in Pensions 1992*, ed. John Turner and Daniel Beller. Washington, D.C.: USGPO, 177–216.

Munnell, Alicia. 1992. "Current Taxation of Qualified Pension Plans: Has the Time Come?" *New England Economic Review* (March/April): 12–25.

Munnell, Alicia. 1991. "Are Pensions Worth the Cost?" *National Tax Journal* 44:393–403.

Munnell, Alicia. 1989. "It's Time to Tax Employee Benefits." *New England Economic Review* (July/August): 49–63.

Munnell, Alicia. 1982. *Economics of Private Pensions*. Washington: The Brookings Institution.

Munnell, Alicia, and Frederick Yohn. 1992. "What is the Impact of Pensions on Savings?" In *Pensions and the Economy*, ed. Zvi Bodie and Alicia Munnell, 115–39. Philadelphia: University of Pennsylvania.

Poterba, James, Steven Venti, and David Wise. 1993. "Do 401(k) Contributions Crowd Out Other Personal Saving?" Working Paper no. 4391, National Bureau for Economic Research, Cambridge, MA.

Quinn, Joseph. 1985. "Retirement Income Rights as a Component of Wealth." *Review of Income and Wealth* 31:223–36.

Reno, Virginia. 1993. "The Role of Pensions in Retirement Income." In *Pensions in Changing Economy*, ed. Richard Burkhauser and Dallas Salisbury, 18–32. Washington, D.C.: Employee Benefit Research Institute.

Rice, Robert. 1966. "Skill, Earnings, and the Growth of Wage Supplements." *American Economic Review* 54:583–93.

Rosen, Sherwin. 1974. "Hedonic Prices and Implicit Markets." *Journal of Political Economy* 82:34–55.

Salisbury, Dallas. 1994. "The Costs and Benefits of Pension Tax Expenditures." In *Pension Funding and Taxation: Implications for Tomorrow*, ed. Dallas Salisbury and Nora Super Jones. Washington, D.C.: Employee Benefit Research Institute.

Schieber, Sylvester. 1990. *Benefits Bargain*. Washington, D.C.: Association of Private Pension and Welfare Plans.

Schieber, Sylvester, and Gordon Goodfellow. 1994. "Fat Cats, Bureaucrats, and Common Workers: Distributing The Pension Tax Preference Pie." In *Pension Funding and Taxation: Implications for Tomorrow*, ed. Dallas Salisbury and Nora Super Jones. Washington, D.C.: Employee Benefit Research Institute, 79–90.

Silverman, Celia, and Paul Yakoboski. 1994. "Public and Private Pensions Today: An Overview of the System." In *Pension Funding and Taxation: Implications For Tomorrow*, ed. Dallas Salisbury and Nora Super Jones. Washington, D.C.: Employee Benefit Research Institute.

Sloan, Frank, and Killard Adamache. 1986. "Taxation and the Growth of Nonwage Compensation." *Public Finance Quarterly* 14:115–38.

Smith, Robert. 1981. "Compensating Differentials for Pensions and Underfunding in Public Sector." *Review of Economics and Statistics* 63:463–68.

Smith, Robert. 1979. "Compensating Wage Differentials and Public Policy: A Review." *Industrial and Labor Relations Review* 32:339–52.

Turner, John, and Daniel Beller. 1992. *Trends in Pensions 1992*. Washington: USGPO.

U.S. Congress, Joint Committee on Taxation. 1993. *Estimates of Federal Tax Expenditures for Fiscal Years 1994–98*. Washington, D.C.: USGPO.

U.S. Congress, Joint Committee on Taxation. 1992. *Estimates of Federal Tax Expenditures for Fiscal Years 1993–97*. Washington, D.C.: USGPO.

U.S. Congressional Budget Office. 1987. *Tax Policy for Pensions and Other Retirement Saving*. Washington, D.C.: USGPO.

U.S. Department of Commerce. 1984. *Statistical Abstract of the United States, 1985*. 105th ed. Washington, D.C.: Bureau of Census.

U.S. Social Security Administration. 1992. "Social Security Area Population Projections: 1992." Actuary study no. 106. Washington, D.C.: USGPO.

U.S. Social Security Administration. 1984. "Social Security Area Population Projections: 1984." Actuary study no. 92. Washington, D.C.: USGPO.

Venti, Steven, and David Wise. 1993. "The Wealth of Cohorts: The Changing Assets of Older Americans." Paper presented at Conference, Public Policy Towards Pensions, Association of Private Pension and Welfare Plans and the Center for Economic Policy Research, Stanford University.

Venti, Steven, and David Wise. 1992. "Government Policy and Personal Retirement Saving." In *Tax Policy and The Economy*. Cambridge, MA: MIT Press.

Venti, Steven, and David Wise. 1990. "Have IRAs Increased U.S. Savings? Evidence from Consumer Expenditure Surveys." *Quarterly Journal of Economics* 105:661–98.

Woodbury, Stephen. 1983. "Substitution Between Wage and Nonwage Benefits." *American Economic Review* 73:166–82.

Woodbury, Stephen, and Wei-Jang Huang. 1991. *The Tax Treatment of Fringe Benefits.* Kalamazoo, MI: Upjohn Institute for Employment Research.

Woods, John. 1989. "Pension Coverage Among Private Wage and Salary Workers: Preliminary Findings from the 1988 Survey of Employee Benefits." *Social Security Bulletin* 52 (October): 2–19.

3

The Wealth of Cohorts: Retirement Saving and the Changing Assets of Older Americans

Steven F. Venti and
David A. Wise

Americans are changing the way they save for retirement. Contributions to personal saving accounts are becoming an increasingly large proportion of retirement saving while contributions to traditional employer-provided pension plans are declining. The proportion of total contributions accounted for by IRAs, 401(k)s, and Keogh plans increased from about 7% to more than 50% during the 1980s. We consider the effect this change has had on the assets of recent retirees and those on the eve of retirement. We find contributions to personal plans have already added appreciably to older Americans' personal retirement assets and, by implication, the effect is likely to be much larger in the future.

The chapter emphasizes older Americans changing assets. The rising popularity of personal retirement saving has fueled the change, and thus to evaluate its implications for the elderly's financial status it is necessary to understand these programs' effect on saving. In earlier research we considered IRAs' effects on savings.[1] Venti and Wise (1992) introduced analysis based on comparing "like families," a version of the cohort analysis structure used in this chapter. Poterba, Venti, and Wise (1994, 1995a) considered the effect on saving of 401(k) and IRA contributions based in part on comparing like families and in part on the "quasi experiment" presented by eligibility for 401(k) plans. This chapter contributes to that line of analysis, but with a different focus, a different methodology, and a broader scope. We direct attention to families just before and just after retirement, and we frame the analysis explicitly in terms of cohorts. The analysis rests primarily on comparing older and younger cohorts of respondents to the SIPP between 1984 and 1991. The cohorts had different lengths of exposure to the personal retirement saving plans introduced in the 1980s. Those already retired in the early 1980s had less opportunity to contribute than those still working when these plans were introduced.

We consider not only whether personal retirement saving contributions substitute for other personal financial assets, as in our previous research, but also whether they substitute for employer-provided pension assets. To understand pensions' effect on saving, we need to understand not only how personal retirement saving relates to other personal financial assets, but also how each of these relates to employer-provided pension assets.

Traditional economic assumptions imply that if employers increase saving for employees through employer-provided pension entitlements, employees save less. Or, if individuals choose to save more through personal retirement saving plans, they save less in other personal financial assets. Or, if individual housing equity increases through unanticipated gains in housing prices, the individual reduces saving in other forms. The net effect on saving of personal retirement saving depends on whether individuals make economic financial decisions in accordance with these assumptions. We find that for the most part these assumptions are inconsistent with observed individual behavior.

1. Background

2. Data

The analysis is based primarily on 1984, 1987, and 1991 data from SIPP. The data are drawn from the 1984, 1985, 1986, and 1990 panels of the survey, with data for the same year sometimes available from more than one panel. The 1984 interview was conducted between September and December 1984, and the 1987 interview between January and April 1987, with approximately 28 months between the two interview periods. Thus in the cohort analysis described below we treat this interval as a two-year period. The 1987 and 1991 surveys were conducted almost exactly four years apart. The 1984 to 1991 period is assumed to span six years.

Each panel contains eight interview waves administered every four months over a 32-month period. We use all the waves containing supplemental topical modules requesting detailed information on assets and liabilities and pension plan coverage: wave 4 of the 1984 panel (administered between September and December 1984), wave 7 of the 1985 panel and wave 4 of the 1986 panel (January to April 1987), and wave 4 of the 1990 panel (February to May 1991). A physical address defines the SIPP household. These households were reformatted into individual family units headed by either a husband-wife pair or a single individual. Thus a single SIPP household may yield several "families" for the present analysis.

We consider the following asset categories:

- Personal financial assets
  - Total
  - Personal (targeted) retirement assets
  - Other personal financial assets
- Employer-provided pension assets
- Social Security assets
- Home equity
- Other nonliquid equity

The analysis deals primarily with personal financial assets and employer-provided pension assets. Table 3A.1 lists each category's components. The table pertains to families aged 65 to 69 in 1991. It reports the proportion of families owning each of the components as well as the asset mean and median values. "Personal retirement assets" include holdings in IRAs, 401(k)s, Keoghs, and life insurance annuities. Respondents were not asked for a 401(k) balance for 1984, and thus 1984 totals do not include 401(k) assets. But the mean (and median) 401(k) family balance would have been quite small at that time. These saving plans are grouped together because each narrowly targets saving for retirement, as opposed to saving for other, presumably more short-term goals. "Other personal financial assets" encompass conventional (non–tax advantaged) saving vehicles, including saving accounts, money market deposit accounts, CDs, NOW accounts, money market funds, U.S. government securities, municipal and corporate bonds, stocks, mutual funds, U.S. savings bonds, and other interest-earning assets. "Total personal financial assets" are the sum of personal retirement assets and other personal financial assets. Home equity is the home's current market value less the unpaid mortgage.

As explained below, the data are used to create means and medians by cohort—all persons who are the same age in a particular calendar year. Thus the same cohort can be followed over successive ages in 1984, 1987, and 1991. However, Social Security and employer-provided pension assets must be calculated from observed benefit payments. Thus wealth in these forms is available only for those who are retired, and we typically consider only those over 65. The present values are obtained by capitalizing the stream of monthly income from each source using sex-specific survival probabilities calculated from mortality tables.[2]

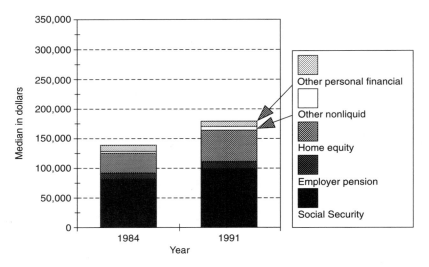

Figure 3.1a
Media assets by year (families aged 65 to 69)

Family Wealth at Retirement

Social Security benefits provide the vast majority of the income of a large fraction of retired Americans, and the present value of expected future benefits is the major component of most elderly families' wealth. In 1991, the median Social Security wealth of families with heads 65 to 69 was about $100,000. (See figure 3.1a.) Median employer-provided pension wealth (including government and military pensions) was only $16,017. Pension wealth is distributed much more unevenly than Social Security wealth—44% of families 65 to 69 had no pension income at all. Median housing equity was $50,000, but housing equity is typically not used to support the elderly's consumption, at least not until quite advanced ages.[3] Median level of other nonliquid assets, such as cars and business equity, was only $5,992. Personal saving through conventional channels represents a very small proportion of most older families' assets; the median level of other personal financial assets was only $7,428.[4] Thus most families, if they spend the income provided by Social Security and employer pension annuities, have almost no liquid, accessible assets to meet unexpected expenditures. More than half of families had neither IRA nor 401(k) accounts, so that median wealth in personal retirement assets was zero.

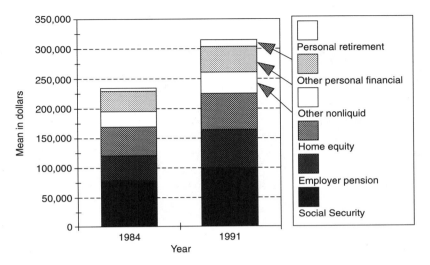

Figure 3.1b
Mean assets by year (families aged 65 to 69)

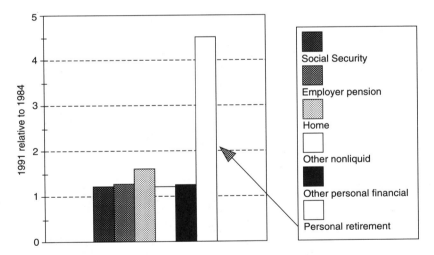

Figure 3.1c
Mean wealth increase, 1984–91 (families aged 65 to 69)

Although the median is the best single measure of the typical family's assets, the components of wealth other than Social Security are highly skewed, so that the means are much larger than the medians. Mean level of other personal financial assets in 1991 was $42,018, more than five times the median. But even mean other personal financial assets are a small fraction of combined Social Security and employer-provided pension assets, as figure 3.1b indicates.

The means, however, reveal IRA and 401(k) assets' increasing importance as a fraction of total personal financial assets. For families aged 65 to 69, personal retirement assets accounted for only 6.6% of total personal financial assets in 1984, but they represented 20.6% by 1991. Personal retirement assets increased more than four-fold between 1984 and 1991, much more than any other component of wealth, as figure 3.1c shows.

Aggregate IRA and 401(k) Saving

Figure 3.2 shows total contributions to IRA and 401(k) accounts over the 1980s. IRA contributions jumped enormously in 1982, as soon as IRAs became available to all wage earners, and increased to a peak of more than

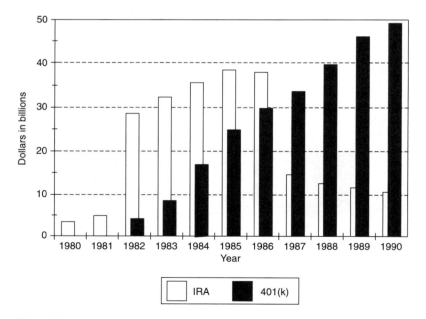

Figure 3.2
IRA and 401(k) contributions

$38 billion in 1985. Contributions dropped dramatically after 1986, when the TRA limited tax deductibility of contributions of families with incomes more than $40,000 per year and single persons with incomes more than $25,000. Even though the legislation affected only 27% of contributors,[5] contributions fell by more than 60%, with a dramatic decline in the contributions even of those unaffected by the legislation. Poterba, Venti, and Wise (1994, 1995a) discuss in detail this decline's implications. By 1990, less than $10 billion was contributed annually to IRA accounts.

Contributions to 401(k) plans increased consistently from their introduction in 1982 to $49 billion in 1990. Extrapolation of past trends would suggest that contributions are now between $60 billion and $70 billion. Figure 3.2 reveals no relationship between IRA and 401(k) contributions, with the annual increase in 401(k) contributions showing little change before and after the decline in IRA contributions beginning in 1987.

Figure 3.3a shows the relationship between these contributions and contributions to other retirement saving plans (excluding Social Security). Contributions to defined-benefit pension plans declined almost 40% in the 1980s, from $48.4 billion in 1980 to $24.9 billion in 1989. This decline

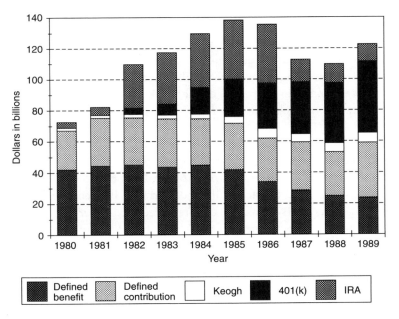

Figure 3.3a
Retirement plan contributions

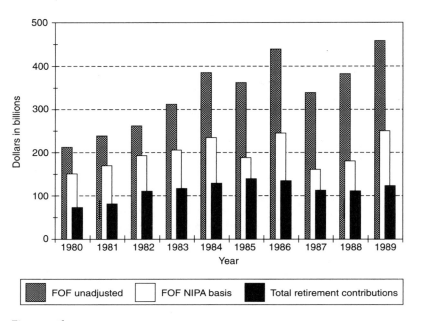

Figure 3.3b
National Flow of Funds saving

was apparently due primarily to the large unexpected returns to pension fund assets over the 1980s, as described in Bernheim and Shoven 1988; it may have also been induced in part by the funding limits imposed by OBRA87, as explained in chapter 7 of the book. The number of participants in defined-benefit plans declined only 9.3% and the number of plans by 10.5% between 1980 and 1989. Contributions to defined-contribution plans remained about the same over the entire period.[6]

Personal targeted retirement saving represented only 7.6% of the total in 1980 but increased to more than 50% of the total by 1989. It seems apparent that if the 1986 legislation had not curtailed IRA contributions, balances in these accounts would have represented a much larger fraction of contributions to all retirement plans, and total contributions would have been substantially larger. The trend in total contributions displayed in figure 3.3a closely follows the trend in IRA contributions.

Figure 3.3b shows total personal saving as measured by the Federal Reserve Board's Flow of Funds (FOF) accounts. These data include contributions to targeted retirement saving plans as well as other saving components. The FOF data are based on direct measurement of the net acquisition of assets and are thus more comparable to the targeted retirement saving components than the National Income and Product Account (NIPA) data, the measure of aggregate personal saving most often cited. The NIPA data estimate saving as the residual between disposable income and personal consumption expenditures. The FOF data include several assets not incorporated in the NIPA definition of saving.[7] Thus, in addition to the more inclusive FOF series, the Federal Reserve Board also publishes a series that attempts to match the components of saving that are in principle included in the NIPA measure—indicated by "FOF NIPA basis" in figure 3.3b. But even after the adjustment, the NIPA and FOF measures often differ by tens of billions of dollars. They are discussed in some detail in Poterba, Venti, and Wise 1995b.

Targeted retirement contributions represent a large fraction of FOF national saving. In 1986, for example, retirement plan contributions accounted for 72.3% of FOF NIPA basis data and 30.9% of the unadjusted FOF series. Both measures generally follow the pattern of targeted retirement saving in figure 3.3a, which in turn follows the pattern of IRA contributions. In particular, both measures show a substantial increase in saving between 1980 and 1986, a noticeable fall after the 1986 legislation, and then a recovery by 1989.

Subsequent analysis assesses the impact of personal retirement saving on older Americans' financial status as they approach and enter retirement and considers two issues. First, using cohort data, we consider the relationship between personal retirement saving and other personal financial assets. Second, we consider the relationship between total personal financial assets and employer-provided pension assets. We direct attention only briefly to the relationship between housing wealth and personal financial assets, but that relationship has been analyzed recently by Hoynes and McFadden (1993), who find little relationship between changes in housing equity and personal financial assets. We rely on their results in making summary judgments about the net effect of personal targeted retirement saving on older Americans' financial assets. In discussing the relationship between housing equity and wealth, Skinner (1991) also concludes little or no relationship exists between housing equity and other financial asset saving.

Personal Retirement Saving and Other Assets: Cohort Analysis

Cohorts and Cohort Data

We begin with a discussion of the principal elements of cohort analysis. A cohort is typically a group of persons born in the same year. Thus those who are a given age in 1984 are also a cohort. Usually in cohort analysis, the same cohort is followed over time. That is, persons who were 50 in 1984 can be observed in 1985, 1986, and so forth. Panel data follows specific individuals over time. For example, the mean wealth of those who were 50 in 1984 can be traced over time, considering the mean wealth of these same individuals in 1985, in 1986, and so forth. From panel data, the cohort means are obtained directly by following the same individuals over time. But cohort means can also be obtained from random population samples in successive years (a series of cross sections). We use the SIPP data in this way, although these data also include a short panel component, following the same people for 32 months. Using these data, mean assets of a random sample of those who were 50 in 1984 are compared to mean assets of another random sample of those who were 51 in 1985, 52 in 1986, and so on.

We have made calculations for 15 cohorts defined by age in 1984: C42, C44, ..., C70. For ease of exposition we usually show data graphically for only a subset of the cohorts. The numerical component of each cohort name is the midpoint of a five-year age interval in 1984, and in fact the cohort is defined by all those in that five-year interval in 1984. For example, C42 refers to the midpoint of the interval that includes people between 40 and 44 in 1984, 41 and 45 in 1985, and so forth.

For illustration, figure 3.4a graphs mean personal retirement saving assets for five cohorts. For each cohort, assets are reported for 1984, 1987, and 1991. For example, the mean of personal retirement assets of cohort C46 was about $1,800 in 1984, $4,500 in 1987, and $11,700 by 1991. Increases for the C52 and C58 cohorts were also large. But the increases for the older cohorts were much smaller. The C70 cohort, which was past typical retirement age in the early 1980s when the programs were introduced, accumulated very little in personal retirement assets. That is, the relationship between age and the accumulation of personal retirement assets depends strongly on the cohort.

Notice that the relationship between age and asset accumulation judged by the cross-section profile is grossly misleading in this case. For example, the difference between the assets of 46- and 52-year-olds in 1984 is much less than the assets actually accumulated by cohort C46 between age 46 (in 1984) and age 52 (in 1991). In figure 3.4a the cross-section relationship between age and assets can be obtained by linking the values reported for a given year. For example, 1991 values are reported for ages 52, 58, 64, 70, and 76, highlighted by the small ovals. Similarly, the 1984 values—for ages 46, 52, 58, 64, and 70—are highlighted by the triangles. In both

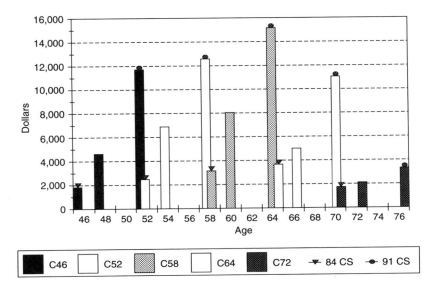

Figure 3.4a
Illustration of cohort data (personal retirement assets)

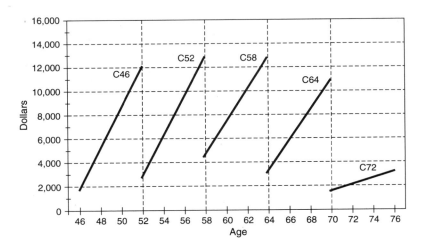

Figure 3.4b
Illustration of cohort data (personal retirement assets—fitted)

cases the cross-section relationship gives a distorted view of the actual accumulation of personal retirement assets with age. This is because the large "cohort effects" are unrecognized in the cross-section relationship.

Different levels of asset accumulation by different cohorts at specific ages provide the core data to evaluate the net saving effect of personal retirement saving contributions. The differences, called cohort effects, can be judged directly by the difference in assets of cohorts that attained a given age in different calendar years. At a given age, different cohorts had different lengths of exposure to personal retirement saving programs widely available beginning in 1982. For example, cohort C46, which attained age 52 in 1991, accumulated much greater personal retirement assets by age 52 than cohort C52, which attained age 52 in 1984 and thus, by that age, had had many fewer years to accumulate these assets. The same is true for cohorts C52 and C58 at age 58, C58 and C64 at age 64, and C64 and C70 at age 70.

To facilitate exposition, we often fit the three data points for each cohort and graph the fitted values, as shown in figure 3.4b. This makes it possible to visualize many more cohorts on the same graph.

Table 3A.2 shows mean personal retirement assets for all 15 cohorts. Each cohort's data are in a separate column, and the asset values moving down the column show the relationship between age and assets within a cohort. The "top" diagonal shows cross-section relationships for 1984, the middle diagonal for 1987, and the lower diagonal for 1991. As figure 3.4 indicates, the differences are extremely large.

Subsequent analysis will consider whether cohort effects like those figure 3.4 shows for personal retirement assets are offset by countervailing cohort effects with respect to other personal financial assets. For example, figure 3.4a shows that those who attained age 52 in 1991 had much larger personal retirement assets than those who reached age 52 in 1984. The key question is whether a reduction in other personal financial assets offset the larger personal retirement assets. If countervailing cohort effects in other personal financial assets offset the personal retirement asset cohort effects, total personal financial assets will show no cohort effects; if they do not, similar cohort effects in total personal financial assets will mirror the personal retirement asset cohort effects. Equivalently, an absence of cohort effects with respect to other personal financial assets will imply that offsetting cohort effects in other personal financial assets do not cancel the personal retirement asset cohort effects. To highlight the cohort effects, we present most evidence graphically. We also use more formal estimates of cohort effects to project younger cohorts' future retirement assets.

Personal Retirement Assets and Other Personal Financial Assets

We begin by considering the assets of all respondents to the SIPP, both contributors and noncontributors. The basic assumption is that younger cohorts—who reached a given age in later calendar years—had longer to contribute to personal retirement accounts, but that in other respects the cohorts are similar (after correcting for earnings differences between cohorts that attained a given age in different years). Thus differences in asset accumulation can be attributed to the differential availability of these programs. It is implicitly assumed that the differences are not due to a systematic trend in the taste for saving. The data for contributors and noncontributors together provide the most compelling evidence on substitution, because these data are not confounded by the potential changing composition of contributors and noncontributors, which may change the two groups' saving propensities over time.

Contributors to personal targeted retirement saving programs are then considered separately from noncontributors. In this case, it is proposed that the cohort differences among contributors result from differences in exposure to the special retirement saving programs. For example, contributors who attained age 52 in 1991 have larger personal retirement assets than contributors who reached age 52 in 1984 because the former group had seven more years to contribute to these programs. These data can be used to judge retirement saving programs' effect on the future asset accumulation of those who participate in such programs. In addition, the cohort effects of contributors can be compared to those among noncontributors. The noncontributor cohort effects might indicate cohort effects that would have obtained in the absence of the special retirement saving programs. That is, it might be assumed that any systematic trend in the taste for saving would be revealed in a cohort effect among noncontributors. The results for the most part show no cohort effects among noncontributors. Comparisons of contributors and noncontributors must be interpreted with caution, however, because the two groups have very different saving propensities, as the data discussed below show. Thus it is questionable whether data for noncontributors can be used to infer the saving of contributors had they not participated in the programs. For contributors, cohort effects are observed with respect to personal retirement assets but not with respect to other personal financial assets. Indeed, for all respondents together, there are no cohort effects with respect to other personal financial assets. Cohort effects are observed only with respect to contributors' personal retirement assets. Thus we believe it unlikely that the results can be attributed to a general shift in the taste for saving over time.

To simplify the graphic exposition, we sometimes show the actual data for "nonoverlapping cohorts," as in figure 3.4a. Or, we present fitted values like those in figure 3.4b. We would like to emphasize the typical family's assets and thus would prefer to use median values. In addition, medians are less subject to random fluctuation due to extreme outliers. As explained above, however, in some instances the medians are not informative (when fewer than 50% of families own an asset), and we present only means.

An issue that arises in the cohort analysis is the appropriate comparison of the assets of those who attained a given age in different calendar years. If our goal were to compare different cohorts' purchasing power, a price index would be the most appropriate measure by which to put different calendar year data on a common basis. Here, however, the issue is not purchasing power but rather the saving that would have occurred in the absence of personal retirement saving programs. There are at least two possibilities: One is to assume that the potential change in other personal financial asset saving if personal retirement saving programs were not available is equal to the percentage increase in this asset category among noncontributors. Averaged over ages 48 to 68, this increase was 3.8% between 1984 and 1991. Another conceptual approach is to base the correction on successive cohorts' nominal earnings, assuming that other personal financial asset saving is based on earnings, and there would have been no real cohort effects in personal financial asset saving in the absence of personal retirement saving programs. The closest empirical approximation to this conceptualization may be an earnings index. To illustrate, we present some results in nominal dollars, but most results are based on values converted to 1984 dollars using the wage and salary component of the Bureau of Labor Statistics Employment Cost Index.

All Respondents: Means

Nominal Values Figure 3.5a shows the mean personal targeted retirement assets of cohorts C46, C52, C58, C64, and C70. Younger cohorts, which attained a given age in a later calendar year and thus at that age

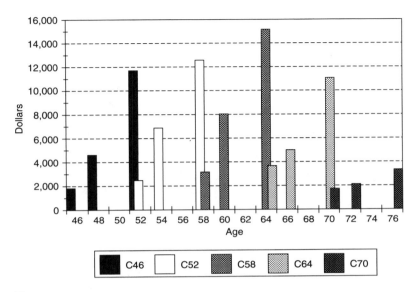

Figure 3.5a
Personal retirement assets (all respondents—five cohorts—means)

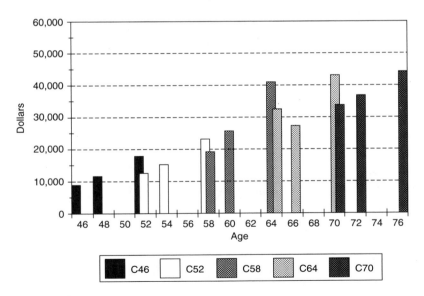

Figure 3.5b
Other personal financial assets (all respondents—five cohorts—means)

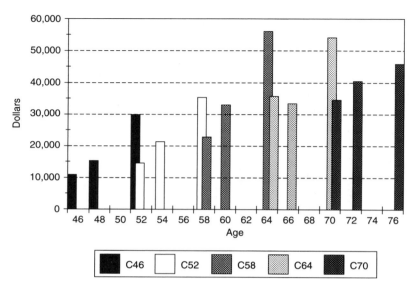

Figure 3.5c
Total personal financial assets (all respondents—five cohorts—means)

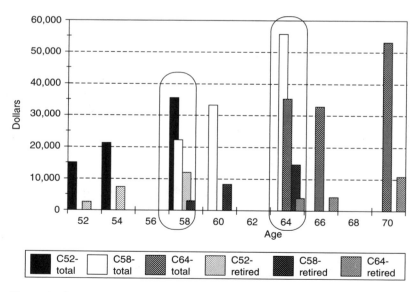

Figure 3.5d
Total personal financial assets versus personal retirement assets (all respondents—selected cohorts)

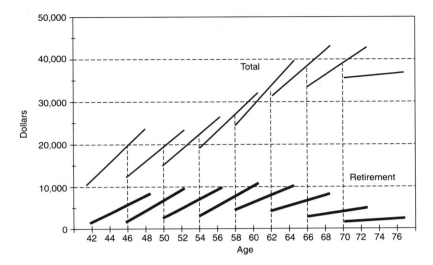

Figure 3.5e
Personal financial assets, total and retirement (means—all respondents—indexed)

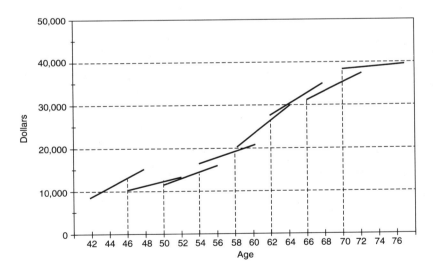

Figure 3.5f
Personal financial assets, other (means—all respondents—indexed)

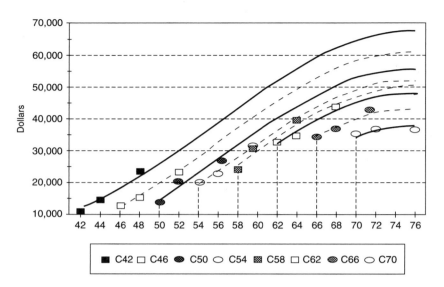

Figure 3.5g
Total personal financial assets (means—both actual and projected)

had longer exposure to the special retirement saving plans introduced in the early 1980s, accumulated much larger personal retirement assets. For example, cohort C58 accumulated the greatest personal retirement assets. Members of this cohort were aged 56 to 60 in 1984 and 54 to 58 in 1982 when the IRA and 401(k) programs were expanded and were aged 62 to 66 when last surveyed in 1991. The C70 cohort accumulated the least personal retirement assets. Members of this cohort were already aged 66 to 70 and past retirement in 1982 and thus were in large part unable to take advantage of the IRA and 401(k) programs.

Figure 3.5b shows the corresponding means of the same cohorts' other personal financial assets. The accumulation of personal retirement assets, described above, differed greatly by cohort. The corresponding accumulation of other personal financial assets also shows a cohort effect, but not one that offsets the retirement asset cohort effect; younger cohorts also have higher levels of other financial assets. Because no reduction in the accumulation of other financial assets offset the rapid accumulation of retirement assets, the accumulation of total personal financial assets also shows a strong cohort effect, with younger cohorts, who attained any age in a later year, typically accumulating more personal financial assets, as figure 3.5c shows. Figure 3.5d shows both total and retirement assets for three cohorts. At age 58, for example, the difference in retirement assets of C52 and C58 can be compared directly to the difference in their total personal assets. The same comparison can be made for C58 and C64 at age 64.

Indexed Values—Fitted Figure 3.5e shows fitted values of total and retirement assets for eight cohorts. The vertical lines aid in comparing the cohort differences in total and retirement assets at given ages. If there were no reduction in the other financial assets of successive cohorts as they increased their personal retirement assets, the difference in the total assets would equal the difference in retirement assets. The average ratio of the total asset difference to the retirement asset difference is 1.16. There is of course some randomness in these ratios. But the data suggest that accumulation of personal retirement assets resulted for the most part in a corresponding increase in total personal financial assets. Figure 3.5f graphs fitted values for other personal financial assets. They reveal essentially no systematic cohort effect.

Indexed Values—Actual and Projected The results above show that each successively younger cohort has greater personal financial assets than the preceding older cohort. What personal financial asset levels will the younger cohorts have accumulated by the time they reach retirement age? Although future asset levels probably cannot be precisely predicted, we believe the data allow plausible projections of the younger cohorts' future assets. We fit the indexed actual cohort means with a specification of the form

$$A_{ic} = \alpha + \beta_c + \gamma_1(Age_i) + \gamma_2(Age_i)^2 + \gamma_3(Age_i)^3 + \varepsilon_{ic} \qquad (3.1)$$

where A represents an asset category (personal retirement assets, other personal financial assets, total personal financial assets), c indexes cohort and i the ith cohort mean. The β_c are cohort effects with $\sum \beta_c = 0$. Thus individual estimates represent deviations from the mean effect, which is set to zero. The specification is intended to fit the age-asset accumulation pattern, allowing the differences in asset levels between successive cohorts to be maintained as the cohorts age, and to cumulate. It is assumed, for example, that the estimated difference between assets of the two youngest cohorts, C42 and C46, will be maintained as the cohorts age. Thus the projected difference at age 76 in the asset levels of cohorts C42 and C70, for example, is given by the difference between C42 and

C44, plus the difference between C44 and C46, plus the difference between C46 and C48, and so forth. Indeed, it is convenient to think of the estimated cohort effects as representing the projected cohort differences at age 76. This assumption likely implies a conservative estimate of the projected cohort differences. Constant percentage differences as the cohorts age, for example, imply much larger age-76 cohort differences.

Table 3.1a shows the estimates. The youngest cohort's projected personal retirement assets (column 1) are $14,076 above the mean, but the oldest cohort's projected assets are $13,103 below the mean, a difference of $27,179. If there were no counterbalancing cohort effects with respect to other personal financial assets, the total personal financial asset cohort effects should approximately parallel the retirement asset cohort effects. The estimates show that the youngest cohort's projected total (column 2) is $16,002 above the mean and the oldest cohort's $14,081 below the mean, a difference of $30,085. The other personal financial asset cohort effects are typically not statistically different from zero. An F-test does not reject the hypothesis that there are no cohort effects, that is, all the individual effects are zero.

Figure 3.5g graphs the projections of total personal financial assets based on equation (3.1). The oldest cohort's age-76 personal financial assets are $37,299; the youngest cohort's projected age-76 assets are $67,385, an increase of more than 80%.

Contributors and Noncontributors Separately: Indexed Means

Indexed Values—Fitted Because only a minority of respondents contribute to a personal retirement saving account—only about 40% of cohorts younger than 65 in 1984 and a much smaller percentage of older cohorts—the larger number of respondents who did not participate and were apparently unaffected by these saving programs dilutes the participants' total savings effect. Thus we also present data for contributors and noncontributors separately. Figures 3.6a through 3.6c show the findings based on means. Again, cohorts who reached a given age in a later calendar year had accumulated much more in personal retirement accounts than cohorts who reached that age in an earlier year. These differences are reflected, for the most part, in corresponding differences in total personal financial assets, as figure 3.6a shows. And, as with both contributors and noncontributors together, the cohort data for contributors' other personal financial assets show essentially no systematic cohort effects. (See figure 3.6b.)

Table 3.1
Projection equation estimated cohort effects, by asset and contributor status

Cohort	Personal retirement assets		Total personal financial assets		Other personal financial assets	
	Coefficient	t-Stat	Coefficient	t-Stat	Coefficient	t-Stat
a. Both contributors and noncontributors—means						
C42	$ 14,076	19.0	$ 16,002	8.2	$ 1,927	1.0
C44	11,085	17.9	12,024	7.3	939	0.6
C46	9,997	17.3	9,568	6.3	−428	−0.3
C48	7,821	14.8	6,556	4.7	−1,264	−0.9
C50	5,759	11.9	4,132	3.2	−1,626	−1.3
C52	3,814	8.6	1,459	1.2	−2,354	−2.1
C54	1,944	4.7	452	0.4	−1,492	−1.4
C56	363	0.9	734	0.7	370	0.4
C58	−1,604	−3.9	−1,682	−1.6	−78	−0.1
C60	−3,815	−8.7	−5,165	−4.5	−1,349	−1.2
C62	−5,813	−12.1	−3,796	−3.0	2,017	1.7
C64	−8,130	−15.4	−5,234	−3.7	2,895	2.2
C66	−10,345	−18.0	−8,766	−5.8	1,578	1.1
C68	−12,049	−19.2	−12,203	−7.3	−154	−0.1
C70	−13,103		−14,081		−981	
b. Contributors—means						
C42	30,138	16.3	31,120	4.4	982	0.1
C44	24,305	15.8	25,331	4.3	1,025	0.1
C46	21,990	15.3	20,567	3.8	−1,423	0.2
C48	17,802	13.5	16,136	3.2	−1,666	−0.3
C50	13,235	11.0	11,451	2.5	−1,784	−0.4
C52	8,697	7.9	5,686	1.3	−3,011	−0.7
C54	4,355	4.2	2,536	0.6	−1,818	−0.5
C56	381	0.4	379	0.1	−2	0.0
C58	−4,140	−4.1	−5,351	−1.4	−1,210	−0.3
C60	−8,972	−8.2	−15,512	−3.7	−6,539	−1.6
C62	−12,970	−10.8	−10,886	−2.4	2,084	0.5
C64	−17,496	−13.3	−10,101	−2.0	7,395	1.5
C66	−21,873	−15.3	−11,122	−2.0	10,751	2.0
C68	−26,299	−16.8	−24,331	−4.1	1,968	0.3
C70	−29,153		−35,903		−6,752	

Table 3.1 (continued)

Cohort	Personal retirement assets		Total personal financial assets		Other personal financial assets	
	Coefficient	t-Stat	Coefficient	t-Stat	Coefficient	t-Stat
c. Contributors—medians						
C42	16,066	11.8	21,522	6.5	−6,078	2.3
C44	12,793	11.3	19,358	7.0	−2,771	−1.2
C46	12,074	10.3	17,811	6.9	−2,955	−1.4
C48	9,936	10.3	14,804	6.2	−2,441	−1.3
C50	7,383	8.3	11,362	5.2	−2,005	−1.1
C52	5,066	6.2	7,053	3.5	−1,964	−1.2
C54	3,103	4.1	4,498	2.4	−1,753	−1.2
C56	910	1.2	163	0.0	−1,370	−1.0
C58	−1,953	−2.6	−3,451	−1.9	−374	−0.3
C60	−5,556	−6.3	−9,896	−5.0	−1,806	−1.1
C62	−7,414	−8.4	−11,095	−5.1	−74	−0.0
C64	−10,617	−11.0	−12,503	−5.3	3,520	1.8
C66	−12,448	−11.8	−15,700	−6.1	5,184	2.5
C68	−14,046	−12.2	−20,652	−7.3	7,186	3.2
C70	−15,297		−23,274		7,701	

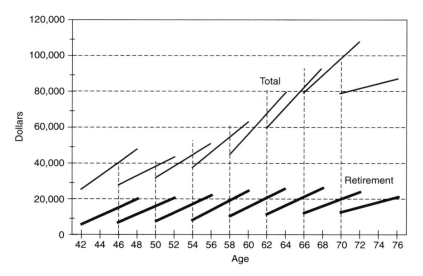

Figure 3.6a
Personal financial assets, total and retirement (means—contributors—indexed)

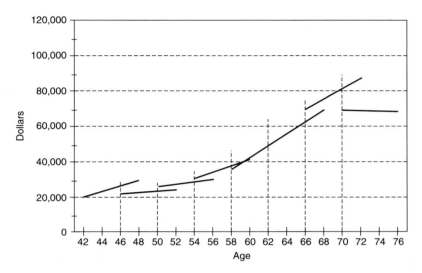

Figure 3.6b
Personal financial assets, other (means—contributors—indexed)

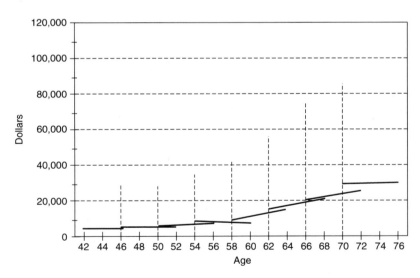

Figure 3.6c
Personal financial assets, other (means—noncontributors—indexed)

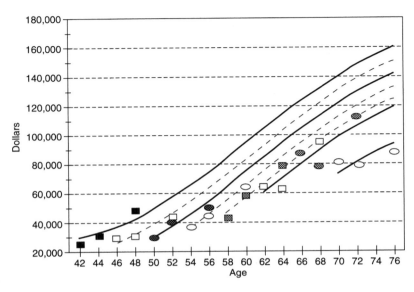

Figure 3.6d
Total personal financial assets (means—contributors—actual and projected)

For comparison, figure 3.6c shows noncontributors' accumulation of personal financial assets. There appear to be no cohort effects among noncontributors at younger ages. At older ages, older cohorts appear to have slightly higher personal financial asset levels, perhaps because a smaller proportion of older cohorts ever contributed to a personal retirement plan, and thus the noncontributors among the older cohorts disproportionately include "savers" who would have contributed to a personal retirement account had these accounts been available. This composition effect is discussed below with reference to table 3.2.

Indexed Values—Actual and Projected   Figure 3.6d shows projected means (indexed to 1984) of contributors together with actual values for selected cohorts. The projected age-76 total personal financial assets of cohort C70 (in 1991) are $93,151; the projected value of the C42 cohort at age 76—18 years hence—is $160,175. As with both contributors and noncontributors, estimated cohort effects for total personal financial assets tend to mirror estimated effects for personal retirement assets, as table 3.1b shows. Esimated cohort effects for other personal financial assets are not typically statistically different from zero. (The estimates, however, reveal an apparent composition effect among older cohorts discussed below.) Thus for participating families the cumulative effect of personal retirement account contributions is very large. Assuming no cohort effect with respect to other personal financial assets, personal retirement assets would increase over the next 18 years from 22% to 50% of the total personal financial assets of age-76 families.

Contributors and Noncontributors Separately: Indexed Medians

Indexed Values—Fitted As mentioned above, the distribution of financial assets is highly skewed so that means are much larger than medians. Thus the median is a much better indicator of the typical family's assets. Medians for all respondents are not informative, however, because the median for personal targeted retirement assets is typically zero. Figure 3.7a shows median total and retirement assets for contributors. Like the means, the medians also show that younger cohorts accumulated much larger levels of personal retirement assets than older cohorts. The larger accumulation of retirement assets was not offset by a corresponding reduction in the accumulation of other personal financial assets (figure 3.7b), which show no substantial offsetting cohort effects. Thus younger contributor cohorts are accumulating much larger levels of total financial assets (figure 3.7a) than their older counterparts.

Figure 3.7c shows the medians for noncontributors. These data show extremely low financial asset levels and essentially no cohort effects at younger ages. As mentioned above, the "apparent" cohort effect for the oldest cohort reflects a composition effect; most of the oldest respondents were noncontributors, and thus had greater assets than younger cohort noncontributors.

Indexed Values—Actual and Projected Like the means, the projected median values of total personal financial assets show very large cohort effects that tend to mirror the cohort effects for personal retirement assets, as table 3.1c shows. Recall that unlike means, the sum of the medians is not the median of the sum, and thus the estimated cohort effects cannot be added across equations. Most of the estimated cohort effects for other personal financial assets are not statistically different from zero, although an apparent composition effect is reflected in the estimated cohort effects among older cohorts. Nonetheless, younger cohorts of participating families are clearly accumulating much more in total personal financial assets than older cohorts. The projected median of current age-76 families (cohort C70 in 1991) is $62,388; the projected accumulation of the youngest cohort by age 76 is $107,138.

Table 3.2
Summary of cohort effects at selected age intervals: percentages and conditional means and medians (1984 dollars), 1984 and 1991

Age interval and data reported	Means		Medians	
	1984	1991	1984	1991
Ages 55–59				
All respondents				
Personal retirement assets	3,456	9,015	—	—
Other personal financial assets	19,271	17,052	—	—
Total personal financial assets	22,729	26,066	—	—
Contributors				
% with personal retirement saving	43	43	43	43
Personal retirement assets	8,215	21,225	5,561	11,997
Other personal financial assets	31,864	31,028	11,997	10,581
Total personal financial assets	40,081	52,254	19,878	28,952
Noncontributors				
% without personal retirement saving	57	57	57	57
Total personal financial assets	9,744	6,590	1,006	921
Ages 60–64				
All respondents				
Personal retirement assets	3,946	10,914	—	—
Other personal financial assets	28,629	27,959	—	—
Total personal financial assets	32,575	38,874	—	—
Contributors				
% with personal retirement saving	38	42	38	42
Personal retirement assets	9,968	25,795	6,300	17,076
Other personal financial assets	51,397	50,160	17,720	16,598
Total personal financial assets	61,365	75,954	26,996	38,691
Noncontributors				
% without personal retirement saving	62	58	62	58
Total personal financial assets	13,468	12,684	2,073	1,645
Ages 65–69				
All respondents				
Personal retirement assets	2,467	8,022	—	—
Other personal financial assets	33,352	29,483	—	—
Total personal financial assets	35,819	37,505	—	—
Contributors				
% with personal retirement saving	19	35	19	35
Personal retirement assets	11,925	24,672	7,245	14,047
Other personal financial assets	62,073	60,753	31,659	27,762
Total personal financial assets	73,998	85,426	40,948	53,636

Table 3.2 (continued)

Age interval and data reported	Means		Medians	
	1984	1991	1984	1991
Noncontributors				
% without personal retirement saving	81	65	81	65
Total personal financial assets	22,708	17,152	9,171	7,446

Note: Based on mean and median regressions controlling for age, education, marital status, and income. The means for each age-saver group are evaluated at the 1987 means of that group's demographic variables. The medians are evaluated at the 1987 medians of the demographic variables. All values are in 1984 dollars.

Summary of Age-Specific Cohort Effects by Contributor Status: Means and Medians

The graphs of the cohort data show the accumulation of assets with age for successively older cohorts. The different levels of asset accumulation by different cohorts at specific ages provide the core data to evaluate the net saving effect of personal retirement saving contributions. As discussed above, the single most informative comparison is for both contributors and noncontributors combined, considering the change in other financial assets (or in total financial assets) as respondents' personal retirement assets increased. Possible changes in the composition of contributors and noncontributors do not confound these data, because the proportion of contributors increased between 1984 and 1991. But comparisons for contributors and noncontributors separately are also informative: We consider the change in contributors' other financial assets (or total financial assets) as their personal retirement assets increased. But other financial assets may have increased or decreased for other reasons as well. One way to judge the effect of other influences is to consider the change in noncontributors' financial assets. As mentioned above, however, because of apparent large differences in saving propensity, noncontributors may be an inadequate control group against which to judge contributors' behavior in the absence of retirement saving programs. And the comparison of cohort data for contributors and noncontributors may be affected by composition effects. For example, the proportion of contributors in the 65–69 age interval increased from 19% to 35% between 1984 and 1991. Thus "saver" families may have disproportionately become contributors, leaving a larger concentration of "nonsavers" in the noncontributor group in 1991. If this were the case, noncontributors would not serve as a homogeneous control group against which to compare the contributors. To help address this changing composition issue we have estimated the

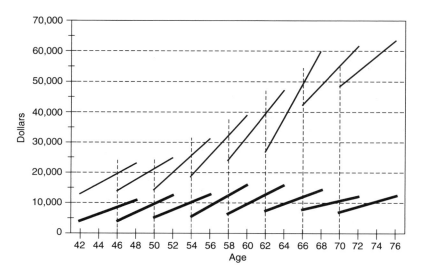

Figure 3.7a
Personal financial assets, total and retirement (medians—contributors—indexed)

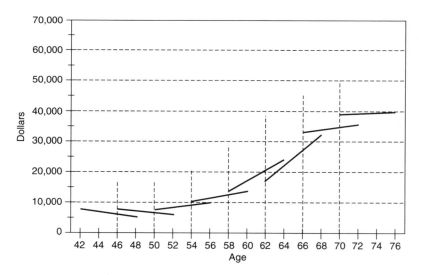

Figure 3.7b
Personal financial assets, other (medians—contributors—indexed)

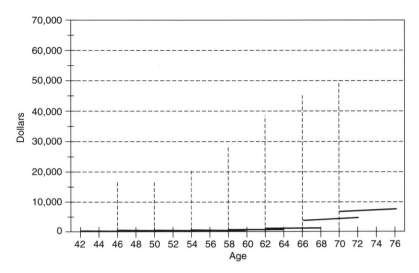

Figure 3.7c
Personal financial assets, other (medians—noncontributors—indexed)

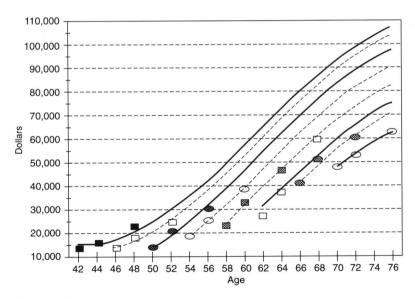

Figure 3.7d
Total personal financial assets (medians—contributors—actual and projected)

mean assets of all respondents—both contributors and noncontributors —and the mean and median assets of contributors and noncontributors separately, controlling for income, age, marital status, and gender of the family head. Table 3.2 shows the 1984 and 1991 means and medians for three age groups spanning typical retirement ages. The table evaluates means at the 1987 means of the income and demographic variables and medians at the medians of those same variables. Thus the estimates reflect values that would have obtained if the income and demographic characteristics of pools of contributors and noncontributors remained at 1987 levels in all years. All values are in 1984 dollars. (The conditional medians are somewhat larger than the unconditional medians. Thus, for example, noncontributors' conditional financial medians may be 50% higher than the overall medians of noncontributors' financial assets.) Tables 3A.3a and 3A.3b show data for all three years and for additional age intervals.

Consider the age 60–64 means, for example. Considering contributors and noncontributors combined, the mean retirement saving assets of families in this age interval in 1984 was $3,946, compared to a mean of $10,914 for those who did not attain this age until 1991. But this large increase in retirement saving assets was not accompanied by a substantial decline in other personal financial assets, which remained virtually unchanged ($28,629 in 1984 and $27,959 in 1991). Consequently, total personal retirement assets increased greatly, from $32,575 to $38,874. For contributors, mean targeted retirement saving increased from $9,968 for the oldest cohort (those in this age interval in 1984) to $25,795 for the youngest cohort (who attained this age interval in 1991). There was little corresponding change in other personal financial assets, however, which declined from $51,397 for the oldest cohort to $50,160 for the youngest cohort. Total personal financial assets increased by 24%, from $61,365 to $75,954. In contrast, noncontributors' assets declined by 6%, from $13,468 to $12,684. Because of means' additive property, the $15,827 increase in contributors' targeted retirement saving assets can be compared to the $14,589 increase in total personal financial assets. Similar trends are revealed for the other age groups.

The medians in table 3.2 show a similar pattern. Typically contributors' personal retirement assets and total financial assets show a large increase, and other financial assets only a small decline. In contrast, noncontributors' median personal financial assets typically declined more than the median of contributors' other personal financial assets, and the percentage decline was typically much greater. Because financial assets are so skewed, the medians provide a better measure than the means of the typical family's wealth. But because medians are not additive, direct comparison between the increases in retirement assets and in total financial assets does not provide an unambiguous measure of the extent of substitution. Tables 3A.3a and 3A.3b show much the same pattern but with some variation among the age intervals and from year to year.

In addition, the tables show the proportion of each age group with a personal retirement saving account. The proportion with retirement accounts does not vary much by age or cohort for those younger than 64. Nor does the proportion vary much for the oldest age group, of which very few in any cohort had accounts. But older cohorts, in the 65–69 and 70–74 age intervals in particular, were much less likely than the younger cohorts to have personal retirement accounts. Thus the decline in the total personal financial assets of noncontributors in the 65–69 age interval (as the proportion in the noncontributor status declined from .81 to .65) may result in part from a composition effect, with "savers" increasingly likely to be contributors. This effect may be reflected in the older cohort data graphed in figures 3.6c and 3.7c, and the data must be interpreted accordingly. But the conditional means and medians should help control for this composition effect. Judging by the proportion of contributors, the data for "preretirement" ages and for the oldest ages are probably not importantly affected by this changing composition in either case.

Personal Retirement Savings and Employer-Provided Pension Assets

Trade-offs between personal retirement saving and other personal financial asset saving may provide the most readily available opportunity for substitution from one form of saving to the other. But personal retirement saving could also substitute for employer-provided pension assets. Those who foresee larger employer-provided retirement benefits may be less likely to contribute to a 401(k) plan or IRA account or to accumulate other personal financial assets. Thus we consider whether families with more pension wealth have less wealth in total personal financial assets.

Two circumstances condition the analysis: First, the SIPP data do not allow calculation of employer-provided pension wealth until a person is retired and receiving pension benefits. The benefit, together with life tables, can be used to determine the present value of expected future pension benefits—pension wealth. Thus cohort analysis as presented above is not suitable in this case. Second, both pension wealth and personal financial asset saving increase with income; thus without controlling for income, those with greater personal financial wealth almost certainly have greater pension wealth as well. We therefore consider the relationship between personal financial assets and pension wealth for those 65 to 69 who have retired and for whom we can determine pension wealth. And we use Social Security wealth percentiles to control for lifetime income.[8] The relationship between Social Security wealth and lifetime income is very nonlinear, with less-than-proportionate increases in Social Security wealth as lifetime income increases. But we believe that the percentile level provides the best available means of grouping people by lifetime income.

Using an analysis of variance framework, we estimate the relationship between pension wealth and three personal financial asset categories: personal retirement assets, other personal financial assets, and total personal financial assets. The specification is of the form

$$A_i = a_i + b_i(\text{Pension Wealth}) + c_i(\text{Education}) + e_i, \tag{3.2}$$

where i indicates the ith Social Security wealth decile and A denotes a personal financial asset category. We control for education because saving is typically found to increase with years of education, given income.

Table 3.3 reports the parameter estimates on pension wealth for each of the personal asset categories for 1984, 1987, and 1991. The estimates are typically small but suggest that a dollar more in pension wealth was associated with from 4 cents less to 19 cents more in total personal financial assets in 1991, although most estimates are not statistically different from zero. Excluding education from the specification yields essentially the same results. And the same results are obtained if home equity is added to the specification, to control for other wealth that could in principle be used to meet financial needs after retirement. Thus we conclude there is unlikely to be much, if any, substitution of personal financial saving for employer-provided pension entitlement.

We obtain essentially the same results when we estimate equation (3.2) separately for those with and without a college degree. If anything, the results are stronger for those with college degrees. That is, the estimated coefficients are somewhat larger for the college educated group. This result is apparently at variance with recent results of Bernheim and Scholz (1993), who find no substitution effect for those without a college degree but a positive substitution effect for those with. Their estimates are based on the Survey of Consumer Finances and pertain to individuals not yet retired. They use an indicator variable for pension coverage, whereas we use pension wealth just after retirement. Their measure of personal assets

Table 3.3
ANOVA estimates of the effect of employer pension wealth on personal financial assets, by social security wealth percentile, asset, and year

Social security wealth percentile	Personal retirement assets		Other personal financial assets		Total personal financial assets	
1984						
1st	−.021	(.010)	−.006	(.050)	−.027	(.053)
2nd	−.000	(.013)	.052	(.061)	.052	(.065)
3rd	−.005	(.015)	.125	(.073)	.120	(.078)
4th	.008	(.016)	−.003	(.077)	.005	(.082)
5th	.028	(.016)	.230	(.075)	.257	(.079)
6th	−.005	(.011)	.159	(.055)	.153	(.058)
7th	−.008	(.012)	.024	(.059)	.016	(.062)
8th	−.012	(.016)	−.112	(.078)	−.124	(.083)
9th	−.008	(.014)	.126	(.067)	.118	(.071)
10th	.006	(.010)	.045	(.048)	.052	(.051)
1987						
1st	.013	(.013)	.074	(.053)	.087	(.056)
2nd	−.001	(.015)	−.040	(.060)	−.041	(.064)
3rd	−.011	(.023)	.054	(.090)	.043	(.096)
4th	−.008	(.020)	−.086	(.078)	−.093	(.083)
5th	.000	(.017)	.173	(.068)	.174	(.073)
6th	.020	(.013)	.208	(.053)	.228	(.056)
7th	.002	(.010)	.009	(.041)	.012	(.043)
8th	.020	(.014)	.027	(.057)	.047	(.060)
9th	.005	(.018)	−.278	(.071)	−.274	(.075)
10th	−.032	(.013)	.278	(.052)	.246	(.056)
1991						
1st	.006	(.020)	.066	(.055)	.072	(.062)
2nd	−.003	(.042)	.003	(.116)	.000	(.131)
3rd	.105	(.039)	.087	(.107)	.192	(.121)
4th	.064	(.030)	.084	(.083)	.147	(.093)
5th	−.016	(.023)	−.023	(.064)	−.039	(.073)
6th	−.029	(.026)	.065	(.071)	.036	(.080)
7th	−.007	(.029)	−.007	(.080)	−.013	(.090)
8th	.054	(.028)	.111	(.078)	.165	(.088)
9th	.057	(.026)	.031	(.071)	.088	(.080)
10th	−.027	(.022)	.039	(.061)	.012	(.069)

includes business equity and property other than primary home, whereas we include only personal financial assets. Our ANOVA (Analysis of Variance) specification also aims to capture lifetime earnings differences and allows for complete interaction by Social Security wealth percentile.

Several other previous studies have considered the impact of employer-provided pensions on personal saving. The early work of Cagan (1965) and Katona (1965) found that those covered by an employer pension save more in other forms. Cagan attributed this to a "recognition effect," whereby pension coverage induces awareness of the need to save for the future. More recently, several studies have sought to update and add to this line of analysis by relating personal saving to expected pension wealth instead of pension coverage. These studies have focused on older persons not yet retired, for whom the pension-saving trade-off may be greatest. The results have been mixed, perhaps because it is difficult to calculate pension wealth accurately for those not yet retired. Munnell (1976) finds a substantial offset, as high as 62 cents for each dollar of estimated pension wealth. Blinder, Gordon, and Wise (1981); Hubbard (1985); and Avery, Elliehausen, and Gustafson (1986), however, find little or no evidence of a trade-off; Diamond and Hausman (1984) find a modest trade-off. Thus these findings would suggest that the trade-off is far from dollar-for-dollar, and the consensus view appears to be little or no effect.

Possibly the principal reservation about the previous studies is the difficulty of constructing an accurate measure of expected pension wealth prior to receipt of pension benefits. Such calculations require assumptions about job mobility, future earnings, time to retirement, and most important, pension plan provisions. The detail necessary to calculate pension wealth is not reported in any of the data used by previous investigators with the exception of the Survey of Consumer Finances used by Avery, Elliehausen, and Gustafson (1986). Thus we have directed attention to recently retired persons and have used Social Security wealth percentiles to control for lifetime income.

Housing Equity

Rapid increases in housing prices led to large increases in home equity in many parts of the country over the 1980s. Figure 3.8 shows data for selected cohorts indexed to 1984 dollars. Substantial cohort effects are apparent, but whether the younger or the older cohort has more housing equity varies with age. Cohorts that reached ages 58, 64, and 70 in 1991 had greater housing equity than the older cohorts who reached these ages

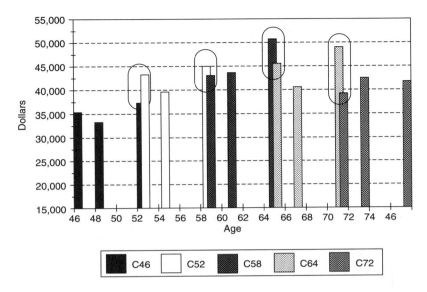

Figure 3.8
Home equity (all respondents—selected cohorts—indexed)

earlier, in 1984. For many, the increase in housing equity was probably an unanticipated windfall gain. Thus even more inducement to reduce other personal financial asset savings might be expected, contrary to the findings reported above. This is typically true for ages above 58. At 52, however, the younger cohort has less housing equity than the older cohort, and this is typically true at ages less than 58. More discussion of cohorts and housing equity with particular attention to the effect of the TRA, which may have encouraged home equity loans, is presented in Poterba, Venti, and Wise 1996.

Notice that figure 3.8 shows an increase in housing equity between 1984 and 1991 for each cohort, even for the cohort that ages from 70 to 76 between 1984 and 1991. Cross-section data, however, show a misleading decline in housing equity at older ages. The 1991 cross-section data, represented by the 1991 values at 52, 58, 64, 70, and 76, show home equity declining after age 64. Older cohorts have less housing equity than younger cohorts, but not because they reduce housing equity as they age.

We have not attempted in this chapter to consider formally the relationship between personal financial asset saving and housing equity. Hoynes and McFadden (1993) have completed an analysis of this issue. They find essentially no relationship between increases in home equity and total personal financial asset saving, based on data from the Panel Survey of Income Dynamics (PSID). They follow the same individuals over an extended time period. The SIPP data follow the same individuals for only 30 months, and the cohort method we use above does not provide a sufficient number of cohorts to meaningfully compare changes in home equity to changes in personal financial assets by cohort. Skinner (1991) also finds little relationship between housing equity and personal financial assets.

Conclusions

Personal targeted retirement accounts are an increasingly important form of saving for retirement. By 1989, contributions to IRA, 401(k), and Keogh accounts exceeded contributions to traditional employer-provided defined-benefit and defined-contribution pension plans. We have emphasized the effect of this form of saving on the financial status of recent retirees and those approaching retirement. Based on comparison of younger and older cohorts, we conclude that, for the most part, the increasing contributions to personal retirement plans have not displaced other financial asset saving. And consequently younger cohorts' real personal financial assets are substantially larger than those of their predecessors. Although any projections must be imprecise, we have made conservative estimates suggesting that age-76 families 18 years in the future will have almost $25,000 more in personal financial assets than current 76-year-old families—about $67,000 versus $43,000. Participating families' personal financial assets will be $67,000 higher at age 76—$160,000 versus $93,000.

Using Social Security wealth percentiles to control for lifetime income, we find that thus far there has been little replacement of employer-provided pension entitlements with personal retirement saving. Nor do we find any reduction in other personal financial asset saving with increases in employer-provided pension wealth. Thus we conclude that, for the most part, recent retirees' personal retirement saving has not replaced employer pension plan saving, nor have employer pensions displaced other personal financial assets. This should not be interpreted to mean that employer pensions have no effect on individual behavior. It seems apparent that employer pensions together with Social Security have led to dramatic declines in typical retirement ages and older Americans' labor force participation. Thus even if pensions have not reduced the amount that employees save in other forms, they surely have reduced the amount that older persons earn. This issue is discussed in some detail in Lumsdaine and Wise 1990.

Because we can find no apparent offset to the increase in personal retirement saving, we believe that this form of saving will not only be an increasingly important component of the wealth of the elderly, but indeed holds the prospect of adding substantially to older Americans' financial status. In particular, personal retirement saving is likely to increase substantially older families' nonannuitized liquid financial saving.

If these trends continue, the baby boom generation will accumulate substantially greater personal financial assets than their older counterparts and thus after retirement will have much larger pools of accessible assets upon which to draw to meet unexpected contingencies.

Notes

Funding for this chapter was provided by the National Institute on Aging through grant number P01-AG05842 and by the Hoover Institution.

1. Results using different data sets and different methodologies are presented in Venti and Wise 1986, 1987, 1990b, 1992. The last paper summarizes the findings of other investigators of this issue (Gale and Scholz 1990; Feenberg and Skinner 1989; and Joines and Manegold 1991).

2. A discount rate of 6% is used. Social Security, railroad retirement, federal employee, and military pensions are indexed by law. About 75% of state and local public employees receive some postretirement benefit increase; about half receive automatic COLAs (Phillips 1992). Postretirement benefit increases in the private sector are less common. Gustman and Steinmeier (1993) found that during the 17-year period ending in 1987, which included a period of high inflation, about 45% of private-sector defined-benefit plans provided some postretirement cost-of-living increase, usually ad hoc. We have indexed Social Security, military pension, railroad retirement, and all government employee pension annuities at 4% annually. Other annuities are not indexed.

3. See Venti and Wise 1989, 1990a, 1991; Feinstein and McFadden 1989; and Sheiner and Weil 1992.

4. The value for 1991 may be an anomaly. Medians in earlier years were about $9,000, and mean values increased from $34,365 in 1984 to $42,018 in 1991.

5. See EBRI 1986.

6. The data show an anomalous increase in contributions to defined-contribution plans from $25.5 billion in 1988 to $34.0 billion in 1989. Preliminary Department of Labor tabulations show a decline to below $25.5 billion in 1990.

7. There are three principal conceptual differences between the FOF and the NIPA definitions of savings. These involve treatment of nonhousing durable goods, state and local government pension reserves, and net savings of corporate firms. For details see Wilson et al 1989.

8. Only those with reported Social Security benefits are included in the analysis.

Table 3A.1
Components of asset categories, proportion of families owning, and mean and median levels, ages 65–69, 1991

Asset category and component	Percentage owning	Mean	Median
Personal (targeted) retirement assets	34.5	$10,992	$ 0
Individual retirement accounts (IRAs)	30.8	7,239	0
401(k) accounts	3.8	617	0
Keogh plans	1.9	1,439	0
Life insurance and annuities	3.0	1,626	0
Other personal financial assets	84.8	42,018	7,428
Saving accounts and CDs	72.2	19,894	3,600
Money market funds, bonds, and securities	13.3	8,007	0
Stocks and mutual funds	21.9	13,219	0
U.S. savings bonds	14.1	548	0
Non–interest-bearing checking accounts	38.4	351	0
Employer-provided pension assets	56.2	62,305	16,017
Pension	34.6	23,276	0
Railroad retirement	2.0	3,483	0
Federal	5.1	9,767	0
State government	2.6	11,550	0
Local government	2.8	3,569	0
Military	7.1	5,251	0
Veterans	5.2	3,891	0
Other	3.0	1,517	0
Social Security assets	88.0	99,682	99,167
Home equity	75.3	64,955	50,000
Equity in other property	81.8	33,855	5,992
Net equity in other property	13.2	7,450	0
Motor vehicle equity	80.6	6,902	3,950
Business equity	5.9	7,180	0
Rental property	7.7	7,961	0
Other properties (vacation, commercial, etc.)	1.4	369	0
Money owed to family	2.6	685	0
Equity in other financial investments	3.5	2,258	0
Money owed to family—business/property sale	2.7	1,049	0

Table 3A.2
Mean personal retirement assets for 15 cohorts (in dollars)

Age	Cohort (age in 1984)														
	42	44	46	48	50	52	54	56	58	60	62	64	66	68	70
42	1,509														
44	4,343	1,426													
46		4,532	1,825												
48	10,369		4,528	2,036											
50		10,391		4,885	1,983										
52			11,694		5,740	2,353									
54															
56					12,030		7,030	2,849							
58						12,494		6,702	3,039						
60							11,174		7,967	4,275					
62								15,130		8,108	4,272				
64									15,033		8,467	3,678			
66										10,820		4,932	3,262		
68											10,612		6,328	2,398	
70												10,999		3,201	1,608
72													7,565		2,036
74														5,374	
76															3,204

Table 3A.3a
Summary of cohort effects at selected age intervals: percentages and conditional means (1984 dollars)

Age interval and data reported	1984	1987	1991
Ages 50–54			
All respondents			
Personal retirement assets	2,772	5,748	9,103
Other personal financial assets	14,456	14,483	13,501
Total personal financial assets	17,227	20,231	22,604
Contributors			
% with personal retirement saving	36	42	46
Personal retirement assets	7,498	13,767	20,413
Other personal financial assets	27,744	27,511	24,024
Total personal financial assets	35,241	41,277	44,436
Noncontributors			
% without personal retirement saving	64	58	54
Total personal financial assets	6,615	5,145	5,390
Ages 55–59			
All respondents			
Personal retirement assets	3,456	6,581	9,015
Other personal financial assets	19,271	18,956	17,052
Total personal financial assets	22,729	25,537	26,066
Contributors			
% with personal retirement saving	43	43	43
Personal retirement assets	8,215	15,325	21,225
Other personal financial assets	31,864	34,953	31,028
Total personal financial assets	40,081	50,279	52,254
Noncontributors			
% without personal retirement saving	57	57	57
Total personal financial assets	9,744	6,916	6,590
Ages 60–64			
All respondents			
Personal retirement assets	3,946	6,923	10,914
Other personal financial assets	28,629	25,153	27,959
Total personal financial assets	32,575	32,076	38,874
Contributors			
% with personal retirement saving	38	41	42
Personal retirement assets	9,968	17,042	25,795
Other personal financial assets	51,397	41,179	50,160
Total personal financial assets	61,365	58,220	75,954

Table 3A.3a (continued)

Age interval and data reported	1984	1987	1991
Noncontributors			
% without personal retirement saving	62	59	58
Total personal financial assets	13,468	14,189	12,684
Ages 65–69			
All respondents			
Personal retirement assets	2,467	4,342	8,022
Other personal financial assets	33,352	31,238	29,483
Total personal financial assets	35,819	35,580	37,505
Contributors			
% with personal retirement saving	19	27	35
Personal retirement assets	11,925	16,037	24,672
Other personal financial assets	62,073	58,129	60,753
Total personal financial assets	73,998	74,166	85,426
Noncontributors			
% without personal retirement saving	81	73	65
Total personal financial assets	22,708	21,253	17,152
Ages 70–74			
All respondents			
Personal retirement assets	1,626	1,834	4,433
Other personal financial assets	34,291	34,469	35,680
Total personal financial assets	35,917	36,303	40,112
Contributors			
% with personal retirement saving	8	15	20
Personal retirement assets	14,698	12,594	22,623
Other personal financial assets	88,181	66,427	89,799
Total personal financial assets	102,878	79,020	112,421
Noncontributors			
% without personal retirement saving	92	85	80
Total personal financial assets	26,585	29,020	25,201
Ages 75–79			
All respondents			
Personal retirement assets	960	1,082	1,778
Other personal financial assets	30,271	29,241	33,360
Total personal financial assets	31,231	30,323	35,138

Table 3A.3a (continued)

Age interval and data reported	1984	1987	1991
Contributors			
% with personal retirement saving	6	7	11
Personal retirement assets	16,305	16,218	19,187
Other personal financial assets	76,484	75,562	69,867
Total personal financial assets	92,789	91,780	89,054
Noncontributors			
% without personal retirement saving	94	93	89
Total personal financial assets	27,025	25,930	31,141
Ages 80 +			
All respondents			
Personal retirement assets	431	575	1,243
Other personal financial assets	27,493	27,949	29,880
Total personal financial assets	27,924	28,524	31,123
Contributors			
% with personal retirement saving	4	4	5
Personal retirement assets	8,551	15,288	25,500
Other personal financial assets	78,271	54,771	76,091
Total personal financial assets	86,812	70,059	101,591
Noncontributors			
% without personal retirement saving	96	96	95
Total personal financial assets	25,166	26,900	27,656

Note: Based on mean regressions controlling for age, education, marital status, and income. The means for each age-saver group are evaluated at the 1987 means of that group's demographic variables. All values are in 1984 dollars.

Table 3A.3b
Summary of cohort effects at selected age intervals: percentages and conditional medians (1984 dollars)

Age interval and data reported	1984	1987	1991
Ages 50–54			
Contributors			
% with personal retirement saving	36	42	46
Personal retirement assets	5,374	8,828	11,542
Other personal financial assets	8,851	8,806	7,701
Total personal financial assets	16,392	20,792	22,883
Noncontributors			
% without personal retirement saving	64	58	54
Total personal financial assets	831	829	721
Ages 55–59			
Contributors			
% with personal retirement saving	43	43	43
Personal retirement assets	5,561	10,051	11,997
Other personal financial assets	11,997	13,274	10,581
Total personal financial assets	19,878	26,918	28,952
Noncontributors			
% without personal retirement saving	57	57	57
Total personal financial assets	1,006	951	921
Ages 60–64			
Contributors			
% with personal retirement saving	38	41	42
Personal retirement assets	6,300	10,954	17,076
Other personal financial assets	17,720	16,800	16,598
Total personal financial assets	26,996	30,832	38,691
Noncontributors			
% without personal retirement saving	62	59	58
Total personal financial assets	2,073	1,834	1,645
Ages 65–69			
Contributors			
% with personal retirement saving	19	27	35
Personal retirement assets	7,245	10,420	14,047
Other personal financial assets	31,659	32,493	27,762
Total personal financial assets	40,948	49,222	53,636

Table 3A.3b (continued)

Age interval and data reported	1984	1987	1991
Noncontributors			
% without personal retirement saving	81	73	65
Total personal financial assets	9,171	8,949	7,446
Ages 70–74			
Contributors			
% with personal retirement saving	8	15	20
Personal retirement assets	7,965	7,753	13,018
Other personal financial assets	43,715	38,972	32,263
Total personal financial assets	58,169	50,713	53,319
Noncontributors			
% without personal retirement saving	92	85	80
Total personal financial assets	14,216	13,815	12,257
Ages 75–79			
Contributors			
% with personal retirement saving	6	7	11
Personal retirement assets	6,184	7,402	10,961
Other personal financial assets	42,655	52,361	36,523
Total personal financial assets	54,756	60,602	57,442
Noncontributors			
% without personal retirement saving	94	93	89
Total personal financial assets	13,297	12,188	12,800
Ages 80+			
Contributors			
% with personal retirement saving	4	4	5
Personal retirement assets	5,445	5,162	9,199
Other personal financial assets	45,564	30,640	39,777
Total personal financial assets	61,278	46,280	63,012
Noncontributors			
% without personal retirement saving	96	96	95
Total personal financial assets	9,493	9,637	8,836

Note: Based on median regressions controlling for age, education, marital status, and income. The medians for each age-saver group are evaluated at the 1987 medians of that group's demographic variables. All values are in 1984 dollars.

References

Avery, Robert B., Gregory E. Elliehausen, and Thomas A. Gustafson. 1986. "Pensions and Social Security in Household Portfolios: Evidence from the 1983 Survey of Consumer Finances." In F. Adams and S. Wachter (eds.), *Savings and Capital Formation: The Policy Options*. Lexington, MA: Lexington Books, 127–60.

Bernheim, B. Douglas. 1987. "The Economic Effects of Social Security: Toward a Reconciliaton of Theory and Measurement." *Journal of Public Economics* 33:273–304.

Bernheim, B. Douglas, and John Karl Scholz. 1993. "Private Saving and Public Policy." *Tax Policy and the Economy* 7:73–110.

Bernheim, B. Douglas, and John B. Shoven. 1988. "Pension Funding and Saving." In Z. Bodie, J. Shoven, and D. Wise (eds.), *Pensions in the U.S. Economy*. Chicago: University of Chicago Press.

Blinder, Alan S., Roger Gordon, and David E. Wise. 1981. *An Empirical Study of the Effects of Pensions on the Saving and Labor Supply Decisions of Older Men*. Princeton, NJ: Mathtech Inc.

Cagan, Phillip. 1965. *The Effect of Pension Plans on Aggregate Saving: Evidence From a Sample Survey*. Occasional Papers no. 95, National Bureau of Economic Research, Cambridge, MA.

Diamond, Peter A., and Jerry A. Hausman. 1984. "Individual Retirement and Savings Behavior." *Journal of Public Economics* 23:81–114.

Employee Benefit Research Institute (EBRI). 1986. "Tax Reform and Employee Benefits." Issue Brief no. 59, October.

Feenberg, Daniel, and Jonathan Skinner. 1989. "Sources of IRA Saving." *Tax Policy and the Economy* 3:25–46.

Feinstein, Jonathan, and Daniel McFadden. 1989. "The Dynamics of Housing Demand by the Elderly: Wealth, Cash Flow, and Demographic Effects." In D. Wise (ed.), *The Economics of Aging*. Chicago: University of Chicago Press.

Gale, William G., and John Karl Scholz. 1990. "IRAs and Household Saving." University of Wisconsin. Mimeographed.

Gustman, Alan, and Thomas Steinmeier. 1993. "Cost of Living Increases in Pensions." In Olivia Mitchell (ed.), *As the Workforce Ages*. Ithaca, NY: ILR Press.

Hoynes, Hilary, and Daniel McFadden. 1994. "The Impact of Demographics on Housing and Non-Housing Wealth in the United States." NBER Working Paper 4666, March.

Hubbard, R. Glenn. 1985. "Personal Taxation, Pension Wealth, and Portfolio Composition." *Review of Economics and Statistics* 67(1):53–60.

Joines, Douglas H., and James G. Manegold. 1991. "IRAs and Saving: Evidence from a Panel of Taxpayers." Federal Reserve Bank of Kansas City Research Working Paper: 91–05.

Katona, George. 1965. *Private Pensions and Individual Saving*. Ann Arbor: University of Michigan Press.

Lumsdaine, Robin L., and David A. Wise. 1994. "Aging and Labor Force Participation: A Review of Trends and Explanations." in Y. Noguchi and D. Wise, eds, *Aging in The United States and Japan*. Chicago: University of Chicago Press, pp. 7–42.

Munnell, Alicia H. 1976. "Private Pensions and Saving: New Evidence," *Journal of Political Economy* 84 (October): 1013–32.

Phillips, Kristen. 1992. "State and Local Pension Benefits." In John A. Turner and Daniel J. Beller (eds.), *Trends in Pensions 1992*. Washington, D.C.: U.S.P. 341–92.

Poterba, James M., Steven F. Venti, and David A. Wise. 1997. "The Effects of Special Saving Programs on Saving and Wealth." Working paper no. 5287, National Bureau of Economic Research, October.

Poterba, James M., Steven F. Venti, and David A. Wise. 1996. "Do Retirement Saving Programs Increase Saving: Reconciling the Evidence." Working paper, April. NBER.

Poterba, James M., Steven F. Venti, and David A. Wise. 1995a. "Do 401(k) Contributions Crowd Out Other Personal Saving?" *Journal of Public Economics* 58:1–32.

Poterba, James M., Steven F. Venti, and David A. Wise. 1994. "401(k) Plans and Tax-Deferred Saving." In D. Wise (ed.), *Studies in the Economics of Aging*, 105–38. Chicago: University of Chicago Press.

Schieber, Sylvester, and John Shoven. 1997. "The Consequences of Population Aging for Private Pension Fund Saving and Asset Markets." M. Hurd and N. Yashiros, eds., *The Economic Effects of Aging in the United States and Japan*. Chicago: University of Chicago Press, 111–130.

Sheiner, Louise, and David N. Weil. 1992. "The Housing Wealth of the Aged," Working paper no. 4115, National Bureau of Economic Research, July.

Skinner, Jonathan. 1991. "Housing and Saving in the United States." Working paper no. 3874, National Bureau of Economic Research. October.

Venti, Steven F., and David A. Wise. 1992. "Government Policy and Personal Retirement Saving." *Tax Policy and the Economy* 6:1–41.

Venti, Steven F., and David A. Wise. 1991. "Aging and the Income Value of Housing Wealth." *Journal of Public Economics* 44:371–95.

Venti, Steven F., and David A. Wise. 1990a. "But They Don't Want To Reduce Housing Equity." In D. Wise (ed.), *Issues in the Economics of Aging*. Chicago: University of Chicago Press, 13–29.

Venti, Steven F., and David A. Wise. 1990b. "Have IRAs Increased U.S. Saving? Evidence from the Consumer Expenditure Surveys." *Quarterly Journal of Economics* 105:661–98.

Venti, Steven F., and David A. Wise. 1989. "Aging, Moving, and Housing Wealth." In D. Wise (ed.), *The Economics of Aging*. Chicago: University of Chicago Press, 9–48.

Venti, Steven F., and David A. Wise. 1987. "IRAs and Saving." In M. Feldstein (ed.), *The Effects of Taxation on Capital Accumulation*. Chicago: University of Chicago Press, 7–48.

Venti, Steven F., and David A. Wise. 1986. "Tax-Deferred Accounts, Constrained Choice and Estimation of Individual Saving." *Review of Economic Studies* 53:579–601.

Wilson, John F., James L. Freund, Frederick O.Yohn, and Walter Lederer. 1989. "Measuring Household Saving: Recent Experience from the Flow-of-Funds Perspective." In R. Lipsey and H. Tice (eds.), *The Measurement of Saving, Investment, and Wealth*. Chicago: University of Chicago Press, 101–152.

4

Government Guarantees of Private Pension Benefits: Current Problems and Market-Based Solutions

Carolyn L. Weaver

Ultimately, the United States could be left only with bankrupt defined benefit plans with the benefits financed directly by taxpayers.

—Zvi Bodie and Robert C. Merton[1]

The alarm has been sounded.

—James B. Lockhart, III[2]

In the past decade, Americans have deposited hundreds of billions of dollars into private pensions, either directly through their contributions to 401(k) plans and other tax-deferred saving plans or indirectly through their participation in traditional employer-sponsored pension plans, known as defined-benefit plans. Annual contributions in 1989 were $105 billion, and pension fund assets exceeded the $2 trillion mark.[3] On the benefit side, close to one-third of elderly Americans received income from a private pension or annuity, with total 1990 payments of $144 billion, and more than half the workforce can expect to receive a pension at retirement.[4] Pension accumulations are now an important component of American workers' wealth, of retired workers' income security, and of investment capital in U.S. financial markets.[5]

The traditional defined-benefit plan, while declining in popularity, remains American workers' primary pension. This kind of plan promises workers an annuity at retirement based on a formula typically related to final salary and years of service. Workers own, make contributions to, or accumulate interest in no individualized accounts; instead, the employer (or plan sponsor) manages a pension fund from which benefits are paid, and these benefits are conditional on the worker meeting the plan's vesting standards and the firm continuing to operate the plan.[6]

Some 27 million people, or about two-thirds of workers covered by private pensions, are covered by a defined-benefit plan, accumulating promises of future benefits amounting to $950 billion in present-value terms.[7] These promises are backed by the assets accumulating in company pension funds, estimated at $1.4 trillion,[8] the net worth of the plans' sponsoring companies, and ultimately, in the case of financial distress or plan sponsor bankruptcy, by a federal insurance program administered by the PBGC.

As noted in more than a few news stories of late, the PBGC is on rocky shoals. According to its most recent annual report, the agency has a past loss (or "accumulated deficit") of $2.9 billion and faces a reasonable prospect of substantially larger losses in the decades ahead.[9] The headlines— "The Coming Pension Bailout," "The Pension Time Bomb," "Pension Plans in Trouble," "Do You Know Where Your Nest Egg Is?"—conjure images of a bankrupt pension insurance program, raising questions not only about the possibility of a saving and loan–style taxpayer bailout but also about the security of the private pension system more generally.[10] In the words of PBGC Executive Director Martin Slate, "concern about the health of the PBGC and the defined-benefit system is widespread."[11]

I begin this chapter by carefully looking at the financial problems facing the PBGC. Drawing on a large body of economic research on government guarantees, I argue that these are long-term problems and stem from the failure to control the incentive problems pension insurance has created. Disincentives to fund benefit promises, reduce pension fund volatility, and avoid unnecessary plan terminations are deeply embedded in the structure of the program set in place in 1974. I then discuss the reforms needed to ensure a viable pension insurance program, one offering true insurance against the risk of pension default within a healthy and flexible retirement income system more generally. I conclude with reflections on the problems of public policies aimed at promoting retirement income security.

The PBGC and Its Finances

Since ERISA's enactment in 1974, a mandatory pension insurance program administered by the PBGC has covered participants in most defined-benefit pension plans.[12] Plan sponsors pay premiums for this insurance, and workers are protected (up to limits set in the law) against the loss of basic retirement benefits if their plan is terminated with insufficient assets to meet outstanding liabilities.[13] In such cases, which usually occur because

Table 4.1
Pension insurance coverage, benefits, premiums, and claims: fiscal year 1993

Coverage	Estimate
Number of plans	64,000
Number of participants (workers and retirees)	32 million
Benefits	
Benefit payments	$722 million
Participants receiving monthly payments	158,000
Participants to receive payments in future[a]	282,000
maximum annual benefit	
—at age 65	$30,802[b]
—at age 55	$13,807[b]
Premiums	
Total paid by plan sponsors	$913 million
Average annual premium per participant	$29
Cumulative Claims, 1975–93	
Number of underfunded terminations	1,848
Liabilities of terminated plans	$8.0 billion
Assets of terminated plans	$3.0 billion
Recoveries from employers	$0.6 billion
Net claims	$4.4 billion
Plan assets/plan liabilities	38%
Recoveries/unfunded liabilities	13%

Sources: Pension Benefit Guaranty Corporation, *1993 Annual Report*; Richard A. Ippolito, "Private Pensions in the U.S. II" (April 29, 1992); and data supplied by the Office of Public Affairs, PBGC, May 1994.
a. Vested workers in plans that have been or are expected to be trusteed. (See note on table 4.2.)
b. 1994 data.

of plan sponsor insolvency, the PBGC steps in as trustee, taking over any assets remaining in the pension fund and guaranteeing the payment of insured retirement benefits.[14] To cover the gap between assets and liabilities in the plans, the PBGC relies primarily on premium income and on investment earnings on the assets it holds; it also has recourse to liability payments from employers.[15]

Table 4.1 summarizes some pertinent information on PBGC activity. As indicated, the PBGC insures the pensions of 32 million workers and retirees in 64,000 (single-employer) pension plans. Since 1974, it has trusteed 1,848 pension plans with benefit liabilities of $8 billion (expressed in present-value terms); of this, $3 billion was offset by pension fund

Table 4.2
Pension insurance claims' experience, fiscal years 1975–93 (in millions of dollars)

Year of termination	Number of plans terminated	Pension liabilities	Plan assets	Recoveries from employers	Net claims	Average net claim per terminated plan
1975–81	824	$ 741	$ 295	$ 129	$ 317	$0.4
1982–87	689	2,694	848	184	1,661	2.4
1988–93	335	4,579	1,871	312	2,396	7.2
Total	1,848	8,014	3,014	626	4,374	
Probable[a]	46	3,645	1,403	616	1,627	
Total	1,894	$11,659	$4,417	$1,242	$6,001	

Source: Pension Benefit Guaranty Corporation, *1992 Annual Report* and *1993 Annual Report*.
a. Termination is expected "based on the occurrence of an identifiable event by year end and the expectation that the distress test will be met or PBGC itself will seek termination of the plan." The figures do not include other terminations the PBGC regards as "reasonably possible" or "near-term, serious risks."

assets and another $600 million was offset by employer liability payments, leaving net claims of $4.4 billion. In 1993, 158,000 people were receiving retirement benefits from the PBGC at an annual cost of $722 million, and more than 250,000 were expecting to receive benefits from the PBGC at retirement.

Table 4.2 summarizes the trends in PBGC claims over the years. As indicated, although the number of terminations of underfunded pension plans has been declining (down from 689 plans in 1982–87 to 335 in the most recent period, 1988–93), net claims against the PBGC have been rising (up from $1.7 billion in 1982–87 to $2.4 billion in the more recent period). Unfunded liabilities per terminated plan are up significantly (about threefold), recoveries from employers as a fraction of unfunded liabilities remain low, and net claims are piling up. Net claims to date (including completed and probable terminations) total $6 billion.[16]

Fiscal 1991 was the kind of year that strikes fear in the hearts of those who worry about pension insurance's future. Amidst the airline industry's continuing restructuring, seven of Eastern Airlines' pension plans and three of Pan American's, covering tens of thousands of workers, were terminated. As table 4.3 shows, their claims for unfunded benefits amounted to $1.3 billion, or more than one-quarter of the claims in the PBGC's history.[17] In the same year, CF&I Steel, Uniroyal Plastics, and Blaw-Knox terminated plans with claims totaling close to one-half billion dollars.

Looking over the PBGC's history, the largest claims are of recent origin and have been concentrated in two industries, airlines and steel. Referring

Table 4.3
Ten companies with largest pension insurance claims (through 1993)

Company	Date of plan termination(s)	Claim (in millions of dollars)	Percentage of all claims	Cumulative percentage of all claims
Pan American Airways	1991	$762.7	15.25%	15.25%
Eastern Air Lines	1991	562.8	11.26	26.51
Wheeling-Pittsburgh (steel)	1985	495.2	9.90	36.41
Sharon Steel	1993	246.5	4.93	41.34
Kaiser Steel	1987	223.0	4.46	45.80
CF&I Steel	1991	218.6	4.37	50.18
LTV (Republic Steel)	1986	205.1	4.10	54.28
Allis-Chalmers (farm equipment)	1985	170.2	3.40	57.68
Uniroyal Plastics (Jesup)	1991	127.2	2.54	60.23
Blaw-Knox (steel)	1991	100.9	2.02	62.24

Source: Office of Public Affairs, Pension Benefit Guaranty Corporation, June 1994.
Note: Claims are insured pension liabilities less plan assets. Figures exclude recoveries from employers.

again to table 4.3, five of the ten largest claims against the PBGC have occurred just since 1991, and eight out of the ten companies filing the largest claims have been in the airline and steel industries. Together, the ten companies listed account for close to two-thirds of all claims against the PBGC.

Where does this leave the PBGC? Because of the miracles of federal budgeting, the PBGC is running a cash flow surplus (meaning premium and other income exceeds annual benefits and other expenses) while slipping further into debt on a net worth basis.[18] (Sounds like the Social Security system.) With assets of $8.4 billion and liabilities of $11.3 billion, the PBGC's "accumulated deficit" at the close of 1993 stood at $2.9 billion.[19] This is the amount, in present-value terms, by which the PBGC's promises to pay future benefits based on terminations to date exceed assets on hand.

PBGC's Slate has described the accumulated deficit as a "long-term deficit" and likened it to a home mortgage: "You might have 30 years to pay it off, but you still have to pay it."[20] Although it certainly is true that the PBGC debt is not due and payable today—indeed, benefit payments to retirees and vested workers in terminated plans can extend for 40 years or longer—this characterization tends to understate the economic and financial consequences of the debt and how its costs are allocated over time; it also greatly understates the size of the PBGC's funding problem.

Accumulating a debt and repaying it over many years amounts to pay-as-you-go financing, which, as is well known, amounts to deficit financing pure and simple: The cost of benefit promises extended and liabilities incurred in the past is redistributed to the future. Quite apart from whether a private insurer operating in a competitive setting could finance its operations this way (which it could not), this is not generally regarded as a sound way to finance a government pension insurance program. By understating the true cost of pension guarantees to today's participants, pay-as-you-go financing creates a clear danger of a taxpayer bailout. The reason, quite simply, is that companies reluctant to pay for their own insurance (on account of expected future claims) and pay for others' past losses can avoid doing so by abandoning their pension plans, or not establishing one to begin with, thereby eroding the insurance pool and exacerbating the financing problem.[21]

In a 1982 article entitled (appropriately) "Guaranteeing Private Pension Benefits: A Potentially Expensive Business," Alicia Munnell, Assistant Secretary for Economic Policy at the Treasury Department and former Vice President of the Boston Federal Reserve Bank, stated: "The existence of a deficiency in assets violates an important PBGC financing principle—namely, that premium rates should be set at such a level as to produce annual revenues which, together with investment earnings and employer liability collections, are sufficient to cover the unfunded benefit claims of plan terminations during the year."[22] Under this principle, the full cost (in present-value terms) of benefit claims stemming from plan terminations in a particular year is allocated to the plans subject to the risk of termination during that year. Adhering to this principle, noted Munnell, would "minimize the necessity for future premium increases and their potentially destabilizing effects on the private pension system."[23]

This financing principle has been violated throughout PBGC's history. Premiums have generally, but by no means always, been set high enough to cover annual benefit outlays but not high enough to meet the present value of new benefit claims. As a result, pension plan participants (and company shareholders) have borne only a small portion of the cost of their insurance protection; the balance has been shifted to future plans, including plans not yet formed.

As to the size of PBGC's financing problem, Zvi Bodie and Robert Merton, among others, have noted that the "accumulated deficit" figure the PBGC reports substantially understates its true liability—that is, the implicit obligations it has assumed on behalf of currently insured plans.

As further discussed below, the PBGC figure completely ignores expected future terminations among currently insured plans, even those terminations considered all but inevitable.[24] Taking into account expected future terminations, the PBGC's financial position is much weaker than implied by the $2.9 billion deficit figure.

Arriving at an economically meaningful measure of PBGC's liability requires looking, first, at its exposure to future losses and, second, at the likelihood these losses will materialize. This information is combined to assess PBGC's expected future claims.

Exposure to Future Losses

The extent of underfunding, that is, the gap between pension fund assets and the present value of outstanding (guaranteed) benefit promises among underfunded plans, is a measure of PBGC's exposure to future losses.[25] Though the great majority of pension plans in the United States are well funded and pose relatively little risk of loss to the PBGC, a significant minority of plans are nevertheless underfunded, some of them substantially so, and the potential for losses is great. PBGC estimates that about one-quarter of insured plans are underfunded, to the tune of $53 billion.[26] A mere 50 companies account for most of this underfunding.[27]

Table 4.4 reports data on the 50 companies with the most underfunded pension plans (dubbed the "iffy 50"). Included in this table are data, as of the end of 1992, on the assets, liabilities, and amount of underfunding (expressed in dollar and percentage terms) for each company's under-funded pension plan(s). The table presents separately data on total and guaranteed benefit liabilities, both expressed in present-value terms.[28]

As this table reveals, the assets of some of the largest pension plans in America fall far short of outstanding pension promises. For example, General Motors' pension promises to workers and retirees in underfunded plans totaled $60 billion at the end of 1992; assets in these plans were just $40 billion, leaving $20 billion (or fully one-third) of benefit promises unfunded. PBGC guaranteed some $57 billion, or about 95%, of GM's pension promises, of which $17 billion was unfunded. Among other major corporations, unfunded guaranteed benefits were close to $2 billion at LTV and Bethlehem Steel, $1 billion at Westinghouse, and $900 million at Chrysler, followed by Uniroyal Goodrich, TWA, Navistar, and American National Can, each with unfunded guaranteed benefits on the order of $400–$500 million. Together, the 50 companies, the table shows, sponsor

Table 4.4
Fifty companies with largest unfunded pension liabilities as of December 31, 1992 (in millions of dollars)

Company	Plan assets	Total pension benefits			Guaranteed pension benefits		
		Benefit liabilities[a]	Amount unfunded	Percentage unfunded	Benefit liabilities[a]	Amount unfunded	Percentage unfunded
Ravenswood Aluminum Corp.	$ 11	$ 106	$ 95	89%	$ 100	$ 89	89%
LTV Corp.	1,273	3,375	2,102	62	3,206	1,933	60
New Valley Corp.	269	698	429	61	663	394	59
Tenneco Inc.	195	444	249	56	422	227	54
Keystone Consolidated Ind., Inc.	95	215	120	56	204	109	53
Loews Corp.	159	328	170	52	312	153	49
Uniroyal Goodrich Tire Co.	517	1,018	501	49	967	450	47
Laclede Steel Co.	115	216	101	47	211	96	45
Rockwell International Corp.	462	842	380	45	806	344	43
Trans World Airlines, Inc.	592	1,071	479	45	1,018	426	42
Bridgestone-Firestone, Inc.	303	547	245	45	520	217	42
Anchor Glass Co.	170	296	126	43	282	111	40
ACF Industries, Inc.	124	214	90	42	203	79	39
Bethlehem Steel Corp.	3,426	5,857	2,431	42	5,564	2,138	38
PacifiCorp	473	736	262	36	699	226	32
White Consolidated Industries, Inc.	253	388	136	35	369	116	32
Clark Equipment Co.	181	276	95	35	262	82	31
Maxxam Inc.	586	888	302	34	844	257	31
General Motors Corp.	39,572	59,754	20,182	34	56,766	17,195	30
American National Can Co.	1,092	1,637	546	33	1,555	464	30

Budd Co.	362	535	173	32	508	146	29
Mack Trucks, Inc.	401	583	183	31	554	153	28
Allegheny Ludlum Corp.	323	466	143	31	442	120	27
Rohr, Inc.	347	493	146	30	468	121	26
Crown Cork & Seal Co., Inc.	840	1,179	339	29	1,120	280	25
Goodrich (B.F.) Co.	386	537	151	28	510	124	24
James River Corp. of Virginia	266	370	104	28	351	85	24
Bull HN Information Systems Inc.	350	483	133	28	459	109	24
Armco Steel Company, L.P.	709	1,037	328	32	915	206	23
National Intergroup, Inc.	532	719	187	26	683	151	22
CSX Corp.	812	1,080	268	25	1,026	214	21
Westinghouse Electic Corp.	3,918	5,189	1,271	24	4,930	1,012	21
Reynolds Metals Co.	943	1,248	304	24	1,185	242	20
PPG Industries, Inc.	924	1,203	279	23	1,143	219	19
Goodyear Tire & Rubber Co.	1,276	1,622	346	21	1,541	265	17
Navistar International Corp.	2,070	2,614	544	21	2,483	413	17
Northwest Airlines, Inc.	1,212	1,523	311	20	1,447	235	16
Woolworth Corp.	546	664	118	18	649	103	16
Allied-Signal Inc.	607	740	133	18	703	96	14
Ceridian Corp.	565	685	120	18	651	86	13
National Steel Corp.	962	1,157	194	17	1,099	137	12
Deere & Co.	1,367	1,617	250	15	1,536	169	11
Warner-Lambert Co.	1,026	1,209	183	15	1,148	122	11
Honeywell Inc.	2,162	2,530	368	15	2,404	242	10
Armco Inc.	1,790	2,088	298	14	1,983	193	10
Chrysler Corp.	8,332	9,692	1,360	14	9,208	876	10

Table 4.4 (continued)

Company	Total pension benefits				Guaranteed pension benefits		
	Plan assets	Benefit liabilities[a]	Amount unfunded	Percentage unfunded	Benefit liabilities[a]	Amount unfunded	Percentage unfunded
Greyhound Lines Inc.	928	1,070	142	13	1,016	88	9
Inland Steel Co.	1,686	1,844	157	9	1,797	110	6
United Technologies Corp.	1,446	1,616	171	11	1,536	90	6
Unisys Corp.	2,748	3,055	307	10	2,902	155	5
TOTALS (in millions)	$89,703	$127,752	$38,049	30%	$121,369	$31,667	26%

Source: Based on Pension Benefit Guaranty Corporation, "Top 50 Companies with the Largest Unfunded Pension Liability," released Nov. 22, 1993. See PBGC 1993d.

Note: This list contains information on each company's unfunded pension plan(s); companies may have other plans that are overfunded, but they are not considered here.

a. Vested benefit liabilities expressed in present-value terms using a common discount rate based on annuity prices at the end of 1992.

less than 1% of the plans the PBGC insures and account for more than 70% of all underfunding.[29]

As table 4.4 also reveals, underfunding is heavily concentrated in the automobile, steel, airline, and tire industries, those with collectively bargained pension plans. Eighty-five percent of underfunding is in plans covering unionized workers.[30]

Judging by the size of companies' unfunded benefit promises—corporate debt, pure and simple—relative to their probable net worth, it would appear safe to say that the pension insurance program is keeping at least some otherwise insolvent companies afloat. As further discussed below, federal pension guarantees tend to increase equity values and subsidize wages in firms in financial distress.[31]

Four caveats are in order before drawing any conclusions about likely losses to the PBGC. First, exposure is not risk. The financial health of the companies on this list—and thus the risk they actually pose to the PBGC —varies widely. Moody's bond ratings, for example, just one of many measures of performance, vary from investment grade to below investment grade among the companies on this list and are rising for some companies and declining for others. Second, exposure (and risk) vary widely year to year.[32] Three companies on the top of PBGC's 1991 list (Blaw-Knox, CF&I Steel, and Jesup Group), for example, were dropped from the 1992 list because their pension plans terminated, and 11 companies were dropped because their pension plans became better funded.[33] Third, it is safe to assume that none of the companies on this list are out of compliance with federal pension law. Through a complex web of transition rules, waivers, and exemptions, some companies can systematically underfund their pension plans, leaving PBGC exposed to the risk of substantial losses.[34] Finally, because underfunding tends to rise rapidly in companies experiencing financial distress,[35] actual claims against the PBGC in the event of plan termination would almost certainly exceed those suggested by the underfunding reported in the table.

With that said, PBGC estimates one-fourth of underfunding is in companies with below-investment-grade bond ratings—financially weak companies that pose a "reasonably possible" risk of terminating their pension plans.[36] Net claims for these plans, were they terminated over the next decade, are estimated at $13–$18 billion.[37] Incorporating this into a 10-year forecast, which assumes other, lesser terminations as well, PBGC projects the accumulated deficit (net of premium income) will reach $14 billion (in real 1993 dollars) in 2003—roughly five times its current size.[38] The

Office of Management and Budget, using a more sophisticated, options-pricing model, estimates that PBGC's "uncovered exposure" to current plans is $40–$60 billion in present-value terms.[39] Unlike the PBGC estimate, the OMB estimate recognizes that even well-funded pension plans in healthy firms pose risks due either to the firms' misfortunes or asset price volatility.

Concern Over an S&L–Style Bailout

Little wonder that an S&L-style taxpayer bailout has crossed more than a few analysts' and commentators' minds.[40] The PBGC is financed entirely by premiums levied on companies that sponsor defined-benefit pension plans; it has no general claim on the federal treasury.[41] Premiums have fallen far short of net claims to date and, at current levels, fall far short of expected future claims. Raising premiums to cover past losses as well as to produce a stream of income capable of meeting future losses presents a clear danger of hastening the retreat, if not igniting an exodus, from defined-benefit plans. Avoiding this outcome, within the context of the current system, could require either significant reductions in benefit guarantees—something Congress has shown great reluctance to approve even with the massive losses in the S&L industry—or direct taxpayer subsidies.

As noted by Richard Ippolito, chief economist at the PBGC, the shift from defined-benefit plans toward defined-contribution plans was "one of the most important developments in private pensions in the 1980s. In 1979, among workers covered by a pension plan, 83% were covered primarily by a defined-benefit plan. By 1988, this share was 66%."[42] Some employers, particularly smaller ones, are eliminating their defined-benefit plans, while new companies, with increasing frequency, are opting for defined-contribution plans instead.

Although researchers debate the underlying causes of this shift,[43] it would appear safe to say that the explosion of defined-benefit plans in the 1950s and 1960s is over and a potentially serious retrenchment is underway. The long-term prospects for the PBGC's revenue base are clearly unfavorable. As figure 4.1 illustrates, the number of insured plans fell sharply (some 40%) between 1985 and 1993, from 110,000 to 64,000 plans, while the number of premium payers grew from 30 million to 32 million. (The number of premium payers includes a growing number of retirees and separated vested workers, masking a declining number of active workers.) According to Ippolito, even if Congress adjusted pre-

Number of plans
Number of participants (000's)

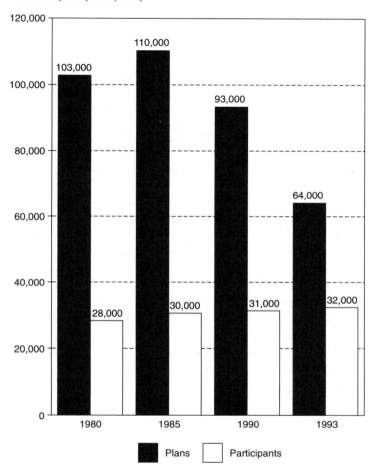

Figure 4.1
PBGC insured plans and participants: selected years
Source: Pension Benefit Guaranty Corporation, *Annual Report*, selected years.
Note: Participants include current workers, former (vested) workers, and retirees.

miums for inflation, total revenues to the PBGC would begin to fall within a decade.[44]

The concern, of course, is that steep increases in the PBGC premium, as currently structured, could accelerate the shift from defined-benefit plans. Currently, plans covered by pension insurance pay a flat charge of $19 per participant annually plus a variable charge of $9 annually per $1,000 in unfunded vested benefits; the premium is capped at $72 per participant, regardless of the extent of underfunding.[45] Although this differs significantly from the flat premium that prevailed until 1988, it is still a far cry from risk-based premiums, which would reflect the differences in expected claims among pension plans and thus, if well designed, provide no particular enticement for high-risk plans to join or deterrent for low-risk plans to remain in the insurance pool.[46]

To see more clearly the problem with the current premium structure, consider the variable-rate premium as an implicit interest rate on unfunded pension debt. At $9 per $1,000 of underfunding, this rate is less than 1%— 0.9% to be precise. Because of the cap on premiums, moreover, companies with the largest unfunded liabilities pay an even lower rate. According to the PBGC, companies affected by the premium cap effectively pay only $3 or $4 per $1,000 of underfunding,[47] resulting in an implicit interest rate of just 0.3%–0.4%. For comparison purposes, as of 1996, commercial lenders were demanding 7%–8% on corporate debt issued by the strongest companies in America; companies with speculative-grade bond ratings (such as some of those on the PBGC's iffy 50 list) were having to pay substantially more than this.[48]

Evidently, the PBGC premium structure targets its transfers on financially weak companies with underfunded pension plans. Premiums are unrelated to the default risk (because they do not vary with the plan sponsor's financial health) and are only partially related to exposure (because they do not vary with the pension fund volatility and vary in only a limited way with the degree of underfunding). For the most underfunded plans, there is no marginal relationship between underfunding and premiums paid. As a result, the premium structure continues to embody perverse incentives for participation and significant cross subsidies among firms—with wealth being transferred from workers and shareholders in healthy firms with well-funded pension plans to those in weak firms with underfunded plans.[49]

In a voluntary pension system, companies cannot be expected to continue establishing and maintaining defined-benefit plans unless—on a company-by-company basis—the expected net benefits of these plans with compulsory insurance exceed the expected net benefits of the next best alternative, which might be a 401(k) or other defined-contribution plan that does not carry pension insurance.[50] The higher the PBGC premium and the more poorly it reflects differences in expected losses, the more likely it is that some companies, namely healthy companies with well-funded plans, will be induced to drop their plans and new companies with good growth prospects will elect not to adopt them. Although a company must be able to meet all its legal liabilities to terminate an ongoing plan, most companies in America are in just such a position, and thousands are exercising this option every year.[51]

From PBGC's standpoint, an eroding premium base is just one potential consequence of raising premiums; another is that PBGC could (and very likely would) be left insuring a riskier set of pension plans with substantially greater exposure to losses. Again, since premiums are not based on risk, healthy companies with well-funded plans (those least likely to make a claim against the PBGC and find pension insurance guarantee least valuable) are most likely to vacate their plans—and the pension insurance system—if rates increase appreciably. This would result in a higher average risk among remaining covered plans and the need for further destabilizing premium increases. As a recent Congressional Budget Office report concluded: "Far-sighted, fiscally sound premium payers will not voluntarily subsidize the pension costs of their competitors indefinitely. Instead, they will terminate their plans and avoid paying these overpriced premiums.... A voluntary federal insurance system that relies heavily on subsidies from one insured firm to another is probably destined for a taxpayer bailout."[52]

PBGC, in other words, like any insurer that does not base premiums on expected losses, must contend with a classic adverse selection problem. Failing to contend with it ultimately could lead to the situation described by Bodie and Merton at the start of this chapter: "The U.S. could be left only with bankrupt pension plans with the benefits financed directly by taxpayers."[53]

A brief review of the PBGC, from its inception in 1974 through its most recent reforms, reveals a history of failed attempts to control the incentive problems created by pension insurance.

Controlling Losses: A History of Failed Attempts

It is well known that an insurer, whether public or private, must control the incentive problems created by insurance, namely the problems of moral hazard and adverse selection, to attract and retain customers and remain financially viable.[54] A substantial body of research—not to mention the presence of a multibillion dollar unfunded liability—suggests the federal government has failed to adequately control the incentive problems pension insurance has created.[55]

It is only a slight exaggeration to say—as Ippolito has said—that when PBGC was created, "the potential for moral hazard was virtually unconstrained."[56] Under the original program, the benefit guarantee was generous, and (until 1976) there were no actuarial reductions for early retirement. Pension participants were thus shielded from the loss of virtually all vested retirement benefits accumulated at the time of plan termination. This undermined worker and union incentives to monitor pension fund performance and the incentive of the companies sponsoring them to ensure that employer promises of future benefits could be met.

This is not to say there were no coinsurance factors in the original pension insurance program. The law contained a maximum insured benefit, for example, but it was high enough that it affected only a small minority of highly compensated workers.[57] More importantly, the amount of workers' pensions actually guaranteed was determined, even for young workers with many years until retirement, based on earnings and service up until the time of plan termination. As a result, there was no protection against the loss of *expected future pension accumulations*—that is, the pensions workers would have earned if their plan had continued and they had remained with the firm. Unfortunately, this coinsurance factor (which can be large and remains in force today) is smallest for workers who, in an unregulated environment, would have had the keenest incentive to monitor pension fund performance—workers nearing retirement with substantial service to the company.[58]

Having weakened plan participant incentives to monitor pension funds, pension insurance simultaneously weakened employer incentives to fully fund pension promises and to take adequate precautions against default. Under the law, a company could terminate its underfunded plan without entering bankruptcy or even demonstrating financial distress, thereby shedding its unfunded pension liabilities to the PBGC in exchange for 30% of the company's net worth. Theoretically, at least, any company whose unfunded liabilities rose above 30% of net worth (or for whom 30% of net worth fell below the value of unfunded benefits) could terminate its pension plan at a profit, leaving the PBGC holding the bag for the difference.[59] Kathleen Utgoff, former executive director of the PBGC, noted that this feature of pension insurance had the remarkable (if predictable) effect of leading "to the termination of underfunded plans by ongoing, solvent employers, an event virtually unheard of prior to the passage of ERISA."[60]

In corporate finance terms, pension insurance amounted to a "put option" which gave firms, in effect, the right to sell pension plan assets plus 30% of net worth to the PBGC for a price equal to the present value of benefit liabilities.[61] Like any option, its value, or expected payoff, varied directly with underlying asset volatility.

Having created this clear moral hazard for plan sponsors, ERISA then allowed companies to retain significant control over funding levels, the riskiness of their pension funds, and the timing of the insured event (plan termination)—that is, over the value of the pension put. Companies could increase the put option's value by reducing funding ratios and investing in riskier assets. Companies choosing to pursue this strategy, of course, would forego the sizable tax advantages to funding their pension funds to the maximum permissible under the law—something that would make sense only for some companies, namely unprofitable, risky companies for whom the tax shelter may have been superfluous and the pension put quite valuable.[62] For them, shareholder wealth would be maximized by minimizing pension fund contributions and investing in the riskiest assets, thus increasing PBGC's exposure to losses.[63]

The dangers firms in financial distress pose to insurers and guarantors are well known. As noted by the Congressional Budget Office, "Firms on the brink of financial failure are extraordinarily dangerous to any insurance pool because their owners have nothing to lose from high-risk business strategies."[64]

PBGC, in effect, stood ready to make good on a portion of failing companies' debt (their unfunded pension debt), which could pile up quickly in the period preceding plan termination. Companies, meanwhile, retained discretion over the timing of plan termination. Firms in financial distress had the incentive to offer increases in compensation in the form of unfunded (insured) pension benefits rather than wages,[65] to reduce or fail to make pension contributions to free resources for other, potentially more profitable uses, and generally to pursue riskier investment strategies —otherwise known as "gambling for resurrection"—which would result in rapid defunding of the pension plan and a rapid increase in PBGC's losses in the event of plan termination. If the gamble paid off and the company survived, PBGC got nothing; if it didn't, PBGC bore a substantial share of the losses.[66]

The termination of Allis-Chalmers' United Auto Workers' pension plan in 1985 provides a particularly vivid example of the debt a company could incur and then transfer to the PBGC. By the time this pension plan was terminated, assets amounted to a mere 1.3% of benefit liabilities—that is, to back up $176 million in guaranteed benefit liabilities, the pension fund had just $2.3 million in assets.[67] More recently, LTV's Republic Steel terminated its pension plan with less than $10,000 in assets to back up $230 million in liabilities.[68]

Importantly, nothing about the premium structure discouraged this type of activity. At a flat $1 per participant annually, the premiums a company had to pay bore no relationship to the claims it might be expected to make on the pension insurance system. Employer incentives to fund accruing benefits, reduce pension fund volatility, and avoid unnecessary terminations were all weakened.

Finally, although PBGC had the authority to monitor the potential for losses, it was severely constrained in what it could (or was required to) do with any information so gained to directly control losses. It could not modify premiums to reflect differences in expected losses across companies or to reflect actual claims experience. It could not dictate changes in company practices to reduce the risks posed to the agency or take any actions to modify contract terms to control exposure.[69] Meanwhile, the government imposed no economically meaningful standards under which severely underfunded plans would be terminated, and there were no circumstances under which benefit guarantees would be frozen or scaled back. PBGC was left with one blunt instrument—involuntary termination —whereby, under certain circumstances, it could seek a court order to terminate a plan and seize any assets remaining in the pension fund. This instrument would be politically difficult and, in some cases, economically inappropriate to use.[70]

As for adverse selection, ERISA attempted to deal with this problem by making the pension insurance program mandatory. This was a temporary solution at best, however, since in the United States the private pension system is voluntary. Requiring sponsors to carry insurance in a world in which companies can choose to offer whatever plan they prefer—a defined-benefit plan with insurance, a defined-contribution plan without insurance, or no plan at all—simply increases the cost of adopting and maintaining defined-benefit plans.

As Alicia Munnell assessed the situation in 1982, "The PBGC's vulnerability stems from its inability to control the actions of plan sponsors. Often it does not even have access to detailed information about a pension plan until the company decides to terminate. Hence, the PBGC will always remain financially vulnerable and the federal government may well end up as the insurer of the nation's private pension system."[71]

On the legislative, regulatory, and judicial fronts, a great deal has changed over the years.[72] The premium structure has been modified to partially reflect exposure (but not the risk of default); funding requirements have been tightened (through stricter minimum-funding rules, faster amortization of unfunded liabilities, and a new full-funding limit); the insured event has been tightened (to require "financial distress" on the part of companies seeking to terminate their plans); the PBGC's claim on employers has been increased to 100% of underfunding; and certainly, the relevant laws and regulations have become far more complex. Unfortunately, the constructive changes (such as the introduction of a variable-rate premium, the financial distress test, and the increased claim on employers) have tended to be too little too late to stem the losses. Other changes lauded as constructive, if not landmark, have tended to be ineffective or counterproductive.

For example, the minimum-funding rules, together with the full-funding limit, have allowed chronically underfunded plans to remain underfunded, have denied companies with well-funded plans the opportunity to make extra contributions during prosperous years, and have forced well-funded plans (overfunded plans in the Internal Revenue Service's view) to defund.[73]

As illustrated in figure 4.2, in real dollar terms, underfunding has risen steadily since the early to mid-1980s, from a low point of $14 billion in 1983 to a high of $53 billion in 1992, while overfunding has fallen from a high of $296 billion in 1985 to a low of $107 billion in 1992. Figure 4.3 shows that funding ratios among underfunded plans have drifted up since the early 1980s, but within a narrow range, while funding ratios for overfunded plans and for all plans combined have fallen markedly (by about one-third).

It is not possible to glance at this data and disentangle the effects of the new rules from those of market developments, such as strong investment returns and declining interest rates since the mid-1980s,[74] but there is ample reason to doubt the new minimum funding rules' efficacy. A 1993 General Accounting Office report, for example, examined a set of underfunded plans and found that in most cases sponsors were making no additional contributions for underfunding. GAO concluded that the rules had been largely ineffective in accelerating the movement of underfunded plans toward full funding.[75] More recently, the PBGC reported that

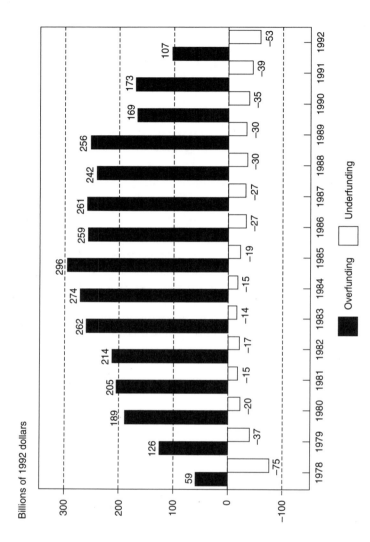

Figure 4.2
Overfunding and underfunding in 1992 dollars, 1978–92
Source: Richard A. Ippolito, "Private Pensions in the U.S. II" (September 2, 1992), and data supplied by the Office
of Public Affairs, Pension Benefit Guaranty Corporation, June 1994.

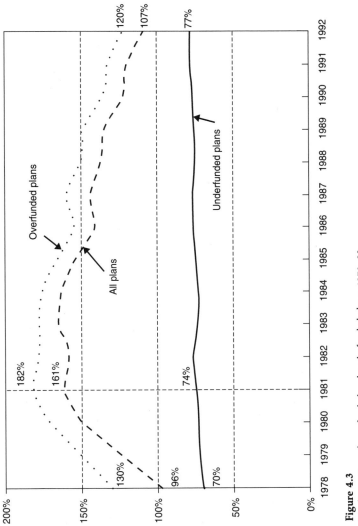

Figure 4.3
Funding ratios of overfunded and underfunded plans, 1978–92
Source: Richard A. Ippolito, "Private Pensions in the U.S. II" (September 2, 1992), and data supplied by the Office of
Public Affairs, Pension Benefit Guaranty Corporation, June 1994.

among the 50 companies with the most underfunded plans in 1989–91, some 40% were making additional contributions for underfunding not even large enough to cover the interest on their unfunded liabilities.[76]

In addition, the increase in the PBGC's claim on employers to the full amount of underfunding, though potentially significant in the unusual event that PBGC terminates a plan before the company files for bankruptcy, is of little value in the more typical case where termination accompanies bankruptcy.[77] The chief problem is that bankrupt companies have little net worth to recover. Also, the priority status ERISA accords to PBGC's 30%-of-net-worth claim, equivalent to a federal tax lien, has been a continuing source of controversy in the courts. The PBGC's new expanded claims have general unsecured status, which is low on the creditor totem pole and easily trumped by foresighted lenders who arrange for security. (Employer liability payments yielded about 11.5 cents on the dollar of unfunded guaranteed benefits in 1988–93, as compared to 10 cents on the dollar in 1982–87.)[78]

Also, certain issues critical to controlling risk and exposure simply remained unaddressed. For example, the impact of pension fund volatility on PBGC's exposure to losses has not been addressed, through either restrictions on asset mix or explicit pricing.[79] To see the potential problem, consider two fully funded pension plans identical in all respects but investment policy: one invests in common stocks and one in fixed-income securities to hedge against unexpected increases in pension liabilities.[80] The first plan has a significantly higher risk of underfunding, exposes the PBGC to greater expected losses, and yet would pay the same flat premium.

In addition, shutdown benefits—a major source of defunding prior to termination—remain unaddressed.[81] Common in the auto and steel industries, shutdown benefits entitle workers to immediate, full retirement benefits when a plant closes. These benefits are generous, payable to workers at any age, and rarely prefunded.[82] Because plant closings are frequently associated with financial distress, payment of shutdown benefits increases liabilities and drains pension assets in plans that have a high likelihood of failing.

Finally, the PBGC still has no authority to directly alter the practices of, or modify the terms of insurance for, plan sponsors that pose an increased risk of loss. As noted by Peter Abken, researcher at the Atlanta Federal Reserve Bank, the PBGC is an "involuntary creditor: it is obligated to provide insurance up to guaranteed-benefit levels, with no power to alter the terms of its insurance or influence the actions of pension plan sponsors."[83] More importantly perhaps, there are still no clear, economically meaningful standards under which severely underfunded pension plans are terminated, and under no circumstances are benefit guarantees frozen or scaled back.

Reviewing the history of the pension insurance program and the various attempts to control losses, Richard Ippolito concludes: "The value of the pension put has been reduced significantly, and the gaming potential in general has been reduced.... Nevertheless, the cross-subsidies remaining in the insurance system are great, and the moral hazard potential is still sizable."[84] David Lindeman, director of corporate policy at PBGC, sums up the current situation this way: "Despite nearly 20 years of experience since the enactment of ... ERISA, the PBGC's control over pension funding remains weak and uncertain and more under the effective control of the insured than of the insurer."[85]

In short, the government has failed to control the incentives the pension insurance program has created. A $2.9 billion past loss ("accumulated deficit") and large projected future losses have resulted. Meanwhile, the adverse-selection problem continues to bedevil those who hope to solve PBGC's ballooning debt and perpetuate the current system by simply raising premiums.[86]

Not Controlled After All These Years?

Coming out of the 1980s, which brought us the S&L crises and revealed the clear dangers of financial crises in other federal guarantee programs, how can the government have failed to secure the pension insurance program? In part, the problem is informational. How does one structure a guarantee program so that those endeavoring to maximize the transfers they receive or minimize the implicit taxes they must bear cannot outsmart the program? Tax and regulatory policy history is riddled with examples of policies rendered useless, or very nearly so, or far more costly than anticipated, by individuals seeking to maximize their well-being subject to new constraints.

Because the federal government supplies pension insurance on a monopoly basis, Congress is unable to learn from other insurers' experience about how best to design, enforce, and price its "contract" and most importantly, how consumers (in this case, pension plan participants) value different contracts relative to their cost. Indeed, Congress's primary source of data on its own program's performance is the federal budget, which is inherently flawed, particularly in its treatment of unfunded liabilities. Noting that "information is the lifeblood of a pension insurance system," the Congressional Budget Office observes that: "Congress finds itself in the same uninformed, disadvantaged position as the participants of defined-benefit plans in the period before the pension insurance program was established. As the manager of the insurance system, the Congress can perceive only dimly the extent to which this program is accumulating unfunded future claims."[87]

In part, moreover (the overwhelming part, in my view), the problem is political and stems from an unresolved conflict over pension insurance's purpose. Congress sees the pension insurance program not just as a mechanism for guaranteeing retirement benefits against default risk but also as a vehicle for subsidizing workers and shareholders in certain companies—which companies being fairly obvious. Nearly two-thirds of all claims against the PBGC as of 1987 were attributable to participants covered by the United Auto Workers and the United Steelworkers of America; union workers as a whole were the recipients of 95% of all claims against the PBGC.[88] At present, plans covering union workers constitute the vast majority of the PBGC's exposure to future losses. The pension insurance program is, and always has been, a form of industrial policy designed to prop up unionized companies in declining or restructuring industries.[89]

The problem is not so much that Congress wants to prop up these companies, but that it wants to do so with, to use Bodie and Merton's phrase, "cheap pension guarantees" administered through the PBGC.[90] Mixed insurance-transfer programs—euphemistically referred to as "social insurance" by proponents—inevitably distort the allocation of resources in the economy and are notoriously poor at targeting scarce resources.[91] In PBGC's case, the system subsidizes wages in failing firms, artificially prolonging the life of inefficient firms at the expense of efficient ones;[92] encourages firms with a greater likelihood of failure to offer compensation in the form of unfunded pension promises the PBGC will likely pay; and, by weakening unions' stake in the long-term viability of firms, makes capital investment in these firms less attractive.[93] As for poor targeting, companies that mismanage themselves into the ground or fail in their gamble for resurrection can line up in the same queue for transfers as otherwise well-managed companies in declining industries; the more generous the pension plan, the greater the subsidies. Efforts to hold on to subsidies for favored firms in the face of financial pressures to erase them have resulted in an ever more complex law with the potential for even greater economic distortions and more perverse wealth transfers.

What Now?

Resolving the inherent conflict between the program's insurance and transfer functions and ultimately restoring its financial integrity will take more than a new and improved funding requirement, tighter controls over pension fund actuaries, or closer monitoring of pension fund performance: It will take separating the insurance functions from the transfer functions and separately financing the latter through the Treasury's general fund.[94] Only in this way can the subsidies now hidden in the system be made visible,[95] their costs controlled, and the distortions they create minimized, thereby giving the insurance program a fighting chance of long-term survival. The PBGC—and the defined-benefit pension system it was created to protect—cannot survive if survival depends on the willingness of healthy companies with well-funded plans to pay for their own insurance plus a portion of other companies' (possibly their competitors) and of past losses of other companies. This has seemed to work as long as it has only because pension insurance is underpriced even for well-funded plans; part of the program's cost has been shifted to the future.[96]

Much is known about how to move toward a system of true insurance against default risk.[97] The two basic approaches are (1) to internalize the costs of employer discretion—that is, permit companies to extend unfunded benefit promises, reduce funding levels, or practice whatever (otherwise prudent) investment strategies they prefer, provided they bear the increased risks and costs they impose on the system; and (2) to limit employer discretion to increase exposure or the likelihood of loss through (enforceable) contract terms requiring or prohibiting certain actions. Risk-based premiums are the essence of the first approach—a means of properly aligning the employer incentives without unduly restricting their ability to respond to changing market conditions. Reduced benefit guarantees (or increased coinsurance terms) and increased priority for pension claims in bankruptcy are other incentive-based reforms, whereby in one case workers and in the other case creditors would exert pressure on companies to properly secure their pension promises.[98]

Examples of the latter approach include requiring companies to collateralize their pension promises, either with assets in the pension fund or some other collateral of the firm, or to hedge their pension liabilities through immunization strategies. Ensuring compliance with these rules would require a monitoring system backed by a set of well-defined criteria specifying the circumstances under which, for example, benefit guarantees would be frozen or scaled back or pension fund assets would be seized.

Unfortunately, knowing what kinds of reforms might be desirable is very different from knowing which reforms, in which combination, would be valued at what price. As a monopoly public supplier, the government has limited knowledge about how to structure the insurance contract to minimize economic inefficiencies, and it has weak incentives to figure it out.[99] As is well known, the incentives to innovate in the public sector are weak, and the incentives to underfund long-term obligations and shift costs to the future are strong. Meanwhile, all the political pressures that brought us the current system exist to perpetuate it. Much like the proverbial dog chasing its tail, the government is unlikely to ever reach the goal of financial viability for the pension insurance program if it pursues that goal through incremental reforms of the current system.

In my view, the government should simply surrender its position as monopoly supplier of pension insurance and shift the insurance (or guarantee) function to the private sector.[100] To control expected losses, private insurers or guarantors would rely on pricing and monitoring to the extent feasible, backed by standards to the extent necessary.[101] Undoubtedly, they would provide a range of contracts to accommodate the range of circumstances in which individual companies (and their workforces) found themselves. Companies would have to convince competing financial institutions, not regulatory authorities (or no one at all), that an investment approach or funding strategy was secure, then bear their decisions' financial consequences. Companies would be free to move among institutions, and this would provide useful information about the kinds of contracts that were valued.

Having said this, the question arises of what, if any, requirements to impose on the contracts. To achieve the benefits of competition and avoid recreating a private-sector PBGC, the regulations should be minimal. For example, the government might require that some fraction of basic retirement benefits be guaranteed in the event of the plan sponsor's dissolution.[102] Insurers and guarantors would then be free to guarantee higher levels of benefits, to pay benefits in circumstances other than the firm's dissolution, and to require any funding level or investment strategy they wished—provided they could structure their contracts to control losses in ways companies were willing to accept and at a cost they were willing to bear.

I see no reason why large commercial insurers, life insurance companies in particular, and financial guarantee firms would not step in to provide basic protection against the loss of retirement benefits—if permitted to do so on commercially viable terms. In contrast to 1974, when apparently no companies were willing to take on the business, a considerable amount of claims experience now exists on which to base decisions on contract terms and pricing; the insured event is no longer under plan sponsors' exclusive control; and a large and sophisticated financial guarantee market and a well-developed secondary market for insurance, or reinsurance market, would allow insurers to protect themselves against insolvency arising from an unusually large claim or a concentration of policies covering plans in a single industry.[103]

Beyond that, the question arises of what to do with pension plans currently not commercially insurable or insurable only at a price that would render them bankrupt—due either to the size of their unfunded liabilities or the likelihood of default. (More than a few of the companies on the "iffy 50" would likely fall into this category.) These companies would require some direct government financing. It makes little sense to take companies that have lawfully amassed huge pension debts and drive them into bankruptcy in the zeal to create a better system in the long run. On the other hand, it makes little sense to protect them from the full brunt of market forces without taking the steps necessary to sharply contain exposure.

In the transition to a new, fully privatized system, the government could continue to cover these companies subject to strict standards governing funding, asset allocation, benefit increases and guarantees, and reporting and monitoring.[104] These standards would be designed to reduce—and certainly to preclude any deliberate increase in—exposure. For example, companies might be required, among other things, to freeze benefit accruals or forego guarantees on benefit increases until their plans became fully funded, hedge their pension fund portfolios against unexpected changes in pension liabilities, use standardized actuarial assumptions in reporting to the federal government, and subject themselves to regular audits of their plans and their overall business operations. To reduce the potential for gaming the system, the insured event might be limited to the firm's dissolution (or, if agreeable to the PBGC, reorganization).[105] Although premiums might continue to be capped on the basis of current risk and exposure, they could be fully adjusted to reflect incremental changes in unfunded liabilities.

This highly regulatory approach is clearly inferior to a pricing solution in that it would surely distort the way these companies do business, but it would control exposure and thus limit the cost to taxpayers. Likewise, although it would maintain insurance protection for benefits already accrued, it would give workers and unions a significant stake in future pension promises' financial viability, not just their size. Companies that reined in their underfunding or in other ways regained their credit standing would be free to buy private insurance at any time, thereby escaping the government-run program's stringent standards.

All new pension plans and the vast majority of existing plans, which are well funded, would be required to purchase protection against the risk of default through commercial insurers or financial guarantors competing for their business. The long-run goal would be to avoid creating a new generation of companies dependent on taxpayers' (and other pension plans') largess to survive and, indeed, to permit future generations to benefit from the availability of true insurance in a competitive marketplace.[106]

Privatizing the supply of pension insurance would not only depoliticize the system but also foster innovation through competition, vital to acquiring and using knowledge and developing new and better products—even insurance products.[107] As noted by Nobel Laureate Friedrich Hayek many years ago, the field of insurance "illustrates perhaps more clearly than any other how new institutions emerge not from design but by a gradual evolutionary process."[108] The best ways of pooling financial risks and transferring income over time—that is, of providing retirement income or insurance against its loss—are more likely to emerge through experimentation in a market system than from careful planning by government. The surge of financial innovation in the United States in the past 20 years, driven to a large extent by pension fund managers' needs within a regulated but still highly competitive market, is testimony to market power in generating and using valuable ideas about how to manage risks.[109]

Concluding Thoughts

The last 20 years has witnessed the proliferation of government policies designed to improve defined-benefit pensions to increase retirement income security.[110] However well meaning, these policies have increased the cost of offering defined-benefit plans, particularly among small companies where job growth is now concentrated, and reduced the likelihood that these plans will be offered.[111]

Even the most ardent defenders of ERISA and the various tax provisions that underpin private pensions must question the extent to which this promotes retirement income security. Workers who derive an increasing share of their retirement protection from 401(k) plans or other defined-contribution plans take on increasing responsibility for managing investment risk—indeed, for retirement income planning generally—and are less able to use (tax-advantaged) pensions to target a level of retirement income in relation to preretirement earnings.[112] Although this is perfectly reasonable and appropriate if it reflects a change in workers' preferences (for example, an increased demand for fully portable pensions in light of, say, an increase in the expected risk of job change), it is quite unreasonable—indeed, it represents a welfare loss to society—if it is induced by government policies that distort worker and employer choice of pension plans. The retirement income system's efficiency would surely be enhanced if the choice of pension plans were the outcome of mutually advantageous agreements between employees and employers, subject to the free interplay of market forces, rather than the by-product of government policy.[113]

From the standpoint of retirement income policy more generally, the government has amassed trillions of dollars in unfunded liabilities due to promises of income security to future retirees. These promises— whether in the form of pension insurance, Social Security, Medicare, or any number of other public programs—are qualified promises; they involve contingencies and risks. As the baby boom generation fast approaches retirement, policymakers would be well advised to focus less on how to increase these promises and more on how to reduce the risks inherent in them.[114]

Notes

The author would like to acknowledge the helpful comments of Zvi Bodie, Richard Ippolito, Robert Mackay, and James Smalhout on an earlier draft of this paper.

1. Bodie and Merton 1993, 208.

2. Lockhart 1992a.

3. These figures include contributions to employer-sponsored pensions and exclude contributions to individual retirement accounts. See Employee Benefit Research Institute 1994a, 16, 30.

4. Benefit payments include lump sum distributions. See EBRI 1994, 9–11; Turner and Beller 1992, 599; Ippolito 1992, 1–2; and Schieber and Goodfellow 1994, 135–36.

5. As of 1989, private pensions held 19% of U.S. corporate equity and 24% of outstanding corporate and foreign bonds (Turner and Beller 1992, 432–33).

6. In the absence of insurance protection, workers are thus exposed to the risk of loss of benefits if their employer terminates the plan with insufficient assets to meet outstanding benefit promises. Workers covered by defined-contribution plans do not bear this risk, as these plans are (absent fraud) always fully funded. Under defined-contribution plans, workers have individual accounts consisting of employer (and, if contributory, employee) contributions and interest earnings, and the total accumulation belongs to the worker after a short vesting period (Ippolito 1986; Bodie, Marcus, and Merton 1988; and Bodie 1990).

7. Coverage data are as of 1989. See EBRI 1992b, 1994a; OMB 1994, 138; and PBGC 1993c. The present value of future benefits includes payments to retirees and separated vested workers, not just active covered workers.

Here and elsewhere, the term "outstanding benefit promises" is used in its legal sense: nominal benefits owed under the plan's benefit formula assuming no future salary growth, discounted at a nominal rate of interest. The present value of nominal benefits would be owed if the plan terminated today—a so-called termination liability. Corporate balance sheets for external reports use this measure of pension liabilities, known as the accumulated benefit obligation (ABO). See Bodie, Kane, and Marcus 1993.

For an alternative view of the pension promise that incorporates workers' expectations of—and employers' implicit promises to pay—future benefits linked to future wage growth, see Ippolito 1986. This latter view of pension liabilities, contained in the economics literature, is consistent with the projected benefit obligation (PBO), which incorporates increases in salary up to the expected date of retirement—a so-called ongoing liability. Corporate income statements use the PBO in computing pension expense.

Generally speaking, prior to legislation in 1987, the tax code permitted pension funds to accumulate assets equal to ongoing liabilities; present law permits them to accumulate assets equal to the lesser of 150% of termination liabilities or 100% of ongoing liabilities. More on this below. See Ippolito 1991.

8. Estimate is from 1993 data and excludes assets of defined-contribution plans and of defined-benefit plans managed by insurance companies (PBGC 1993c and EBRI 1994a).

9. PBGC 1993a; OMB 1994; Estrella and Hirtle 1988; Hirtle and Estrella 1990; and Lewis and Cooperstein 1993.

10. See, among others, Smalhout 1992; Samuelson 1993; and Dunkle 1993.

11. Slate 1993a.

12. The PBGC has two insurance programs, one covering 64,000 single-employer plans and one covering about 2,000 multiemployer plans (collectively bargained plans involving more than one employer). This chapter deals exclusively with the single-employer program. As noted below, the two programs are fundamentally different in design and have quite different financial outlooks.

For helpful summaries of the single-employer program and PBGC operations, see US CBO 1993; EBRI 1992a; McGill 1984; and U.S. House of Representatives 1993, sec. 14.

13. PBGC insures all "basic" retirement benefits vested prior to termination, where basic includes retirement annuities being paid or owed at termination. (The insured amount is phased in for benefits in effect for less than five years.) The maximum benefit guarantee is $2,567 monthly ($30,802 annually) for a worker age 65 in 1993, actuarially reduced for benefits drawn before 65. (An exception is shutdown benefits, discussed below, which entitle workers to full retirement benefits at any age when a plant is closed.) The amount of benefits payable by the PBGC is calculated and fixed in nominal terms at the time of termination, which may be many years before a worker retires and monthly payments commence (McGill 1984, 582–89; PBGC 1993a; and Ippolito 1989, 78–83).

14. To terminate an underfunded pension plan, a plan sponsor must meet one of four financial distress tests: (1) It has filed for bankruptcy under Chapter 7; (2) It has filed for reorganization under Chapter 11, and the court has determined the company cannot successfully reorganize and stay in business unless the plan is terminated; (3) It demonstrates it cannot meet its debts and stay in business unless the plan is terminated; or (4) It demonstrates pension costs are "unreasonably burdensome" because of a declining workforce. PBGC is also

authorized to terminate a pension plan involuntarily under certain circumstances, as discussed below. See ERISA sec. 4041(c)(2) in Albergo and Domone 1993.

15. Employers are liable to the PBGC for the full amount of unfunded benefit liabilities. (Prior to the Pension Protection Act of 1987, the employer's liability was capped at 30% of the company's net worth.) The PBGC is authorized to recover its claim not only from the employer terminating the pension plan but also from any other corporations under common control. See Keating 1991, 69–70; and Wald and Kenty 1991, 305–6. In the past decade, liability payments have yielded only about 11 or 12 cents on the dollar of unfunded benefits. See PBGC 1993c, 4.

16. As noted in the table, PBGC defines "probable terminations" narrowly and excludes plans that pose a risk of loss that is "near-term, serious" (using the language of the PBGC's 1992 annual report) or "reasonably possible" (using the language of the 1993 annual report). See PBGC 1992a, 10, 36; and PBGC 1993c, 8, 40.

The multiemployer program, by contrast, has an accumulated surplus due to past terminations and is running annual surpluses. Under this program, which covers mine workers, truck drivers, and construction workers, for example, PBGC does not take over a pension plan in financial distress; instead it makes loans to insolvent pension plans to help meet benefit payments. Benefit guarantees are well below those in the single-employer program (about one-half the level for workers with the same years of service and the same age); in addition, benefit increases occurring within five years of the PBGC intervention are not guaranteed. Employers desiring to withdraw from the pension plan must pay a proportionate share of any unfunded liabilities (Utgoff 1992; Munnell 1982; McGill 1984; and PBGC 1992a).

17. The figure encompasses claims for unfunded benefits excluding recoveries of employer liability payments (referred to as gross claims) (Ippolito 1992; EBRI 1992a, 14; and PBGC 1992a, 4.

18. According to the US CBO (1993, 25), "PBGC has reduced the reported federal budget deficit by $2.2 billion since 1981—even as it was accumulating a deficit of $2.5 billion." The problem is that the budget uses a cash basis method of accounting, recognizing premiums when received but ignoring obligations incurred to pay benefits in the future. The problem of interpreting PBGC's true short- and long-range financial condition is further complicated by the budget's short time frame and the fact that there is an off-budget account and an on-budget account for the PBGC, with the former making payments to the latter. For an excellent discussion, see US CBO 1993, 23–26. See also OMB 1993, 182–85; OMB 1994, 138; and U.S. House of Representatives 1993, 1103–4.

19. PBGC 1993c, 1. Liabilities for terminated plans are discounted to the present using a common interest rate, whereas liability and claims figures shown in tables 4.1 and 4.2 were discounted at the time of plan termination. For a helpful discussion of the data contained in PBGC's financial statements, see EBRI 1992a. For an interpretation of the data and an analysis of their limitations, see US CBO 1993 and Bodie and Merton 1993.

20. Slate 1993b.

21. See discussion below on the requirements for (and potential drawbacks of) voluntarily terminating a well-funded defined-benefit plan.

Importantly, this discussion pertains to allocating costs and aggregate pricing of pension insurance over time, not across companies at a point in time (or the extent of cross subsidies among companies or the degree to which premiums are based on risk). As a group, pension plans have not paid the full cost of their insurance in terms of expected losses. This has implications for PBGC's long-term viability quite independent of whether, for example, the system continues to embody cross subsidies among firms. The PBGC cannot recover past losses from future premiums unless it continues to underprice pension insurance relative to expected future claims (thus amassing new past losses) or it exploits its power, inherent in the mandatory insurance requirement, to erode the benefits to employees and employers of maintaining their defined-benefit plans. That companies can terminate their plans inherently limits this power.

Proponents of the "social insurance" view of pension insurance sometimes obscure the distinction between allocating costs over time and across companies. See, for instance, EBRI 1992a, 24, where the system is said to be "solvent as long as there are sufficient funds to allow cross subsidies."

22. Munnell 1982, 35–36. Of course, the PBGC, like any insurer, must contend with periodic unanticipated losses arising from inherent uncertainty about future claims. Losses, per se, are not an indication of a breakdown in financing (or pricing); persistent losses—and projected future losses—are.

23. Munnell 1982. Under the principle Munnell enunciated, PBGC would be self-financing over time, a view generally believed to be consistent with congressional intent. See US CBO 1993, 5–6.

24. Bodie and Merton 1993. See also Estrella and Hirtle 1988; and Lewis and Cooperstein 1993.

25. Actually, even well-funded plans expose PBGC to future losses because of pension fund volatility. More on this below.

26. PBGC 1992a, 1993c.

27. PBGC 1993d.

28. About 95% of benefit liabilities are guaranteed.

29. PBGC 1993c, 1993d.

30. Ippolito 1992, 21. Ippolito goes on to note that "virtually all large claims processed by the PBGC have been [on account of] sponsors of flat-benefit plans covering union workers." Some 95% of flat-benefit plans are chronically (and legally) underfunded. These plans account for 20% of outstanding guaranteed benefits but represent more than two-thirds of the PBGC's exposure to losses. OMB 1993, 182; and Ippolito 1989, 107–12. More on this below.

31. See Kane 1989 for a discussion of this problem in the context of the S&L crisis and Smalhout 1992 for an analogy between the "secretly insolvent" S&Ls of the early 1980s and the "secretly insolvent" pension plan sponsors of the 1990s.

32. Exposure is particularly sensitive to interest rate movements (whether actual or assumed)—the higher the interest rate used to discount future benefits, the lower the present value of benefit liabilities and the higher the funding ratio. The US GAO (1992), for example, evaluated a sample of about 17,000 large plans in 1987 and found that a 1% reduction in the interest rate doubled the amount of unfunded liabilities and increased the number of under-funded plans by 65%. In a separate study, Ippolito (1989) found that exposure varied by as much as 85% (from $26 billion to $126 billion in real dollars) in a span of just five years, 1979 to 1984, with most of the variation attributed to changes in long-term nominal interest rates. The sensitivity of exposure to interest rates, of course, implies that plan actuaries' choice of interest rate assumptions can have a dramatic impact on reported underfunding and required funding contributions. See Munnell 1982; Ippolito 1989, 144–47; and US GAO 1992, 20–25.

33. PBGC 1992b.

34. Under the provisions of ERISA and the Internal Revenue Code, flat-benefit plans covering unionized workers are almost always underfunded, and the extent of underfunding can be increased without violating the law. These plans base benefits on a flat dollar amount per year of service, and this amount is generally increased with every contract negotiation (typically every three years). Because these increases apply to past years of service as well as to future, they increase past-service liabilities, which can be funded over long periods. Each benefit increase creates a new layer of past-service liabilities. Moreover, the Internal Revenue Code does not permit firms to anticipate these increases through additional pension fund contributions.

Final salary plans, by contrast, are almost always overfunded on a termination basis. These plans are required to take into account future wage growth in determining pension contributions. See US CBO 1993, 16–20; Ippolito 1989, 107–12; OMB 1993, 182; and Schmitt and Falk 1993, 4.

Also, as a general matter, ERISA allows pension plans to amortize unfunded liabilities over a period of years depending on the cause of underfunding. Although 1987 legislation shortened amortization periods, these rules generally apply prospectively (to increases in underfunding after 1987), and the legislation included special transition rules for large, integrated firms in the steel industry. Also, although the legislation created new minimum funding rules, firms with large unfunded liabilities have been able to skip contributions by using credits for past contributions above the minimum, for improved investment returns, or for gains resulting from changes in actuarial assumptions.

35. Companies in financial distress seek waivers of minimum contributions from the IRS (and can avoid making any contribution for a year or longer while awaiting an IRS determination); close plants and lay off workers, triggering special early retirement benefits, such as shutdown benefits, that are rarely prefunded; defer required contributions if a bankruptcy court permits (as did LTV, Continental Airlines, and CF&I Steel); and, in some cases, simply fail to make required contributions. All these actions deplete or slow the accumulation of assets while liabilities climb. (LTV's Republic Steel plan terminated with $7,700 in assets against $230 million in liabilities after its workers "with large unguaranteed benefits exercised their cash-out option en masse (Bodie 1992, 37)." Firms in financial distress can also change actuarial assumptions to reduce reported liabilities and required contributions. Firms have even increased benefits while in bankruptcy. (TWA and Continental Airlines added $150 million to unfunded benefits while in bankruptcy). See PBGC 1992a, 11; Ippolito 1989, 117–25, 132–44; US CBO 1993, 19–20; US GAO 1992, 1993; and Abken 1992.

It should be noted that tax laws sometimes prevent companies from making the contributions necessary to remove themselves from the "iffy 50" list. The law limits total contributions that can be made by a company that sponsors both a defined-benefit and a defined-contribution plan; companies violating this limit are subject to a 10% excise tax and the loss of tax deductibility for excess contributions. Loews Corporation, for example, complained that this limitation prevented it from contributing millions of dollars to the pension plan of its Lorillard Tobacco Co. subsidiary, one of the most underfunded plans on the 1992 list. See Vise 1993.

36. See PBGC 1993c; and Slate 1994, 2.

37. PBGC adjusts the higher figure to reflect the more detailed information available for some plans (PBGC 1993c, 8, 40).

38. PBGC 1993c, 9. PBGC prepares two other forecasts based on the assumption that future claims' experience mirrors past experience—the average experience over either the program's history (the most optimistic forecast) or the most recent 12 years (the middle forecast).

39. This is the present value of expected claims net of expected premium income for currently insured plans. See OMB 1994, 133–38. For more on the methodology, see Lewis and Cooperstein 1993. See also Hirtle and Estrella 1990.

40. While downplaying, but not denying, the S&L analogy, Martin Slate said, "We are talking about a situation that by its very nature will worsen and ultimately affect our ability to serve workers and retirees and the taxpaying public if we do not address the problems now (Slate 1993b)." See also Abken 1992; Bodie 1992; Bodie and Merton 1993; US CBO 1993; and Schmitt and Falk 1993.

In Senator Robert Dole's words, "Even in terms of the S&L fiasco, these deficit figures are staggering." He went on to say "if there is one thing Congress learned from the thrift crisis, it is that early action is necessary to stop the problem in its tracks and stem the exposure of the American taxpayer" (Lockhart 1992a)."

41. PBGC is authorized to borrow up to $100 million from the federal treasury. This authority has been used only once: initially, when the PBGC borrowed $100,000 for organizational expenses, and the loan was repaid from the proceeds of the first premiums. See ERISA sec. 4005(c) in Albergo and Domone 1993; and McGill 1984, 602.

42. Ippolito 1995, 27. Between 1979 and 1989, the number of active workers covered primarily by a defined-contribution plan more than doubled, from 6 million to 15 million, while the number covered primarily by a defined-benefit plan dropped from 29 million to 27 million (EBRI 1993). See also EBRI 1992b; and Clark and McDermod 1990.

43. Three developments have been identified as underlying the shift from defined-benefit plans, none of which appear transient: the shift in employment away from large unionized firms in the manufacturing sector, where defined-benefit plan coverage has been highest; increased federal regulation, which has tended to increase the cost and reduce the net benefits of offering defined-benefit plans; and the introduction of 401(k) plans, which present employees and employers with a closer substitute for defined-benefit plans. See Ippolito 1995, Clark and McDermod 1990; and Gustman and Steinmeier 1992.

As Ippolito elaborates, 401(k) plans permit not only tax-deductible employer contributions but also, uniquely, voluntary pretax contributions by workers and matching contributions by employers. Workers have more freedom to achieve desired saving goals, and firms can encourage certain workers to remain with the firm.

44. Ippolito 1992, 24.

45. See EBRI 1992a for the premium structure over the years.

46. As discussed below, risk-based premiums play a critical role in controlling moral hazard; by making it more costly to engage in a risk-increasing activity, the insurer reduces the likelihood that the insured will engage in that activity. On the role of risk-based premiums in pension insurance and how they might be structured, see, among others, Sharpe 1976; Ippolito 1989; Pesando 1982; and Bodie and Merton 1993. For an excellent discussion in the context of deposit insurance reform, see Bentson and Kaufman 1988.

47. PBGC (1993f).

48. A more precise measure of the risk would be the credit spread, or the difference between the actual interest rate charged and a risk-free rate, such as the rate on comparable (same maturity) Treasury securities.

49. For recent empirical estimates of actuarially fair premiums (and thus the implicit subsidies inherent in the current premium structure), see Lewis and Pennacchi 1993; Van Derhei 1990; and Hirtle and Estrella 1990. On the wealth transfers implicit in pension insurance and ERISA more generally, see Ippolito 1987, 1988.

50. Because a company wishing to drop pension insurance must also terminate its defined-benefit plan, it must consider not just the expected savings in insurance costs, but also the wealth losses that would be imposed on workers and retirees (in the form of foregone expected benefit accruals); the lost potential bonding effects of its defined-benefit plan, whereby the plan may encourage long tenure among workers and allow the company to make investments in workers it otherwise may not find profitable; and the transactions costs. New firms contemplating a defined-benefit plan with (absolutely or relatively) overpriced insurance face only the issue of bonding, and this is a less serious consideration given the availability of 401(k) plans.

51. About 10% of plans terminate annually in what is called a standard termination. The number of completed terminations in 1992 was 7,900, See PBGC 1992a, 5. Under the law, employers may terminate their plans either by buying annuities from a commercial insurer or (if agreeable to participants) by making lump sum payments for the full amount of outstanding benefit promises. This requires that the plan be fully funded at the time of termination (Wald and Kenty 1991, 294–98).

52. US CBO 1993, 5. As Abken has noted, the adverse selection problem PBGC faces is even more acute than the one facing deposit insurers, because deposit taking is a "core function" of the banking business, and relinquishing a bank charter and becoming a nondeposit financial intermediary is far more costly than relinquishing an employee-benefit plan. Abken 1992, 13–14.

53. Bodie and Merton 1993, 208. In another article, Bodie concludes: "There is still a substantial danger that the PBGC will become like the Federal Savings and Loan Insurance Corporation (FSLIC), that is, another government insurance program run amok." Bodie, "Commentary," in Sniderman 1992, 161.

For an opposing view, see EBRI 1992a, which argues that there is no need for a taxpayer bailout because the total overfunding in the U.S. pension system is ample to cover " pockets of underfunding" and, in any event, PBGC promises are not backed by the full faith and credit of the federal government. (ERISA sec. 4002(g)(2) explicitly states, "The United States is not liable for any obligation or liability incurred by the corporation.")

As the CBO notes, however, " This argument ignores the fact that the assets of overfunded plans do not belong to the government and that merely proposing a transfer of these assets to underfunded plans could trigger a massive exodus of overfunded plans from the DB insurance system." See US CBO 1993, 15. Few doubt, moreover, that guaranteed pension payments to retirees would be cut in the event of a PBGC funding shortfall—although future payments could well be at risk.

54. Moral hazard refers to the problem that arises when insurance, by shielding individuals from some or all of the losses stemming from a risk, dilutes the insureds' incentives to take precautions against incurring that loss. The fuller the protection against losses, the weaker the incentives to take precautions (or the greater the willingness to take risk), and the greater the likelihood of losses.

Adverse selection refers to the problem that arises if, because of information problems or statutory prohibitions, the insurer is unable to set premiums to closely reflect the losses an individual is expected to impose on the system—low-risk individuals will tend to drop out of the insurance pool, choosing instead to self-insure. This results in a higher average level of risk (and larger expected losses) on the part of those remaining in the pool.

For analyses of the demand for insurance, monitoring problems, agency costs, and private incentives to solve incentive problems, see Hirschleifer and Riley 1979; Harris and Raviv 1978; Jensen and Meckling 1976; and Mayers and Smith 1982.

55. This section draws on the work of Ippolito 1989, 1988; Bodie and Merton (1993); Abken (1992); Munnell (1982); Sharpe (1976); Treynor (1977); and Marcus (1987). See also Utgoff 1992; Keating 1991; and Niehaus 1990.

56. Ippolito 1989, xi.

57. The percentage of workers affected is estimated to be less than 5% of age-65 retirees. See Ippolito 1989, 75–76.

58. The guaranteed benefit is a fixed-dollar (nominal) annuity payable until death. As Ippolito notes, coinsurance factors can be very large if evaluated in terms of the loss of expected future pension wealth. According to his estimates, these losses have generally ranged from 25% to 35%, depending on prevailing interest rates, and are largest for workers in the middle of the age-service distribution. See Ippolito 1989, 19–26, 174, 182. Also, because PBGC is a creditor of bankrupt sponsors, other unsecured creditors in bankruptcy proceedings can be viewed as coinsurers of pension insurance (US CBO 1993, 13).

59. In addition to those mentioned above, other factors that would weigh against immediate termination include possible litigation, damaged labor relations, and, given forbearance on the PBGC's part, the possibility that it would be more profitable to hold this option than to exercise it. See Munnell 1982 and Bulow, Scholes, and Menell 1983.

60. Utgoff 1993, 148.

61. See Sharpe 1976; Treynor 1977; Marcus 1987; and Bodie, Light, et al. 1987.

62. Bodie, Light, et al. 1987. As Utgoff has observed, the irony of this "two-track incentive scheme" is that workers in weak companies most "needed the protection of assets set aside in a pension trust," since workers in healthy companies were already "protected by the ability and the obligation" of plan sponsors to make benefit payments. See Utgoff 1993, 148–49.

63. As noted by Sharpe (1976), incentives to pursue this strategy would disappear with risk-based premiums.

64. US CBO 1993, 29. This was vividly illustrated by the S&L crisis, well described by Kane (1989) and Barth (1991).

65. And workers, facing the possible loss of jobs, had the incentive to accept these pension offers, knowing that if the company failed, PBGC would largely protect them. As Senator James M. Jeffords has observed: "Companies and unions continue to use PBGC not just as the insurer of last resort, but more as a silent partner with deep pockets at contract negotiations for wages and benefits" (Taylor 1993, 308). See also Bulow, Scholes, and Menell 1983 on how ERISA's enactment shifted contract negotiation focus from pension contributions to pension benefits.

66. US CBO 1993, 12. See also Akerlof and Romer 1994, 2, for a discussion of how government guarantee programs can create incentives for companies "to go broke for profit at society's expense (to loot) instead of to go broke (to gamble for success)."

67. This company never received a funding waiver or violated any minimum funding rules; it operated a flat-benefit plan with a relatively old workforce and granted frequent benefit increases (Ippolito 1989, 39, 114; and Utgoff 1992, 151).

68. Bodie 1992.

69. The PBGC did not even oversee the operations of the plans it insured; the Department of Labor and the Internal Revenue Service performed this function. This remains the case today.

70. Under the law, PBGC could (and still can) terminate a plan if, among other things, the ultimate loss to PBGC "may reasonably be expected to increase unreasonably" if the plan is not terminated. (ERISA sec. 4042(a)(4) in Albergo and Domone 1993.) Such a standard, if it

can be called such, is not tied to any well-specified or economically meaningful criterion (such as expected claims' exceeding 30% of net worth or the firm's net worth falling below a certain level) and leaves the PBGC with discretion it would be politically reluctant to exercise. Attempting to terminate a giant underfunded plan that was meeting all the funding requirements in the law—simply because of the risk of default—would put the PBGC in the position of imposing real wealth losses on workers, entering into costly litigation with other creditors, and potentially hastening the plan sponsor's bankruptcy. Because the PBGC was not a commercial insurer with profits and losses to contend with, because the federal budget did not reflect the long-range implications of short-term decisions, and because the PBGC was authorized, not required, to terminate plans in this circumstance, PBGC was unlikely to exercise this instrument except in the most unusual circumstances.

71. Munnell 1982, 47.

72. For a review of the legislative changes in the Single-Employer Pension Protection Amendments of 1986 and the Pension Protection Act of 1987, see Utgoff 1993 and Ippolito 1989, especially appendix E. Two significant administrative decisions were made and enforced over the years: (1) actuarially reducing the benefit guarantee for benefits drawn before 65 (except in the case of shutdown benefits) and (2) aggressively prohibiting follow-on plans—successor plans designed to offset the pension losses to workers when a company terminates its underfunded plan and puts the liability onto the PBGC.

73. The full-funding limit no longer permits companies to fund 100% of ongoing liabilities (unless this is less than 150% of termination liabilities). As a result, many well-funded plans (about one-half, according to Bodie and Merton [1993]), especially those with relatively young workforces, will be precluded from making any contributions for several years. This amounts to an implicit tax on defined-benefit plans that will make defined-contribution plans relatively more attractive. See Ippolito 1991.

74. For earlier periods, Ippolito has performed the kind of study necessary to isolate the effects of regulation. In a careful empirical analysis of funding ratios in 1950–81, he found that "ERISA exerted no independent effect on underlying funding ratios in the average private pension plan ... the most underfunded plans prior to ERISA became relatively more underfunded...." See Ippolito 1989, 106; and 1988.

75. US GAO 1993. As James Lockhart puts it, "companies whose plans are billions of dollars underfunded have taken multiyear funding holidays" (Lockhart 1992b).

76. PBGC 1993e.

77. On the problems and potential solutions, see Lindeman 1993 and Keating 1991.

78. PBGC 1993c.

79. This is a top concern in Bodie, "Commentary," in Sniderman 1992 and Bodie and Merton 1993. More generally, see Sharpe 1976 and Bulow, Scholes, and Menell 1983.

80. For more on the hedging or immunization strategies available for managing pension fund risk, see Bodie and Merton 1993; and Bodie, Kane, and Marcus 1993.

81. According to the GAO, a 1991 internal PBGC study found shutdown benefits may have accounted for more than one-quarter of the agency's accumulated deficit in 1990 (US GAO 1992, 28).

82. According to Utgoff (1993, 149), shutdown benefits can add "$100,000 or more to the present value of benefits for each worker who qualifies." PBGC pays unreduced benefits (up to the maximum in the law) to workers receiving shutdown benefits, regardless of age,

while actuarially reducing the benefit guarantee for workers who draw regular retirement benefits before 65. (The reduction is roughly half for workers retiring at 55) (Ippolito 1989, 78–80, 152).

As for the lack of prefunding, the actuaries assume that a plant closing has a small, often zero, probability of occurrence and thus the payments contingent on this event are not fully valued in calculations of plan liabilities. See US GAO 1992, 27–28.

83. Abken 1992, 13.

84. Ippolito 1989, 86. He concludes, "No private insurance firm would willingly operate the pension insurance system under the current inadequate, albeit reformed, rules and prices."

85. Lindeman 1993, 74. He continues: "In addition, the PBGC's insurance premiums have little relationship to its exposure and risk. These failings might not matter if in the case of bankruptcy there were rigorous and indisputable consequences for companies and for pension beneficiaries. But there are not. The exact status of PBGC in bankruptcy remains uncertain."

In describing the "black magic of deposit guarantees" in the context of the S&L crisis, which applies well to pension insurance guarantees, Kane (1989, 4) said: "We must understand that deposit insurance is not strictly insurance at all. This is because the FSLIC guarantees are not written against a specified set of risks whose actuarial potential to destroy the institution's financial viability can be calculated in advance. Because the guarantee contract does not limit the set of unfavorable events to which the guarantor's credit is exposed, and because the degree of effective risk can be increased by the guaranteed party, deposit insurance represents an unconditional third-party guarantee of a firm's capacity to repay a particular class of its debts."

86. The Uruguay Round General Agreement on Tariffs and Trade (GATT) legislation improved the financing of underfunded plans and helped shore up the PBGC. The legislation, among other things, required faster funding of new pension liabilities, larger minimum contributions for underfunded plans with relatively high benefit disbursements, and use of more uniform actuarial assumptions, and it gradually removed the cap on the variable-rate premium, leaving the basic flat premium at $19 per participant. The legislation also contains a number of compliance and disclosure reforms. For brief summaries, see PBGC 1993e, 1993f, 1993g.

Despite the legislation's "get tough" appearance, no attempt is made to relate premiums to risk or in other ways to create proper incentives for employers (and unions) to keep pension promises in line with companies' ability to pay and plan sponsors' ability to manage pension fund volatility. Companies with underfunded plans would still be charged an implicit interest rate on pension debt substantially below the rate commercial lenders demand on ordinary corporate debt—the marginal rate wouldn't just fall as underfunding rose—and premiums would still be unrelated to the plan sponsors' creditworthiness. Well-funded plans would be free to increase risk and exposure—or, for that matter, reduce them—with no effect on premiums. The pension insurance systems' fundamental structure, which is at once highly regulatory and highly redistributive, would remain intact.

87. US CBO 1993, 33.

88. Ippolito 1987, 1988. See also discussion below regarding subsidies to firms with ongoing pension plans.

89. See Utgoff 1993. See also Michael S. Gordon's statement in Ippolito 1989, 264, in which he notes ERISA emerged in "the era of Chrysler and Lockheed bailouts" and argues that "the supposition that Congress was prepared to accept loss of jobs and further industrial decline in return for sound insurance principles is preposterous."

90. Bodie and Merton 1993, 224.

91. See EBRI 1992a for an explanation (and endorsement) of the social insurance view of pension insurance. See also Buchanan 1968 on how the mixed purposes of Social Security created a system that was, at once, inequitable, inefficient, and unsound.

92. Utgoff (1990, 158), reports that the termination of the Wheeling-Pittsburgh pension plans reduced funding costs by enough to allow a "permanent increase in wages of $3 per hour." For the S&L/deposit insurance analogy, see Kane 1989.

93. This conclusion is based on Ippolito's model of efficient underfunding of pension plans in unionized companies. See Ippolito 1987, 1988.

94. The transfer functions would include past losses and other sunk costs (those that cannot be avoided by actions taken now), such as a portion of the probable losses associated with currently underfunded plans. More on this below. For more on sunk costs, see US CBO 1993, 27–28.

95. Importantly, transfers are not just those already made and thus obvious. They are embedded in the current premium structure, funding rules, amortization schedules, and every other program aspect, which together permit some companies, particularly those in financial distress, to systematically underfund their pension promises and increase the PBGC's exposure. Returning to the put-option analogy, the put option's value is substantially greater for these companies, artificially raising the value of firm equity and subsidizing wages.

96. Ignoring past losses, Hirtle and Estrella (1990) estimate that a flat premium of $44 per participant annually, more than double the average premium of $21 paid in 1990, would cover expected losses. In this model, which retains the two-tiered premium structure in present law, actuarially fair premiums would range from $28–$46 per participant for well-funded plans (those with funding ratios over 125%) to $83–$259 for underfunded plans (those with funding ratios below 100%). Using an options-pricing model to estimate the value of pension insurance for a random sample of 20 firms, Lewis and Pennacchi (1993) report that pension insurance is underpriced for all firms in the sample, including both underfunded plans in weak companies and overfunded plans in strong companies. Also, as discussed above, because of mandatory coverage, the program can extract some of defined-benefit plans' efficiency gains that would otherwise accrue to workers and shareholders.

97. See, especially, Ippolito 1989; Bodie and Merton 1993; Lindeman 1993; and Keating 1991. Among government reports, see especially US CBO 1993. Many insights can also be gained from the work of Kane (1989), Barth (1991), and Bentson and Kaufman (1988) on deposit insurance reform.

98. Reduced benefit guarantees could be coupled with increased disclosure to plan participants of the consequences of underfunding and termination. See David Walker's suggestions in Krystof 1993. See also Pesando 1982 on increased disclosure as an alternative to pension insurance.

99. See Leonard and Zeckhauser 1983.

100. Others who have endorsed privatization, or risk-based premiums brought about (in whole or in part) through private supply, include Ippolito (1989); Pesando (1982); Sharpe (1976); Smalhout (1993); and Bodie (1994). See also US CBO 1993 for a discussion of the privatization option.

101. On the advantages of pricing over regulation, see Zeckhauser in his comments on Bulow 1983. Also, on how the failure to use explicit risk-based pricing may result in implicit

risk-based premiums through less efficient, more restrictive regulatory standards, see Bentson and Kaufman 1988.

102. Making dissolution of the firm the insured event was first recommended by McGill (1970). Ippolito (1989, 197) has likened paying off claims outside of firm failure to "paying life insurance benefits to individuals who are in poor health but not necessarily fatally ill."

Ippolito also makes an interesting suggestion that private contracts offer renewable-term insurance. He argues that firms should not find their premiums rising simply because they are going into financial distress; premiums should be set initially to reflect plan sponsor risk characteristics and then modified only to reflect plans sponsor actions that change their risk classification (such as lowering funding levels or changing their line of business) or to reflect overall claims experience. See Ippolito 1989, 178–79.

103. As noted by the CBO, PBGC's low premiums and comprehensive coverage may also have deterred private insurers in the early 1970s. See US CBO 1993, 41.

In the Ippolito model, a private industry group that both reinsured pension insurance policies and handled the problem of catastrophic losses, such as those that might be occasioned by a prolonged recession, would back up the reinsurance market. The industry group would levy a surcharge on insurers to build a reserve for covering the losses stemming from a bunching of claims or catastrophic losses.

104. In the Ippolito model, the industry group (not the government) would serve as the insurer of last resort for commercially uninsurable companies, which would be put in an assigned risk pool and subject to strict rules to reduce exposure (lower benefit guarantees and strict funding and asset allocation rules). Companies outside the pool would subsidize them. Another option, discussed by US CBO (1993), is for the government to assume the function of insurer of last resort and to try to limit losses in the ways suggested above. Others would go further. Pesando (1982) argued against creating pension insurance, suggesting that disclosure requirements, possibly coupled with minimum-funding requirements, would be preferable. Ippolito (1987) proposed repealing pension insurance.

105. Ippolito (1989) suggested this as a way of controlling the gaming associated with the timing of termination.

106. In the S&L context, see Kane 1989, 185.

107. Citing Hayek (1983, 68), competition is "like experimentation in science, first and foremost a discovery procedure ... a process in which people acquire and communicate knowledge.... It merely leads, under favorable conditions, to the use of more skill and knowledge than any other known procedure."

108. Hayek continued, "Providing against risks by insurance is not the result of anyone's ever having seen the need and devising a rational solution" (1960, 291).

109. "To make the best available knowledge at any given moment the compulsory standard for all future endeavor," Hayek said, "may well be the most certain way to prevent new knowledge from emerging" (1960, 292).

110. Utgoff 1990; Clark and McDermod 1990; and Weaver 1994.

111. For data on the administrative costs of defined-benefit plans by firm size and the relative cost of defined-benefit and defined-contribution plans for small firms, see findings of Hay/Huggins Co. report cited in Utgoff 1991. See also EBRI 1993.

112. Pesando 1982, Ippolito 1995, and Bodie 1990. As Ippolito notes, workers covered by 401(k) and other defined-contribution plans typically receive lump sum distributions when

they change jobs and typically do not roll these distributions over into other tax-deferred savings arrangement, such as IRAs.

113. On the desirability of tax and regulatory neutrality, see Ippolito 1990.

114. Weaver 1994 further develops this theme.

References

Abken, Peter A. 1992. "Corporate Pensions and Government Insurance: Deja Vu All Over Again?" *Economic Review* (March/April 77(2)):1–16.

Akerlof, George A., and Paul M. Romer. 1994. "Looting: The Economic Underworld of Bankruptcy for Profit." University of California-Berkeley. Manuscript.

Albergo, Paul F., and Dana J. Domone. 1993. *ERISA: The Law and the Code*. Washington, DC: BNA Books.

Barth, James R. 1991. *The Great Savings and Loan Debacle*. Washington, DC: The AEI Press.

Bentson, George J., and George C. Kaufman. 1988. "Regulating Bank Safety and Performance." In *Restructuring Banking and Financial Services in America*, ed. William S. Haraf and Rose Marie Kushmeider. Washington, DC: The AEI Press, 63–99.

Bodie, Zvi. 1994. "What the Pension Benefit Guaranty Corporation Can Learn From the Federal Savings and Loan Insurance Corporation." Cambridge, MA: Harvard Business School. Manuscript.

Bodie, Zvi. 1992. "Is the PBGC the FSLIC of the 1990s?" *Contingencies* (March/April 1992): 34–38.

Bodie, Zvi. 1990. "Pensions as Retirement Insurance." *Journal of Economic Literature* 28(1):28–49.

Bodie, Zvi, Alex Kane, and Alan J. Marcus. 1993. *Investments*. Homewood, IL: Richard D. Irwin, Inc.

Bodie, Zvi, Jay O. Light, Randall Morck, and Robert A. Taggart, Jr. 1987. "Funding and Asset Allocation in Corporate Pension Plans: An Empirical Investigation." In *Issues in Pension Economics*, ed. Zvi Bodie, John B. Shoven, and David A. Wise, 15–47. Chicago: University of Chicago Press.

Bodie, Zvi, Alan J. Marcus, and Robert C. Merton. 1988. "Defined Benefit vs. Defined Contribution Pension Plans: What are the Real Tradeoffs?" In *Pensions in the U.S. Economy*, ed. Zvi Bodie, John B. Shoven, and David A. Wise, 139–60. Chicago: University of Chicago Press.

Bodie, Zvi, and Robert C. Merton. 1993. "Pension Benefit Guarantees in the United States: A Functional Analysis." In *The Future of Pensions in the United States*, ed. R. Schmitt, 194–234. Philadelphia: University of Pennsylvania Press.

Bodie, Zvi, John B. Shoven, and David A. Wise, eds. 1988. *Pensions in the U.S. Economy*. Chicago: University of Chicago Press.

Buchanan, James M. 1968. "Social Insurance in a Growing Economy: A Proposal for Radical Reform." *National Tax Journal* 21 (December): 386–95.

Bulow, Jeremy I., Myron S. Scholes, and Peter Menell. 1983. "Economic Implications of ERISA." In *Financial Aspects of the United States Pension System*, ed. Zvi Bodie and John B. Shoven. Chicago: University of Chicago Press.

Clark, Robert L., and Ann A. McDermod. 1990. *The Choice of Pension Plans in a Changing Regulatory Environment*. Washington, DC: The AEI Press.

Dunkle, Tom. 1993. "Insufficient Funds: Pension Plans in Trouble." *Insight* (April 4).

Employee Benefit Research Institute (EBRI). 1994a. In *Pension Funding and Taxation*, ed. Dallas L. Salisbury and Nora Super Jones. Washington, DC: Employee Benefit Research Institute.

Employee Benefit Research Institute. 1994b. "Questions and Answers on Employee Benefit Issues." *EBRI Issue Brief* no. 150 (June). Washington, D.C.: Employee Benefit Research Institute.

Employee Benefit Research Institute. 1993. "Pension Evolution in a Changing Economy." *EBRI Special Report* no. 141 (September). Washington, DC.: Employee Benefit Research Institute.

Employee Benefit Research Institute. 1992a. "PBGC Solvency: Balancing Social and Casualty Insuance Perspectives." *Employee Benefit Notes* 126 (May).

Employee Benefit Research Institute. 1992b. "Changing Roles of Defined Benefit and Defined Contribution Plans." *Employee Benefit Notes* 13 (December).

Estrella, Arturo, and Beverly Hirtle. 1988. "Estimating the Funding Gap of the Pension Benefit Guaranty Corporation." *Federal Reserve Bank of New York Quarterly Review* (Autumn) 13(3):45–59.

Gustman, Alan, and Thomas Steinmeier. 1992. "The Stampede to Defined Contribution Plans." *Industrial Relations* 31 (Spring): 361–69.

Harris, Milton, and Arthur Raviv. 1978. "Some Results on Incentive Contracts with Applications to Education and Employment, Health Insurance, and Law Enforcement." *American Economic Review* 68 (March): 20–30.

Hayek, Friedrich A. 1983. *Law, Legislation, and Liberty: The Political Order of a Free People*. Vol. 3. Chicago: University of Chicago Press.

Hayek, Friedrich A. 1960. *The Constitution of Liberty*. Chicago: University of Chicago Press.

Hirschleifer, Jack, and John G. Riley. 1979. "The Analytics of Uncertainty and Information: An Exploratory Survey." *Journal of Economic Literature* 17 (December): 1375–1421.

Hirtle, Beverly, and Arturo Estrella. 1990. "Alternatives for Correcting the Funding Gap of the PBGC." New York: Federal Reserve Bank of New York.

Ippolito, Richard A. 1995. "Toward Explaining the Growth of Defined Contribution Plans." *Industrial Relations*, 34(1):1–20.

Ippolito, Richard A. 1992. "Private Pensions in the U.S. II." Manuscript prepared for International Symposium on Welfare and Market Mechanisms, April, at University of Tokyo.

Ippolito, Richard A. 1991. "The Productive Inefficiency of the New Pension Tax Policy." *National Tax Journal* 44(3):405–17.

Ippolito, Richard A. 1990. *An Economic Appraisal of Pension Tax Policy in the United States*. Homewood, IL: Richard D. Irwin, Inc.

Ippolito, Richard A. 1989. *The Economics of Pension Insurance*. Homewood, IL: Richard D. Irwin, Inc.

Ippolito, Richard A. 1988. "A Study of the Regulatory Effects of ERISA." *Journal of Law and Economics* 31 (April): 85–125.

Ippolito, Richard A. 1987. "Pension Security: Has ERISA Had Any Effect?" *Regulation*, no. 2:15–22.

Ippolito, Richard A. 1986. *Pensions, Economics, and Public Policy*. Homewood, IL: Published for the Pension Research Council, Wharton School, University of Pennsylvania by Dow-Jones Irwin.

Jensen, Michael C., and William H. Meckling. 1976. "The Theory of the Firm: Managerial Behavior, Agency Costs, and Ownership Structure." *Journal of Financial Economics* 3 (October): 305–60.

Kane, Edward J. 1989. *The S&L Insurance Mess: How Did it Happen?* Washington, DC: The Urban Institute Press.

Keating, Daniel. 1991. "Pension Insurance, Bankruptcy and Moral Hazard." *Wisconsin Law Review* 65:65–108.

Krystof, Kathy M. 1993. "Pension System Reform Seen." *Los Angeles Times*, 15 May.

Leonard, Herman B., and Richard J. Zeckhauser. 1983. "Public Insurance Provision and Non-Market Failures." *The Geneva Papers on Risk and Insurance* 8(27):147–57.

Lewis, Christopher M., and Richard L. Cooperstein. 1993. "Estimating the Current Exposure of the PBGC to Single-Employer Pension Plan Terminations." In *The Future of Pensions in the United States*, ed. R. Schmitt, 247–76. Philadelphia: University of Pennsylvania Press.

Lewis, Christopher M., and George G. Pennacchi. 1993. "Is Federal Pension Insurance Fairly Priced?" Washington, DC: Office of Management and Budget. Manuscript.

Lindeman, David C. 1993. "Pension Plagues and the PBGC." *The American Enterprise* (March/April) 4(2):72–80.

Lockhart, James B. III. 1992a. "Pensions—Preempt the Crisis Now." *Washington Post* (April 28).

Lockhart, James B. III. 1992b. Testimony before the House Ways and Means Committee Subcommittee on Oversight (August 11), Washington, DC: Government Printing Office.

Marcus, Alan J. 1987. "Corporate Pension Policy and the Value of PBGC Insurance." In *Issues in Pension Economics*, ed. Zvi Bodie, John B. Shoven, and David A. Wise, 48–76. Chicago: University of Chicago Press.

Mayers, David, and Clifford W. Smith, Jr. 1982. *Toward a Positive Theory of Insurance*. New York: New York University Press.

McGill, Dan M. 1984. *Fundamentals of Private Pensions*. Homewood, IL: Richard D. Irwin, Inc.

McGill, Dan M. 1970. *Guaranty Fund for Private Pension Obligations*. Homewood, IL: Richard D. Irwin, Inc.

Munnell, Alicia H. 1982. "Guaranteeing Private Pension Benefits: A Potentially Expensive Business." *New England Economic Review* (March/April): 24–47.

Niehaus, Gregory R. 1990. "The PBGC's Flat Fee Schedule, Moral hazard, and Promised Pension Benefits." *Journal of Banking and Finance*, 14(1):55–68.

Office of Management and Budget (OMB). 1994. *Fiscal Year 1995 Budget of the U.S. Government: Analytical Perspectives*. Washington, DC: Government Printing Office.

Office of Management and Budget, Executive Office of the President. 1993. *Budget Baselines, Historical Data and Alternatives for the Future*. Washington. DC: Government Printing Office.

Pension Benefit Guaranty Corporation (PBGC). 1993a. "Terminations." *PBGC Facts* (February).

Pension Benefit Guaranty Corporation. 1993b. "PBGC Solvency," *PBGC Facts* (July).

Pension Benefit Guaranty Corporation. 1993c. *1993 Annual Report*. Washington, DC: Pension Benefit Guaranty Corporation.

Pension Benefit Guaranty Corporation. 1993d. "Top 50 Companies Show Continued Growth in Pension Underfunding." *PBGC News*, Nov. 22.

Pension Benefit Guaranty Corporation. 1993e. "Pension Funding Reforms." *PBGC Facts* (September).

Pension Benefit Guaranty Corporation. 1993f. "PBGC Premium Reforms." *PBGC Facts* (September).

Pension Benefit Guaranty Corporation. 1993g. "Retirement Protection Reforms." *PBGC Facts* (September).

Pension Benefit Guaranty Corporation. 1992a. *1992 Annual Report*. Washington, DC: Pension Benefit Guaranty Corporation.

Pension Benefit Guaranty Corporation. 1992b. "Pension Underfunding Growth Continues in PBGC's Top 50 List." *PBGC News*, November 19.

Pesando, James E. 1982. "Investment Risk, Bankruptcy Risk, and Pension Reform in Canada." *Journal of Finance* 37(3):741–49.

Samuelson, Robert J. 1993. "Pension Time Bomb." *Washington Post*, March 4.

Schieber, Sylvester J., and Gordon P. Goodfellow. 1994. "Pension Coverage in America: A Glass Two-Thirds Full or One-Third Empty?" In *Pension Coverage Issues for the '90s*, ed. Richard P. Hinz, John A. Turner, and Phyllis A. Fernandez. Washington, DC: U.S. Department of Labor.

Schmitt, Ray, and Gene Falk. 1993. "Are Pension Guarantees Another Savings and Loan Collapse in the Making?" *CRS Report for Congress* no. 93–121 EPW, Feb. 1. Washington, DC: Congressional Research Service.

Sharpe, William F. 1976. "Corporate Pension Funding Policy." *Journal of Financial Economics* 3: vol 3, no. 3 183–93.

Slate, Martin. 1994. Remarks before the Committee on Ways and Means, U.S. House of Representatives, April 19.

Slate, Martin. 1993a. Remarks before the ERISA Industry Committee, Washington, DC, June 8.

Slate, Martin. 1993b. Remarks before the United Steelworkers of America, Washington, DC, July 13.

Smalhout, James. 1993. "Avoiding the Next Guaranteed Bailout." *The Brookings Review* (Spring): 12–15.

Smalhout, James. 1992. "The Coming Pension Bailout." *The Wall Street Journal*, June 19.

Sniderman, Mark S., ed. *Government Risk-Bearing*. Proceedings of a Conference held at the Federal Reserve Bank of Cleveland, May 991 (1993), Norwell, MA. and Dordrecht: Kluwer Academic Publishers.

Taylor, Andrew. 1993. "Pension Woes Raise Specter of Thrift-Style Bailout." *Congressional Quarterly* (Feb. 13): 307–8.

Treynor, Jack L. 1977. "The Principles of Corporate Pension Finance." *Journal of Finance* 32(2):627–38.

Turner, John A., and Daniel J. Beller. 1992. *Trends in Pensions 1992.* Washington, DC: Government Printing Office.

U.S. Congressional Budget Office (USCBO) 1993. *Controlling Losses of the Pension Benefit Guaranty Corporation.* Washington, DC: Government Printing Office.

U.S. General Accounting Office (USGAO). 1993. "Most Underfunded Plan Sponsors Are Not Making Additional Contributions." Testimony before the Subcommittee on Oversight, Commitee of Ways and Means, U.S. House of Representatives, April 20.

U.S. General Accounting Office. 1992. "Hidden Liabilities Increase Claims Against Government Insurance Program." Report to the Employment and Housing Subcommittee, Committee on Government Operations, U.S. House of Representatives, December.

U.S. House of Representatives. 1993. Committee on Ways and Means. *1993 Green Book: Overview of Entitlement Programs.* Committee Print 103–18.

Utgoff, Kathleen P. 1993. "The PBGC: A Costly Lesson in the Economics of Federal Insurance." In *Government Risk-Bearing*, ed. Mark S. Sniderman, 145–46. Boston: Kluwer Academic Publishers.

Utgoff, Kathleen P. 1991. "Toward a More Rational Pension Tax Policy: Equal Treatment for Small Business." *National Tax Journal* 44(3):383–91.

Utgoff, Kathleen P. 1990. "The Proliferation of Pension Regulations." *Regulation* (Summer): 29–38.

Van Derhei, Jack. 1990. "An Empirical Analysis of Risk-Related Insurance Premiums for the PBGC." *The Journal of Risk and Insurance* 57(2):240–59.

Vise, David. 1993. "Firms Stuck Between IRS and U.S. Pension Agency." *Washington Post*, February 13.

Wald, Martin, and David E. Kenty, eds. 1991. *ERISA: A Comprehensive Guide.* New York: John Wiley and Sons.

Weaver, Carolyn L. 1994. "Income Security Policy for an Aging Society: Balancing Interests and Controlling Risks Across Workers and Retirees." In *Economic Security, Intergenerational Justice, and the Elderly in North America*, ed. Vernon Greene, Theodore Marmor, and Timothy Smeeding. Washington, DC: The Urban Institute.

5   The Growth of 401(k) Plans: Evidence and Implications

James M. Poterba

The 1980s witnessed important changes in the structure of pension arrangements. After decades of growth, the number of defined-benefit plans stabilized and then began to fall. Defined-contribution plans, in contrast, continued to grow rapidly. The most dramatic growth in the defined-contribution sector was concentrated among 401(k) plans. These plans, which enable workers to defer compensation and accumulate assets at pretax rates of return, first became available in 1978. By 1989, 17.3 million workers participated in these plans. Contributions to 401(k) plans represented more than half of all defined-contribution plan contributions in 1989, and they were nearly twice as great as the flow of contributions to defined-benefit plans.

This chapter presents background information on 401(k) plan growth, then explores several questions about the interaction among 401(k) plans, other pension arrangements, and household saving. The first of five sections describes 401(k) plan basic provisions, including their tax treatment and nondiscrimination rules that apply to them. The subsequent section presents data on the growth of 401(k) participation and contributions during the last decade, along with summary information on the characteristics of current 401(k) participants. This section also examines the effect of various 401(k) plan provisions on participation and contribution behavior.

The third section addresses the interaction between 401(k) plans and other types of pension arrangements, in particular describing what is known about whether 401(k) plans have displaced other pension plans. The following section explores a parallel question, the extent to which 401(k) contributions displace other forms of household saving and presents evidence suggesting very little substitution between 401(k) contributions and other saving. The final section concludes and outlines several policy issues raised by 401(k) plan growth.

The Structure of 401(k) Plans

Legislation established 401(k) plans in 1978, but their use expanded rapidly after the Treasury Department issued clarifying regulations in 1981. These plans, established by employers, allow employees to contribute before-tax dollars to qualified retirement plans. Participants in 401(k) plans can defer income tax liability on their contributions. Assets in 401(k) accounts accumulate tax-free, and income from these plans is taxed when the funds are withdrawn. Prior to 1987, employees could contribute up to $30,000 each year to a 401(k) plan. In 1986, the Tax Reform Act (TRA) reduced the limit to $7,000 beginning in 1987 and instituted indexation for inflation in subsequent years. The contribution limit for 1993 was $8,994, for 1996, $9,400.

Employers may choose to adopt several additional features of 401(k)s. First, employers can match employee contributions. A 1987 survey of employers with 401(k) plans, conducted by the General Accounting Office (1988a), found that 51% of firms with 401(k) plans match employee contributions, and conditional on matching, more than two-thirds provided at least a 25% matching contribution. The Massachusetts Mutual Insurance Company (1991) found that 20% of plans had match rates of 100% or more, while 29% had no employer matching. A more recent but smaller survey of 401(k) plans by Papke, Petersen, and Poterba (1996) found that nearly 90% of participants in responding 401(k) plans have their contributions matched at rates of at least 25 cents per dollar contributed, and one-third receive match rates of 100% on at least part of their contributions.[1]

A second important feature of many 401(k) plans is a hardship withdrawal provision that enables participants to access funds in the plan, in some cases with a penalty payment. The John Hancock Financial Services (1993) survey of 401(k) plan participants suggests that many at least consider the possibility of using 401(k) assets for preretirement expenses. Although 98% of the sample respondents indicated that they planned to use their 401(k) as a retirement saving vehicle, 27% suggested that they might use the funds for educational expenses, 27% for medical expenses, and 12% for home purchase. Such withdrawals have tax consequences, because the withdrawal is treated as taxable income in the year received.[2] In many plans, employees may also borrow funds from their 401(k) accounts. Even when the plan includes these provisions, however, participants seem to take advantage of them relatively infrequently.

Section 401(k) plans usually allow participants significant discretion in how they invest their assets. Typical investment options include a stock fund, a bond fund, and a money market fund. VanDerhei (1992) presents information on asset allocation in 401(k) plans based on 1989 IRS Form 5500 filings. His tabulations show that common stock accounts for 21% of the asset value in 401(k) accounts, but insurance company products, primarily GICs, account for 41% of value. Since prospective returns on GICs are likely to be less attractive than those in the late 1980s, the portfolio composition of 401(k) accounts may shift away from these investments during the 1990s.

To avoid the possibility that tax-deferred saving plans with employer matching could be used to channel additional compensation primarily to high-income employees, Congress enacted a series of nondiscrimination tests 401(k) plans must satisfy. These regulations restrict the share of each year's contributions to 401(k) plans that can be made by "highly compensated employees." Until 1986, the average percentage of salary deferred by the highest-paid third of the participant group could not exceed the greater of (1) 150% of the average deferral percentage (ADP) for other eligible employees, or (2) the lesser of 250% of the ADP for other employees, and the other-employee ADP plus 3%.

TRA further limited tax-deferred benefits to highly compensated employees by changing the structure of antidiscrimination provisions and adding specific 401(k) nondiscrimination tests to the general rules prohibiting discrimination in contributions and benefits. Since 1986, the ADP of highly compensated employees has been limited to (1) 125% of the ADP for all other eligible employees, or (2) the lesser of twice the ADP for all other employees, and the ADP for all other employees plus two percentage points.[3] For example, if the highly compensated group's ADP is 6%, and the ADP for the non–highly compensated group is 4%, the plan would pass the test because it satisfies the second criterion. If it were 6.5%, the plan would fail. Even though under criterion (2) 6.5% is less than twice 4%, it is more than two percentage points higher than the ADP for non–highly compensated workers. TRA also added a second test, the actual contribution percentage (ACP) test, which applies a similar set of restrictions to the combined employee after-tax and employer contributions to the plan.

If a 401(k) plan fails to satisfy the ADP or ACP tests, the firm can either make additional contributions on behalf of lower-paid employees, so-called helper contributions, or restrict contributions by highly compensated employees. Helper contributions include qualified, nonelective employer contributions (QNCs) and qualified matching contributions (QMACs). As a result of these contributions, the stated match rate in some 401(k) plans is a lower bound on the effective match rate for participants outside the highly compensated group.

The Massachusetts Mutual Life Insurance (1991) survey of 401(k) plans provides evidence on the importance of ADP testing. This survey found that 81% of plans passed the ADP test without any correction such as helper contributions. The most important difference between plans that passed the ADP test and those that did not initially pass was the participation rate of non—highly compensated employees: 70% at firms that passed, 57% at firms that required correction. Papke, Petersen, and Poterba (1996) present evidence suggesting that although most plans satisfy the non-discrimination tests, high-wage employees do tend to contribute a higher share of their wages to 401(k)s than do their low-wage counterparts.[4]

Participation in and Contributions to 401(k)s

This section summarizes data on 401(k) plan growth during the 1980s. It begins with aggregate statistics on number of participants in these plans and flow of contributions, then explores the characteristics of participants. (Andrews 1992 presents a more detailed discussion of some of these issues.) The last subsection discusses the interaction between characteristics of particular 401(k) plans, such as the employer match rate, and the rate of employee participation.

Aggregate Trends

Table 5.1 shows the rapid growth of 401(k) plans during the last decade. Between 1984 and 1989, the number of plans more than tripled, and the number of participants more than doubled.[5] Contributions increased even more than the number of participants, even though TRA limited the maximum contribution. Annual contributions to 401(k) plans began at a low level in 1982, then increased continuously, reaching $46 billion in 1989.

The U.S. Department of Labor (1993) provides data on 401(k) plan assets, income, and outlays, tabulated from IRS Form 5500 filings for plan year 1989. The tabulations show that 401(k) plans with at least 100 participants had total assets of $334 billion. The Form 5500 filings also provide important data on the mix of contributions between employers and employees. In 1989, when contributions to 401(k) plans with more than 100 participants totaled $41.5 billion, participants contributed just over half ($22.7 billion).

Table 5.1
Growth of 401(k) plans

Year	Plans (in thousands)	Participants (in millions)	Contributions (in billions of 1989 dollars)
1983	1.7	4.4	n.a.
1984	17.3	7.5	19.5
1985	29.9	10.3	28.0
1986	37.4	11.6	33.0
1987	45.1	13.1	36.2
1988	68.1	15.5	41.3
1989	83.3	17.3	46.1

Note: Table A4 in *Trends in Pensions 1992*, augmented with data from table E19 of U.S. Department of Labor (1993), *Private Pension Plan Bulletin*. Dollar amounts in 1989 dollars have been computed using the Consumer Price Index.

Participant Characteristics

Aggregate rates of 401(k) eligibility and participation given eligibility can be computed from the SIPP. Poterba, Venti, and Wise (1995) present information from the 1984, 1987, and 1991 SIPPs; the summary tabulations are reproduced below:

	1984	*1987*	*1991*
Workers eligible for 401(k)	13.3%	20.0%	34.7%
Participation given eligibility	58.1	62.6	70.8
Overall participation rate	7.7	12.5	24.6

This analysis is limited to households with heads between ages 25 and 65 and excludes households with self-employment income. These tabulations show that by 1991, almost one-quarter of these households participated in a 401(k).

Table 5.2 disaggregates eligibility and participation patterns by age and income, using data from the 1991 SIPP. Eligibility for a 401(k) increases with income but is not strongly related to age. Given eligibility, participation is unrelated to age and is above 60% for all income groups. The relationship between income and 401(k) participation shown in the table is due largely to the relationship of eligibility to income. The tabulations suggest the diffusion of 401(k) plans may have the greatest effect on persons who will retire in several decades, rather than in the next few years.

Table 5.2
401(k) eligibility and participation in 1991

Income (in thousands of dollars)	Age category				
	25–35	35–45	45–55	55–65	All
Percentage eligible for 401(k)					
<10	5.1	11.2	2.1	7.9	6.4
10–20	14.8	20.2	16.5	14.4	16.6
20–30	30.2	34.6	27.6	20.9	29.7
30–40	40.1	42.8	32.8	36.5	39.0
40–50	38.9	46.0	48.7	37.7	43.7
50–75	51.3	53.9	56.4	51.9	53.8
>75	51.2	47.1	52.5	37.0	48.1
All	31.4	39.2	35.9	28.9	34.7
401(k) participation rate given eligibility					
<10	79.8	58.4	72.5	85.2	70.8
10–20	63.2	67.7	51.5	68.3	63.0
20–30	70.3	59.8	57.6	49.0	61.7
30–40	74.1	63.7	58.5	72.5	67.3
40–50	73.8	68.7	81.6	67.8	72.9
50–75	76.1	67.2	75.1	84.0	73.3
>75	86.2	83.8	88.1	85.7	85.8
All	73.5	67.7	72.3	72.3	70.8

Source: Poterba, Venti, and Wise 1994. Tabulations are based on 1991 Survey of Income and Program Participation.

Workers between ages 35 and 45 have the highest eligibility rale, more than ten percentage points higher than that of workers aged 55–65.[6]

Participation rates in 401(k) plans are substantially greater than those of other voluntary retirement saving plans. This suggests that some features of the 401(k) program—for example, the often-generous employer match rate or the link to the workplace, which can encourage all workers to participate together—are important aspects of the plans.

Participation in 401(k) plans is also highly persistent. Papke, Petersen, and Poterba (1996) present information on the participation rate in 401(k) plans in both 1987 and 1990 for firms that offered plans in both years. The data show a very strong correlation across years. Although this is not definitive evidence individuals are participating year after year, since in principle a 60% participation rate in the individual years 1987 and 1990 could be achieved with as little as 20% of the firm's workers participating in both years, other evidence suggests that individual behavior is highly persistent. Kusko, Poterba, and Wilcox (1994) show that at the firm they analyzed, the probability an individual who in a given year contributes to the 401(k) plan will contribute again the next is greater than 99%. This finding is conditional on being employed at the firm in the next year, so it overstates the degree of persistence among all contributors. Nevertheless, it is consistent with the view individuals do not often reconsider the decision to contribute to a 401(k) plan. It is also consistent with the view that saving through payroll deduction, for example, through 401(k) plans, is a form of self-control, a point developed in more detail by Shefrin and Thaler (1988).

401(k) Plan Characteristics and Participation Rates

One of the central questions about 401(k) plans, as well as other types of tax-deferred retirement saving programs, is plan contribution sensitivity to tax and other incentives, particularly the employer match rate. This subsection describes the results of a number of studies that have investigated the correlation between match rates and eligible employee participation and contribution decisions.[7]

Poterba, Venti, and Wise (1994) draw on General Accounting Office survey data to examine correlations among match rates, participation, and contribution levels. They find some evidence of higher participation rates when employers match contributions. No evidence in the GAO data, however, suggests that as match rates increase once positive, the employee participation rate increases. The evidence does suggest contribution rates, measured as a fraction of employee compensation, rise as the match rate increases. Employees at firms that do not match contributions contributed an average of 3.5% of salary to the 401(k) plan; those at firms with match rates of more than 100% contributed an average of 8.6% of salary.

Papke, Petersen, and Poterba (1996) conduct a similar analysis using the relatively small sample of 401(k) plans in their survey. They find a statistically significant positive effect of matching on plan participation rate, although once again, it is difficult to distinguish the marginal effects of match rate changes once this rate is positive. The predicted effect of a 50% employer match rate is a 10% increase in participation.

Three other studies have examined the effects of match rate changes on the share of salary contributed to the 401(k) plan. Papke (1992) analyzes plan level data from IRS Form 5500 filings and finds that how much changes in the match rate affect the contribution rate depends on the level of the match rate. At low levels of matching, match rate increases appear to raise the share of salary contributed, although at high match rates, there appears to be a negative effect. Andrews (1992) studies data from the May 1988 CPS, which includes information on whether, and what fraction of salary, an individual contributes to a 401(k), and whether the plan includes a corporate match. The CPS does not include information on the match rate. Andrews finds a positive relationship between participation and the presence of a match, but a negative relationship between the contribution rate and matching.

The Kusko, Poterba, and Wilcox (1994) analysis of individual participation and contribution decisions based on employee records for a single large employer provides a different perspective on this issue. The data set used includes information on individual contributions in several consecutive years when the plan in question offered substantially different employer match rates. The findings show relatively little change in either participation or contribution behavior in response to large changes in the matching provisions. This study also shows a nontrivial share of 401(k) contributors, in this case about one in five, were making the maximum possible contribution to the 401(k) plan and therefore faced some limits on their ability to adjust contributions in response to changes in the match rate.

This discussion suggests that research on the link between plan provisions and employee behavior has yet to reach definitive conclusions. Since plan characteristics should in part be determined by employee preferences, it is difficult to interpret cross-sectional evidence relating plan attributes to contribution or participation rates. Further work is needed to explore these issues.

Did 401(k) Plans Replace Other Private Pension Plans?

Although 401(k) plans differ from other traditional pension plans in many respects, they are formally characterized as a type of defined-contribution (DC) pension plan. The growth of 401(k) plans during the 1980s coincided with a sharp reversal of growth trends for defined-benefit (DB) plans, and to a lesser extent for non-401(k) DC plans. The time profile of contributions to 401(k) and other pension plans raises a question about the interaction among these plans: Have 401(k)s simply replaced other private pension arrangements? This section begins by explaining the regulatory and other factors that likely affected the growth rate of DB and non-401(k) DC pension plans during the 1980s. It then presents evidence

drawn from the Papke, Petersen, and Poterba (1996) survey on the inter-
actions between these various pension arrangements.

The Changing Complexion of Pension Arrangements in the 1980s

Table 5.3 shows that the relative flows of contributions to DB and DC
pension plans changed substantially during the 1980s.[8] The table also
shows the number of DC and DB pension plans, number of participants in
these plans, and level of contributions to these plans since 1975. The
number of DC plans more than doubled between 1975 and 1982, then
rose by 43% again between 1982 and 1989. The number of DB plans
increased during the 1975–82 period, but the increase was slower than
that for DC plans. Between 1982 and 1989, however, the number of DB
plans actually declined. The number of participants in DB plans peaked in
1984, and the number of active participants (those not retired) peaked in
1981. In contrast, the number of DC plan participants increased throughout the 1980s. The number of DC participants grew more slowly than the
number of plans.

The last column in table 5.3 tracks contributions to DC and DB pension
plans. The disparity between the contribution series is even more dramatic than between the number of participants or the number of plans. In
constant 1989 dollars, DC plan contributions increased from $35.4 billion
in 1980 to $80.1 billion in 1989, with 401(k) contributions accounting
for $46.1 billion of the 1989 total. Contributions to DB plans, however,
peaked at $64.1 billion in 1980 and 1981, then declined to only $24.9
billion by 1989.

Contributions to DC plans grew rapidly largely because of the growth
of 401(k) plans. Without them, contributions to DC plans amounted to
only $34.0 billion in 1989, only slightly more than that year's contri-
butions to DB plans. In some years in the late 1980s, non-401(k) DC
plan contributions were less than DB plan contributions.[9] From the standpoint of assessing how the growth of 401(k)s has affected private saving,
an important but possibly unanswerable question is whether the contributions that flowed to 401(k) plans would have flowed to another DC
plan if 401(k)s had not been available.

The trends described in table 5.3 resulted from several coincident developments. Bernheim and Shoven (1989) argue that high investment returns
on existing DB plans reduced required contributions to DB plans in the
mid-1980s. Chang (1991) argues a decline in employers' desire to offer DB
plans, largely due to regulation, accounts for the shrinking number of plans.

Table 5.3
Trends in pension plans, participants, and contributions

Year	Plans (in thousands)	Participants (in millions)	Contributions (in billions of 1989 dollars)
Defined-contribution plans (of which 401(k) Plans)			
1975	207.7	11.5	29.5
1976	246.0	13.5	30.9
1977	281.0	15.2	32.5
1978	314.6	16.3	35.0
1979	331.4	18.3	35.4
1980	340.8	19.9	35.4
1981	378.3	21.7	38.7
1982	419.5	24.6	40.0
1983	426.6(1.7)	29.1(4.4)	44.9
1984	435.4(17.3)	32.9(7.5)	51.8(19.5)
1985	462.0(29.9)	35.0(10.3)	61.3(28.0)
1986	545.0(37.4)	36.7(11.6)	66.0(33.0)
1987	570.0(45.1)	38.3(13.1)	66.0(36.2)
1988	584.0(68.1)	37.0(15.5)	68.0(41.3)
1989	599.0(83.3)	36.5(17.3)	80.1(46.1)
Defined-benefit plans			
1975	103.3	33.0	55.8
1976	114.0	34.2	62.1
1977	121.7	35.0	63.8
1978	128.4	36.1	52.5
1979	139.5	36.8	69.3
1980	148.1	38.0	64.1
1981	167.3	38.9	64.1
1982	175.0	38.6	62.2
1983	175.1	40.0	57.6
1984	168.0	41.0	56.3
1985	170.2	39.7	48.4
1986	172.6	40.0	37.6
1987	163.1	40.0	32.5
1988	146.0	40.7	27.6
1989	132.5	40.0	24.9

Note: Numbers were converted from current dollars using the Consumer Price Index. Data are drawn from U.S. Department of Labor 1993.

These factors, as well as sectoral shifts from industries that had historically offered DB plans to those that had historically offered DC plans, explain the changing pattern of contributions.[10]

The changing regulatory treatment of DB and DC pension plans began in 1974 with ERISA, which imposed minimum plan standards for participation, vesting, and retirement, as well as requirements for funding past service liability. It also established the PBGC to insure pension benefits to employees in DB plans and financed this insurance program with taxes on existing plans. ERISA placed a lower regulatory burden on DC plans, which were subject only to the minimum plan standards that also affected DB plans.

Legislation since ERISA has raised PBGC premia, required faster funding of liabilities, and penalized employers for claiming excess assets of terminated DB plans. In 1982, TEFRA imposed faster vesting schedules for lower-paid employees in so-called top-heavy plans. TRA imposed a 10% excise tax on excess pension plan assets that revert to an employer upon plan termination. Subsequent legislation raised this tax to 20%, effective in 1990, and to 50% if the employer does not transfer a portion of the excess assets to a replacement plan or increase terminating plan benefits.

OBRA87 increased the basic PBGC premium from $8.50 to $16.00 per participant and added a variable premium that depends on the plan's degree of underfunding. It also limited the tax deduction for plan contributions to 150% of the plan's termination liability. Chang (1993) argues that these changes reduced employer contributions to DB plans. The net effect of these tax and regulatory changes is a marked increase in the administrative cost of, and a decrease in the benefits to employers from, establishing DB pension plans. These factors undoubtedly contribute to 401(k) and other DC plans' popularity, particularly at small companies, since 1986.

Survey Evidence on the 401(k) Replacement Hypothesis

The substitution among 401(k) plans, DB plans, and other DC pension plans cannot be studied using the household level data sets that form the basis for much of the research on 401(k)s and household saving. These data sets, such as the SIPP and CPS, do not collect sufficiently detailed information on respondents' pension arrangements. In addition, neither contains any information on the pension arrangements at the respondent's firm before the 401(k) option became available.

To investigate the degree of substitution between 401(k) plans and other employer-provided retirement saving arrangements, and to obtain firm-level information on these plans more generally, Papke, Petersen, and Poterba (1996) surveyed a stratified random sample of firms with 401(k) plans in 1987.[11] We asked 401(k) plan administrators about their plans' origins, in particular whether it replaced another pension plan for covered employees. We also inquired about various detailed plan provisions, including participation rates, employer matching rules, loan and hardship withdrawal plan provisions, and whether the plan had been affected by antidiscrimination rules.

Table 5.4 summarizes the survey responses. Forty-five percent of the responding firms, representing 37% of the 401(k) participants in our survey, indicated that another pension plan was converted to the 401(k). Two percent of the responding firms (one firm) reported that DB pension plans were terminated and replaced with a 401(k). Many more firms reported they converted previous thrift plans or profit-sharing plans to 401(k)s. These findings, although based on a small sample, suggest that at least a substantial fraction of 401(k) plans did not replace previous plans.[12] A more difficult question these findings do not resolve concerns the change in the level of funding of other pension plans since the sponsoring firm initiated the 401(k) plan.

The prevalence of conversions from thrift plans to 401(k)s can be attributed to 401(k)s' more attractive features. Contributions to thrift plans were made on an after-tax basis, so 401(k)s provide the added benefit of tax deferral. In addition, until TRA tightened the limits on both 401(k) contributions and withdrawals, 401(k)s offered a highly liquid and tax-favored means to accumulate assets. Under the pre-1986 limit on 401(k) contributions of $30,000 per year, and with federal marginal tax rates of 50% on high-income individuals, the incentives to defer income and accumulate savings at the pretax rate of return were substantial.

The survey responses indicate that 401(k)s are typically supplemental plans, added to preexisting DB (63%) or DC (19%) plans. Our question on the fraction of 401(k)-eligible workers also covered by other pension arrangements at the firm provides a direct test of whether 401(k) plans have replaced all other pension coverage. In 1990, 82% of the participants in 401(k) plans were also covered by another DB plan at the same firm, and 30% were also covered by another DC plan. These responses are not exclusive: 401(k) eligibles could be covered by both another DC plan and a DB plan. The 401(k) was the only retirement plan for covered workers at 19% of the firms, representing 10% of the participants.

Table 5.4
401(k) plan initiation decisions

	Simple average	Participant-weighted average
Date when 401(k) plan started		
Before 1981	14%	19%
1981–83	16	30
1984–86	51	42
Since 1986	19	15
New plans[a]	55	63
Type of plan converted:[a]		
Thrift/saving	53	49
Profit sharing	40	50
Other	7	1
Why was plan started?		
Supplement primary DC plan	19	14
Supplement primary DB plan	63	66
Replace primary DC plan	9	6
Replace primary DB plan	2	17
Optional tax-deferred saving plan	58	59
Is the 401(k) the primary retirement plan?	26	6
Percentage of 401(k) eligibles also covered by		
Defined-benefit plan		
1986	85	88
1990	73	82
Defined-contribution plan		
1986	37	32
1990	36	30
Percentage of 401(k) eligibles for whom the 401(k) *is the only retirement plan*		
1986	5	4
1990	19	10

Source: Papke, Petersen, and Poterba 1996.
a. Denotes tabulations based on 33 rather than 43 responses.

Another form of evidence on 401(k) plans' prevalence as sole pension vehicles can be computed from U.S. Department of Labor (1993) tabulations. Fourteen percent of the assets of 401(k) plans with at least 100 employees were held in plans that represented the only pension plan the employer sponsored.[13] This suggests that 401(k)s that could have completely displaced other retirement saving vehicles account for a relatively small share of 401(k) activity.

The differences between the participant-weighted and plan-weighted results in table 5.4 suggest important differences between the roles 401(k) plans play at large and small firms. Small firms are more likely to rely on 401(k)s as their primary retirement vehicle and to have initiated their 401(k) plan in recent years. The 401(k) was the only retirement plan for 14% of the workers at firms that started their 401(k) plans in 1986 or later, compared with only 7% of the workers at firms with plans that started before 1986. Although 18% of the plans that began before 1986 are primary retirement plans, 40% of the post-1986 plans are primary plans.

Do 401(k) Contributions Displace Other Private Saving?

The foregoing discussion suggests 401(k)s have not grown primarily by crowding out other pension plans. This makes it difficult to argue that the decline in other pension contributions is a result of the diffusion of 401(k)s. A related issue concerns the interaction between 401(k) contributions and other forms of private saving. Are contributions to 401(k) plans made from funds households would otherwise have saved through different channels? An accumulating body of evidence, summarized in this section, suggests that contributions to 401(k) plans represent new saving.[14]

The net saving effect of 401(k) contributions can be investigated by exploiting the quasi-experimental differences in household exposure to 401(k) saving opportunities. One test in this spirit compares assets accumulated by individuals of similar age and income but in different birth cohorts, who have therefore been able to save through 401(k) plans for different lengths of time, using data from the SIPP for 1984, 1987, and 1991. Because age, income, and other characteristics of the three cross sections are similar, one would expect saving balances also to be similar. The different cohorts do face different historical patterns of asset returns, but for households with relatively little wealth, this should not have had much effect on observed holdings. The critical differences between these cohorts, from the standpoint of retirement saving accounts, are that the

Table 5.5
Median 401(k) and other financial asset balances, 1984–91 (in 1987 dollars)

	1984	1987	1991
Families with 401(k)s:			
Total financial assets	$—	$8,566	$9,808
Non-401(k) assets	3,723	2,587	2,498
401(k) assets	—	3,145	4,424
Debt	1,153	1,247	1,240
Families without 401(k)s:			
Total financial assets	3,570	3,602	3,312

Note: Tabulations are from various years of the Survey of Income and Program Participation. This table summarizes results in Poterba, Venti, and Wise 1995. Because the entries are medians, the sum of 401(k) and non-401(k) assets does not necessarily constitute total financial assets. Households with IRAs are excluded from the analysis to control for heterogeneity in household saving behavior.

1984 sample had only about two years (1982 to 1984) to accumulate 401(k) balances, while the 1987 sample had about five years, and the 1991 sample about nine years.[15]

Table 5.5 presents summary statistics on the total financial asset holdings of 401(k) and non-401(k) participants in various years, along with the amount held in 401(k) accounts.[16] The table shows non-401(k) assets do not decline as 401(k) assets increase. The total financial assets of families with 401(k) accounts increased greatly between 1984 and 1991, but their non-401(k) financial assets changed little. These results do not support the view 401(k) participants have dissaved through other channels.

The growing importance of 401(k) plans provides a second quasi-experimental way to assess the net effect of retirement saving programs. Assuming that 401(k) eligibility is largely exogenous—the result of decisions by employers—then comparisons between non-401(k) asset accumulation by those eligible and not eligible provides another way to assess the 401(k) saving effects. This approach views 401(k) eligibility as the treatment in a natural experiment to evaluate the saving effect of a plan with 401(k) tax incentives, employer payroll deductions, and provisions. In this case the key question is whether families eligible for a 401(k) in a given year had larger total financial asset balances than families not eligible, or, equivalently, whether non-401(k) financial assets declined enough to offset eligible families' 401(k) contributions.

Table 5.6 presents the results of this comparison using data from the 1991 SIPP. The table disaggregates households into various income

Table 5.6
Median financial assets, 401(k) eligibles vs. not eligibles, 1991

Income level (in thousands of dollars)	Eligible for 401(k)	Not eligible for 401(k) (in dollars)
<10	$ 2,033	$ 1,378
10–20	4,045	1,997
20–30	5,499	2,558
30–40	8,683	3,256
40–50	14,470	6,206
50–75	26,093	10,080
>75	51,080	29,842

Source: Tabulations from the 1991 Survey of Income and Program Participation, presented in Poterba, Venti, and Wise (1995).

categories to control for income-related differences in 401(k) eligibility. It presents median total financial assets for 401(k)-eligible and ineligible households in each income group. If families reduced saving in other forms when they became eligible for a 401(k) plan, the typical family eligible for a 401(k) in 1991 should have accumulated less wealth in other, non-401(k) financial assets than the typical ineligible family. This is not the case. The median total financial assets of 401(k)-eligible families with incomes above $75,000, for example, is $51,080, whereas the median for families in this income group who were not eligible is only $29,842. These data show no substitution of 401(k) contributions for other financial-asset saving.

Conclusions and Implications of 401(k) Growth

401(k) plans have grown more rapidly than any other type of pension arrangement during the last decade. The participation rates of eligible employees at firms that offer 401(k) plans are high, typically near 70%. Because most U.S. households have relatively little accumulated financial wealth, for many 401(k) plan participants, their plan assets are a substantial and growing fraction of their net worth. The primary assets of a median household reaching retirement today are Social Security, accumulated net worth in an owner-occupied home, and (possibly) an employer-provided pension. If present trends toward the expansion of 401(k)s continue, the assets in 401(k) plans will represent an important component of retirement saving for the next century's retirees.

Because 401(k) plans differ in some respects from traditional DB and DC pension plans, their growing importance raises several new issues for pension policy. One important difference between 401(k)s and other arrangements is that individuals typically have more discretion in investing their 401(k) assets than in investing DB or non-401(k) DC assets. This can have important consequences for 401(k) assets' long-term growth. There is some evidence, presented for example in VanDerhei 1992, that 401(k) assets are invested more conservatively than assets in traditional DB plans. Since the expected return on equities is greater than that on bonds, lower equity exposure in 401(k) plans will imply slower growth of plan assets as participants move toward retirement, and consequently lower average levels of retirement income than if the plan assets had been invested differently. It is not clear what role, if any, this suggests for public policy. Since many 401(k) participants have little experience in making investment decisions, encouraging education about the risks and returns from investing could be warranted.

A second important difference between 401(k)s and traditional pension plans is that participants have more discretion in withdrawing assets through lump sum distributions. This raises one of the key issues about the link between 401(k) growth and future retirees' financial health: Will 401(k) assets remain in these plans until participants retire? Several analyses of the patterns of lump sum distributions from current plans,[17] although plagued with data difficulties, provide some evidence on their role in long-term financial planning. Although many lump sum distributions are not reinvested in a dedicated retirement saving vehicle such as an IRA, some evidence exists that larger distributions are more likely to be reinvested.

These findings are consistent with a behavior pattern in which individuals, typically young ones with brief tenures at 401(k)-providing firms, receive relatively small distributions and spend them or reinvest them outside the retirement saving system. Individuals who receive larger distributions, typically older and nearer retirement, are more likely to roll over these distributions into another saving vehicle. Salisbury (1993) notes that recent changes in lump sum distributions' tax treatment are likely to affect these payments' disposition. Further research on the link between individual characteristics, the incidence of 401(k) lump sum distributions, and the disposition of these distributions is one of the top priorities for research on this aspect of the retirement saving system.

Notes

This chapter was originally prepared as a paper for the APPWP/CEPR Conference on Public Policy Toward Pensions, Washington, DC, October 7–8, 1993. It was written while the author was a fellow at the Center for Advanced Study in the Behavioral Sciences and draws on several earlier collaborative research studies supported by the National Institute of Aging and the National Science Foundation.

1. Many 401(k) plans provide high employer match rates up to a fixed fraction of salary (often 5%) contributed to the plan. After reaching this matching limit, employees may still make unmatched contributions provided they have not reached the IRS contribution limit.

2. Leaving a firm that offers a 401(k) plan can trigger a withdrawal if an individual has a relatively small 401(k) account balance and the employer chooses to terminate the account. The plan balance is then transferred to the participant as a lump sum distribution, which the recipient can either reinvest in a tax-free account such as an IRA or treat as current taxable income.

3. TRA defined highly compensated employees as those more than 5% owners, officers earning more than $45,000 per year, employees earning more than $75,000, and employees earning more than $50,000 and in the top 20% of paid employees.

4. An earlier survey by Buck Consultants (1989) found somewhat greater difficulty in complying with the ADP tests. For the 1988 plan year, only 60% of the plans represented in that survey passed the ADP test without corrective action.

5. Participation in a plan indicates only that an employee has a 401(k) account, not that he made a contribution in a given year. Most 401(k) participants do make contributions, however.

6. Andrews (1992) presents a detailed analysis of the relationship between individual characteristics and the probability that an employer offers a 401(k) plan.

7. The U.S. General Accounting Office (1988b) tabulates participation rates by a number of 401(k) plan characteristics other than the employer match rate; no strong patterns emerge from this analysis.

8. This section draws heavily on Papke, Petersen, and Poterba (1996).

9. Silverman (1992) presents further details on the shifting importance of DB and DC pension plans.

10. Bloom and Freeman (1992) suggest that a shift-share analysis of the change in pension plan coverage as a function of the workforce's demographic, industrial, and unionization composition can explain approximately half the coverage decline during the 1980s.

11. The survey response rate was disappointingly low, with just over 5% of surveyed firms responding. This suggests caution in evaluating the results. Papke, Petersen, and Poterba (1996) present evidence, however, that the attributes of responding plans are similar to those in other, larger surveys of 401(k)s.

12. Some firms that have started pension plans for the first time since 401(k)s became available may have chosen 401(k) arrangements instead of other options; these firms will not show up as replacements in the survey. Andrews (1992) reports tabulations from IRS Form 5500 data showing that for 3.4 million of the 13.1 million 401(k) participants in 1987, the 401(k) was the primary pension plan.

13. Section 401(k) plans with at least 100 participants accounted for $41.5 billion of the $46.1 billion of 401(k) contributions in 1989. They presumptively account for most of the participants in 401(k) plans as well.

14. This section draws heavily on Poterba, Venti, and Wise 1995.

15. Because of the rapid growth of 401(k) availability during the 1980s, many of those who participated in these plans in later years had been eligible only for a few years.

16. Poterba, Venti, and Wise (1995) disaggregate financial asset balances by age and income.

17. Studies of the disposition of lump sum distributions include Andrews 1991; Chang 1993; Fernandez 1992; and Yakoboski 1993.

References

Andrews, Emily S. 1992. "The Growth and Distribution of 401(k) Plans." In *Trends in Pensions 1992*, ed. J. Turner and D. Beller. Washington, DC: U.S. Department of Labor, 149–76.

Andrews, Emily S. 1991. "Retirement Savings and Lump Sum Distributions." *Benefits Quarterly* 2:47–58.

Beller, Daniel J., and Helen H. Lawrence. 1992. "Trends in Private Pension Plan Coverage." In *Trends in Pensions 1992*, ed. J. Turner and D. Beller. Washington, DC: U.S. Department of Labor, 59–96.

Bernheim, B. Douglas, and John B. Shoven. 1988. "Pension Funding and Saving." In *Pensions in the U.S. Economy*, ed. Z. Bodie, J. Shoven, and D. Wise. Chicago: University of Chicago Press, 85–111.

Bloom, David E., and Richard B. Freeman. 1992. "The Fall in Private Pension Coverage in the United States." *American Economic Review* 82(2): 539–45.

Buck Consultants. 1989. *Current 401(k) Plan Practices: A Survey Report*. Secaucus, NJ: Buck Consultants.

Chang, Angela. 1993. "Tax Policy, Lump Sum Pension Distributions, and Household Saving." Federal Reserve Bank of New York. Mimeographed.

Chang, Angela. 1991. "Explanations for the Trend Away from Defined Benefit Pension Plans." Congressional Research Service Report 91-647 EPW.

Fernandez, Phyllis A. 1992. "Preretirement Lump Sum Distributions." In *Trends in Pensions 1992*, ed. J. Turner and D. Beller. Washington, DC: U.S. Department of Labor.

John Hancock Financial Services. 1993. *Insights into Participant Behavior: Defined Contribution Plan Survey*. Boston: John Hancock Financial Services.

Kusko, Andrea L., James M. Poterba, and David W. Wilcox. 1994. "Employee Decisions with Respect to 401(k) Plans: Evidence from Individual-Level Data." Working paper no. 4635, National Bureau of Economic Research, Cambridge, MA.

Massachusetts Mutual Life Insurance Company. 1991. *401(k) Survey Report*. Springfield, MA: Massachusetts Mutual Life Insurance Company.

Papke, Leslie. 1992. "Participation in and Contributions to 401(k) Plans: Evidence from Plan Data." Working paper no. 4199, National Bureau of Economic Research, Cambridge, MA.

Papke, Leslie, Mitchell Petersen, and James M. Poterba. 1996. "Did 401(k)s Replace Other Employer-Provided Pensions?" In *Advances in the Economics of Aging*, ed. D. Wise. Chicago: University of Chicago Press, 219–240.

Poterba, James M., Steven F. Venti, and David Wise. 1995. "Do 401(k) Contributions Crowd Out Other Personal Saving?" *Journal of Public Economics* 58(1):1–32.

Poterba, James M., Steven F. Venti, and David Wise. 1994. "401(k) Plans and Tax-Deferred Saving." In *Studies in the Economics of Aging*, ed. D. Wise. Chicago: University of Chicago Press, 105–138.

Salisbury, Dallas. 1993. "Policy Implications of Changes in Employer Pension Protection." In *Pensions in a Changing Economy*, ed. Employee Benefit Research Institute. Washington, D.C.: EBRI.

Shefrin, Hersh M., and Richard Thaler. 1988. "The Behavioral Life-Cycle Hypothesis." *Economic Inquiry* 26(4):609–43.

Silverman, Celia. 1992. "Changing Roles of Defined Benefit and Defined Contribution Plans." *Employee Benefit Notes* 13 (December): 1–4.

Turner, J. and D. Beller, eds. 1992. *Trends in Pensions 1992*. Washington, DC: U.S. Department of Labor.

U.S. Department of Labor. Office of Research and Economic Analysis. 1993. *Private Pension Plan Bulletin*. Washington, D.C.: U.S. Department of Labor.

U.S. General Accounting Office. 1988a. *401(k) Plans: Incidence, Provisions, and Benefits*. Washington, DC: General Accounting Office.

U.S. General Accounting Office. 1988b. *401(k) Plans: Participation and Deferral Rates by Plan Features and Other Information*. Washington, DC: General Accounting Office.

VanDerhei, Jack. 1992. "New Evidence that Employees Choose Conservative Investments for Their Retirement Funds." *Employee Benefit Notes* 13 (February): 1–3.

Yakoboski, Paul. 1993. "New Evidence on Lump-Sum Distributions and Rollover Activity." *EBRI Notes* 14 (July): 6–8.

6

Abandoning the Nest Egg? 401(k) Plans and Inadequate Pension Saving

Andrew Samwick and
Jonathan Skinner

A whole generation of people are going to wake up years from now and say, "God, I wish I had known when I was 32 that I should have been putting this money in."

Myron Mintz, Chair, PBGC, quoted in Vise 1993

One of the fundamental changes in the U.S. pension system has been the shift toward DC pension plans, and in particular toward 401(k) pension plans. Until the early 1980s, the typical pension was a DB plan in which the employer guaranteed a fixed nominal retirement payment that depended on the employee's tenure and earnings history at the company. In DC pension plans, employers and employees typically contribute to the worker's pension fund, which is then distributed when the worker leaves the firm. The fastest growing component of DC plans is the 401(k), which is self-directed in the sense that the employee can make additional pretax contributions and determine how his or her pension contributions will be invested. Between 1981 and 1989, the number of workers with a primary DC plan rose from 6 million to 15 million; by contrast, the number of workers with primary DB plans fell from 30 million to 27 million (Silverman 1993).

Although DC plans in general, and 401(k) plans in particular, provide a great deal of latitude for employees to control their pension plan size and composition, in some cases they allow eligible workers to eschew making any kind of pension contribution whatsoever. Furthermore, when employees who have made DC contributions change jobs, they often spend the lump sum proceeds of their pension from the former employer. Employees may use the pension distributions to buy a boat or car or to take a vacation (Schultz 1993). The prospect of eligible workers who don't contribute to pensions and workers who spend the proceeds of their pensions when they change jobs has created concern that a sizable fraction of Americans will retire with minimal or nonexistent pension wealth. As one commissioner at the Securities and Exchange Commission put it, "Using retirement assets to fund current consumption could be laying the foundation for future disaster."[1]

In response to concern about employees dipping into 401(k) retirement assets, some observers have proposed returning to DB plans with mandatory coverage to ensure adequate retirement benefits for all covered workers (*Washington Post* 1993). One need not return to DB plan mechanisms to ensure mandatory coverage, however. One congressional proposal provided for a voluntary minimum 401(k) contribution rate of 3% for eligible workers; in return, the firm would become exempt from onerous reporting requirements under federal nondiscrimination laws.[2] Alternatively, the government could simply mandate minimum contributions to 401(k) plans among eligible workers, a proposal similar to that suggested by the President's Commission on Pension Policy (1981). Finally, alternatives exist to the prevailing treatment of 401(k) accounts at job separation. Currently, workers separating from jobs are allowed to spend all of their 401(k) balances (less taxes and penalty). A frequently discussed alternative would be to transfer the lump sum distributions directly to a pension "clearinghouse" that would free the former employer from record-keeping duties and discourage employees from spending the distributions before retirement.

What effect would such restrictions on 401(k) contributions and distributions have on American workers' pension saving? Presumably, mandating minimum contribution limits and sharply restricting lump sum disbursements would increase pension saving for those who don't contribute to their 401(k) or who are planning to buy a boat with their 401(k) distributions. On the other hand, such mandates might not achieve the goal of attaining financial security for those with inadequate retirement resources for at least two reasons. First, many 401(k)-eligible workers who aren't contributing may already have an existing primary pension plan or be relatively affluent in terms of nonpension saving. The anecdotal evidence about eligible employees who don't contribute to their DC plans may reflect only a small fraction of total workers, especially in comparison to those workers ineligible for any pension plan. Second, instituting minimum contribution guidelines or rollover restrictions could cause some firms to drop their pension plan altogether, either because of additional costs to the employers or because of employee resistance to restrictions on lump sum distributions.

This chapter considers how mandated contribution limits and rollover restrictions would affect U.S. workers' retirement income. To analyze the distribution of pension entitlements among current workers, we utilize the *Survey of Consumer Finances 1989* (SCF) and the supplemental *Pension Provider Survey* (PPS). The SCF provides detailed information on the income and wealth of a representative cross section of households and a special sample of high-income households drawn from tax files.[3] The employers of SCF respondents covered by pensions were subsequently interviewed, and the PPS recorded the full summary plan descriptions of the pension plans. Our detailed information on roughly 800 pension plans held by 1,000 workers allows us to determine how mandated minimum pension contributions or rollover restrictions would affect pension income adequacy among a representative sample of the working population.

In this chapter, we focus on three basic results. First, workers eligible for 401(k)s who do not contribute to them and have no alternative pension plan make up between 2% and 3% of the workforce.[4] By contrast, roughly 50% of American workers have no pension coverage at all. In both income and wealth, those who do not contribute to their pension plans appear to be somewhat better off than those ineligible to contribute to any plan. One puzzle is why 401(k)-eligible workers who neglect to contribute appear to generate so much public concern relative to the much larger group of people ineligible for any type of pension.[5]

Second, imposing a 3% or 5% minimum contribution for those eligible for 401(k) plans would improve financial security among the 5%–10% of the pension-eligible workforce with the least-generous anticipated pension income; overall, however, the effects would be quite modest. For example, under a 3% mandatory minimum contribution rate, we estimate that the annuitized pension stream at or below the 10th percentile of workers covered by a pension would increase from $5,438 under current law to $6,340, an increase of $902 annually. Above the 50th percentile, a mandated minimum contribution would have little or no effect; in the aggregate, pension benefits are predicted to rise by less than 2%.

Third, we show that mandating a minimum 50% rollover of preretirement lump sum distributions would increase retirement income by roughly 10%–25% for those in the bottom half of pension income distribution who switch jobs. The effects among workers with higher pension incomes (and those who remain with their employers for a long time) would be much smaller.[6] Firm or worker behavioral responses could largely attenuate these increased levels of pension benefits. Suppose that a 50% minimum rollover provision were enacted that allowed workers to withdraw only half their 401(k) between jobs, and as a consequence the number of enrollees decreased a uniform 5%, because either workers or employers opted out of their 401(k) plans. Then the simulated gains in retirement income would be reduced by 30% on average and by more than 50% in the distribution's lowest quartile. In sum, mandated minimum pension rollover provisions could potentially enhance retirement income if firm and employee behavioral responses are minimal.

In the sections below, we consider each policy question in turn. The next section addresses patterns of eligibility among 401(k) contributors. Following that, we examine how minimum contribution levels for 401(k)s would affect retirement annuities. A later section estimates the effects of minimum rollover provisions. The final section concludes with additional discussion of pension policy and saving behavior.

Patterns of Eligibility and 401(k) Contributions among U.S. Workers

DC plans, and in particular 401(k) plans, have become an increasingly important component of American worker pension coverage. Beller and Lawrence (1992) reported that the fraction of participants in private pensions who had a primary DC plan increased from 13% in 1975 to 32% in 1987. Samwick (1993b) used household data from the PPS to show that covered workers with a DC plan as the primary or supplemental plan increased from 21.5% in 1983 to 39.3% in 1989. The fraction of covered workers relying solely on DC plans doubled from 9.5% to 19.6% during the same period.

A large fraction of this growth came from the increase in coverage of 401(k) plans. Participants in such plans grew from 17% of the covered population in 1984 to 37% in 1988 (Silverman 1993). Among private-sector workers covered by pension plans in 1993, 35% were covered only by a 401(k) plan and another 19% were covered by a 401(k) plan in addition to another type of pension plan (U.S. Department of Labor 1994).

Despite these dramatic changes in DC coverage, Kruse (1991) showed that little of the overall shift was due to actual terminations of DB plans with replacement by a new DC plan.[7] Using more recent data, however, Papke (1995) found some offset of DB for DC plans among smaller employers, who are most likely to find DB administrative costs onerous. Still, the majority of 401(k) plans were likely to have supplemented existing DB or DC plans rather than replace them, so workers who do not contribute to a 401(k) plan may well be covered under an alternative DB or DC plan.

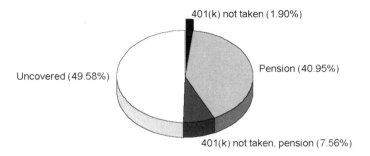

Figure 6.1
Pension status of workers, 1991
Source: SIPP, calculations by William Gale.

William Gale of the Brookings Institution has kindly provided a break-down of 401(k) eligibility and participation status using SIPP data from early 1991. The SIPP data ask specifically about the existence of a 401(k) plan offered by employers, then whether the worker participates in the plan. Figure 6.1 breaks down pension status among workers who were full- or part-time employees in 1991, weighted to be representative of the overall population. Nearly 50% of workers were not covered by any pension ("Uncovered"). Another 41% actively participated in pensions ("Pension"). This group either had no option of contributing to a 401(k), or if they were eligible, they contributed. The remaining category, con-stituting 9.5% of the working population, was eligible for a 401(k) but did not contribute. The majority of this latter group, 7.6% of the workforce, were participating in other DB or DC pension plans, even if they did not contribute to their 401(k) ("401(k) not taken, pension"). Most likely their 401(k) plans were supplemental to their primary, non-401(k) plan. The final group, constituting only 1.9% of the workforce, were eligible for a 401(k), did not contribute, and had no other pension plan available ("401(k) not taken"). CPS data suggest a somewhat higher percentage, closer to 4% of the workforce.[8] This group is the subject of concern because they are not accumulating pension resources. Note that this figure is a snapshot at a point in time; it is likely that of this group, some fraction will subsequently contribute to a pension fund as they change jobs or as retirement looms larger (just as some now contributing will likely discontinue in the future).

Consider the group of workers who do not actively participate in any pension plan. Nearly 50% of the workforce cannot be active participants because they are ineligible for a pension, and an additional 2%–4% are eli-gible but do not participate. Put another way (taking 3% as the midpoint estimate), for every 18 workers without pensions, only one does not contribute to his or her 401(k) plan. The other 17 workers simply have no pension plan available to them.

From these calculations, one might be tempted to conclude that leading financial regulators' concerns about 401(k)-eligible workers raiding their nest eggs are overblown. Two factors could militate against such a conclusion. First, workers not covered by pension plans may have alternative sources of financial security at retirement, such as a greater amount of private wealth accumulation or generally higher income levels (and consequently higher Social Security payments). Hence, the small percentage of the population who are eligible for 401(k)s but do not contribute could in fact be the most likely candidates for destitute retirements, justifying policy concerns about this group. We consider this hypothesis below. Second, although the 7.6% of workers who do not contribute to their 401(k) plans may have alternative pension plans, those pensions might provide inadequate retirement benefits, meaning that this group would still be at risk for inadequate retirement income. Examining this question requires the more detailed analytical framework introduced in the next section.

Returning to the first issue, we would like to examine income and wealth for workers conditional on their pension coverage. The SCF provides the most comprehensive data on income, wealth, and pension entitlements. We would like to identify workers who are eligible for a 401(k) but do not contribute. Unfortunately, the SCF is not so specific and identifies workers only as responding they are eligible for a pension but do not participate, so this group may include more than just 401(k) nonparticipants.

The first row in table 6.1 presents the proportion of workers who fall into each of the pension eligibility or participation categories according to the SCF. Of the total number of workers aged 25–64, 4.8% are eligible for a pension plan but do not contribute. As noted above, this number should (theoretically) be comparable to the 2% reported in the SIPP or the 4% in the CPS. However, the SCF questionnaire is less specific in discerning whether the respondent misunderstands the question or whether the worker is in fact eligible but does not participate.

The third column of row 1 shows 38% of the workforce is not covered by any pension plan. This number from the SCF seems small relative to other tabulations of pension coverage.[9] We also report the fraction of workers covered by any pension plan (58%), the percentage with a secondary 401(k) plan (6%), and the percentage with a primary 401(k) plan (6%).

Table 6.1
Other financial resources of workers by pension coverage and 401(k) enrollment (all employed workers 25–64 in 1989)

	All workers	Not covered by pension plan: eligible	Not covered by pension plan: not eligible	Covered by any pension plan	Have secondary 401(k) plan	Have primary 401(k) plan
% of workers age 25–64	100.00	4.74	37.71	57.55	6.25	5.73
% of workers age 25–44	100.00	5.17	39.96	54.87	5.87	6.05
% of workers age 44–65	100.00	3.89	33.24	62.87	6.99	5.09
Median income age 25–44	$23,000	$20,000	$14,040	$27,000	$35,000	$30,000
Median income age 45–64	$21,000	$21,000	$12,000	$25,000	$44,720	$24,960
Median net worth age 25–44	$34,800	$17,300	$14,100	$50,850	$99,850	$48,810
Median net worth age 45–64	$98,170	$72,630	$75,140	$108,970	$149,000	$188,700

Notes: Figures represent authors' calculations using the 1989 Survey of Consumer Finances. Top row is the percentage of the 73.25 million employed workers aged 25–64 described in each column. Next two rows break that age range into two age-specific subgroups. Other rows are dollars values in 1989.

The question remains, are people who do not contribute to their 401(k) plan worse off, in terms of wealth or income, than people not eligible for pension coverage? Row 4 of the table reports median income for each of these worker groups after adjusting for differences in age. For those aged 25–44, median income of workers without pension eligibility is $14,040, but median income for those covered by any pension plan is $27,000; the highest median income, $35,000, is reported for people with a secondary 401(k) plan (results are similar for the older workers). Workers who are eligible for pension plans but do not contribute have a somewhat lower median income than those who do contribute ($20,000 versus $27,000) but have higher median incomes than those not eligible for pensions at all ($20,000 versus $14,040). For older workers, median income of those eligible but who do not contribute, $21,000, is closer to median income for pension participants ($25,000) than for those who are ineligible for pensions ($12,000). In short, median income for people who eschew pension participation is somewhat lower than for those who participate, but it is substantially higher than for those not eligible for coverage at all. People who do not contribute to a 401(k) are likely to have higher incomes and hence higher Social Security benefits at retirement compared to those not eligible for pension coverage.

A somewhat different story emerges for median household net worth, measured in the SCF as the sum of all real and financial assets less all household debt. Median net worth for those 25–44 who are eligible for pensions but don't participate is $17,300, compared to $14,100 for those not covered by pension plans. By contrast, among participants in pension plans, median wealth is $50,850. It might appear the decision not to participate in a pension (even when eligible) could reflect differences in propensities toward saving more generally.[10]

In sum, there is little evidence the group of eligible workers who do not participate in their pension plans are worse off than the group of workers ineligible for pensions. If anything, the group of eligible nonparticipants has earnings more closely related to those of workers who participate in pensions. On the other hand, nonparticipants show a much lower taste for wealth accumulation than their participating counterparts.[11]

These simple tabulations may mask the possibility some workers contribute only small fractions of their income to a 401(k), so they appear as pension participants, even though their retirement income prospects are dim. In the next section, we consider the impact of mandatory contributions on the magnitude and distribution of retirement income, using as an example a proposal to mandate a minimum 3% contribution rate for any self-directed 401(k) pension plan.

Mandating Minimum 401(k) Contributions: A Simulation

What is the impact of mandating employers (or workers) contribute a specific minimum fraction of employees' (or their own) salary to a 401(k)? The answer depends on a number of factors that could affect pension coverage, including age, earnings history, tenure, and the type of plan. In this section, we abstract from such issues to isolate the impact of a contribution mandate, holding constant (or integrating over) the wide variety of earnings outcomes among workers, different ages and cohorts, and the composition of their pension. To do this, we use a methodology developed in Samwick 1993a and extended in Samwick and Skinner 1996 that uses the PPS's detailed pension formulas to simulate pension entitlement distribution for a representative sample of current workers. Our analysis examines the full distribution of pension entitlements, rather than just the mean, because much current policy debate concerns potential impact of reforms on workers with the least-generous pension entitlements.

We simulate the distribution of pension incomes using the following strategy. Consider a representative individual with average earnings at age 42 in 1989 ($32,863) and with continuous work experiences from ages 31–65. We simulate a total of 2,000 earnings histories assuming that the logarithm of earnings follows a random walk with a quartic drift with age and a 1% annual productivity growth.[12] The standard deviation of annual innovations to the logarithm of earnings is conservatively assumed to be 10%.[13] From this set, we randomly assign to each pension plan a number of earnings histories proportional to the population weight of all workers in the sample covered by that plan. In other words, if the weighted number of workers with pension plan A is 10 times the number of workers covered by pension plan B, we assign 10 random earnings histories to pension plan A for every earnings history for plan B.[14]

We then calculate pension entitlements for each plan for all its assigned earnings histories. Because some concern over 401(k) plan growth stems from the greater responsibility employees must take for investing their pension funds, we also simulate DC plan investment performance using historical capital market data from Siegel (1992).[15] For each year of each of the 2,000 earnings histories, we randomly assign a year of real-asset returns from 1900 to 1990 for investments in short-term bonds, long-term bonds, and stocks.[16] Also associated with each earnings history is a randomly chosen portfolio share that averages one-third in each asset but varies considerably across earnings histories.[17] By imposing the same share of assets on the individual for the entire time, we ensure the greatest degree of variance across workers in their rates of return on their DC plans (i.e., workers do not learn to become better investors over time). We assume an inflation rate of 4% per year and discount rate of 3% for computing present values of real dollars.

In calculating percentages of people eligible for 401(k)s, percentages who don't contribute, and percentages who have no other pension plan besides the 401(k), we use the SIPP tabulations reported in figure 6.1, because the questions in the SIPP pertain more directly to 401(k) plans. We must specify the characteristics of pension plans for those who do not participate because we need to simulate the counterfactual of what would happen in the event of a mandatory 3% or 5% contribution rate. Because the policy not taken is unobserved in the data, we randomly assign to noncontributors 401(k) plans from among those who do contribute. If the randomly chosen plan is more generous than the spurned 401(k) plan, it will tend to place mandatory contribution limits in a more favorable light.

Simulating the distribution of resulting pension benefits for a large number of individual workers corresponds to taking the mathematical expectation over four variables: (1) realizations of earnings over the individual's working life, (2) the pension plan, out of 800 different plans, in which he or she is enrolled, (3) how much the worker contributes to the 401(k) plan, and (4) the rate of return the individual receives on the DC plan investment. We abstract from any correlation (suggested in table 6.1) between lifetime income and the type of plan, amount contributed, or manner in which DC balances are invested. This allows us to compare directly mandatory contribution requirement effects on retirement income, albeit for a universe of "representative" workers with median earnings at age 42.[18]

Table 6.2 shows the percentile distribution of the simulated annuitized pension benefits, only for those eligible for a 401(k). The first column shows the annual actuarially fair pension benefit (in 1989 dollars) that would result under current pension characteristics, contribution rates, and earnings patterns.[19] The median benefits are $19,569, reflecting both the real annual one percentage point productivity gains assumed in the earnings realizations and the fact that many 401(k)-eligible workers are also covered under a DB plan (or another DC plan), so they tend to be among the workers with the best pension compensation packages. The top number in the first column, $0, reflects the absence of any pension benefit for

Table 6.2
Annuitized pension income under 3% and 5% minimum contribution rule to 401(k):401(k)-eligible only (in 1989 dollars)

Percentile of pension benefits	Current law	3% minimum contribution	5% minimum contribution	3% minimum contribution, unit elastic pension demand
5th	$ 0	$ 4,570	$ 6,374	$ 4,110
10th	5,305	6,637	8,272	6,087
25th	10,693	11,002	11,860	10,558
50th (median)	19,569	19,569	19,788	19,442
75th	31,819	31,819	31,861	31,534
90th	47,701	47,710	47,701	47,411
Mean	23,896	24,294	24,768	23,941

Notes: Unit elastic demand requires that pension coverage be randomly reduced to keep mean benefits over all workers (not just those eligible for 401(k) plans) constant after the minimum contribution is imposed. Minimum contribution limits relate to 3% or 5% of gross earnings in each year.

the worker whose pension is in the 5th percentile of those eligible for the 401(k), because roughly 6% of 401(k)-eligible workers do not participate and have no other pension plan available.[20] The 10th-percentile annuitized pension benefit, $5,305, is roughly one-quarter of the median pension. By contrast, for the (fortunate) 90th-percentile worker, the annuitized value of pension benefits is $47,701. Despite the fact that each of these simulated workers earned $32,863 at age 42, variations in subsequent (or previous) earnings draws, differences in investment returns and low pension contribution rates, and heterogeneity in the type of pension plan (or combination plan) lead to very large variations in pension income at retirement.

Suppose a mandatory overall contribution rate equal to 3% of earnings were imposed for 401(k)s. For example, if previously the employer had contributed 1% and the worker 1%, total contributions must now rise to 3%.[21] Column 2 of table 6.2 shows the impact of such a mandate. Not surprisingly, the reform would have the largest impact on those workers with the lowest pension benefits. For the 5th-percentile workers, benefits would rise from $0 to $4,570, a substantial increase in retirement resources. However, the dollar benefits of the 3% minimum contribution rule would fade rapidly at higher points of the pension income distribution; workers are predicted to gain $1,332 (25%) at the 10th percentile but only $309 (2.9%) at the 25th percentile. The largest impact would clearly be on those with the least-adequate pension plans. Even so, outside the bottom decile of those eligible for 401(k)s, the magnitude of the effect would not be large, with the 5th percentile worker not even attaining the annuitized pension income received by the 10th percentile worker under the current law ($5,305). In the aggregate, mean pension benefits would rise by only 1.7%.

Column 3 of table 6.2 shows how a 5% minimum contribution would affect annuitized pension income. At the 5th percentile, pension income would increase substantially, from $0 to $6,374, while the 10th percentile worker would receive pension income 56% higher than under current law. The increase in pension benefits would be quite small for workers above the median pension benefit. But even with a 5% mandatory contribution rate, pension benefits would still show a substantial degree of variation, with the annuitized annual pension income at the 90th percentile more than five times that at the 10th percentile. Again, this variation would be caused not by inadequate contribution rates, but by differences in earnings realizations, rates of return on investment, and the type and generosity of 401(k) and other (DB or DC) pension plans held by those who are eligible for 401(k)s.

To this point, we have not considered possible behavioral responses to mandatory contribution requirements. Firms might respond by dropping their 401(k) plans, either because employers would not want to absorb the additional contribution costs, or because employees would not want their after-tax wages to decrease, through either mandatory employee contributions or the lower gross wages employers might offer as a trade-off for increased employer contributions. Theoretically, mandates could increase overall pension income inequality if enough firms (or employees) dropped their 401(k) plans in response to the mandate. Although little is known about the elasticity of demand (or supply) for such plans, we can measure the magnitude of the behavioral responses under the assumption that total contributions to pension plans would remain unaffected. In other words, we hold constant total pension saving by assuming that the probability that firms would drop their DC plans increases proportionally to the expense of providing the 3% mandated contributions.[22] Of course, some workers who no longer were eligible for 401(k) pensions would have other pensions available, so they would not be left bereft of pension coverage.

Column 4 of table 6.2 shows the impact of these behavioral effects following the imposition of a 3% minimum contribution rate. Most of the decline in pension income would occur among those with the least-adequate pension coverage (since the mandate would most affect their plans). The assumed behavioral effects would reduce the estimated gains at the 5th percentile by 10%, but at the 10th percentile by roughly 40%. Allowing pension coverage to fall to maintain a steady mean pension income under a 5% minimum contribution would yield a pension income at the 5th percentile equal to $4,660 (compared to $4,110 for a 3% minimum), implying that increasing the minimum contribution much beyond 3% would generate little added security for the bottom of the distribution, given a sufficiently large behavioral response. Note also that the behavioral response assumed here would entail reductions in coverage uniformly at all pension income levels; if firms could discriminate between high- and low-income workers, the minimum contribution's impact would be curtailed among lower-income workers even further, leading to a possibly unchanged degree of pension inequality.

The impact of a 3% or 5% mandated minimum 401(k) pension contribution would be similar for the entire sample of all pension-eligible workers, with results shown in table 6.3. However, because of the larger universe of workers, the 5th percentile pension benefit under current law would be $2,570 rather than zero. (Four percent of this larger group is not participating in any pension plan.) At higher percentiles of the pension distribution, the mandates would have little effect. Under the 3% mandated contribution, for example, the 25th percentile pension benefits would rise from $9,942 to $10,166, an increase of only 2.3%.

Table 6.3
Annuitized pension income under 3% minimum contribution rule to 401(k): all pension-eligible workers (in 1989 dollars)

Percentile of pension benefits	Current law	3% minimum contribution	5% minimum contribution	3% minimum contribution, unit elastic pension demand
5th	$ 2,570	$ 4,618	$ 6,035	$ 4,253
10th	5,438	6,340	7,706	5,896
25th	9,942	10,166	11,113	9,941
50th (median)	17,969	17,988	18,341	17,813
75th	30,963	30,963	30,989	30,704
90th	49,076	49,076	49,076	48,862
Mean	23,461	23,775	24,291	23,491

Notes: Unit elastic demand requires that pension coverage is randomly reduced to keep mean benefits over all workers (not just those eligible for 401(k) plans) constant after the minimum contribution is imposed. Minimum contribution limits relate to 3% or 5% of gross earnings in each year.

In sum, the mandated pension contribution rule would succeed in raising pension income among those at or below the 10th percentile of the pension distribution, but employer and employee behavioral responses could attenuate or even eliminate these improvements in pension income distribution. In the next section, we consider whether a different approach —mandating minimum rollover amounts—might have a larger overall impact on pension benefits at retirement.

Mandated Rollover Provisions

In 1990, nearly $50 billion in pension assets were distributed prematurely, prior to age 59 1/2 (Yakoboski et al. 1994a). In the same year, aggregate personal saving was $175 billion, so the disposition of these pension distributions (whether saved or spent) can have a potentially large impact on aggregate saving. Of these annual distributions, only half are estimated to have been rolled over into qualified retirement accounts such as IRAs; the rest were spent or invested in household durables (such as houses).[23] What would be the impact of a mandated minimum rollover, which for simplicity we assume to be 50% of the lump sum distribution? This section uses the same large sample of pension plans to examine how such a mandate would affect retirement income.

We assume the worker changes jobs at ages 41 and 51 and holds the third job until age 65, at which point the worker retires. To focus just on job interruption impact on pension benefits, and to exclude complicating effects of possible lower wages following job separation, we assume earnings and the type of pension plan are unaffected by the job switch. In other words, it is as if the worker's pension plan is stopped at age 41 (and 51) and restarted.

Among all pension-eligible workers, median annual retirement income would be $12,720 when the worker rolled over 100% of pension assets into a qualified account, compared to only $8,530 when the worker consumed all of the lump sum distributions, or a difference of 49%.[24] Column 1 of table 6.4 presents annual pension income distribution under the assumption that half the (simulated) individuals roll over their entire lump sum distribution into a qualified IRA, which is then accumulated forward using the worker's assigned portfolio allocation and market returns. The other half of workers are assumed to spend all their lump sum distributions. Not surprisingly, such differences in saving behavior substantially widen variation in pension income; at the 10th percentile of workers (many of

Table 6.4
Annuitized pension income under restricted DC rollover spending: all pension-covered
workers switch jobs at 41 and 51 (in 1989 dollars)

Percentile of pension benefits	Current law: half of preretirement distributions rolled over, half consumed	50% minimum rollover on all preretirement distributions	50% minimum rollover, 5% reduction in DC coverage	50% minimum rollover, 10% reduction in DC coverage
5th	$ 0	$ 0	$ 0	$ 0
10th	2,405	2,976	2,548	1,980
25th	5,575	6,253	5,915	5,701
50th (median)	10,383	11,817	11,460	11,025
75th	19,044	20,524	20,247	19,799
90th	31,750	33,465	33,175	32,799
Mean	14,531	15,621	15,287	14,930

Notes: In column 1, half of the simulated individuals spend all their pre-retirement lump sum
distributions, while the other half of the simulated individuals roll their distributions into
tax-qualified accounts with the same asset portfolio and (random) returns. In columns 2–4,
simulated individuals who previously had rolled over all of their distribution continue to
do so, while simulated individuals who once spent their distributions now save half in tax-
qualified accounts and spend the other half.

whom presumably have spent their lump sum distributions at ages 41
and 51), annual retirement income would be only $2,405.[25]

Column 2 of table 6.4 reports the potential distribution of annual pension income under the assumption that the half of the population who had
previously rolled over nothing now must deposit 50% of their lump sum
distributions into a qualified IRA account (the mandate has no effect on
those who had previously rolled over all their distributions). The effects
would be substantial through the entire pension distribution. At the 10th
percentile, pension income would rise by $571, or 24%, while at the
75th percentile, pension income would rise by $1,480, or 8% of initial
pension income. This policy's aggregate effects on average benefits would
be roughly five-and-a-half times larger than those of a 3% minimum contribution rate. Of course, these results would be specific to workers who
moved twice after age 40. More mobility would strengthen the results,
less would weaken them.

Behavioral effects could attenuate the mandate's impact substantially.
Because we have little information on how such a mandate would affect
provision of (and enrollment in) 401(k) plans, we assume a 5% reduction
in DC coverage in response to the mandate. A mandatory rollover of 50%

would attenuate the gains in pension income by 30% on average and more than 50% in the bottom quartile. A 10% reduction in DC coverage would leave the lowest 5% of the distribution worse off than under the status quo. Once again, knowing the magnitude of this behavioral effect is critical in evaluating how such a mandate might affect overall saving behavior.[26]

Conclusion and Discussion

Concern has increased over the possibility of workers covered just by 401(k) pension plans neglecting to save for retirement and finding, too late, that they have insufficient economic resources to fund their retirement. This chapter has attempted to gauge the importance of this potential problem and evaluated two possible policy solutions to the problems inherent in 401(k) and other pension plans. In particular, we considered how mandated contribution rates for 401(k) plans and mandated 50% rollovers of premature lump sum distributions would affect both the level and distribution of pension benefits in the working population. First we found between 2% and 4% of the workforce do not contribute to a 401(k) plan and have no other pension coverage. Second, mandated minimum contribution rates of 3% and 5% would have relatively little impact on retirement income, except among the bottom 5th to 10th percentile of the pension distribution. By contrast, a mandated rollover would have a much larger impact on the entire distribution of pension recipients, raising average pensions by more than five times the (dollar) impact of the 3% mandate. In both cases, behavioral effects—firms or workers might decide to drop 401(k) plans because of mandated contributions or rollover limits—could sharply reduce these mandates' impact, although we know little about the correct elasticity of demand or supply for pension plans such as 401(k)s.

This chapter has focused solely on the level and distribution of retirement income, as if source of income were the only determinant of worker financial well-being. Focusing just on pension income, however, is sure to be too restrictive, since a higher pension income at retirement is likely to be matched by lower disposable income while younger. The problem is that the counterfactual is not well defined: What happens when the worker spends the dollar not contributed to the pension fund? As one report conjectured about lump sum distributions that are spent: Some consumption, such as home purchase or increased education, may enhance retirement income security. Some consumption may be necessitated by current economic hardship, i.e., a worker is laid off and needs the money to cover his or her family's current living expenses. Other consumption may result from a desire for current gratification combined with a lack of foresight.... (Yakoboski et al. 1994a, 3)

If lump sum distributions are used to purchase a house or increase education, it is not clear that forcing workers to roll over their accumulated distributions would enhance welfare. Even if the worker's objective is simply to spend the money on a vacation rather than save for retirement, one must still take the position that policy makers in Washington, D.C., are not in a better position to determine the optimal trade-off between current consumption and retirement income. Alternatively, policy makers must provide a convincing rationale for subsidizing the accumulation of assets for retirement but not for other purposes the workers themselves might value more. By the same token, a mandate to contribute 3% or 5% of earnings to a 401(k) would likely be reflected in at least a partial reduction of take-home earnings, and it is not entirely clear what should be considered the best level of saving for retirement given that such saving reduces current income.[27] We estimate the impact of various pension reforms on a narrowly defined measure of pension inequality that is explicitly not a measure of economic well-being over the entire lifetime but is nonetheless informative about future financial security in retirement.

The calculations presented above have focused on how policy mandates for pension contributions might affect the pension income among the roughly 50% of the workforce eligible for pensions. Neither mandates of minimum pension contributions nor rollover restrictions would enhance the pension benefits of the 50% without any coverage at all, leading to something of a paradox: Why the intense concern about 401(k)-eligible workers who don't contribute, when many more workers cannot contribute simply because they have no access to a pension plan?[28] In other words, the policy proposals evaluated in this chapter could, at best, improve pension income for less than 5% of workers but would leave the remaining uncovered workers, constituting half the workforce, entirely unaffected (or even worse off if the reforms affected nonpension workers' income adversely). If pension policy's goal is to improve retirement income for those with the least-generous retirement income prospects, then expanding the base of workers eligible for pensions might be more effective than encouraging eligible workers to contribute more to their pension plans.

Notes

We are indebted to William Gale, Syl Schieber, and Paul Yakoboski for very helpful suggestions. Samwick is grateful to the National Institute on Aging for financial support.

1. J. Carter Beese, as quoted in Schultz 1993.

2. H.R. 4534, 101st Congress.

3. See Kennickell and Woodburn 1992 and Kennickell and Shack-Marquez 1992 for descriptions of the SCF 1989.

4. The lower estimate comes from the SIPP, the higher from more recent data from the CPS
(U.S. Department of Labor 1994).

5. The President's Commission on Pension Policy (1981) was an exception.

6. Our estimates parallel earlier results by VanDerhei (1992).

7. Other studies that have analyzed the trend from DB to DC plans include Gustman and
Steinmeier 1992; and Ippolito 1990. Evidence cited in Silverman 1993 suggests a flattening
of the trend toward DC plans.

8. U.S. Department of Labor 1994 tabulates the CPS data from 1993.

9. Beller and Lawrence (1992) and U.S. Department of Labor (1994) present more detailed
tabulations of pension coverage. Samwick (1993b) discusses the SCF data's comparability to
that of other surveys. The simulation framework below deals explicitly with this discrepancy.

10. Another comparison is between those who are eligible but decline to participate and
those with a 401(k) primary plan, the idea being that nearly all pension plans in which participants can decline to participate are 401(k)s. Median net worth is lower for those who do
not participate: $17,300 versus $48,810 among ages 25–44, and $72,630 versus $188,700
among ages 45–64 (table 6.1). Once again, there appear to be systematic differences in
wealth accumulation patterns between those who do and do not elect 401(k) participation,
even after controlling for the modest differences in income between the two groups.

11. Unfortunately, because of the SCF's reporting convention, we cannot separately identify
people who had a primary pension plan but did not contribute to 401(k)s.

12. We estimated the parameters of the drift component of the wage process from the
March 1989 CPS by regressing the logarithm of annual earnings on age, age^2, age^3, and age^4
for full-time, white male workers. Murphy and Welch (1990) show that a quartic specification
matches the empirical age pattern of earnings more accurately than a quadratic specification
using just age and age^2. More specifically, the quadratic specification overstates the reduction or reversal of real-wage growth near retirement. Using such a specification would bias
downward DB benefits based on the last three to five years of nominal earnings.

13. Using a large sample of individual labor market histories taken from young men's Social
Security earnings records, Topel and Ward (1992) find that the evolution of wages within
jobs closely approximates a random walk. They estimate the standard deviation of the permanent innovation in log earnings to be about 13%. Using similar methods but earnings histories of workers of all ages from the *Panel Study of Income Dynamics*, Samwick (1993a) also
obtains an estimate of 13%.

14. Because the SIPP provides a more accurate estimate of the groups of pension-covered
workers in table 6.1 (no 401(k), secondary 401(k), primary 401(k)), we stratify the sample of

plans in the PPS by these three categories, use the sample weights from the SCF to get a representative sample of the plans in each group, then construct a population for each of the three groups in proportion to that group's prominence in the SIPP. The two groups that have 401(k)s are further split into contributors and noncontributors, with the former contributing 6% (the SCF-conditional mean rate of voluntary contributions).

15. See Samwick and Skinner 1996 for a more detailed discussion of asset returns.

16. To capture the persistence of shocks to asset returns (e.g., bull and bear markets), we assign the years from 1900 to 1990 to ages in the earnings history at five-year intervals and randomize the initial duration at age 31. Assigning ten-year intervals had little impact on the results below.

17. The shares are assigned by drawing three random numbers {a, b, c} from a uniform distribution and assigning the shares as a/z, b/z, c/z, where $z = a + b + c$. For a further discussion of portfolio allocations of pension funds, see Papke 1992.

18. See Samwick and Skinner 1996 for a more detailed description of our approach. In that paper, we compared DB and DC plans by simulation using both the "representative worker" approach discussed here, and a more complicated approach that allowed for different types of workers to hold different types of pension plans. Our results from those simulations showed little difference for the two approaches, suggesting that the "sorting" effects may be of second-order importance.

19. All dollar amounts in the text are in constant 1989 dollars. The consumer price index increased by 27.3% between March 1989 (the date of the survey) and March 1996.

20. That is, 1.9% of all workers do not contribute to their 401(k) plan and are not otherwise covered by a pension plan, and one-third of all workers are 401(k) eligible, so of those eligible, roughly 6% are assumed not to receive any benefits at retirement. Note that this 6% figure is likely to overestimate the true uncovered sector. Although 6% may not contribute in a given year, many will likely be covered in subsequent jobs.

21. For calculating the retirement income annuity, it does not matter whether the employer or the employee increases the overall contribution rate to 3%.

22. As noted above, whether the firm drops the plan or whether workers request dropping the plan would be irrelevant in this case, although for ease of exposition we refer to firms as dropping coverage.

23. The Employee Benefit Research Institute (EBRI) estimates that about half of all lump sum distributions are transferred to a tax-deferred saving account such as an IRA. However, premature distributions are more likely to be small, and smaller lump sum payments are less likely to be rolled over and more likely to be spent. Hence the fraction of premature distributions rolled over may be smaller than 50%, as is also suggested by the EBRI tabulations of the CPS (see Yakoboski et al. 1994a). On the other hand, IRS data on tax penalties paid on premature pension distributions in 1991 suggest that $14.4 billion was distributed prematurely and not rolled into a qualified account (Statistics of Income, Individual Returns, 1991). For further discussion of premature pension distributions, see Chang 1992.

More recent data compiled by EBRI from the April 1993 CPS sheds more light on this issue (Yakoboski et al. 1994b). According to the data, the percentage of people reporting they used the lump sum distribution for at least some tax-qualified saving rose from 34% at ages 31–40 to 62% at ages 51–60. (Forty-three percent of the older age group contributed all their distribution to tax-qualified saving, with an additional 9% placing all their distributions in non–tax qualified saving.) The percentage reporting that they used some of the distribution for consumption declined from 43% at ages 31–40 to 23% at ages 51–60. Also see Hewitt Associates 1992.

24. This figure is comparable to the 55% calculation by VanDerhei (1992), who assumed four jobs rather than the three assumed above.

25. The 5th percentile of this distribution is zero because, in addition to the 4% who do not contribute to their 401(k) (and only) pension plan, some DB plans yield no entitlement if the worker changes jobs several times. Additionally, comparing median benefits of $12,720 (i.e., complete rollover) with median benefits from table 6.3 of $17,969 for uninterrupted tenure shows job switching's partial impact on pension benefits from DB plans. Samwick and Skinner 1996 discusses both topics in greater detail.

26. We also performed these simulations for just the 401(k)-eligible workers, with similar (and more magnified) effects. One potential problem with the simulations as presented above is that we may have insufficient information about lump sum distributions for DB plans. Yakoboski et al. (1994a) suggest that roughly two-ninths of DB plans offer lump sum distributions for vested workers.

27. Bernheim (1994), for example, has suggested that most families save only one-third the amount necessary to maintain retirement income.

28. Recent proposals by the Clinton administration such as the Retirement Savings and Security Act (April 11, 1996) included provisions to encourage small businesses to sponsor 401(k) plans.

References

Beller, Daniel J., and Helen H. Lawrence 1992. "Trends in Private Pension Plan Coverage." In *Trends in Pensions 1992*, ed. John A. Turner and Daniel J. Beller. Washington, DC: U.S. Department of Labor.

Bernheim, B. Douglas. 1994. *The Merrill Lynch Baby Boom Retirement Index*. New York: Merrill Lynch & Co. New York: Merrill Lynch, Pierce Fenner of Smith, Inc July.

Chang, Angela E. 1992. "Tax Policy, Lump-Sum Pension Distributions, and Household Saving." Massachusetts Institute of Technology. Cambridge, MA. Manuscript.

Gustman, Alan L., and Thomas L. Steinmeier. 1992. "The Stampede Toward Defined Contribution Pension Plans: Fact or Fiction?" *Industrial Relations* 31 (Spring): 361–69.

Hewitt Associates. 1992. *Early Retirement Windows, Lump Sum Options, and Postretirement Increases in Pension Plans: 1992*. Lincolnshire, IL: Hewitt Associates.

Ippolito, Richard A. 1990. "Pension Plan Choice, 1979–1987: Clarifications and Extensions." Pension Benefit Guaranty Corporation. Washington, DC. Manuscript.

Kennickell, Arthur B., and Janice Shack-Marquez. 1992. "Changes in Family Finances from 1983 to 1989: Evidence from the Surveys of Consumer Finances." *Federal Reserve Bulletin* 78 (January): 1–18.

Kennickell, Arthur B., and R. Louise Woodburn. 1992. "Estimation of Household Net Worth Using Model-Based and Design-Based Weights: Evidence from the 1989 Survey of Consumer Finances." Board of Governors of the Federal Reserve System, Washington, DC. Manuscript.

Kruse, Douglas L. 1991. "Pension Substitution in the 1980s: Why the Shift Toward Defined Contribution Pension Plans?" Working Paper no. 3882, National Bureau of Economic Research, Cambridge, MA.

Murphy, Kevin M., and Finis Welch. 1990. "Empirical Age-Earnings Profiles." *Journal of Labor Economics* 8 (April): 202–29.

Papke, Leslie E. 1995. "Does 401(k) Introduction Affect Defined Benefit Plans? *National Tax Association Proceedings 1994*, 173–77.

Papke, Leslie E. 1992. "Asset Allocation of Private Pension Plans." In *Trends in Pensions 1992*, ed. John A. Turner and Daniel J. Beller. Washington, DC: U.S. Department of Labor.

President's Commission on Pension Policy. 1981. *Coming of Age: Toward a National Retirement Income Policy* (February 26, 1981). Washington, DC: Government Printing Office.

Samwick, Andrew A. 1993a. "Wage Risk Compensation Through Employer-Provided Pensions." Massachusetts Institute of Technology, Cambridge, MA. Manuscript.

Samwick, Andrew A. 1993b. "The Effect of the Tax Reform Act of 1986 on Pension Coverage: Evidence from Pension Provider Surveys." National Bureau of Economic Research, Cambridge, MA. Manuscript.

Samwick, Andrew A., and Jonathan Skinner. 1996. "How Will Defined Contribution Pension Plans Affect Retirement Income?" Dartmouth College, Hanover, NH. Manuscript.

Schultz, Ellen E. 1993. "Your Money Matters: Raiding Pension Money Now May Leave You Without a Piggy Bank for Retirement." *The Wall Street Journal*, April 7.

Siegel, Jeremy J. 1992. "The Real Rate of Interest from 1800–1990: A Study of the U.S. and the U.K.," *Journal of Monetary Economics* 29(2):227–52.

Silverman, Celia. 1993. *Pension Evolution in a Changing Economy*. EBRI Special Report no. 141. Washington, DC: Employee Benefit Research Institute.

Topel, Robert H., and Michael P. Ward 1992. "Job Mobility and the Careers of Young Men." *Quarterly Journal of Economics* 107 (May): 439–79.

U.S. Department of Labor. 1994. *Pension and Health Benefits of American Workers: New Findings from the April 1993 Current Population Survey*. Washington, DC: U.S. Government Printing Office.

VanDerhei, Jack. 1992. *Pensions, Social Security, and Savings*. EBRI Issue Brief no. 129. Washington, DC: Employee Benefit Research Institute.

Vise, David A. 1993. "A Pensionless Future? Workers at Risk as Firms Abandon Plans." *Washington Post*, May 13.

Yakoboski, Paul, et al. 1994a. *Retirement Program Lump-Sum Distributions: Hundreds of Billions in Hidden Pension Income*. EBRI Issue Brief no. 146. Washington, DC: Employee Benefit Research Institute.

Yakoboski, Paul, et al. 1994b. *Employment-Based Retirement Income Benefits: Analysis of the April 1993 Current Population Survey*. EBRI Issue Brief no. 153. Washington, DC: Employee Benefit Research Institute.

Washington Post. 1993. "Paying for Retirement." Editorial, May 14.

7 The Consequences of Population Aging on Private Pension Fund Saving and Asset Markets

Sylvester J. Schieber and
John B. Shoven

Background

In the United States the group of people born from 1946 through 1964 has come to be known as the baby boom generation. After World War II, U.S. birth rates jumped to a level significantly above long-term trends and stayed above generally expected levels until the mid-1960s, and there fore the number of people born from 1946 to 1964 constitutes an unusually large segment of the total U.S. population. Because of its size, the baby boom generation has affected various facets of the social structure more significantly during its lifetime than other comparably aged segments of the population.

For example, as the baby boomers entered the education system, they placed new demands on it. Between 1951 and 1954, the number of five- and six-year-old children in the primary education system jumped by 70%. From 1950 to 1970, when the last of the baby boomers were in primary school, enrollments jumped from 21 million to 34 million students.[1] Then, as smaller cohorts of children reached school age, school enrollments began to fall off, stabilizing to 28 million students by 1975.[2] As they came into the primary school system, the baby boomers created a fantastic demand for expanded educational services; as they exited the system, staffing positions were eliminated and schools closed as student bodies were consolidated.

Counting kindergarten, the typical primary and secondary education program in the United States takes 13 years. The leading edge of the baby boomers—those who did not immediately pursue postsecondary education—began to enter the workforce in significant numbers by 1964. The Vietnam conflict slowed the entrance of the oldest baby boom males, as many of them had a period of military service prior to entering the civilian workforce permanently. Of course, many baby boomers also pursued a college education. Thus, the baby boomers really began to enter the workforce in earnest toward the end of the 1960s and throughout the 1970s. Between 1970 and 1986, the U.S. labor force grew at a compound rate of 2.60% per year. By 1985, the youngest of the baby boomers were 21, and those who were going to enter the workforce had done so. In the latter half of the 1980s, the U.S. workforce grew at an annual rate of 0.45 percent per year.[3]

The aging process and the evolving patterns of retirement behavior among workers are predictable, thus it is possible to anticipate the baby boom generation's retirement. Because of its earlier disruptive effects on other aspects of the socioeconomic fabric, it is important to consider, as far in advance of their retirements as possible, the implications of the baby boomers' retirements on existing social and economic institutions meant to handle them. Social Security and employer-sponsored tax-qualified retirement plans provide the two largest sources of cash income for retirees today. Policymakers have focused much more attention on the Social Security system's long-term status than that of the employer-sponsored pension system.

Social Security Funding and the Baby Boom Generation

For some time, policy makers have been aware that the baby boom generation will pose particular challenges for the Social Security program, traditionally run largely on a pay-as-you-go basis. The 1983 Social Security amendments, anticipating the special burden that baby boomers' retirements would place on workers in the future, included provisions for accumulating a substantial trust fund to prefund some of the benefits promised to the boomers. In other words, the baby boom generation was expected to prefund a larger share of its own Social Security benefits than prior generations had. The amendments also reduced the benefits promised to the baby boom generation by gradually raising the age at which full benefits would be paid to age 67 after the turn of the century.

Shortly after the amendments' passage, Social Security actuaries estimated that the Old-Age, Survivors, and Disability Insurance (OASDI) trust funds would grow from around $27.5 billion in 1983 to about $20.7 trillion in 2045 (see figure 7.1). The actuaries expected the trust funds to have resources available to pay promised benefits until the youngest of the baby boomers reached 100. The first projections after the amendments' passage predicted that OASDI trust funds would be solvent until at least 2063.

Billions of dollars

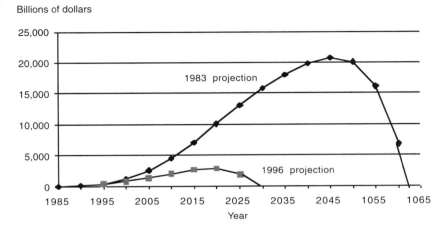

Figure 7.1
Projected OASDI trust fund accumulations (in current dollars by year of estimate)
Source: Harry C. Ballantyne, "Long-Range Projections of Social Security Trust Fund Operations in Dollars," Social Security Administration, *Actuarial Notes* (October 1983), no. 117, p. 2, and *1996 Annual Report of the Board of Trustees of the Federal Old-Age and Survivors Insurance and Disability Insurance Trust Funds* (June 1996), p. 180.

In almost every year since 1983, estimates of the accumulations in the OASDI trust funds have been revised downward. The most recent projection, published in April 1996 and shown in figure 7.1, suggests the trust funds will accumulate to only about $2.5 trillion around 2020 and then decline to a zero balance some time during 2029. At that time baby boomers will range in age from 65 to 83. Although their numbers will be declining, significant numbers will still depend on their retirement benefits to meet ongoing needs.

An alternative way to look at Social Security financing is to segment it into periods. Table 7.1 reflects the Social Security actuaries' April 1993 long-term OASDI financing projections broken into three 25-year periods. For the most part, the first 25-year period from 1994 to 2018 will precede the bulk of the baby boom's claim on the program. The first baby boomers will be eligible for early retirement benefits in 2008, and only about half of them will have attained age 62 by 2017. In addition, if the increases in the actuarial reductions for early retirement benefits and delayed retirement have any effect, the baby boomers will proceed into retirement somewhat more slowly than prior generations. Even on a purely pay-as-you-go basis, the tax revenues funding OASDI benefits are expected to

Table 7.1
Social security income and cost rates as projected under current law

Period	Income rate[a]	Cost rate[a]	Over or under (−) funding as percentage of income rate
1994–2018	12.74	12.63	0.86
2019–2043	13.10	16.89	−28.93
2044–2068	13.26	18.11	−36.58

Source: *1996 Annual Report of the Board of Trustees of the Federal Old-Age and Survivors Insurance and Disability Insurance Trust Funds* (1996), p. 22.
a. The income rate is the ratio of OASDI revenues to taxable payroll. The cost rate is the ratio of OASDI expenditures to taxable payroll.

exceed outgo as late as 2010. Over the 25-year period starting in 1994, OASDI has projected revenues about 3% above projected outlays.

As the baby boom moves fully into retirement, Social Security's financing situation is projected to turn decidedly negative. During the second 25 years reflected in table 7.1, the period when the majority of the baby boomers expect to get the majority of their lifetime benefits, projected outlays under OASDI exceed projected revenues by nearly 30%. In other words, every bit of evidence available today indicates that Social Security will not be able to provide the benefits currently being promised to the baby boom generation on the basis of existing funding legislation. Although it is impossible to anticipate exactly how OASDI projections might change over the next five or ten years, assuming no change in legislative mandates, the recent history of continual deterioration in the program's projected actuarial balances leads us to conclude the future may turn out even worse than we now anticipate.

In some regards, the challenge we face in revising our Social Security financing commitments goes beyond simply restoring the pay-as-you-go actuarial balance to the OASDI programs. During 1994, the Bipartisan Commission on Entitlement and Tax Reform looked at Social Security commitments as part of the larger total entitlement commitments embedded in current law. Figure 7.2 presents the results of their analysis. The commission found total federal revenues had been relatively constant at roughly 19% of GDP over the last 25 years or so. In 1970, approximately one-quarter of total federal revenues were devoted to entitlement programs. By 1990, their share had grown to about 10% of GDP. The commission's projections of entitlement spending under current law, however, suggested that by 2030, federal entitlement program spending would equal 20% of GDP, more than the share of GDP taxpayers have been

Percentage of GDP

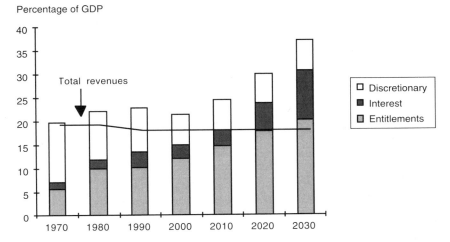

Figure 7.2
Federal outlays and revenues as a percentage of gross domestic product
Source: Bipartisan Commission on Entitlement and Tax Reform, *Interim Report to the President*
(Washington, D.C.: U.S. Government Printing Office, 1994), p. 7.
Note: Medicare and Social Security outlays follow the Medicare and Social Security Trustees'
"best estimate." Medicaid outlays are assumed to reflect demographic changes and increases
in health care costs that underlie Medicare projections. All other spending and revenues are
assumed to follow Congressional Budget Office projections through 1999 and to grow in
proportion to the overall economy thereafter.

willing to allocate to the federal government over the last 20 years.
(OASDI cash benefits account for more than one-third of current total
federal entitlement spending.) Commission projections suggest we must
not only rebalance our major entitlement programs but also significantly
constrain them from current-law levels to operate them with aggregate
budget levels the public is willing to support.

The recent history of major Social Security legislative adjustments,
specifically the 1977 and 1983 amendments, suggests that when benefit
promises exceed program revenues, at least part of the program's rebalancing comes in the form of reduced benefits for retirees. Any reductions
in future benefit promises will to some degree reduce the aggregate claim
Social Security benefits will make on future economic output. Widely
varying approaches have been proposed to deal with Social Security's
funding imbalance under current law. For example, the Social Security
Advisory Council, which focused specifically on OASDI's underfunding
during their deliberations between 1994 and 1996, considered three
options to deal with the system's projected underfunding. The first would

leave the current benefit structure basically intact, restoring balance to the system by raising additional revenues to finance these benefits. The second would curtail benefits under the current system to live within the currently legislated payroll tax rates and add a second-tier mandatory savings program to be administered through the Social Security Administration. The third would significantly restructure the current system, and workers would contribute a portion of their payroll taxes to a Personal Security Account (PSA).

The PSA would be an individual account like an IRA or a 401(k), which many workers in our society already use, but it would differ from those accounts in that participation in the program would be mandatory. A portion of the worker's share of the payroll tax channeled into the accounts would finance them. This would amount to 5% of covered payroll, approximately half the current tax used to finance retirement benefits under Social Security. PSAs would be subject to some restrictions, but they would be under the sole direction of the workers who owned them. The young survivors and disability programs would be left intact and would continue to be financed and administered through Social Security.

Under the PSA proposal, the part of the payroll tax not rebated to workers for PSAs would continue to fund Social Security retirement benefits. The current benefit structure would remain in place for individuals already retired and receiving Social Security benefits or workers grandfathered under the existing system—that is, workers over age 55 at the date of transition. Ultimately the total benefits paid to retirees would come from the system's two separate tiers. The first tier would be the basic, flat benefit provided through Social Security. For individuals with a relatively full career of covered earnings, this benefit would be roughly equal to $410 in 1996 dollars, indexed by the growth in average wages for future years. In retirement, benefits would be indexed by the CPI. Accumulations in the PSA would finance the remaining benefits.[4]

A number of changes under the PSA proposal have implications for both individual and national savings. Under current law, Social Security actuaries estimate the present value of benefits that would be paid over the next 75 years is $21.3 trillion. The assets now in the trust fund plus the tax income and interest that would accrue to the OASDI trust funds over the next 75 years have an estimated value of $18.8 trillion. The problem we face in financing current-law benefits is that, in present-value terms, benefit obligations exceed the resources to pay those benefits by $2.5 trillion over the projection period. Stated alternatively, the actuaries estimate that if we had an extra $2.5 trillion in the Social Security trust funds today, at tax rates now in effect we would have sufficient resources to pay the benefits promised under current law for the next 75 years. This $2.5 trillion shortfall in Social Security funding is not carried on our government balance sheet as formal debt, although current provisions in the Social Security Act define it as a statutory obligation. It differs from formal federal debt in that Congress has reserved the right to redefine the provisions of the Social Security Act at any time. In other words, Congress can renege on the $2.5 trillion with the public having no legal recourse. The issue of political recourse, if such a prospect were to arise, is a different matter.

If the PSA proposal were enacted today, with a transition to the modified program to begin in 1998, the estimated present value of OASDI obligations over the next 75 years would drop immediately to $14.6 trillion, $6.7 trillion less than the obligations under current law. Because a portion of the payroll tax would no longer be going into the trust funds, the estimated present value of current assets plus future income for the trust funds would also fall, to $14.7 trillion. Over the 75-year period, the estimated resources to pay benefits would exceed estimated obligations by $114 billion. In other words, we would convert the $2.5 trillion present-value deficit into a $114 billion surplus.

Under this proposal, the PSA balances themselves would become a tremendous repository of national savings. In 1998, the year that the proposal calls for the modified system to be implemented, these accounts would accumulate $115 billion in today's dollars. By 2002, they would break the half-trillion-dollar mark; by 2010, the $1.5 trillion dollar mark in 1996 dollars; and by 2030, the year the current system is projected to deplete its funds, they would hold $3.5 trillion. By the end of the transition, the balances in the PSAs would equal 1.7 times gross domestic product. In other words, the PSA proposal would not only eliminate the current system's unfunded liability, it would also significantly reduce the government's overall future obligations while simultaneously increasing the wealth holdings of America's workers. To accomplish this tremendous feat, a cost must be borne by someone.

The proposed PSA transition financing mechanism would spread the cost of moving from the current Social Security system to the modified system over roughly 70 years. The transition could be accomplished in a shorter time, but a much smaller number of our citizens would bear the cost, raising serious intergenerational equity questions. Although they favor financing the transition with a consumption tax, such as a national sales tax, PSA proposal proponents, lacking the machinery to collect such a tax, have settled on an incremental, temporary payroll tax as the financing mechanism. Under the 70-year transition, the payroll tax would increase roughly 1.5 percentage points on covered earnings. Granted there is a great reluctance to increase the tax burden on anyone today, we nonetheless cannot escape the laws of arithmetic: The only way to increase saving through Social Security reform is to have workers actually put some of their money in the bank. The transition financing required to move from an unfunded retirement system to one significantly funded would let workers do just that while also letting the Social Security program pay off previously earned benefits. PSA proposal proponents believe workers will be willing to pay a 1.5% "liberty tax" on their wages if they perceive they are getting real value in return and this assures their retirement security.

Because the proposed transition from the current system to a modified system stretches over 70 years, the proposal also requires some transitional borrowing—that is, the issuance of "liberty bonds." In 2005, the amount of the borrowing would be the equivalent of 1.5% of covered payroll; by 2010 the rate of borrowing would drop to 1%. Between 2030 and 2035, we would begin to pay off the liberty bonds and completely pay them off between 2065 and 2070. In present-value terms, the liberty bonds' accumulated value in 1995 dollars would peak at slightly less than $650 billion around 2032. Critics of the proposal have characterized the potential issuance of the liberty bonds as a massive new federal borrowing program. In fact, the liberty bonds would only convert some of the current system's unfunded obligations temporarily to more formal government debt. The accumulated borrowing, at its peak, would be less than one-quarter of the unfunded obligations we face under current law. In this regard, the PSA proposal would significantly reduce total government obligations. The liberty bonds would merely be a temporary mortgage to allow the equitable elimination of existing statutory liabilities. At no time during the transition would the accumulated liberty bonds total more than 25% of the accumulated balances in the PSAs. Although the proposal would convert some statutory liabilities into more formal debt instruments, it would also create a tremendous pool of saving that could easily absorb the liberty bonds plus other expanding forms of financial investments.

To solve our country's growing entitlement dilemma, we must shrink entitlement programs, not merely balance them on some actuarial basis. Both of the Social Security Advisory Council's other proposals would also balance the program's financing and obligations. But the proposal that would maintain the current benefit structure would eliminate only a minuscule portion of the total projected obligations under current law—less than 1%. The proposal that would scale back the benefits provided through the traditional program to fit within the current payroll tax rates, supplemented with a mandatory savings program, would reduce obligations somewhat more—about 11.6% over the next 75 years. The entitlement commission's projections suggest entitlements would have to be cut in half by 2030 to be held to the 1990 share of GDP allotted to them. Though the PSA proposal doesn't get that far, it would reduce current-law obligations by 31.5% over the 75-year projection period. The challenge is to find solutions to our national entitlement financing problem that not only restore balance to these programs but also restore balance at levels taxpayers will support.

Employer-Sponsored Retirement Plan Funding and the Baby Boom Generation

In the general context of retirement policy it is interesting that there is so much consternation about Social Security's long-term prospects and the potential underfunding of benefits for the baby boom generation but hardly any concern about the funded pension system's long-term prospects. A review of the effects of recent legislation and contributions to employer-sponsored retirement plans suggests there may be reason for concern on the pension front as well.

Employer-sponsored retirement programs typically operate in a significantly different environment than the federal Social Security program. Although the federal government operates its own employer-sponsored retirement programs largely on a pay-as-you-go basis, most state and local governments prefund retirement obligations on some basis, and ERISA and the Internal Revenue Code (IRC) require private employers to fund their retirement obligations on the basis of rules laid out therein.

ERISA became law in 1974. Its purpose was to provide more secure retirement benefits for all participants in tax-qualified plans. Among other things, ERISA established rules for including workers in plans, specified when they had to be guaranteed a benefit, and required benefits be funded on a schedule. For a plan to qualify for retirement plan tax preferences in the IRC, it must meet certain requirements to assure benefits being promised are actually provided. All plans operate under fiduciary requirements seeking to assure they prudently invest plan assets solely for the purpose of providing the benefits they promise. In addition, ERISA requires plan trustees to disclose relevant financial and participation data to the government periodically so the plan's ongoing viability and operation can be assured.

Defined-contribution plans have straightforward funding requirements. On the date the plan rules require a contribution, the employer must make a contribution to the plan equal to the obligation. In this case, the employer is not obligated to make any additional contributions for prior periods. The plan's ability to provide an adequate retirement benefit depends heavily on the size of the periodic contributions and the investment returns to plan assets.

Defined-benefit plans have somewhat more complicated funding requirements because such plans promise future benefits. If a worker enters a firm at age 25, works until age 65 and is retired under the plan for 20 years before dying, his span of life under the plan is 60 years. Essentially, under ERISA funding requirements for defined-benefit plans, the employer gradually contributes enough to the plan so the promised benefits will be fully funded when a worker retires. An actuarial valuation of the plan's obligations and assets and specific funding minimums and maximums specified in the law determine the annual contribution to the plan. The funding minimums assure that employers are laying aside money to pay promised benefits, the funding maximums that they do not make extraordinary contributions to the plan simply to avoid paying federal taxes.

Given these seemingly strong funding and disclosure requirements, it may seem odd to worry about the funding of employer-sponsored pension obligations, at least those of private plan sponsors. The problem is an inherent neurosis in federal law governing pensions between the provisions aimed at providing retirement income security on the one hand and limiting the value of the preferences accorded pensions in the federal tax code on the other. From ERISA's passage in 1974 until the early 1980s concerns about benefit security held the upper hand in determining federal policy toward pensions. Since 1982, policies aimed at limiting tax leakages related to employer-sponsored retirement plans have played the dominant role. Though a number of tax law changes since 1982 have affected defined-contribution plans, they have affected defined-benefit plans somewhat more profoundly. This was especially true of OBRA87.

Defined-benefit plans have a special appeal for workers because they promise a level of benefits regardless of financial market gyrations. Over the years, such plans have had a special appeal for employers because they have provided the flexibility to fund promised benefits actuarially over their employees' working lives. Traditionally, actuarial funding allowed employers to fund in advance benefits that increase steeply at the end of workers' careers. Through 1987 employers were allowed to fund up to 100% of the projected benefits that would be paid to a worker at retirement based on his or her current tenure, age, and actuarial probabilities of qualifying for a benefit. OBRA87 dropped the full-funding limits for defined-benefit plans from 100% of ongoing plan liability to 150% of benefits accrued to date.

OBRA87's new funding limits had the effect of delaying the funding of an individual's pension benefit relative to prior law. Table 7.2 helps show the implications of the revised funding standards. For purposes of developing this example, we assumed a worker begins a job at a firm at age 25 earning $25,000 per year. We assumed the worker's pay would increase at a rate of 5.5% per year throughout his or her career. This individual participates in a defined-benefit plan that pays 1% of final average salary at age 65. We assumed accumulated plan assets would earn a return of 8% per year.

The column labeled "Projected unit credit contribution rate" shows the contribution rate, as a percentage of the worker's salary, required to fund this individual's benefit at retirement under the projected unit-credit funding method. The other four contribution rates show what effect imposing a funding limit of 150% of accrued benefits would have on workers at four different points in their careers. The column labeled "Age 25" was developed assuming the worker is covered by the more restrictive funding limit throughout his or her career. The "Age 35," "Age 45," and "Age 55" columns were developed assuming the new funding limit was not imposed until the individuals had already participated in the plan for 10, 20, and 30 years respectively.

For the worker covered by OBRA87 throughout his or her career, the full-funding limits mean that the plan sponsor's contributions to the plan during the first half of the career, until age 45, will be less than if the plan were being funded on an ongoing basis. Of course lower contributions early in the career mean that contributions in the latter half would have to be higher to fund the plan's promised benefits. In this particular example, the plan contribution rate during the worker's early to mid-50s would have to be more than twice the contribution rate under the projected unit-credit funding method.

For the worker not hit by the contribution limits until ten years into the career, the imposition of the contribution limit implies that the employer would subsequently have a nine-year contribution holiday when no contributions would be made. In this case, the accrued benefit would have to catch up with the level of funding accomplished early in the career. Again,

Table 7.2
Effects of OBRA87 full-funding limits on contribution rates for workers at ages when implemented

Age	Pay	Projected unit-credit contribution rate	Contribution rates at various ages under funding limit of 150% of accrued benefit			
			Age 25	Age 35	Age 45	Age 55
25	$ 25,000	4.2%	0.9%	4.2%	4.2%	4.2%
26	26,375	4.3	0.9	4.3	4.3	4.3
27	27,826	4.4	1.0	4.4	4.4	4.4
28	29,356	4.5	1.1	4.5	4.5	4.5
29	30,971	4.6	1.2	4.6	4.6	4.6
30	32,674	4.7	1.4	4.7	4.7	4.7
31	34,471	4.8	1.6	4.8	4.8	4.8
32	36,367	4.9	1.8	4.9	4.9	4.9
33	38,367	5.0	2.0	5.0	5.0	5.0
34	40,477	5.2	2.3	5.2	5.2	5.2
35	42,704	5.3	2.6	0.0	5.3	5.3
36	45,052	5.4	2.9	0.0	5.4	5.4
37	47,530	5.5	3.2	0.0	5.5	5.5
38	50,144	5.7	3.5	0.0	5.7	5.7
39	52,902	5.8	3.9	0.0	5.8	5.8
40	55,812	5.9	4.4	0.0	5.9	5.9
41	58,882	6.1	4.9	0.0	6.1	6.1
42	62,120	6.2	5.4	0.0	6.2	6.2
43	65,537	6.4	6.0	0.0	6.4	6.4
44	69,141	6.5	6.7	1.8	6.5	6.5
45	72,944	6.7	7.4	7.4	0.0	6.7
46	76,956	6.8	8.2	8.2	0.0	6.8
47	81,188	7.0	9.1	9.1	0.0	7.0
48	85,654	7.2	10.0	10.0	0.0	7.2
49	90,365	7.3	11.1	11.1	0.0	7.3
50	95,335	7.5	12.3	12.3	0.0	7.5
51	100,578	7.7	13.5	13.5	1.5	7.7
52	106,110	7.9	15.0	15.0	15.0	7.9
53	111,946	8.1	16.5	16.5	16.5	8.1
54	118,103	8.2	18.2	18.2	18.2	8.2
55	124,599	8.4	16.2	16.2	16.2	0.0
56	131,452	8.6	14.6	14.6	14.6	10.8
57	138,682	8.8	13.4	13.4	13.4	10.5
58	146,309	9.1	12.6	12.6	12.6	10.3
59	154,356	9.3	12.0	12.0	12.0	10.3
60	162,846	9.5	11.5	11.5	11.5	10.2

Table 7.2 (continued)

Age	Pay	Projected unit-credit contribution rate	Contribution rates at various ages under funding limit of 150% of accrued benefit			
			Age 25	Age 35	Age 45	Age 55
61	171,802	9.7	11.3	11.3	11.3	10.3
62	181,251	9.9	11.2	11.2	11.2	10.4
63	191,220	10.2	11.1	11.1	11.1	10.5
64	201,737	10.4	11.1	11.1	11.1	10.7

the contribution rate in the mid-50s would be more than twice what it was under projected unit-credit funding. For the worker not hit until age 45, the contribution holiday would be shorter, but the same general effect of delaying retirement funding would significantly increase late-career contribution requirements given the level of promised benefits. Finally, for the worker not hit until age 55 by the new funding limit, the contribution holiday would be only one year, and though contributions during the remaining career would be higher than under projected unit-credit funding, the implications would be far less significant than in the previous cases.

In 1988, when OBRA87 funding limits took effect, the leading edge of the baby boom generation was age 42. The trailing edge was age 24. OBRA87 has had the gross effect of significantly delaying the funding of the baby boom generation's defined-benefit retirement promises. Given the significant numbers of workers falling within the baby boom cohorts, OBRA87 has created an overall slowdown in pension funding. As this legislation was being considered, The Wyatt Company analyzed its 1986 survey of actuarial assumptions and funding covering 849 plans with more than 1,000 participants to estimate the effects of the new funding limits. It found 41% of the surveyed plans had an accrued benefit security level of 150% or greater. All of these plans would have been affected by the new limit had it been in effect for 1986 and could not have made deductible contributions. For a subset of 664 plans for which they could estimate the marginal effects of the new limits, 40% would be affected by the new proposal, compared with only 7% under prior limits.[5]

In its 1987 survey of actuarial assumptions and funding, The Wyatt Company reported 48% of the plans had an accrued benefit-security ratio of 150% or more. Because plans at this funding level cannot make deductible plan contributions, the percentage of plans overfunded by this measure should decline over time. In its 1992 survey, Wyatt found only 37%

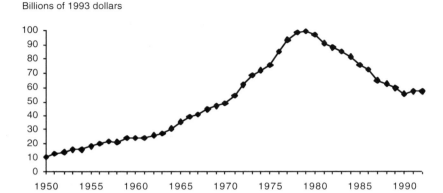

Billions of 1993 dollars

Figure 7.3
Real employer contributions to private pension and profit-sharing plans
Source: Derived by the authors from the National Income and Product Accounts.

of large defined-benefit plans had accrued benefit-security ratios of 150%
or greater.[6]

OBRA87 significantly limited the funding of defined-benefit plans, but
it was only one of several pieces of legislation that affected the funding
of tax-qualified retirement plans after 1981. In 1982, TEFRA reduced and
froze for a period of time the dollar funding and contribution limits for
both defined-benefit and defined-contribution plans. TEFRA also established new discrimination tests which had the practical effect of lowering
contributions for many plans. The next year's Deficit Reduction Act extended the freeze in funding and contribution limits TEFRA established.
In 1986, the TRA again reduced and froze funding and contribution limits
for tax-qualified plans. Finally, OBRA93 included provisions that reduced
the amount of an individual employee's compensation that could be considered in funding and contributing to tax-qualified plans. OBRA93's
provisions have the practical effect of further limiting the funding of
employer-sponsored retirement programs.

Figure 7.3 shows the annual employer contributions to private pension
and profit-sharing plans dating back to just after World War II. Contributions gradually increased through the early 1970s then escalated as
ERISA was passed and implemented. But around the time the federal
government started passing the various restrictive tax measures affecting
employer-sponsored retirement plans, contributions began to decline. By
1990, employer nominal contributions to these plans were about 15%

below contribution levels in the early 1980s and in real terms were about 45% below the level at the end of the 1970s. On an inflation-adjusted basis, contributions in 1990 were at about the same level they had been in 1970, four years before ERISA's passage.

Most of the past decade's pension legislation has evolved within the context of short-term fiscal considerations. The need to raise revenues to reduce the federal government's deficit has delayed the funding of the baby boom generation's pension benefits with virtually no consideration of the long-term impact on benefit cost or viability. Although the Social Security Act established a board of trustees to oversee the OASDI financial operations and requires the board report to Congress on the programs' financial and actuarial status, no similar oversight body identifies pending problems with the funded pension system and warns policymakers about them. Retirement plan sponsors are individually required to disclose their plans' current funding status periodically, but the evolving policy focus pushing plan sponsors to fund for only current obligations hardly encourages individual planning for longer-term contingencies. In the aggregate, public policymakers have completely ignored tax policy's long-term implications on pension funding to minimize short-term structural imbalances underlying federal fiscal policy. In the following sections we attempt a longer-term view of pension funding.

Methodology of Current Study

This section briefly outlines the underlying methods, assumptions, and inputs used to develop the estimates presented in the next section. Projections of the U.S. pension system require a long-term projection of the population and workforce, and their respective characteristics. For purposes of this exercise, we were not interested in developing a long-term demographic and labor force projection model. To develop such a model would have been a more Herculean undertaking than we were prepared to commit to in the time available. Second, we felt the nature of our projection might lead to comparisons with the long-term Social Security projections and thought it would make sense to have the same underlying demographic and workforce characteristics as utilized in those projections. Thus we began with Social Security's 75-year projections of the U.S. population, which gave us population estimates by single-year attained ages between 0 and 99 for each of the projection years. We also started with their projections of the workforce in each year, distributed in five-year age cohorts.

From published data and our own computations developed using the Internal Revenue Service Form 5500 for pension reporting plus computations from the March 1992 CPS and the 1991 SIPP, we developed age- and sex-specific rates of participation, vesting in, and receipt of benefits from defined-benefit and defined-contribution plans. We developed age and sex-specific distributions of tenure in current job, important for projecting the vesting rates of participants in pension plans. We also developed estimates of total wages for the economy's private, state and local, and federal sectors from Bureau of Economic Analysis data published in the NIPA. Estimates of age and sex-specific pay levels were developed.

We used the IRS Form 5500 files in conjunction with data from the Employee Benefit Research Institute's *Quarterly Pension Investment Report* (QPIR) to estimate the starting total distribution of assets and contributions between defined-benefit and defined-contribution plans. We also used the QPIR data to estimate the distribution of financial assets held by plans across various forms of investments. Table 7.3 shows the resulting distribution of assets by plan type. Focusing on the private defined-benefit and defined-contribution plans in this paper, we note with interest the relatively large amount of cash and other short-term investments these pension funds hold, despite the long-run nature of the funds themselves. Equities, which have a superb track record over long holding periods, amount to only 36% to 41% of the total portfolio. Given historic returns, the pension funds would be better off with a larger stake in stocks. Table 7.3 also shows our assumed real rates of return for the different asset cat-

Table 7.3
Asset allocation of pension plans as of July 1992 (in percentage points)

Type of plan	Equities	Bonds	GICs	Real estate	Cash
Private defined benefit	36 %	33 %	0 %	15 %	16 %
Private defined contribution	41	14	13	6	26
Federal defined benefit	44	44	1	6	5
Federal defined contribution	30	70	0	0	0
State and local defined benefit	44	44	1	6	5
State and local defined contribution	33	49	5	8	5
Real return rate	5.0	2.0	1.2	2.0	0.0

Blended real rate for private defined benefit plans: 2.76

Blended real rates for private defined contribution plans: 2.65

Sources: Asset allocation: EBRI's Quarterly Pension Investment Report; rates of return: authors' assumptions.

egories. The numbers are loosely based on the information in Ibbotson 1993, although we are admittedly conservative.[7] Ibbotson reports that the geometric average real rate of return for the Standard and Poor's 500 stock portfolio over the years 1926–92 was 7.0%. The corresponding average real rate of return on long-term corporate bonds was 2.3%, while it was 0.5% for short-term Treasury bills. We have no corresponding data for GICs, which are fixed-income contracts typically issued by insurance companies and featuring a somewhat shorter maturity than long bonds. As the reader can see, we have consistently assumed rates of return somewhat below the long-run averages Ibbotson calculated.

The Social Security population projection was distributed by age, sex, and workforce participation for each year of the projection. Our analysis distributed the workforce into three separate sectors: private employment, state employment, and federal employment. The working population was further distributed by tenure and pension participation status. In each year of the projection the population and workforce were rolled forward one year with appropriate mortality decrements and workforce adjustments to account for job leavers, entrants, and changers. We made an underlying assumption there was 14% turnover of workers between jobs each year.

We developed projections separately for private-employer plans, state and local defined-benefit plans, and the federal employee thrift plan. In each case, we developed separate projections for defined-benefit and defined-contribution plans, then aggregated them. For example, in the projection for the private sector, we estimated total employer contributions to private plans were 2.8% of payroll, approximately 30% of which has been going into defined-benefit plans in recent years. We estimated employee contributions to private plans to be 1.75% of payroll, with slightly less than 2% going to defined-benefit plans. Based on Form 5500 files of plans with 100 or more participants, we estimated employer contributions to defined-contribution plans were 1.13 times employee contributions to those plans.

In the initial year, benefits were estimated from Form 5500 files and the QPIR data. Going forward, benefits were estimated on the basis of workers covered by a pension and passing into immediate retirement starting at age 54, at which age we assumed 3.7% of existing workers would retire. By age 80, we assumed all remaining workers would retire. For workers who terminated their employment under a defined-benefit plan, we assumed if they were vested they would be paid a deferred benefit at age 65. We calculated the accrual rate of the benefit formula for those working until the age of full retirement benefits to be 1.25% of final salary per year of service on average. For those receiving a deferred benefit it was 1.00% of final salary per year of service. We assumed that 40% of workers participating in a defined-contribution plan who terminated prior to retirement would take a lump sum benefit and use it for some purpose other than meeting their retirement needs. Under defined-contribution plans, benefits generally commence at retirement and are paid out as an annuity over a maximum of 30 years.

Economic assumptions in large part drive future contributions and trust fund accumulations. Our assumptions on inflation, 4.0% per year, and wage growth, 5.1% per year, correspond with those used in the Social Security projections under the second option for saving the system discussed above.

Baseline Projections for the Private Pension System

Table 7.4 shows our current combined projections for defined-benefit and defined-contribution private pension plans. Under our forecast assumptions, the total private pension system assets continue to grow in nominal terms for the next 60 years. However, this growth is slowing almost continuously. For instance, in 1993 the benefits (payouts) of the defined-benefit and defined-contribution private plans combined are 83% of total contributions. This means, of course, that there is a net inflow of funds into the total system, even without taking into account the investment return on the $3 trillion asset pool. However, by the year 2006 benefits are projected to be 102.4% of contributions, and we expect that aggregate benefits will continue to outstrip contributions for the entire remaining period through 2065. By 2025 benefits are projected to be 163% of contributions.

If inflation and asset returns match our assumptions, the value of pension assets will continue to climb, albeit at slowing rates, until peaking (in nominal terms) in 2052. In real or relative terms, however, pension assets are projected to peak and begin to fall much earlier. Our model indicates the ratio of pension assets to total payroll (at 1.25 in 1994) will climb modestly until reaching a peak of 1.36 in 2013. The ratio is projected to fall after 2014 and drop below 1.0 for the first time in 2038. Real inflation-adjusted pension assets would peak in 2024 with our baseline assumptions.

The important story from our analysis is that pensions could gradually cease to be the major engine of aggregate saving they have been for the past 20 years or more. Figure 7.4 shows the private pension system's total real saving (projected contributions less benefits plus real inflation-adjusted asset returns) relative to the economy's projected total private

Table 7.4
Combined private defined-benefit and defined-contribution projections for selected years, 1992–2065 (all dollar amounts in billions)

Year	Assets	Benefits	Contributions	Investment income	Net inflow	Real net inflow	Total payroll	Saving/payroll
1992	2,870	86	105	181	201	86	2,313	0.037
1993	3,070	93	112	194	214	91	2,465	0.037
1994	3,284	99	120	207	228	97	2,626	0.037
1995	3,512	107	128	221	242	102	2,794	0.036
1996	3,754	116	136	236	257	107	2,971	0.036
1997	4,011	125	145	252	272	112	3,157	0.035
1998	4,283	135	154	269	288	117	3,351	0.035
1999	4,571	145	164	286	305	122	3,555	0.034
2000	4,876	154	174	304	323	128	3,771	0.034
2005	6,664	231	231	413	413	147	5,013	0.029
2010	8,913	347	303	549	505	149	6,580	0.023
2015	11,606	517	392	710	585	121	8,532	0.014
2020	14,662	751	504	891	644	57	10,993	0.005
2025	17,964	1,056	648	1,088	680	(39)	14,121	−0.003
2030	21,399	1,430	838	1,287	694	(162)	18,243	−0.009
2035	24,889	1,876	1,089	1,482	695	(300)	23,683	−0.013
2040	28,287	2,427	1,414	1,660	647	(485)	30,725	−0.016
2045	31,281	3,140	1,824	1,807	491	(760)	39,643	−0.019
2050	33,097	4,088	2,341	1,865	118	(1,206)	50,892	−0.024
2055	32,466	5,345	2,999	1,766	(580)	(1,879)	65,212	−0.029
2060	27,411	6,972	3,847	1,363	(1,762)	(2,858)	83,641	−0.034
2065	15,172	9,038	4,945	462	(3,630)	(4,237)	107,513	−0.039

Real saving/payroll

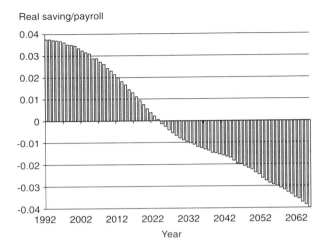

Figure 7.4
Potential real saving of private pensions relative to total private payroll for the years 1992–2065 (assuming current plan characteristics and contribution rates persist)

payroll for 1992 to 2065. We use total payroll as the scaling factor simply because it is a readily available by-product of the Social Security forecasting operation. Figure 7.4 shows that under our assumptions the pension system would continue to generate significant investable funds for the U.S. economy for the next 20 years or so. In fact, the decline would be very minor for about the next 10 years, then would steepen considerably. By 2024, the pension system is projected to cease being a net source of saving for the economy and in fact to become from that point increasingly a net dissaver. By 2040, the net real dissaving would be more than 1.5% of payroll, and by 2065 the negative saving is projected to reach almost 4.0% of payroll. The pension system's change from a large net producer of saving to a large absorber of saving or loanable funds will likely have profound implications for interest rates, asset prices and the economy's growth rate.

It should be emphasized the prediction's timing of the change in pensions from net buyer of assets to net seller is very sensitive to our assumptions about rates of return earned on pension investments as well as to the assumed level of pension contributions. However, we feel that the pattern of figure 7.4 is almost inevitable; only the timing could be somewhat different than pictured. If investment returns exceed our fairly conservative assumptions, then the decline of pension saving will be delayed and more modest. Still, the demographic structure is such that it will by necessity occur. It is not even realistic to view this as a negative development. After all, pension assets are accumulated to provide the resources the elderly need in retirement. It is only natural that when we have an extraordinarily large number of retirees, the private pension system's real assets will shrink, and the system will at least temporarily cease being a source of new investment funds for the economy.

One concern that all this may raise is the impact on the prices of pension assets, mainly stocks and bonds. We share that concern to some degree but cannot predict the size or timing of any effect. One thing to note in this regard is that although the pension system will become a less important purchaser of securities, it will not become a net seller for quite a while. As noted earlier, our model predicts benefits will first exceed contributions in 2006. However, at that point the annual investment income (dividends, interest, and capital gains) on the $7 trillion portfolio should approximate $450 billion in nominal terms and $170 billion in real terms. There would be no reason to be net sellers of assets at that time and, in fact, we would suppose pensions will still be accumulating assets then. Under our conservative assumptions, the pension system will more likely begin to be a net seller in the early part of the next century's third decade. This could depress asset prices, particularly since the U.S. demographic structure does not differ greatly from those of Japan and Europe, which also will have large elderly populations at that time. The asset-price effect, if it occurs, would also likely affect all long-term assets. We think high real interest rates could depress the prices of stocks, bonds, land, and real estate. Although this might suggest that a good investment for this period would be short-term Treasury bills, the effect, if it occurs, is likely to be gradual and last for decades. In the 20th century, the longest stretch of time over which Treasury bills outperformed equities was about 15 years. We have little else to go on, but we certainly are not advocating that long-term investors invest in short-term instruments to ride out this demographic tidal wave. In fact, it is our opinion that far too many people invest in short-term instruments for long-term accumulations.

Under our baseline assumptions, the outlook for defined-contribution plans is relatively optimistic. Our model shows defined-contribution plan assets growing relative to economy-wide aggregates over the next 30 years or so, then stabilizing at the relatively larger level. Using total economy-wide payroll as our scaling factor, defined-contribution assets are now about 37% of one year's payroll. We project those assets to climb to 52% of payroll by 2000, to 70% by 2010, and to level out at about 85% for 2025 and beyond. The defined-ontribution system by its nature is not susceptible to running out of assets and, indeed, we do not project any such occurrence. The private defined-contribution system would be a modest net source of saving in the economy even in the period with the maximum number of baby boom retirees.

With our baseline assumptions, however, private defined-benefit plans would experience significant net outflows (dissaving). Benefits under these plans already exceed contributions; in fact, they are roughly three times contributions. The robust investment returns of the past decade or so have permitted and in fact compelled this. If investment returns drop to our conservative figures and if firms contribute a total of 2.8% of payroll to pension plans, then defined-benefit plan real assets will begin to fall immediately. Defined-benefit pension assets (now 88% of the economy's total payroll) would fall to 77% of total payroll by 2000, 66% by 2010, and 42.5% by 2025. The net flow of funds into the defined-benefit plans (or savings) would be positive, but only in nominal terms. Even nominal defined-benefit saving would become negative by 2025, and the entire stock of defined-benefit plan assets would be exhausted by 2043.

This is not a forecast of doom for the defined-benefit plans; it is simply a "what if" exercise. If by magic our rate-of-return assumptions proved to be precisely accurate, employers would be forced to increase their pension contributions above the 2.8% of aggregate payroll we have assumed or to curtail the pension benefits they offer workers. Although existing workers' vested benefits cannot be cut, certainly changes in plan design can reduce the accrual of new benefits. This tough choice of higher costs or lower pension benefits would occur long before 2043, when the model says that defined-benefit plan assets would be exhausted. Government regulators and pension actuaries would sound the alarm, decades, we hope, before the forecast could come true. The problem may become apparent, and the tough choice may have to be faced very early in the next century. We are concerned that employers may have gotten used to the very low contributions many have had to make to defined-benefit plans in recent years thanks to an extraordinary performance by financial markets and the constraints the federal regulatory environment imposes on funding. When they face their pension plans' higher long-run funding costs under more normal return realizations, they may choose to curtail the benefits they offer. It is also possible that at just about the time this is being resolved, we as a society will have to acknowledge the fact that Social Security is not in long-run equilibrium; once again, the choice will be either to raise taxes or lower benefits. In this sense, both Social Security and the funded private defined-benefit pension system will likely face cost pressure to scale back retirement benefits.

Alternative Projection Scenarios

As the discussion above suggests, the baseline scenario we have developed here is not sustainable. ERISA funding requirements would not permit the contingency of the whole private defined-benefit pension system running out of assets while accruing massive unfunded liabilities. If private employers were to face the prospect that they could not meet future benefit obligations, ERISA would require they either contribute additional funds to their plans or curtail the benefits being offered under them. Current contribution and accrual rates in the face of the workforce's demographic structure will require that contributions to plans increase or that benefits be curtailed.

A number of scenarios can be considered in terms of employers increasing contributions to cover accruing benefit obligations. In one, employers would delay increased funding for some time but ultimately would increase defined-benefit funding sufficiently to pay the benefits the current benefit structure implies. In another, employers would increase their contribution rates in the very near future to a level that would indefinitely sustain private-sector defined-benefit plans at approximately current levels of funding relative to liabilities. The former strategy would create the risk that when we reach the point where employers must increase their contributions, they will discover that they are not able or willing to make such a large commitment, and covered workers would then have very little time to adjust their personal saving to make up for the cuts in their pension benefits. The latter strategy would require such a large immediate shift in contributions to plans that employers might not be able to adjust other commitments and sustain the plans. The best strategy for minimizing the risk of benefit reductions would seem to be to increase contributions gradually to a level that would sustain the system. We developed a series of simulations to test these alternative approaches.

In recent years, private-employer contributions to defined-benefit plans have averaged about 2.8% of private-sector payroll (note that this is all private-sector pay, not just pay in covered employment). In what we

Real saving/payroll

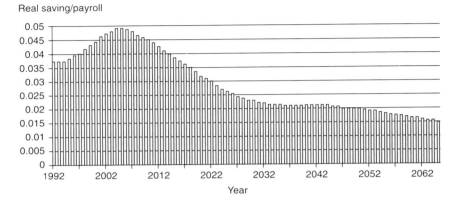

Figure 7.5
Potential real saving of private pensions relative to total private payroll for the years 1992–
2065 (assuming current plan characteristics persist and contribution rates rise)
Source: Watson Wyatt Worldwide.

consider the most likely scenario that would have employers remaining committed to their defined-benefit plans, we assumed contributions began to rise in 1995, increasing at a rate of 0.015% of payroll per year until the contribution rate equaled 4.5% of payroll. Under these assumptions, the assets in defined-benefit plans would remain at a relatively constant level in comparison to payroll over the 75-year projection period. Figure 7.5 shows the pattern of real saving in this scenario. Under this scenario the pattern of real pension saving to payroll would increase as employer contributions to defined-benefit plans were increasing but would decline over the remainder of the period, although the net real saving would be positive in every year. In other words, private pensions would contribute to net savings throughout the period but would take on diminished importance as the baby boomers claimed their retirement benefits.

Under this scenario, the private-sector defined-benefit pension system would have sufficient assets to pay benefits until the baby boom generation has completely passed on. In 2065, assets relative to payroll would be down about 4% from the current ratio and would be declining ever so slightly. In other words, under this funding scenario private-sector defined-benefit plan assets would make it through the baby boomers' retirement period and last indefinitely beyond that. Over almost all of the projection period, however, employer contributions under this scenario would be 60% higher than they are today. The alternative would be reduced benefits.

In the original Social Security Act in 1935 and all subsequent amendments, Congress has maintained the option of changing the law at any time, including the option to reduce benefits that might have been accrued under the definitions of prior law. Federal law does not allow employers the same flexibility in the administration of their defined-benefit programs. ERISA requires benefits accrued under a defined-benefit plan be paid unless the funds in the plan are exhausted, in which case the PBGC assumes payment of the benefits up to the guaranteed minimums under its benefit insurance program. Any discussion of employers reducing benefits to cope with the situation we have pictured here does not insinuate that employers might, at some future time, refuse to meet their legal obligations under their defined-benefit plans. We are suggesting that by reducing benefits, employers could curtail accruals under the plans, which would reduce the benefits anticipated by workers who expect their retirement plans to continue to operate in accordance with current benefit provisions.

Benefit reductions to bring plans back into balance in relation to current funding rates could occur relatively late in workers' careers, when the heaviest accrual of benefits under defined-benefit plans occurs. For example, a worker who begins a job at age 30, is covered by a defined-benefit plan, and is eligible to retire at age 60 would receive only 60% of expected benefits from the plan if it were terminated after 23 years of covered service. In the last quarter of the career, more than 40% of the benefit would be earned under the plan if it were to be continued. Stated alternatively, many plan sponsors could readily achieve the savings needed to bring benefit promises into balance with current funding rates by curtailing their defined-benefit plans when the baby boomers were within a decade of their anticipated retirement dates and substituting lower-cost defined-benefit or defined-contribution plans. Of course, baby boomers would then have less retirement income than the private pension system's current structure now implies.

Conclusions

The major finding of this chapter is that the national saving the private pension system generates can be expected to decline from current levels, gradually for about a decade, then far more steeply. With our conservative assumptions about the rate of return earned by pension assets, the pension system would cease to be a source of saving roughly in 2024. It is our opinion that this indeed will happen, although there is considerable uncertainty about the timing.

We also find the defined-benefit portion of the private pension system faces a tough choice. Our model shows the system would run out of money in 2043 if it were funded according to our assumptions and if rates of return were consistent with those we have projected. Obviously, the system will not be allowed to run out of money. However, the model is implicitly predicting that either corporate pension contributions will have to be substantially raised or pension plans scaled back. It is highly unlikely current low contribution rates, caused by the high realized rates of return on financial assets over the past decade, can be sustained.

We have briefly speculated about the impact of the pension system's reduced saving on asset prices. Even though we think the change will be less dramatic than our baseline model predicts because of adjustments in contributions and plan design, we still feel the demographic structure is such that a major change in pension saving will occur. The timing and magnitude of the effect on asset prices is impossible to determine. Capital markets are worldwide, interest rates are determined by both supply and demand, and forecasts of financial rates of return some 30 or more years into the future are futile. However, the population bulge we call the baby boom caused considerable strain on the U.S. education system in the 1950s and 1960s. Absorbing those people into the workforce was a challenge in the 1970s and early 1980s and may have been a factor in slowing the growth in worker productivity. It is probably safe to say the same numerous cohort will strain the economic system once again during their retirement years, roughly 2010 to 2050.

Notes

The authors would like to thank Dean Maki and Linda Moncrief for their valuable research assistance and Henry Aaron and Tatsua Hatta for their helpful comments. Any remaining errors are our responsibility.

1. U.S. Bureau of the Census, *Historical Statistics of the United States, Colonial Times to 1970*, (1975) Bicentennial Edition, Part 1, Washington, DC, p. 368.

2. U.S. Bureau of the Census, *Statistical Abstract of the United States* (111th edition), Washington, DC, 1991, p. 132.

3. U.S. Bureau of the Census, *Historical Statistics of the United States, Colonial Times to 1970*, (1975) Bicentennial Edition, Part 1, Washington, DC, p. 127, and *Statistical Abstract of the United States* (111th edition), Washington, DC, 1991, p. 384.

4. For a full discussion of this proposal, see Sylvester J. Schieber, "A Proposal to Establish Personal Security Accounts as an Element of Social Security Reform as Considered by the

Social Security Advisory Council," testimony before the Senate Finance Committee, Subcommittee on Social Security and Family Policy, March 25, 1996.

5. The Wyatt Company, *The Compensation and Benefits File*, Washington, DC (November 1987), vol. 3, no. 11, p. 4.

6. The Wyatt Company, *Survey of Actuarial Assumptions and Funding, 1992*, Washington, DC, 1992, p. 4.

7. Ibbotson Associates, *Stocks, Bonds, Bills and Inflation, 1993 Yearbook: Market Results for 1926–1992*, Chicago, 1993.

8   Managing Public-Sector Pensions

Ping-Lung Hsin and
Olivia S. Mitchell

Public employee pension plans play a key role in the nation's retirement income system. In the mid-1990s, public-sector workers' pension
systems held close to $1 trillion in assets—about the same as private-
sector defined-benefit plans—and covered more than 13 million active
and retired employees of state and local governments, school systems,
police and fire groups, legal and correctional systems, and other groups as
well.[1] As these plans have grown, interesting questions have arisen as to
what kinds of benefits they pay, how much they cost to operate, and how
they are managed. In this chapter we first discuss some general aspects of
public-sector pensions, then narrow the focus to address policy concerns
specific to public-sector plans. Of particular interest is how public pension
plans are managed and to whom these systems should be responsive as
they mature.

Public Pension Plan Benefit Promises and Funding Behavior

Like many private-sector workers, state and local employees covered by
public employee retirement plans tend to have defined-benefit pensions.[2]
In this type of retirement plan, a worker accrues retirement benefits according to a specified formula that depends on one's age at retirement, salary,
and years of service. Public-sector plans differ from private plans in some
key ways, however, as demonstrated in periodic surveys collected by the
U.S. Bureau of Labor Statistics and summarized in table 8.1.[3] For instance,
state and local workers tend not to face minimum age and/or service
requirements to participate in the plans but must meet longer vesting
requirements; in contrast, private-sector participants are more likely to be
required to have a certain age and service, but generally vest sooner.

    Retirement and benefit promises are somewhat different across private
and public pensions as well, as is evident from table 8.1. Early retirement

Table 8.1
Public and private defined-benefit pension plan design features (percentage of full-time pension plan participants)

	Public (1990)		Private (1989)	
1. Participation: minimum age and/or service requirement	10		66	
2. Vesting: Cliff	99		89	
Full > 10 yrs		45		38
Full > 5		47		44
Other		7		7
3. Early retirement permitted	88		97	
Eligibility based on:				
Service alone		24		6
Age alone		5		6
A55 + S10		9		43
A + S other		50		42
4. Normal retirement				
Service alone	36		8	
S30		22		7
Age alone	4		43	
A62		—		6
Age + service	53		37	
A55 + S30		13		1
A62 + S10		3		10
A + S = 85		—		6
5. Benefit formulas				
Dollar amount basis	13		22	
Earnings basis	82		75	
Career		—		11
Terminal		13		64
Five years used		19		81
Three years used		69		16
Other		22		13
Other basis	5		3	
Percentage of pay per year of service	72		54	
<1.25		2		12
1.25–1.74		19		25
1.75–2.00		4		5
2.00+		44		12
Other		3		—
6. Benefits integrated with Social Security	32		63	

Table 8.1 (continued)

	Public (1990)		Private (1989)	
7. Average pension replacement rates:				
Annuity as a % of final earnings				
At 20 years of service				
Salary 15K	34		23	
Salary 25K	34		20	
Salary 35K	34		20	
At 30 years of service				
Salary 15K	52		35	
Salary 25K	52		30	
Salary 35K	44		30	
8. Prevalence of postretirement increases				
Automatic	50		NA	
Full increase		27		NA

Sources:
Item 1: BLS (1992), p. 94; BLS (1990), p. 196.
Item 2: BLS (1992), p. 89; BLS (1990), p. 196.
Item 3: BLS (1992), p. 84; BLS (1990), p. 198.
Item 4: BLS (1992), p. 83; BLS (1990), p. 197.
Item 5: BLS (1992), pp. 76–7; BLS (1990), pp. 201 and 203.
Item 6: BLS (1992), p. 79; BLS (1990), p. 204.
Item 7: BLS (1992), p. 81; BLS (1990), p. 206.
Item 8: BLS (1992), p. 87; BLS (1990), p. 207.
Notes:
—   Not reported by BLS because fraction less than 0.5%.
NA   Not available from BLS.
BLS   Bureau of Labor Statistics.

is less readily available in the public sector, with only 88% of these employees having early retirement as an option, versus 97% of private covered participants. In the public sector only 9% can retire early on attaining age 55 with 10 years of service, whereas 43% may retire early in the private sector on meeting these conditions. On the other hand, normal retirement in the public sector is available on attaining somewhat fewer years of service than in private plans. Public pensions are somewhat more likely to base benefits on earnings, 82% versus 75%, though both types of plans rely heavily on the final three to five years' worth of earnings to determine the pay basis for the benefit formula. Partly because Social Security does not cover many public employees, these participants have benefit formulas that provide a somewhat larger percentage of pay per year of service: in public plans the modal percent is 2% or higher per year of service, while in private plans the modal figure is around 1.5%. In the resulting benefit structure, the pension generates a higher replacement rate, or benefit as a percentage of preretirement pay, in the public as compared to the private sector. The Bureau of Labor Statistics data imply that a retiring public-sector worker receives a pension annuity 40%–70% higher than his private-sector counterpart, depending on his service and earnings level.[4]

Given the benefit promises a defined-benefit pension plan specifies, it falls to pension actuaries to estimate what these benefits mean in present-value terms and to specify a pattern of required contributions. A pension plan is said to be funded on a *flow* basis if annual actual contributions equal annual required contributions. The pension system is said to be funded on a *stock*, or *cumulative*, basis if it holds assets sufficient to cover the expected value of benefits promised based on past employment under the plan (*past service costs*) as well as benefits earned by virtue of the current year of work (*normal costs*). If pension plan total assets equal cumulated liabilities, the defined-benefit plan is said to be fully funded; on the other hand, if liabilities exceed assets, the plan is said to be underfunded. (Conversely, if assets exceed liabilities, the plan is overfunded; see Mitchell and Smith 1994).

Public policy has focused on underfunding of private-sector defined-benefit plans for more than two decades. Specifically, corporate bankruptcy, which in the event of an underfunded pension calls into question the likelihood of receiving one's pension benefits, generates concern. The 1974 passage of ERISA, which sought to ensure that private employers fully fund their defined-benefit promises, explicitly recognized this risk. The law tried to achieve full funding by requiring corporations meet normal cost contribution requirements as well as fund a portion of past service costs over time, and also by guaranteeing a portion of the defined-benefit promise for private-sector employers.

In contrast to the private-sector regulatory structure, ERISA does not cover public employee plans, and many are not required to prefund their benefit promises fully. Whether public pension plans should be funded is a matter of some controversy. Some contend that (essentially) no funding is optimal based on the belief there is virtually no risk that a public entity will go bankrupt (Mumy 1978). On the other hand, even if public-sector default risk was low in the past, this may not be true in the future.[5] Furthermore, public-sector workers face shrinking tax bases, rising pension benefit payouts, and growing retiree populations, under which circumstances unlimited taxing authority may not be readily exercised in years to come.

Arguments in favor of well-funded public pensions tend to rely on the observation that underfunding is not costless—rather it imposes risks on various stakeholders, who in turn will demand a risk premium to bear this uncertain promise. For example, unionized public-sector employees will seek to bargain wage premiums when their defined-benefit plans are less than fully funded (Smith 1981; Mitchell and Smith 1994), and unfunded pension benefit obligations may be reflected in state and local government borrowing capabilities (e.g., Inman 1986).[6] A related concern is that some evidence shows that pension/state budget links have grown closer of late, with states meeting budget shortfalls by deferring public pension plan contributions directly, or by altering actuarial assumptions used to compute the required contributions (Mitchell and Smith 1994). It is essential therefore to investigate why some public-sector pension plans prefund their promised benefits, while others do not.

Public Pension Plan Management and Authority Structures

To learn more about public-sector plan funding and management patterns, it is fruitful to think about the funding decision-making process in three stages.[7] First, we investigate the decision-making structure of public-sector pension plans. Second, we inquire how different management structures affect endogenously determined funding requirements. Third, we ask how these endogenously determined funding requirements in turn influence funding results.

Investigating these questions requires a reliable data source on public pensions, a need recently met by the development of surveys collected by the Public Pension Coordinating Council following public plan reporting standards developed by the Government Accounting Standards Board (GASB).[8] The PENDAT data file used for this empirical analysis is a nationwide survey of 325 public employee retirement systems covering 476 state and local pension units, 199 general employee pension plans, 31 teacher plans, 66 police/firefighter plans, and 29 other plans (Zorn 1994). In 1992 these plans held $791 billion, or 86% of the total amount of state and local pension plan assets, and included 11 million members, or 83% of the total covered sector.

Looking first at these public-sector plans' funding status, figure 8.1 indicates they held on average 75% of the assets required to meet *stock* funding requirements—that is, the plans had three-quarters of the assets

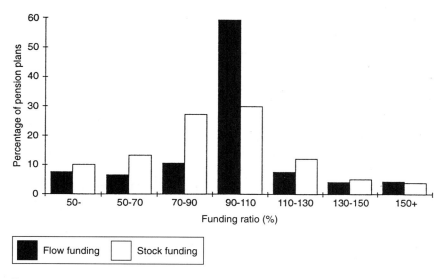

Figure 8.1
Flow and stock funding ratios of state and local pension plans in 1992

needed to meet cumulative projected benefit obligations. Even more of the plans met *flow* funding requirements, meaning that they contributed enough to meet current annual required contribution levels. In general, the PENDAT file indicates that underfunding is not a widespread problem among responding state and local plans, though there are pockets of funding problems across the sample.

Other aspects of the public pension plan universe appear in table 8.2, which summarizes the management structure of public-employee retirement systems. These state and local pension systems are controlled by a board of trustees whose size averages eight trustees but ranges from three to fourteen. The board's size also varies by administrative jurisdiction: state-administered systems appear slightly larger with nine trustees per board, while locally administered public plans have seven trustees on average. As a rule, about half the public pension trustees are appointed (45%), often by the governor, and one-third are elected by participants. Locally administered plans tend to have more elected participants than state-run plans, and all have about the same fraction of ex officio members (e.g., state treasurer, superintendent of schools, etc.). In general, public pension boards are heavily reflective of political inputs, with 60%–70% of the trustees selected either directly by politicians or indirectly by virtue of their ex officio status.

Table 8.2
Public employee pension system management

	Total	State administered	Locally administered
Average number of trustees on pension board	7.8	9.0	7.4
Selection method for trustees			
Appointed	45%	60%	46%
Elected by participants	34	23	38
Ex-officio	16	17	16
Trustee authority over			
Investments	90%	75%	95%
Benefits	73	77	72
Actuarial assumptions	85	91	83
Administrative budget authorized by			
Pension board	56%	29%	67%
Legislature or other[a]	44	71	33
Administrative expenses paid for by			
Pension board[b]	38%	26%	43%
Employer	62	75	57
Number of in-house staff per 100 active members	1.7	2.6	1.4
Administrative budget (dollars/year) per active member	$509	$173	$655
Number of systems reporting	325	85	240

Source: Adapted from Hsin 1994.
a. Administrative expenses authorized mostly by city councils/county commissioners if not by legislatures.
b. Administrative expenses paid for by the pension board from contributions or investment income.

The authority these boards exercise also varies by subject area, as table 8.2 makes clear. Most boards make decisions over investments, but the pattern varies across employer type: locally administered plans give their trustees authority more often than state-run plans. In both groups about three-quarters of the boards make decisions regarding benefits.

Even more interesting are the large reported differences in authority over actuarial assumptions. Most trustee boards at the state level make decisions concerning these crucial inputs to the funding process, and almost as many do so at the local level. This is important because recent studies call attention to the very important role seemingly small differences play in key actuarial assumptions, which in turn can dramatically influence reported funding requirements. For example, one such assumption is the defined-benefit plan's forecast for *salary growth*, needed to project anticipated benefits, which will depend on workers' final pay. Logically, a plan that uses a low salary growth rate will require employers to contribute relatively small amounts to fund the plan (holding other things equal). This could produce funding problems if the low earnings growth projections systematically understate workers' actual pay increases, particularly near retirement.

Also of key importance for funding purposes is the *assumed interest rate* used to discount future pension benefits. Since these benefit flows must be paid for dozens of years into the future, small changes in interest rate assumptions can have substantial impact on funding requirements. Thus one expert concluded that "varying the interest rate assumption by two percentage points around a 7% baseline results in pension cost changes ranging from more than a 60% increase to nearly a 40% decrease" (VanDerhei 1994, 79). This is beginning to attract policymakers' attention, as the press recently reported: "[There is] a new, get-tough attitude by the Securities and Exchange Commission and other government agencies toward corporations that have not contributed enough money to their pension funds. Specifically, the companies are accused of using outlandishly high interest rate assumptions in projecting how much the funds will earn" (McGinn 1993).

Some have argued the most critical actuarial assumption is actually a third, composite statistic called the *spread rate*, which is the real discount implied by differencing the nominal wage growth and interest rate forecasts. This, too, like the other actuarial assumptions, is in the purview of most trustee boards and is necessary to determine required pension. Of course, trustee boards' authority over these key pension assumptions may not imply they are selected with any particular contribution goal in mind. On the other hand, recent policy discussions have suggested that pension managers may be unable to select their funding assumptions independently, finding instead that they must reduce required contribution amounts in times of financial duress (Verhovek 1990; Durgin 1991). Whether this is a substantive issue is an empirical question. Turning to the evidence, PENDAT plans appear at first glance to use interest rate and salary growth rate assumptions that move in tandem (table 8.3). In particular, state plans use both high earnings growth and high interest rate assumptions, but together these imply a spread rate of about 2% in real terms, similar to the spread rate the local plans' assumptions imply (both of which are lower when taken separately). Although these tabular findings might appear

Table 8.3
Public-employee pension plan assumptions and funding patterns

	Total	State administered	Locally administered
Actuarial assumptions			
Interest rate (%)	7.8	8.0	7.7
Salary growth rate (%)	5.7	6.2	5.6
Spread rate (%)	2.0	1.9	2.1
Extent of pension funding[a]			
Flow-funding ratio (%)	100.8	91.8	85.2
Stock-funding ratio (%)	90.9	84.4	94.3
Number of systems	476	133	343

Source: Adapted from Hsin 1994.
a. The flow-funding ratio refers to the ratio of the employer's actual contributions in a given year relative to the employer's required contribution in that year. The stock-funding ratio refers to the ratio of accumulated assets in the pension plan to the PBO (see Zorn, 1994).

comforting in that there is no clearcut evidence of strategically chosen rates to minimize employer contribution obligations, it is important to re-ask this question using multivariate analysis to isolate the empirical determinants on which actuarial assumptions are based, while holding constant other factors that vary across plans.

Determinants of Public Pension Plan Actuarial Assumptions

Prior research studies on public pension plan behavior have focused on the determinants of underfunding, rather than on the underlying assumptions used to set funding targets. One theory, the "bonding hypothesis," proposes that an underfunded pension promise can be thought of as similar to a bond purchased by employees from their firm. Through the bond, an employer can avoid the potential of an employee "holdup," which might arise if employees can unite to extract high compensation from the firm (Ippolito 1986). Although this model was first developed to discuss private pension plan sponsors, the public-sector analogy is that taxpayer residents with large investments in both public and private property would stand to lose from this type of threat and would be more likely to offer an underfunded pension the stronger the public employee union.

A second hypothesis offered to explain public pension underfunding rests on taxpayer myopia. According to this view, pension underfunding arises when politicians hide the full cost of labor services from voters

(Inman 1982, 1986). Both models imply public plan funding is lower when reporting requirements are minimal but rises if pension boards are more closely monitored via reporting and disclosure requirements.

Neither hypothesis has been tested concurrently with public employee pension data, and the few existing studies employ very small data sets. Marks et al. (1988) examined 45 state-administered plans in 1978 and report an inverse correlation between union status and public pension funding. A more recent study by Mitchell and Smith (1994) used a small sample of state-administered pensions (42 plans) surveyed in 1989; these authors concluded pension promises were better funded when employees were not unionized and when a state experienced above-average economic growth. In addition, the study found that public pension plans' past funding practices are perpetuated, so that pension systems with high ratios of stock funding also maintained persistently high flow-funding ratios. Mitchell and Smith's analysis also examined the endogeneity of required pension contribution levels, whereas previous analysts assumed that actuarial computations of required contributions could safely be assumed to be exogenous. In the first study to include both state and locally administered public pension plans, funding was found to respond to pension governance structures as well as factors examined in other studies (Mitchell and Hsin 1994). Information from 1990 showed public pension funding fell in times of fiscal stress in the state and when employees were more heavily represented on the trustees' board.[9]

Prior studies on this topic all share the shortcoming that the analysis assumes that the annual required pension contribution amounts employers must make to their public pension plans are determined independently of political and economic pressures.[10] Generally the dependent variable used to analyze funding behavior is either the gap between actual and required contribution levels or their ratio. However, contribution levels may not be exogenous if they embody strategically chosen actuarial assumptions responsive to the public employer's financial condition. As a result, it is necessary to examine whether these assumptions are endogenous, and what effect endogeneity might have on employer pension contributions in public sectors.

We address these questions using a multivariate model of the determinants of pension system actuarial assumptions; of particular interest are the interest rate and the spread rate assumed by a public pension plan board:

$$Y_j = a_0 + a_1 X + a_2 Z + e_1 \quad (j = 1, 2).$$

Explanatory variables include factors reflecting pension board governance and reporting practices (X), namely the fraction of pension trustees elected by participants, based on previous research with earlier PENDAT surveys (Mitchell and Hsin 1994) that suggested participant trustees may be more cautious in their actuarial assumptions, inasmuch as their own pension benefits are at stake. We also include an interaction between this variable and the locale's degree of fiscal stress, a factor Mitchell and Smith (1994) found to influence funding outcomes, to ascertain whether fiscal stress also influences the choice of actuarial assumptions directly. (We represent fiscal stress with an excess unemployment term measured as the deviation between recent and five-year average unemployment.) In prior research we also found some evidence that boards behaved more conservatively on pension funding when required to carry liability insurance (Hsin and Mitchell 1994). In the present context, the question is whether a term controlling for board members' insurance status affects choice of actuarial assumptions as well.

Other control variables incorporate factors representing economic and other pressures on public pension plans. One hypothesis is that unionized plans and plans with a history of poor funding might use higher-than-average interest and spread rates. Another is that public plans with better past funding and better investment returns might strategically set higher interest and spread rates. In addition to plan type variables (teacher, firefighter/police), it is useful to ask whether public plans in states that prohibit state budget deficit carryovers from one year to the next are more likely to use higher-than-average interest assumptions (NASBO 1992). If so, it implies that the actuarial assumptions used in computing contributions owed to the public employee pension plan could be responsive to other fiscal conditions.

Table 8.4 shows the results of the multivariate empirical analysis. The evidence shows, first, that a plan's interest rate and spread rate assumptions are lower when pension trustee boards are more heavily composed of elected participants, holding other things constant. Furthermore, this tendency is somewhat stronger when the state's fiscal situation falters. Although the estimated magnitudes of the effects are not large, the results still imply that funding requirements are endogenously determined as they depend heavily on the actuarial assumptions trustees select. As a result, prior studies that ignore this endogeneity have biased estimates of their funding equations.

Although various reporting and insurance variables employed in the regression appear not to affect assumptions utilized, the evidence in the

Table 8.4
Determinants of public pension plan actuarial assumptions (standard errors in parentheses)

	Assumed interest rate	Implied spread rate
Pension plan governance and reporting practices		
Fraction of pension trustees elected by participants	-0.003^a	-0.002^b
	(0.001)	(0.001)
Pension board elected by participants' fiscal stress[b]	-0.001	-0.003^a
	(0.001)	(0.001)
Board must carry liability insurance	0.08	0.07
	(0.07)	(0.08)
Board must issue free-standing pension report	0.07	0.02
	(0.07)	(0.08)
Frequency of independent valuation reports	-0.01	0.11
	(0.16)	(0.18)
Economic and other pressures on public pension plans		
Plan unionized	0.18^a	-0.05
	(4.94)	(0.09)
Adjusted stock-funding ratio of public pension plan	-0.01^a	-0.004
	(0.001)	(0.001)
Plan investment returns (five-year average)	0.01	-0.001
	(0.02)	(0.02)
Fiscal pressure: excess unemployment	0.10^a	0.11^b
	(0.04)	(0.05)
State permits budget deficit carryover	-0.24^a	0.06
	(0.07)	(0.08)
Plan primarily for teachers	-0.07	-0.16
	(0.12)	(0.17)
Plan primarily for police and firefighters	-0.28^a	-0.22^a
	(0.07)	(0.08)
R^2	24.8	14.1

Notes: [a] indicates significance at the 0.05 level and [b] at the 0.10 level; 1-tail tests on all coefficients except 2-tail tests on union, teacher plan and elected trustees. Sample Ns are 418 and 309 respectively. The stock-funding figure is adjusted to use a common interest rate and spread rate across plans using the method developed in Mitchell and Smith 1994. Equations also include a constant term and variables indicating missing pension-return and stock-funding figures (Hsin 1994).

second panel of table 8.4 highlights the influence of economic and other pressures on public pension plans. Specifically, unionized plans appear to use somewhat higher interest rates, though they also use higher wage projections so that the effect on spread rates is not statistically significant. Additionally, the results show public pension plans with higher past cumulative funding rates also report using lower-than-average interest and spread rate assumptions in computing ongoing pension contribution requirements.[11] This suggests that well-funded plans tend to select conservative actuarial assumptions, whereas poorly funded plans choose assumptions reducing required pension contributions. The magnitudes of these effects are fairly small, though the results are statistically significant.

External factors also influence the choice of actuarial pension assumptions, in particular the effect of regional fiscal stress. Interest and spread rates are statistically significantly higher when plans operate in areas with unusually high unemployment, lowering required pension contributions. This result supports the contention that the economic environment influences pension contributions. Other factors behave more or less as anticipated, with one interesting and not particularly intuitive finding that plans primarily serving police and firefighters tend to use more conservative assumptions. More research on this plan type would be useful in future research.

Taking the results as a whole, the factors most consistently associated with public pension trustees' choice of pension assumptions concern how the board is chosen, the plan's funding and investment history, and fiscal stress. These findings certainly do not prove that all public pension trustees predictably select assumptions to minimize pension contributions. However, they do suggest that actuarial assumptions are not exogenous when pension contributions are set. To look further at this issue, we next consider how these strategic influences on pension assumptions affect in turn public employers' pension contribution patterns.

Empirical Analysis of Public Pension Contributions

Earlier we suggested that studies that ignore actuarial assumption endogeneity might misestimate pension plan funding behavior's true determinants. In this section we posit that this bias can be examined using a multivariate analysis of actual employer annual pension contributions.[12] Specifically, we relate actual to required public plan contributions controlling on variables X and Z described above:

Actual Contributions $= b_0 + b_1 X + b_2 Z + b_3$(required contributions) $+ e_2$.

Controlling required contributions reflects the fact that plans increase contribution amounts as required levels rise; indeed some prior studies divide actual by required contributions, but we do constrain this coefficient to be unity in this model. If, as posited earlier, actuarial assumptions influence required contributions, we expect that the parameters b_1 and b_2 will be biased when required contributions are included in the equation. Conversely, the full effect of plan governance and economic and fiscal pressures on contribution levels is expected to be larger when b_3 is constrained to be equal to 0. We test this hypothesis next.

Empirical estimates of this regression equation appear in table 8.5, with the first column representing the unconstrained and the second column the constrained model. Focusing on the equation that controls for required contributions first, the results suggest that most explanatory variables have few statistically significant effects on public employers' actual contributions. When required contributions rise by 1% of payroll, employers' actual contributions rise by 0.7%, holding other things equal. This point estimate suggests that increases in state and local pension plan liabilities are not fully funded. The results also imply that actual contributions are lower when states cannot carry over budget deficits, suggesting that public pension plans are sometimes residual claimants on public-sector resources.[13]

These effects may be contrasted with those in the second column of table 8.5, where the full effect of explanatory variables on employers' pension payments includes these factors' direct influence on contributions as well as their indirect effects via the choice of actuarial assumptions. As hypothesized, the pattern of estimated coefficients is quite different. For example, having elected trustees now proves to have a strong positive effect on payments, one which becomes more potent in times of fiscal stress. Even controlling for board composition, higher-than-average fiscal pressures now have a strong negative impact on contributions. Permitting a carryover of state budget deficits increases state contributions, and this effect is statistically significant. These findings are consistent with the last section's suggestion that public pension contribution determinants may be incorrectly assessed unless the endogeneity of the so-called "required" pension amount is taken into account. In general, therefore, this is corroborating evidence that public pension plan sponsors may respond to changes in their economic environments by adjusting what they report as their required contribution amounts. In other words, models of public pension financing strategies should take into account the influences of

Table 8.5
Determinants of public pension plan actual contribution amounts (standard errors in parentheses)

	Actual contributions	Actual contributions
Required pension contributions (% of payroll)	−0.71[a]	
	(0.05)	
Pension plan governance and reporting practices		
Fraction of pension trustees elected by participants	0.004	0.06[a]
	(0.02)	(0.02)
Pension board elected by participants' fiscal stress[b]	0.01	0.05[a]
	(0.01)	(0.02)
Board must carry liability insurance	1.18	1.78
	(0.99)	(1.36)
Board must issue free-standing pension report	0.60	1.13
	(1.04)	(1.42)
Frequency of independent valuation reports	−8.56[a]	−12.37[a]
	(2.46)	(3.35)
Economic and other pressures on public pension plans		
Plan unionized	1.25	−1.27
	(1.21)	(1.64)
Adjusted stock-funding ratio of public pension plan	−0.02	−0.05[a]
	(0.01)	(0.02)
Plan investment returns (five-year average)	−0.10	0.07
	(0.30)	(0.41)
Fiscal pressure: excess unemployment	−0.83	−1.14[b]
	(0.60)	(0.63)
State permits budget deficit carryover	1.82[b]	2.78[a]
	(1.03)	(1.40)
Plan primarily for teachers	−2.10	−2.43
	(1.54)	(2.09)
Plan primarily for police and firefighters	1.46	8.65[a]
	(1.21)	(1.51)
R^2	62.5	29.5

Notes: [a] indicates significance at the 0.05 level and [b] at the 0.10 level; 1-tail tests on all co-efficients except 2-tail tests on union, teacher plan and elected trustees. Sample Ns in both columns are 241. Stock-funding figures are adjusted to a common interest rate and spread rate using the Mitchell and Smith (1994) method. Equations also include a constant term and variables indicating missing pension return and stock funding (Hsin 1994).

economic and governance factors not only on actual contribution ratios, but also on required funding targets as well as actuarial assumptions used to construct funding targets.

Discussion

This chapter has argued that public-employee pension systems deserve attention from pension specialists for many reasons, not the least of which is that these public plans play a substantial role in providing retirement income for millions of public-sector workers. For many reasons, however, these public plans have become increasingly expensive in recent years, and in some cases, system benefits have even been reassessed as pension budgets have grown larger than available tax revenues.[14] The present discussion contributes to the analysis of public pension plans' long-term viability by focusing on an important but understudied aspect of public pension management, namely the actuarial assumptions central to determining whether a public pension is fully funded. The findings here suggest that better management and accountability structures would help state and local pension plans, particularly in keeping benefit promises and improving funding patterns.

Notes

Hsin is an Associate Research Fellow at the Chung-Hua Institute for Economic Research in Taipei, Taiwan. Mitchell is the International Foundation of Employee Benefit Plans Professor of Insurance and Risk Management and Executive Director of the Pension Research Council at The Wharton School, as well as Research Associate at the National Bureau of Economic Research. The authors acknowledge research support from The Wharton School and the Pension Research Council, though conclusions and interpretations are those of the authors and do not reflect official policy of any of the institutions with which they are affiliated.

1. These statistics exclude plans covering the military, federal civil service workers, and of course participants in the national Social Security system. For further information on national-level public plans see VanDerhei 1994; other data issues are discussed by Gustman and Mitchell (1992).

2. This section draws on Hsin 1994; Mitchell and Hsin 1994; ad Mitchell and Smith 1992, 1994.

3. Table 8.1 compares state and local employee pension data with private-sector pension information gathered from plans sponsored by medium and large employers; see Bureau of Labor Statistics 1993, 1994 for a discussion of the various sampling frames.

4. For a complete picture of well-being in retirement, it would be necessary to compare the full retirement package of public and private workers, a task beyond the scope of the present work. See Schmitt, Merck, and Neisner 1991.

5. This concern has been strengthened by recent public budget crises (e.g., the District of Columbia); see Verhovek 1990.

6. In addition, the literature suggests that underfunded pensions will be capitalized into local property taxes (Inman 1982, 1986; Epple and Schipper 1981, and workers may seek to evade payroll taxes (e.g., Mesa-Lago 1989).

7. This section draws on Hsin 1994.

8. The majority of large state and local plans in the 1992 PENDAT file conform to GASB Statement no. 5 (GASB 1986), which specifies that public pension plans must report assets at market value and measure liabilities according to a concept known as the PBO. The PBO includes five types of prospective pension liabilities, as noted in Mitchell and Smith 1992: benefits pledged to currently retired employees, benefits pledged to vested terminated employees (based on past service and salary levels), benefits payable to vested active employees (based on current service and salary), benefits payable to nonvested active employees who may vest in the future, and benefits that will be earned by current workers resulting from future salary increases. The plan's PBO changes over time, reflecting new expected benefit accruals; these yearly accruals are termed the plan's "normal cost." To be sound actuarially, the employer's annual contributions to the plan must meet normal cost and amortize any past unfunded pension liabilities; see Zorn 1991.

9. Grosskopf, Hayes, and Porter-Hudak (1988) examined 393 Illinois municipalities in the 1970s and reported that actual pension contributions fell when the rate of return on pension assets rose. Most other factors, including the level of unionization, were not statistically significant in that sample.

10. Mitchell and Smith (1994) explored potential endogeneity of actuarial assumptions using a smaller, 1989 survey of state-only plans and found little evidence to support this hypothesis.

11. These are computed using standardized actuarial figures; see Mitchell and Smith 1994.

12. This section draws on Hsin and Mitchell 1994 and Hsin 1994.

13. The negative effect to independent valuation reports is not readily explained.

14. In fiscal 1993, California public pensioners lost their cost-of-living clauses with funds thus generated earmarked to "reduce employer contributions in fiscal year 1992–1993 and subsequent fiscal years until those amounts are depleted (cited in Melbinger 1992, 23; see also Verhovek 1990)."

References

Bureau of Labor Statistics (BLS), U.S. Department of Labor. 1992. *Employee Benefits in State and Local Governments, 1990.* Washington, DC: Government Printing Office.

Bureau of Labor Statistics (BLS), U.S. Department of Labor. 1990. *Employee Benefits in Medium and Large Firms, 1989.* Washington, DC: Government Printing Office.

Durgin, H. 1991. "Politicians Grabbing Pension Assets." *Pensions and Investments,* July 8.

Epple, Dennis and Katherine Schipper. 1981. "Municipal Pension Funding: A Theory and Some Evidence." *Public Choice* 37(1):141–78.

Governmental Accounting Standards Board (GASB). 1986. "Disclosure of Pension Information by Public Employee Retirement Systems and State and Local Governmental Employers." In *Statement No. 5 of Governmental Accounting Standards Board.* GASB.

Grosskopf, S., K. Hayes, and S. Porter-Hudak. 1988. "Pension Funding and Local Labor Costs." *Southern Economic Review* 54(3):572–82.

Gustman, Alan and Olivia S. Mitchell. 1992. "Pensions and the U.S. Labor Market." In *Pensions and The U.S. Economy*, ed. Z. Bodie and A. Munnell, 39–87. Philadelphia: Dow Jones Irwin.

Hsin, Ping-Lung. 1994. "Funding and Administrative Efficiency of State and Local Government Pension Plans." Ph.D. diss., Cornell University.

Hsin, Ping-Lung and Olivia S. Mitchell. 1994. "The Political Economy of Public Sector Pensions: Pension Funding Patterns, Governance Structures, and Fiscal Stress." *Revista de Analysis Economico* (July), 9(1):151–68.

Inman, Robert P. 1986. "Appraising The Funding Status of Teacher Pensions: An Econometric Approach." *National Tax Journal* (March) 39(1):21–33.

Inman, Robert P. 1982. "Public Employee Pensions and the Local Labor Budget." *Journal of Public Economics* 19(1):49–71.

Ippolito, Richard A. 1986. *Pensions, Economics and Public Policy.* New York: Dow Jones Irwin.

McGinn, Daniel. 1993. "To Guard Pensions, Shield Actuaries." *New York Times*, Dec. 26.

Melbinger, Michael S. 1992. "The Possibility of Federal Regulation of State and Local Government Retirement Plans." *Employee Benefits Journal* 17(4):23–27.

Mesa-Lago, Carmelo. 1989. *Ascent to Bankruptcy: Financing Social Security in Latin America.* Pittsburgh, PA: University of Pittsburgh Press.

Mitchell, Olivia S., and Ping-Lung Hsin. 1994. "Public Pension Plan Governance and Performance." Working paper, National Bureau of Economic Research, Cambridge, MA.

Mitchell, Olivia S., and Robert S. Smith. 1994. "Pension Funding in the Public Sector." *Review of Economics ad Statistics* 76(2):278–90.

Mitchell, Olivia S., and Robert S. Smith. 1992. "Public Sector Pensions: Benefits, Funding and Unionization." In *Industrial Relations Research Association Papers and Proceedings of the 44th Annual Meetings*, 126–33. Madison, WI: Industrial Relations Research Association.

Mumy, Gene. 1978. "The Economics of Local Pensions and Pension Funding." *Journal of Political Economy* 86(3):517–27.

National Association of State Budget Officers (NASBO). 1992. "State Balanced Budget Requirements: Provisions and Practice." Mimeographed.

Schmitt, Ray, Carolyn L. Merck, and Jennifer A. Neisner. 1991. "Public Pension Plans: A Status Report." Congressional Research Service Report no. #91-813 EPW.

Smith, Robert Stewart. 1981. "Compensating Differentials for Pensions and Underfunding in the Public Sector." *Review of Economics and Statistics* 63(3):463–68.

VanDerhei, Jack. 1994. "Funding Public and Private Pensions." In *Pension Funding and Taxation*, ed. Dallas Salisbury and Nora Jones, 59–104. Washington, DC: Employee Benefit Research Institute, 1994.

Verhovek, S. H. 1990. "States are Finding Pension Funds Can Be a Bonanza Hard to Resist." *New York Times*, Apr. 22.

Zorn, Paul. 1994. *Survey of State and Local Government Employee Retirement Systems*. Government Finance Officers Association, Washington, DC.

Zorn, Paul. 1991. *Survey of State and Local Government Employee Retirement Systems*. Government Finance Officers Association, Washington, DC.

9 Retirement Income Adequacy at Risk: Baby Boomers' Prospects in the New Millennium

Sylvester J. Schieber

This chapter evaluates the implications of potential changes to our retirement system on workers' ability to prepare for their retirement needs and assesses how workers' saving levels might have to change and how retirement income levels might change under a variety of alternative policy scenarios. The analysis is developed in the context of a life cycle model of saving in which workers save during their working years to accumulate sufficient assets to maintain the standards of living achieved during their preretirement years. Clearly there are other motivations for saving than those considered here—for example, the desire to accumulate precautionary resources to cover the cost of unexpected events during one's lifetime, the desire to leave an inheritance to descendants, and so forth—but this analysis focuses purely on the need to save for retirement and the implications of potential changes in our retirement system on the need for individuals to alter their personal saving behavior. Saving for other purposes would have to be accumulated in addition to those intended to meet retirement consumption needs.

The underlying motivation for the analysis developed here is that we may face some curtailment of various aspects of our retirement system over the next couple of decades. If that occurs, many workers will almost certainly have to adjust their personal work, consumption, and savings decisions over the remainder of their lifetimes, which raises questions about the implications of alternative changes to retirement programs for various kinds of workers. This chapter assesses the implications of a limited number of specific policy changes that would affect the Social Security retirement program and employer-based pensions.

The next section briefly summarizes evidence that elements of our retirement system will have to be modified in coming years. The third section briefly describes two generalized measures of income adequacy that can be used to assess retirement program effectiveness and the implications of changes. In the fourth section, a conceptual model is used in evaluating the need for personal savings and gauging what standards of living for workers at various points in the economic spectrum are achievable in retirement under a variety of currently operational retirement programs. In the fifth, a number of potential changes to Social Security and the implications for personal saving needs and retirement standards of living are examined. In the sixth section, potential changes to employer-based retirement plans are evaluated. The final section presents a series of conclusions drawn from the analysis. Throughout the presentation, special attention is paid to outcomes at various levels of economic well-being.

The analysis here is constrained to the situation workers face and will face as the retirement system evolves. In this regard, the analysis does not treat the special problems married couples face when one partner dies and leaves behind a survivor. Although survivors' benefits are extremely important, addressing that issue involves redistributing payments from the total retirement package differently over time than we do now. The focus is on the overall level of benefits rather than on the timing of payment patterns. We do present one case that shows how payments made to a retiree couple will vary when the worker selects a joint-and-survivor benefit that will pay the worker's survivor three-fourths of the worker's benefit, so in a limited way I do touch on the issue.

Background

Concern over the U.S. retirement system's long-term stability will increase as the baby boomers—the large group of individuals born between 1946 and 1964—become the elder boom of the early 21st century. The impact of this generation's move into retirement should not be underestimated; the baby boomers' retirement will affect public as well as private retirement income programs in significant ways and will most probably have ripple effects throughout the whole economy. In our earlier analysis in this volume, Schieber and Shoven suggest that Social Security's underfunding may lead to benefit curtailments for baby boomers. Likewise, we suggest that the recent slowdown in the funding of employer-sponsored pensions may lead to benefit rollbacks from the retirement system's second leg.[1]

In addition to questions about formal retirement programs, concerns are also rising that the baby boomers' personal saving rates are inadequate to meet their retirement needs. On the individual saving front, Douglas

Bernheim argues that the typical baby boom household saving rate is only one-third of that required to accumulate sufficient assets to maintain the household's preretirement standard of living in retirement. Bernheim characterizes his conclusion as a best-case scenario that overstates the adequacy of the baby boomers' preparation for retirement.[2] Alan Auerbach and Laurence Kotlikoff observe that under current policy the oldest third of the baby boom generation will be able to sustain the same level of non-medical consumption as current retirees but those born in the last third will be limited to lower consumption levels.[3]

Examinations of each retirement system component raise concerns about the baby boom generation's provision for their retirement needs. In addition, there are concerns about the aggregate claim the baby boomers will make on our total economy and whether their retirement claims can be met on a basis satisfactory to them and to workers who will have to support them. The baby boomers' withdrawal from the workforce could lead to a contraction of our economic capacity, or at least a slowing in the rate of growth to which we have become accustomed, and there is even a chance that their claims against the working-age population will be more than future workers will be willing to bear. The boomers' retirement will make claims through upward pressures on the payroll tax as they draw Social Security benefits and downward pressures on financial markets as they sell their accumulated assets by cashing in their pension promises and selling other assets accumulated during their working lives. These possibilities suggest that today's workers will have to either lower their current standard of living while working or accept a reduced standard of living when they retire.[4]

If the baby boomers today are developing their retirement aspirations by looking at the current generation of retirees, then our retirement income security system must certainly change. The three-legged stool of Social Security, employer-based retirement plans, and personal saving will have to adjust for the baby boomers to achieve benefit levels our retirement system currently provides; apparently, either each leg will have to be cut back from the level of current promises or else current and future generations of workers will have to contribute more to these plans as they approach retirement. Of course, we may ultimately pursue some combination of reductions in benefit promises and increases in worker contribution rates as the ultimate solution. As we look at alternative approaches for dealing with this problem, one question we must consider is, What are the implications of alternative changes in retirement policy on workers and retirees in both the near and long term?

Our extremely diverse workforce reflects the melting-pot population that makes up U.S. society. In some regards, the baby boom generation is becoming even more diverse than earlier generations. As baby boomers age, we seem to be evolving increasingly into a society of haves and have nots, with educated workers benefiting from highly rewarded positions in a world hungry for technical and professional know-how while those with less education or other specialized capabilities increasingly compete in world labor markets characterized by low levels of real compensation. Because each component of our retirement system is based on participation during the working career, any changes we make to the retirement system can have widely varying consequences on workers' ability to provide for retirement needs at different positions along the economic spectrum.

Establishing Measures of Retirement Income Adequacy

The history of organized retirement plans in the United States is relatively recent. Industrial pensions existed before the 20th century but were not widely available until after World War II. Social Security was not enacted until 1935, and the first retirement benefits were not paid under it until 1940. With the growth of organized retirement plans, it became important to define goals for these plans to achieve in terms of providing a sufficient income stream for recipients to maintain acceptable living standards in retirement. Although the goals themselves are sometimes quite specific, there is little explicit discussion on how or why they were developed. For example, the Committee on Economic Security that developed the Social Security Act for Franklin D. Roosevelt's administration in 1935 felt that "payment of benefits at a rate ... approximating 50% of previous average earnings is socially desirable,"[5] although no justification was provided for reaching that particular threshold. Over the years, considerable effort has been devoted to developing income goals by which retirement plans can be judged. These goals can be separated into two classes: One looks at absolute levels of income required in retirement to provide for minimal levels of need; the other considers the level of income required to maintain the preretirement standard of living during retirement.

Absolute Standards of Need

The concept of minimal economic needs goes back at least two centuries to Adam Smith, who classified consumer goods as "either necessaries or luxuries." He classified necessaries as "not only the commodities which are indispensably necessary for the support of life, but whatever the custom of the country renders it indecent for creditable people, even of the lowest order, to be without."[6] Although this concept of minimal need is specific, it is neither absolute nor universal. For example, Smith explained that in late 18th-century England, leather shoes had become a necessity, and that no creditable person would be seen in public without them. Yet in Scotland, custom had rendered them a necessity for men but not for women. Thus women could still walk about barefooted without embarrassment. And in France they were a necessity to neither men nor women. So Smith's concept includes not only the minimum level of goods needed to survive, "but those things which the established rules of decency have rendered necessary."[7]

Jumping to the latter half of the 20th century, President Lyndon Johnson's war on poverty in the early 1960s required some measure of families' minimal needs against which the war could be assessed. Originally, measures of minimal needs were set somewhat arbitrarily, but they ultimately led to the federal government's development of the official poverty lines based on food consumption budgets.[8]

Many analysts over the years have criticized the use of official poverty standards as a measure of minimally adequate income. One criticism is that the standards are based on cash income available to families and exclude the value of in-kind income provided through programs like food stamps, Medicaid, Medicare, housing assistance, and the like. Another is that they are based on food consumption patterns that persisted 40 years ago, resulting in measures of need too low to cover life necessities. With the criticisms has come a series of proposed alternatives to the poverty measures that would generally result in higher poverty standards than the current official poverty lines.[9]

Even if we were to move to the higher thresholds that result from using more contemporary consumption patterns, the absolute measures of need would still be minimalist income levels to consider when designing a comprehensive retirement income system across the income spectrum. Absolute standards of need are valuable, however, because they establish an income floor below which public policy should not allow retirees to fall. They are also important in the context of retirement income policy considerations that might reduce either pension or Social Security benefits. Elderly poverty rates, over the years, have responded to increasing retirement benefits, especially between 1967 and 1974. Significant reductions in existing benefits at the bottom of the income spectrum, even on a prospective basis for future retirees, could portend increases in poverty, especially among the lower third of the income distribution.

Preretirement Living Standards: Measures of Adequacy

Even if precise definitions of minimal need within the range of income levels specified by the official poverty line or alternatives could be agreed upon, many people would still find such income levels to be woefully inadequate to meet their needs in retirement. Indeed, public policymakers have prescribed a retirement income objective significantly higher for many retirees than that implied by the concepts of minimum absolute need inherent in the various poverty thresholds. In 1965, Congress enacted the Older Americans' Act, which listed first among 10 objectives for the nation's older people that they enjoy "an adequate income in retirement in accordance with the American standard of living."[10] Although federal lawmakers established this lofty goal, they failed to define it concretely. Public policy analysts have helped define what has become a widely accepted standard against which retirement income levels can be judged, namely that "the implicit or explicit goal is the maintenance of preretirement standards of living."[11]

The President's Commission on Pension Policy in 1981 embraced this goal. The commission's final report indicated that "preretirement living standards should be measured in terms of preretirement disposable income ... income that would need to be replaced for different income groups."[12] Although maintaining preretirement living standards has become generally accepted as a public policy goal over the years, this does not mean that the federal government has assumed, or intends to assume, the responsibility of providing retirement income levels that maintain every worker's preretirement standard of living during their retirement years.

Future Retiree Income Prospects in the Face of Current Policies

Although future policies may fully fund current retirement promises being held out to the baby boom generation, it is highly probable at least some current promises will be curtailed. Indeed, a number of legislative proposals introduced during the 1994 and 1995 sessions of Congress called for future reductions in Social Security benefit levels. Benefits can be reduced in these programs in a number of ways, and the potential for such cuts raises questions about their impact on future retirement income adequacy. Thus, concepts of absolute and relative income adequacy are useful tools to assess various proposals to deal with our retirement programs' underfunding. Before we assess these proposals, however, we should understand what current retirement programs promise.

A Conceptual Model of Income Adequacy

Dan McGill et al. developed a life cycle income and saving model as a tool for designing and assessing pension plans and saving targets that will allow workers to maintain their preretirement standard of living in retirement.[13] The model allows for alternative wage growth paths, rates of inflation, and returns on assets. Saving can be divided during the working career among Social Security, employer saving, and personal saving. Work-related expenses are subtracted from wage income in deriving the portion of earnings available for consumption. The model provides for special expenses incurred during the retirement period, such as medical expenditures, and can accommodate different ages at which workers begin to accumulate retirement benefits outside of Social Security and different retirement ages.

The model calculates required personal saving rates and retirement income replacement rates for hypothetical workers at different starting wage levels. A number of parameters are specified, including starting age at which retirement accumulation begins, assumed inflation rate, rate of growth in wages (with variable rates being possible over the career), rate of return on retirement saving, whether the employer provides an employee health benefit plan and a retiree health benefit program, whether the worker is married, and level of survivor benefit under an optional joint-and-survivor benefit.

The model described here was developed for comparative purposes so that the personal saving required by a range of hypothetical workers and their potential retirement income levels could be compared under a variety of retirement plans and a range of assumptions. The model can be modified, however, to take into account alternative benefit structures than those that currently exist under Social Security or the employer-based pension system. By comparing benefits and required saving rates under current policy simulations with those under a range of alternative policy options, we can get an idea of what various policy options will imply for different kinds of workers.

Baseline Estimates of Retirement Income Delivery Under Current Policy

The overwhelming majority of U.S. workers today participate in Social Security. Most also participate in an employer-sponsored retirement plan for some of their career and earn supplemental benefits to Social Security.

Periods of participation, contribution requirements, and levels of generosity in employers' contributions to the plans vary among those who participate. To understand what current policy and practice provide, we must look at what current workers would get from these plans if they remained in their jobs until retirement in the context of a worker's ability to accumulate sufficient retirement wealth to maintain a preretirement standard of living after retirement.

Throughout this analysis we use consistent assumptions for a number of variables. We assume a constant rate of inflation of 4% per year, nominal wage growth of 5% per year, and interest returns on saving at 6% per year. We also assume individuals can save for retirement on a pretax basis and the returns accumulated by those retirement savings are not taxed until distributed at retirement as an indexed annuity. In some cases, workers will not be able to accumulate sufficient assests on a pretax basis by retirement to maintain their preretirement standard of living. In other cases, workers with similar preretirement wage patterns can easily accumulate sufficient retirement assets on a pretax basis to meet their retirement needs. This analytic result merely indicates the inconsistency in the current federal income tax treatment of retirement savings. We assume the workers whose benefits we simulate begin working in Social Security–covered employment at age 22 and work until age 62, when they retire. Throughout the initial set of baseline scenarios, we assume we are dealing with a single worker. After working through the initial set of scenarios, we present an abbreviated analysis for married couples. Throughout much of the discussion we assume the workers considered have employer-sponsored health benefits while working and in retirement. In the first scenario we perform a separate set of calculations involving no employer-sponsored retiree health benefit to provide a sense of the potential added personal saving responsibility the absence of such a benefit puts on a worker.

Baseline Case with No Employer-Provided Pension or Retirement Saving Plan

In the first scenario, we assume our worker never accumulates any benefits throughout his or her career from an employer-sponsored pension or saving plan. Because there is no employer-sponsored benefit in this case, the worker alone must accumulate any necessary savings in addition to Social Security. We estimated the saving rates required at three alternative starting ages: 22, 32, and 42. We know some workers have long time horizons and low discount rates and begin to save relatively early in their careers, and other workers are more myopic, have high discount rates and put off retirement saving until much later in the career.

For this analysis we assume that any saving accumulated will be in pretax dollars and the interest accruing on the accumulated assets will not be taxable until the worker retires and begins to receive retirement income. For a self-employed individual, contributions to a Keogh plan might offer sufficient opportunity to accumulate the level of assets we imply in this analysis. A worker employed by a firm that offers no pension will likely have a more limited opportunity to save on a pretax basis at levels needed to meet the retirement goals laid out here, although such a worker may have opportunities to realize the inside buildup on a pretax basis afforded pension participants. If this analysis has a bias, it is that it would understate the extent of savings required by a worker not covered by a tax-qualified retirement plan.

The starting ages at which savings are assumed to commence are each set in a current time frame. In other words, the individual who begins saving at 22 is assumed to have embarked on a career in 1994. The one who starts saving at age 32 is assumed to be 10 years into a career at that time, and the one beginning at age 42 is halfway through a career then. In addition to presenting a number of alternative starting ages, we also show a number of alternative wage levels at the time the retirement saving commences. Some of the higher salary levels for the youngest would be relatively rare, but not impossible.

Table 9.1 presents the results of the first scenario under our assumptions. The youngest worker beginning to save at the lowest income level would have to save about 8.9% of his or her gross pay each year during the career to maintain the preretirement standard of living beyond age 62. At the highest wage levels in the table this young worker would have to be saving 18.5% of pay. For the low-wage worker who puts off saving until age 32, required savings would increase to 11.1%; if saving is put off until age 42, the saving rate has to be 13.5% per year. At the high-income end of the spectrum the delay in saving has an even greater impact on the saving rates. Delaying saving 10 years, until age 32, raises the saving rate from 18.5% to 23.5%, and delaying it until age 42 raises it to 30.6% of pay. Saving nothing until age 32 or 42 and then beginning to lay aside one-fifth to one-third of pay would be extremely painful in most cases and thus unlikely.

Table 9.1

Saving rates required during working career at different ages of saving commencement and replacement of preretirement income for workers without an employer-sponsored retirement benefit under current Social Security law

Salary level when saving begins	Required savings rate as percentage of pay when			Retirement income replacement of final pay when		
	Saving starts at age 22	Saving starts at age 32	Saving starts at age 42	Saving starts at age 22	Saving starts at age 32	Saving starts at age 42
$12,500	8.9%	11.1%	13.5%	63.9%	61.8%	59.6%
15,000	10.9	13.7	17.1	66.4	63.7	60.5
20,000	12.7	16.1	20.3	67.4	64.2	60.1
25,000	13.6	17.2	21.9	67.5	64.0	59.4
30,000	14.3	18.1	23.1	67.7	64.0	59.1
40,000	15.5	19.6	25.2	68.4	64.4	58.9
50,000	16.3	20.7	26.8	67.8	63.5	57.5
60,000	16.9	21.4	27.8	67.0	62.6	56.3
70,000	17.8	22.5	29.3	67.1	62.5	55.7
80,000	18.5	23.5	30.6	67.4	62.5	55.4

Source: Watson Wyatt Worldwide. Dollar amounts stated in 1994 dollars.

At the $12,500 pay level, a worker just commencing retirement saving at age 32 would have to save 25% more per year during the remaining years of his or her career than the worker who began to save at age 22. The low-wage worker just beginning to save at age 42 would have to save 52% more as a share of pay than the worker who began to save at the outset of a career. At the high end of the income spectrum shown in the table, starting to save at age 32 would boost the annual saving requirement 27% per year relative to beginning to save at age 22, and starting only at age 42 would raise the annual savings ante 65%. The saving effect is somewhat greater at the higher income levels because Social Security provides a smaller relative benefit for high-wage workers than for those with lower career wages. And while the basic assumptions here do not provide for the worker to begin saving for retirement outside of Social Security until age 32 or 42, they do provide for the worker's participation in Social Security over a full career from ages 22 to 62.

Table 9.1 also shows the extent to which retirement income in this scenario would replace wages earned in the year immediately before retirement. The replacement rate levels do not decline consistently from one wage level to the next as might be expected, and may be somewhat flatter than expected across the income spectrum for reasons relating to the structure of Social Security benefits across the wage spectrum and relative work expenses. At the low-wage end of the spectrum, work expenses account for a larger share of preretirement earnings that need not be replaced by retirement income in a relative-income standards measure but Social Security benefits are relatively high. At the high end of the income spectrum, Social Security benefits are relatively low, but work expenses are relatively much less than for low-wage earners, which means more income is directed towards consumption while working and drives up the income replacement required to maintain the working-period standard of living during retirement.

At the lowest wage levels presented, the replacement of less than 70% of preretirement earnings may allow retirees to maintain their prior standards of living, but 70% of $12,500 today would fall short of current poverty lines and even farther behind more realistic measures of retirees' needs. In our projections we are assuming 1% real wage growth over time, but recent history suggests that the lowest real wage gains in our economy have been occurring at the low-wage end of the workforce. At the highest wage levels, the replacement rates suggest incomes many would find acceptable, but workers at those income levels, willing to live on incomes less than half the level they had attained prior to retirement, would be unlikely.

Table 9.1 compares the saving rates of workers who begin to save for retirement at different ages who are at the same nominal pay level when they commence to save. In this analysis, workers horizontally across the table have very different lifetime earnings levels. Alternatively, we could compare the required saving rates and retirement income levels for workers whose lifetime earnings levels were equivalent but who commence to save for retirement today or some time in the future. For example, we could measure what would happen to a cohort of 22-year-olds today where individuals within this cohort, on any given lifetime pay profile, begin to save today, wait 10 years to commence saving, or wait 20 years to do so. Our underlying assumptions are wages will grow 5% per year in an economy experiencing price inflation at a rate of 4% per year. Thus, our 22-year-old worker who earns $15,000 today would be earning $24,443 in nominal dollars or $16,569 in today's constant dollars at age 32. The respective amounts at age 42 would be $39,799 or $18,303. In this latter case, the worker who delayed saving until age 32 or 42 would have a higher real wage when he or she commenced to save

Table 9.2

Saving rates required during working career at different ages of saving commencement and replacement of preretirement income for workers without an employer-sponsored retirement benefit under current Social Security law

Salary level at age 22	Required savings rate as percentage of pay when			Retirement income replacement of final pay when		
	Saving starts at age 22	Saving starts at age 32	Saving starts at age 42	Saving starts at age 22	Saving starts at age 32	Saving starts at age 42
$12,500	8.9%	14.4%	20.0%	63.9%	57.5%	54.1%
15,000	10.9	16.5	22.5	66.4	60.1	55.9
20,000	12.7	18.4	25.0	67.4	62.1	57.4
25,000	13.6	19.4	25.4	67.5	62.8	57.4
30,000	14.3	20.1	27.0	67.7	63.5	58.7
40,000	15.5	21.6	29.1	68.4	64.1	59.0
50,000	16.3	22.4	29.4	67.8	64.3	58.0
60,000	16.9	23.0	30.7	67.0	64.2	57.8
70,000	17.8	24.0	32.2	67.1	64.1	57.2
80,000	18.5	24.8	32.9	67.4	63.9	56.0

Source: Watson Wyatt Worldwide. Dollar amounts stated in 1994 dollars.

than if saving started at age 22. Regardless of when the worker commenced saving in this case, however, he or she would have the same lifetime real wages as the other comparison workers.

Table 9.2 shows the results of the estimates of the saving and replacement rate targets for a cohort of workers turning age 22 in 1994 under assumptions that the workers begin to save at ages 22, 32, or 42. The saving and replacement targets reflected in table 9.2 for workers who begin to save at age 22 exactly match the results shown in table 9.1, as the projection periods exactly correspond in the two cases. In the cases shown in table 9.2 where the workers begin to save later in their careers, the required increases in the saving rates and the declines in the projected replacement rates are somewhat larger than in table 9.1, because the workers beginning to save at ages 32 or 42 in table 9.2 on each pay line of the table have somewhat higher real lifetime wages than their counterparts in table 9.1. As a result, the later savers in table 9.2 will tend to get slightly smaller replacement of preretirement earnings from Social Security than those in table 9.1. Thus, fulfilling the goal of maintaining the preretirement standard of living during retirement will require higher saving rates during the saving period. Of course, the higher saving rate itself during the working period lowers the preretirement disposable income target that defines the replacement rate levels attained in equilibrium.

As indicated earlier, this first scenario assumed the worker was covered by an employer-sponsored health benefit plan both before and after retirement. It is not uncommon for employers who provide no pension to offer a health-benefit plan to active workers. It would be extremely rare that an employer would offer a health-benefit plan to retirees but provide no pension or retirement saving plan. If the employer is not willing to offer a retirement benefit that can be funded while a worker is contributing to the firm's bottom line, why would that same employer offer to a former worker who is no longer contributing anything to the firm a benefit that cannot be funded?

It is well known that health costs are generally higher for older people than for younger ones. Although older people may consume more health care services than younger ones, it is not clear that doing so reflects an actual improvement in their standard of living. For example, getting care for an arthritic knee may make the older person feel better than not getting care and thus improve the overall utility of the individual getting the care but does not improve the person's utility relative to 15 years earlier when the arthritis was not a factor.

If a worker faces the prospect of not receiving an employer-sponsored retiree health benefit, then he or she must save at a higher rate to accumulate the necessary resources to finance retirement health insurance. In estimating the potential cost of acquiring such health insurance, we assume retirees will be able to purchase it at group rates. In developing the group rates, we first estimate the actuarial cost of group plans currently being sponsored by a cross section of private-sector employers. This is adjusted to account for administrative costs related to the plans. We estimate separate rates for those between the ages of 55 and 64 and for those over age 65. The first group rate applies to individuals prior to being eligible for Medicare and the second encompasses the Medicare population. We assume health care costs would rise in the future at 6%, or 2% more than our assumed inflation rate and 1% more than our wage growth assumption.

Table 9.3 shows the required saving rates under the scenario where a worker receives only Social Security and has no employer-sponsored retiree health benefits, compared to where such benefits are provided. At the lowest income level, the required amount of saving doubles over the earlier projection. Expecting someone earning $12,500 per year to be saving 18% to 27% of pay is not credible. The added savings burden as a

Table 9.3
Saving rates required during working career at different ages of saving commencement and replacement for workers with and without an employer-sponsored pension or retiree health benefit under current Social Security law

Salary level when saving begins	Saving begins at age 22		Saving begins at age 32		Saving begins at age 42	
	with retiree health benefits	without retiree health benefits	with retiree health benefits	without retiree health benefits	with retiree health benefits	without retiree health benefits
$12,500	8.9%	18.2%	11.1%	21.9%	13.5%	26.6%
15,000	10.9	18.7	13.7	22.7	17.1	27.9
20,000	12.7	18.6	16.1	22.8	20.3	28.5
25,000	13.6	18.3	17.2	22.6	21.9	28.4
30,000	14.3	18.2	18.1	22.6	23.1	28.5
40,000	15.5	18.4	19.6	23.0	25.2	29.3
50,000	16.3	18.7	20.7	23.4	26.8	30.0
60,000	16.9	18.9	21.4	23.7	27.8	30.5
70,000	17.8	19.4	22.5	24.4	29.3	31.6
80,000	18.5	20.0	23.5	25.1	30.6	32.7

Source: Watson Wyatt Worldwide. Dollar amounts stated in 1994 dollars.

percentage of pay declines at each successively higher income level. At the very highest income levels considered, the added burden of having to provide one's own retiree health insurance requires only a couple of percent of pay in added saving, because the plan costs each retiree the same regardless of income level.

Each percentage increase in saving during the working career reduces preretirement consumption by a comparable percentage. Increases in saving during the working career also mean the consumption it displaces does not have to be replaced in retirement. Thus, the increases in saving required for workers to provide for their own postretirement health benefits imply comparably reduced replacement rates at retirement. An alternative way to look at this discussion would be to redefine pay under the two scenarios. In the first scenario, the worker is getting cash wages plus the accruing entitlement to a retiree health benefit. Since that benefit is earned over the working career, one can argue the value of that accruing benefit should be included in the measure of earnings. If we were to do that, the earnings levels for workers expecting to get retiree health benefits would be much higher than those reflected in table 9.3. From this perspective, an employer who sponsors a retiree health benefit program as part of a lifetime compensation package forces the worker to save for retirement health insurance during the working career. One problem with retiree health benefits, however, is that employers cannot prefund them. Since the forced savings for the workers these plans imply cannot be matched with real accumulations of assets to fund them, many employers have abandoned previously offered health benefit plans because they have become too expensive to operate on a pay-as-you-go basis.

Baseline Cases with Pensions or Retirement Saving Plans

The baseline scenarios in which workers receive no employer-sponsored retirement benefits are interesting, but they probably do not reflect the situation the majority of workers face today. Although pension coverage and retirement saving may be uncommon at the lowest wage levels, they are widely prevalent at middle- and upper-income levels. It is important to consider these employer-based retirement programs when we begin to evaluate the implications of changing any elements of the retirement income security system.

To understand the level of potential benefits that existing retirement plans generate requires that we look at a distribution of existing plans. To develop such an analysis, we use a group of actual plans surveyed during 1993 by Watson Wyatt. Approximately 560 firms are included in the database on which this analysis is based. The firms surveyed were predominantly larger firms, most having more than 1,000 employees, and half having more than 5,000 employees. Larger firms often have multiple plans because they have different benefits across different operating units, classes of workers (e.g., union versus nonunion), and so forth. Because larger firms often sponsor multiple plans, the respondents in this survey were asked to identify the retirement plans that best represented the benefits provided to nonunion, salaried workers in their companies. The survey respondents do not constitute a random sample of plans offered by all companies or even large companies, but we believe the survey respondents and their retirement plans generally represent the range and type of plans private employers offer today. Because survey participants are predominantly larger firms, defined-benefit plans are more prevalent in our sample than among firms generally.

In developing the analysis of employer-sponsored retirement plans, we use economic assumptions consistent with those delineated earlier. We assume the inflation rate would be a consistent 4% per year; workers' wages would grow at 5% per year; and the interest rate would be 6% per year for calculating returns on retirement plan assets and for calculating annuities. Throughout the analysis, we calculate benefits on a projected basis assuming that current plans and Social Security continue to provide benefits according to current formulas. To give a sense of the distribution of benefits generated by existing plans, we develop calculations for plans at the 15th, 40th, 65th, and 90th percentiles of benefit generosity.

Defined-Benefit Plans

In assessing the level of benefits defined-benefit plans provide, we use all the defined-benefit plans recorded in the survey whether or not they were supplemented by a defined-contribution plan, because most employers would consider the defined-benefit plan the primary plan for providing a career benefit for long-service workers even when offered a combination of plans. Also, estimating the benefits the defined-benefit plans generate allows the derivation of the required saving rate required to accumulate adequate resources to maintain preretirement standards of living after they retire from the workforce. There are 455 plans included in the calculations presented here.

Table 9.4 shows the level of benefits generated by the defined-benefit plans alone for retirements at age 62 with two different periods of service under the plans. The table reflects the benefit levels the plans provide as replacement rates relative to final annual wages for a single-life annuity. For workers retiring at age 62 with 30 years of service under these plans, the benefits provided range from slightly more than one-fifth to slightly more than one-half of final earnings. For workers retiring with 20 years of service under the plans, the benefits range from roughly 14% of pay to 34%. In each case, the benefits at higher wage levels provide a somewhat higher replacement of preretirement earnings than for lower-wage workers, reflecting the common practice of coordinating employer-sponsored benefits with Social Security's redistributive benefit structure.

As in the case where no pension benefit is available for workers, where a pension is offered it is possible to estimate the saving rate that will allow the worker to maintain his or her preretirement standard of living in retirement. Table 9.5 shows the personal saving rates required for a worker who began to accumulate retirement savings other than Social Security at age 32 in 1994 and who would work until age 62 under defined-benefit plans at various percentile levels of generosity as described above. In this

Table 9.4
Replacement of final earnings by defined-benefit plans for workers retiring at age 62 with either 20 or 30 years of service

Years of service at retirement	Plan percentile ranking	Replacement rates for workers with initial pay levels of			
		$12,500	$20,000	$50,000	$80,000
30	15th	20.5%	20.8%	23.5%	25.3%
	40th	27.8	28.3	31.8	34.5
	65th	33.7	34.4	37.7	40.0
	90th	45.8	46.2	48.1	50.3
20	15th	13.9	14.4	16.3	17.6
	40th	18.6	19.0	21.2	22.7
	65th	22.6	23.1	25.2	26.9
	90th	30.8	30.8	32.1	33.7

Source: Watson Wyatt Worldwide.

analysis, we assume that the employer provides a retiree health benefit for the worker.

In this case as before, the required saving rates generally increase for higher-wage workers relative to their lower-wage counterparts under each pension plan. The more generous the defined-benefit plan, the less the worker would have to save on his or her own at each wage level. Social Security and pension benefits combined are sufficiently generous at the 90th percentile level that the lowest-wage workers for whom calculations were done would have to save less than 1% of pay outside the pension plan. Certainly in the more generous plans, the required saving rates would seem readily achievable. A participant in the 65th percentile plan at a salary level of $12,500 would be required to save 3.6% of pay, less than $9 per week. At the 15th percentile plan level the required saving on the part of the lowest-wage worker shown would jump to $20 per week. If workers more fully understood what saving rates were required to meet their retirement goals, they might be willing to save at the levels implied even with the less generous plans, but it is unlikely that many have a reasonable appreciation of the rate of saving they should be generating.

The replacement rate targets in table 9.5 are relatively flat across the wage spectrum for workers covered under each of the individual plans. Each of the plans offers benefits reasonably within the range of replacement rate targets employed by many professional designers of retirement plans to augment Social Security as it is currently structured. The reader should keep in mind, though, that attaining the replacement rate targets

Table 9.5
Saving rates required to maintain preretirement standards of living and replacement of final earnings from all retirement income sources for workers retiring at age 62 with 30 years of service under defined-benefit plans at varying levels of generosity

Salary when saving and pension coverage begin	Required personal saving rate associated with the pension plan at the				Retirement income replacement of preretirement earnings at the			
	15th percentile	40th percentile	65th percentile	90th percentile	15th percentile	40th percentile	65th percentile	90th percentile
$12,500	6.6%	4.9%	3.6%	0.9%	66.4%	68.0%	69.3%	72.0%
15,000	9.1	7.5	6.1	3.5	68.3	70.0	71.3	74.0
20,000	11.4	9.7	8.4	5.8	68.8	70.5	71.9	74.5
25,000	12.4	10.7	9.4	6.8	68.8	70.5	71.9	74.4
30,000	13.1	11.4	10.0	7.5	69.0	70.7	72.1	74.5
40,000	14.5	12.7	11.4	9.0	69.5	71.3	72.6	75.0
50,000	15.5	13.6	12.3	10.0	68.8	70.6	71.9	74.2
60,000	16.0	14.1	12.8	10.5	68.0	69.9	71.2	73.5
70,000	17.0	15.0	13.7	11.4	68.0	70.0	71.2	73.5
80,000	17.8	15.8	14.5	12.2	68.1	70.2	71.4	73.7

Source: Watson Wyatt Worldwide. Dollar amounts are stated in 1994 dollars.

implies that most workers be required to make some personal contribution toward the retirement accumulation outside the defined-benefit plan in which they are participating.

Table 9.6 shows the saving rates and replacement rate targets for a worker who had not begun to save individually for retirement or established coverage under a pension plan at one of four varying levels of generosity until reaching age 42 in 1994. Comparing the results in table 9.5 to those in table 9.6 leads to some interesting observations. For example, saving rates must rise more for the worker who has delayed getting into the more generous plan than for one who has delayed getting into one that is less generous, because it is more expensive to miss a year of participation in a generous plan than to miss one in a less generous plan. At the $80,000 salary level, the personal saving rate would have to increase 1.7 times for starting to save and participate in the 90th percentile plan at age 42 rather than 32. At $40,000, the saving rate would have to increase 1.8 times; and at $20,000, it would have to increase 4.9 times the earlier rate. By comparison, the respective saving increases for a worker getting into only the 15th percentile plan at age 42 would be 2.4 times the saving rate for the $12,500 per year worker who got in at the younger age; for the $80,000 worker, the difference would be 1.4 times. Although the relative saving increases are more moderate in the less generous plans, because of the outside saving rates required with these plans under any circumstances, an individual who does not begin saving for retirement until the early 40s has a steep hill to climb.

The replacement rate targets in table 9.6 generally fall in the lower part of the range plan designers strive for in crafting retirement plans. The target replacement rates tend to be reduced more at higher wage levels by shortening the participation period from 30 to 20 years than at the lower wage levels, because workers in both scenarios are assumed to have a full career under Social Security and because Social Security makes up a larger portion of the benefit of the lower-wage workers than of those in the higher wage brackets.

Stand-Alone Defined-Contribution Plans

In assessing the level of benefits defined-contribution plans potentially provide, we use plans in firms where the employer sponsored only defined-contribution plans, because we could then be relatively certain the plan was not a supplemental plan meant to augment a more generous retire-

Table 9.6
Savings rates required to maintain preretirement standards of living and replacement of final earnings from all retirement income sources for workers retiring at age 62 with 20 years of service under defined-benefit plans at varying levels of generosity

Salary when saving and pension coverage begin	Required personal saving rate associated with the pension plan at the				Retirement income replacement of preretirement earnings at the			
	15th percentile	40th percentile	65th percentile	90th percentile	15th percentile	40th percentile	65th percentile	90th percentile
$12,500	9.4%	8.0%	6.8%	4.4%	63.7%	65.1%	66.3%	68.7%
15,000	12.9	11.5	10.3	8.0	64.7	66.1	67.3	69.6
20,000	16.0	14.7	13.5	11.2	64.3	65.7	66.9	69.2
25,000	17.5	16.1	14.9	12.7	63.8	65.2	66.4	68.6
30,000	18.5	17.1	15.9	13.8	63.6	65.0	66.2	68.4
40,000	20.6	19.1	17.9	15.8	63.6	65.0	66.2	68.3
50,000	21.9	20.5	19.3	17.3	62.4	63.8	65.0	67.0
60,000	22.8	21.4	20.2	18.1	61.3	62.7	63.9	66.0
70,000	24.2	22.7	21.5	19.5	60.8	62.3	63.5	65.5
80,000	25.4	23.9	22.7	20.7	60.6	62.1	63.4	65.4

Source: Watson Wyatt Worldwide. Dollar amounts are stated in 1994 dollars.

ment benefit. We identify 107 such plans whose benefits we could calculate and compare.

Defined-contribution plans are much more likely to require employee contributions than defined-benefit plans. For years, thrift plans have provided for employer contributions based on matching employee contributions made to the plan. Since the early 1980s, the growth of 401(k) plans has made these employer-matching provisions in plans much more common. For example, in a 1991 U.S. Labor Department survey of private-sector firms with more than 100 employees, 48% of full-time employees in the firms were participating in one or more defined-contribution plans sponsored by their employer. The same survey also found that 44% of the full-time workers were enrolled in a plan with a cash or deferred arrangement—that is, a 401(k) plan. The employer made all contributions to the retirement or savings program for only about 16% of the workers covered by a defined-contribution plan in these medium- and larger-sized establishments.[14]

The Profit Sharing 401(k) Council of America annually surveys profit-sharing and 401(k) plans, gathering information on plan characteristics. Their 1993 plan year survey covering 557 firms reported average employer contributions in cases where the employer offered no defined-benefit plan. In those companies where the employer made all contributions, the average contribution rate was 8.5% of annual payroll. In the combination plans, the average was 5.8% of payroll, and in the cases where the match was zero or on a fixed basis, the average was 3.4% of payroll.[15]

The interesting aspect of the matching requirements under the 401(k) arrangement is that workers' full participation can significantly augment the benefits the employer provides. Variations in matching rates also cause some confusion in scaling overall plan generosity. For example, different workers might reach different conclusions about the relative generosity of two 401(k) plans when comparing one that provides a 100% match of employee contributions up to 3% of pay to one that provides a 50% match of up to 8% of pay. For the employee who wants to contribute less than 6% of pay to the plan, the 100% match is clearly superior, because it generates a greater employer contribution than the 50% match even though the marginal employer contributions above 3% of pay are zero. For the employee who wants to contribute more than 6% of pay, however, the plan offering the 50% match would be more generous because it generates higher employer contributions between 6% and 8% of pay.

In assessing potential retirement income employer-sponsored defined-contribution plans could generate where no defined-benefit plan is available, we assume employees contribute at a level that would generate the maximum employer contributions to the plans. In this regard, we are exaggerating the benefits these plans are likely to provide to many workers because not all participate at a level that generates a maximum employer match. In addition, some contributions and accumulated assets leak from these plans over time as some workers cash out some of their retirement saving to finance consumption prior to retirement. On the other hand, we assume employees would not contribute to their plans if there was no employer match. Some employers offer no match at all, and in many cases where an employer does match, many workers contribute beyond the level at which contributions are matched. Thus, in cases where contributions going into a 401(k) plan were unmatched, we attribute no accumulating value to the employee's unmatched contributions to the plan. In this regard, we underestimate the value of the benefits these plans are likely to provide to many workers. Even in cases where there is no 401(k) match, we know from our own data that half of eligible workers regularly participate in the plans. For the sample of defined-contribution plans analyzed according to our assumptions we calculate how much of final earnings an annuity would replace if purchased with the accumulated savings. Table 9.7 shows the results of these calculations.

The earlier discussion about defined-benefit plans provided, at various income levels, information comparable to that presented for defined-contribution plans in table 9.7. Many defined-benefit plans are coordinated with Social Security, which means workers at different wage levels will receive different relative levels of benefits from the plans. For the most common forms of defined-contribution plans among private-sector employers today, such benefit variations across benefit levels are not an explicit part of the plans' design. In actuality, however, contemporary defined-contribution plans may deliver benefits in a pattern that more

Table 9.7
Replacement of final earnings by stand-alone defined-contribution plans for workers retiring at age 62 with 20 or 30 years of service under the plans

Years of service	Replacement rate from plans with percentile ranking by plan generosity			
	15th	40th	65th	90th
30	19.5%	26.1%	34.2%	45.6%
20	12.4	16.5	21.6	28.9

Source: Watson Wyatt Worldwide.

closely corresponds to the structure of defined-benefit plans than their stated features suggest because more higher-wage workers participate in them.

Comparing the results in table 9.7 with those shown earlier in table 9.4 for defined-benefit plans suggests stand-alone defined-contribution plans can generate retirement income similar to that generated by commonly available defined-benefit plans.[16] In the earlier analysis of defined-benefit plans, we looked at the level of individual savings required to supplement pension benefits so workers could maintain their preretirement standard of living in retirement. Because today's popular defined-contribution plans require significant individual contributions, it may seem strange to separately identify the individual savings needed to meet the retirement income targets. The defined-contribution plans we have been evaluating, however, are merely one of several alternative vehicles for accumulating retirement income. There is no reason to believe, under the assumptions we have postulated, that defined-contribution plans by themselves would be any more likely to generate adequate retirement income without supplemental saving than defined-benefit plans. Indeed, many plans analyzed here permit workers to save additional amounts on a tax-preferred basis, although employers do not subsidize these amounts with matching contributions. In this regard, these plans would require workers to augment them with additional saving, just as defined-benefit plans do.

Because stand-alone defined-contribution plans can replace preretirement income at levels relatively comparable to those of defined-benefit plans, in the interest of brevity, we do not present the full results of the analysis here. In general, we found that to match preretirement income levels, participants in the stand-alone defined contribution plans would have to save beyond the rates at which the employer matches contributions. The outside saving rates required matched up quite consistently with those reported earlier in the discussion of defined-benefit plans.

Although the required saving rates in defined-benefit plans and saving required beyond the match in defined-contribution plans showed comparability, replacement rate calculations yielded somewhat different results in the two cases. The replacement rates under the stand-alone defined-contribution scenario must take into account that the worker is saving some of his or her potential disposable wages as a plan participant. Where workers contribute their own money to an employer-sponsored plan, preretirement saving rates directly affect postretirement replacement rates, because the preretirement savings lower the preretirement income levels that must be matched. The replacement rates for participants in the stardalone defined-contribution plans were consistently two to six percentage points lower than the earlier results presented in table 9.6 where we calculated replacement rates for participants in defined-benefit plans. The difference is that in defined-contribution plans, the worker must contribute directly to the retirement plan in most cases to achieve the calculated replacement rates; the overwhelming majority of defined-benefit plans involve no employee contributions. This defined-contribution scenario has roughly equal potential to provide postretirement income as the earlier one under defined-benefit plans, but because many workers are unwilling to make moderate contributions, even where the employer matches them generously, the defined-contribution scenario is often less successful.

Defined-Benefit and Defined-Contribution Plans Operating Together

The majority of employers that currently offer a defined-benefit plan also offer their workers a defined-contribution plan. Today, virtually all large employers whose defined-benefit plan is typically the most significant supplement to Social Security in workers' retirement portfolios also offer some form of defined-contribution program.

To assess the levels of benefits in this environment, we analyzed retirement benefits provided by 313 employers sponsoring both a defined-benefit and a defined-contribution plan, assessing total potential benefits under the combined arrangements. Again, in many of the defined-contribution plans analyzed, employers match employee contributions but also allow additional contributions above the level the employer matches. In this case, as earlier, we assume the participants would contribute at the rate that would maximize the employer contribution but would not contribute above that amount. We did not include in this analysis employers that provided no employer contribution, nor did we include cases where the employer makes discretionary profit-sharing contributions only.

Table 9.8 shows the replacement of final earnings under the combined plans for workers retiring at age 62 with 20 or 30 years of service. Once again, we based replacement rate estimates on a single life annuity compared to the final annual wage. The results here are similar to those reported earlier for defined-benefit plans alone in that each of the combined plans pays a somewhat higher benefit at higher income levels because the pension benefit is integrated with Social Security. Considerably more generous benefit levels are projected here than where defined-

Table 9.8
Replacement of final earnings by defined-benefit and defined-contribution plan combined for workers retiring with 20 and 30 years of service at age 62

Years of service at retirement	Plan percentile ranking	Replacement rates for workers with initial pay levels of			
		$12,500	$20,000	$50,000	$70,000
30	15th	46.8%	46.9%	49.2%	51.2%
	40th	54.7	54.8	58.6	60.7
	65th	62.9	63.5	66.4	68.3
	90th	75.9	76.4	79.8	82.9
20	15th	30.4	30.6	31.6	33.5
	40th	35.8	35.9	38.0	39.6
	65th	41.3	41.6	43.4	44.8
	90th	49.8	49.6	51.6	53.5

Source: Watson Wyatt Worldwide.

benefit plans were considered alone or where a defined-contribution plan was the only plan offered. At the 90th percentile the worker retiring with 30 years of service who participated fully in the defined-contribution plan would appear to have sufficient income from employer-sponsored benefits alone to attain a standard of living in retirement above those of some of the earlier target rates discussed.

Table 9.9 shows saving rates required beyond employer matches to match preretirement income levels, and the percentage of final earnings replaced under combined defined-benefit and defined-contribution plans for workers retiring with 30 years of service at age 62. In this case, many workers would have to save nothing beyond the employer matching levels in the supplemental defined-contribution plan, even those in the 15th percentile plans and at the lowest wage rates. Within the plans, however, workers would often be contributing 6% to 8% of pay to achieve the levels of income replacement the table reflects.

The high replacement rates table 9.9 reflects suggest workers participating fully in the more generous of the plans employers offer today may actually raise their standard of living when they retire. An alternative perspective, however, is that workers eligible to participate in supplemental defined-contribution plans need not necessarily participate to the full extent employers offer to achieve adequate retirement incomes. Some workers participating in the 65th and 90th percentile in table 9.9 could elect not to contribute to the saving plan in some years or consistently to

Table 9.9
Replacement of final earnings by defined-benefit and defined-contribution plans combined for workers retiring at age 62 with 30 years of service at varying levels of plan generosity

Salary when saving and pension coverage begin	Required saving rate beyond employer matching in the combined DB and DC plans at the				Retirement income replacement of preretirement earnings at the			
	15th percentile	40th percentile	65th percentile	90th percentile	15th percentile	40th percentile	65th percentile	90th percentile
$12,500	0.0%	0.0%	0.0%	0.0%	66.9%	70.0%	75.6%	84.4%
15,000	1.3	0.0	0.0	0.0	70.1	71.4	73.4	82.2
20,000	3.6	1.9	0.0	0.0	70.6	72.4	74.3	79.4
25,000	4.6	2.8	0.9	0.0	70.6	72.4	74.3	78.2
30,000	5.4	3.4	1.6	0.0	70.7	72.6	74.5	77.6
40,000	6.8	4.8	3.0	0.0	71.2	73.3	75.0	78.0
50,000	7.7	5.6	3.9	0.9	70.5	72.6	74.3	77.3
60,000	8.3	6.2	4.5	1.4	69.7	71.8	73.5	76.6
70,000	9.2	7.1	5.4	2.3	69.7	71.8	73.5	76.7
80,000	10.1	7.9	6.2	3.0	69.9	72.0	73.7	77.0

Source: Watson Wyatt Worldwide. Dollar amounts are stated in 1994 dollars.

contribute less than the maximum amount the employer matches and still have a retirement income adequate to maintain preretirement consumption levels. Another consideration is our assumption that workers participating in these plans will be eligible for a retiree health benefit many of them will not actually receive. Our earlier analysis of not having a retiree health benefit suggests that most workers covered by a combination of defined-benefit and defined-contribution plans over a significant portion of their working careers will not confront the potential overpensioning table 9.9 implies.

Table 9.10 shows the results of the analysis for the worker who does not enter the plans and begin saving for retirement until age 42. In this case, which may be more common than the prior scenario, employer-sponsored plans do not offer as rich an opportunity to become over-pensioned as they do for 30 years of participation. In most cases, the worker would need to save in addition to participating in the defined-contribution plan to the extent of employer matching. In the middle- and upper-wage levels shown in the table, workers in the 15th percentile plan would be required to undertake what most would consider substantial savings. At the $40,000 wage level, the worker would have to save about $450 per month beyond a $100 per month contribution to the employer-based saving plan, which would generate an employer contribution of $100 to the plan. At the $80,000 level, the worker would need to save at least $1,200 per month beyond what he contributes to the plan for the employer to match.

In this case the replacement rates tend to be more progressive in the plans at the less generous end of the spectrum and somewhat flatter at its more generous end. In some regards the model may be overly conservative in estimating what workers can receive from the combined Social Security and employer-based retirement plan system. In this example and in the earlier ones, we assume the worker who begins coverage under an employer-sponsored plan at age 42 has no accumulated retirement savings from prior jobs. Because of the widespread prevalence of employer-sponsored retirement saving plans today, many workers who enter their major career job in their late 30s or early 40s have substantial retirement plan accumulations from prior participation in earlier employer-sponsored retirement saving plans.

Implications of Marital Status

Table 9.11 shows the effects of being single versus being married to a spouse who is a homemaker. We assume in both cases the worker would

Table 9.10
Replacement of final earnings by defined-benefit and defined-contribution plans combined for workers retiring at age 62 with 20 years of service at varying levels of plan generosity

Salary when saving and pension coverage begin	Required saving rate beyond employer matching in the combined DB and DC plans at the				Retirement income replacement of preretirement earnings at the			
	15th percentile	40th percentile	65th percentile	90th percentile	15th percentile	40th percentile	65th percentile	90th percentile
$12,500	1.9%	0.3%	0.0%	0.0%	65.2%	66.8%	67.1%	69.0%
15,000	5.5	3.9	2.2	0.0	66.2	67.7	69.4	71.6
20,000	8.6	7.1	5.4	3.0	65.7	67.3	69.0	71.4
25,000	10.2	8.5	6.9	4.5	65.2	66.8	68.5	70.9
30,000	11.3	9.5	7.9	5.5	64.9	66.6	68.3	70.7
40,000	13.4	11.5	9.9	7.5	64.8	66.6	68.2	70.6
50,000	14.8	12.9	11.3	8.9	63.5	65.4	67.0	69.4
60,000	15.6	13.8	12.2	9.7	62.5	64.3	65.9	68.4
70,000	17.0	15.1	13.6	11.0	62.1	63.9	65.5	68.0
80,000	18.1	16.3	14.8	12.2	61.9	63.7	65.3	67.8

Source: Watson Wyatt Worldwide. Dollar amounts are stated in 1994 dollars.

Table 9.11
Saving and replacement rates for a single worker and a married worker with a nonworking spouse necessary to maintain preretirement standards of living in retirement when retiring at age 62 with 30 years of service

Salary when saving and pension coverage begin	Saving rate required		Replacement rate at age 62	
	Single	Married with nonworking spouse	Single	Married with nonworking spouse
$12,500	2.5%	0.0%	64.5%	69.0%
15,000	5.1	0.1	66.4	68.3
20,000	7.4	2.5	66.9	69.6
25,000	8.5	4.0	66.7	69.5
30,000	9.4	5.2	66.7	69.4
40,000	11.0	8.0	67.1	69.2
50,000	12.0	9.6	66.2	68.1
60,000	12.7	10.2	65.3	66.7
70,000	13.8	11.7	65.1	66.1
80,000	14.8	13.1	65.2	65.9

Source: Watson Wyatt Worldwide.

begin pension coverage and retirement accumulation at age 32 and retire at age 62, and the pension plan covering the worker provided 1% of final salary per year of covered service at retirement. We also assume the worker would receive a retiree health benefit. The only difference in the two cases is that one worker has a homeworker spouse and the other is single. In the married household, we assume the worker and spouse were the same age and the worker would choose a joint-and-survivor benefit at retirement that would pay the surviving spouse 75% after the worker's death.

The results in the table suggest there is less difference than one might initially expect between the replacement rates or saving rates of couples versus single workers. Across the pay spectrum the table shows, the married couple's saving rates would actually be less than the single person's. At the lowest pay levels, the difference would be 2.5%. In middle income levels the differences in saving rates would range around 4%–5%. At the highest income level shown, the difference would be 1.7%. The married couple would need to save less than the single individual primarily because of the spouse benefit Social Security would provide. Couple replacement rates would be somewhat higher than those for the single worker for essentially the same reason. Higher in the income spectrum, however, the difference diminishes somewhat because "purchasing" the joint-and-survivor option would reduce pension benefits the couple would receive. Across the income spectrum, however, differences in the target income rates in retirement would generally be separated by one to two percentage points.

Married households in which both spouses are employed are not analyzed separately. If both spouses have full-career jobs, their individual work expenses and work-related taxes will parallel those of individual workers. If each participates in a retirement program and saves in accordance with a plan to allow each individually to maintain their living standard in retirement, their combined retirement incomes should allow them to maintain their combined preretirement standards of living. For married couples where one spouse, typically the wife, works only part time temporarily to cover special expenses that arise—for example, the children's college expenses—it hardly seems appropriate to include such income as part of the normal preretirement standard of living. If, on the other hand, one spouse works throughout a career but receives no employer-sponsored pension, the model suggests such households should have markedly higher saving rates. But that should be the household's concern. An employer, in designing its pension or retirement savings program for its own workers, should not have to cover the contingency that other employers may not develop adequate programs.

Future Retirement Income Prospects in the Face of Social Security Changes

Each year, Social Security actuaries develop 75-year income and cost projections for the OASDI programs. They break the results of those projections into 25-year segments. Table 9.12 spells out the 25-year segments

Table 9.12
Projected income and cost rates for the OASDI trust funds

Period	OASDI income rate	OASDI cost rate	Balance	Balance as percentage of income
1994–2018	12.68	12.38	0.31	2.36%
2019–2043	13.06	16.95	−3.89	−29.79
2044–2068	13.25	18.22	−4.98	−37.51

Source: *1995 Annual Report of the Board of Trustees of the Federal Old-Age and Survivors Insurance and Disability Insurance Trust Funds*, p. 112.

from the most recent report and illustrates the potential impact the baby boom generation will have on Social Security. For the most part, the first 25 years can be thought of as the baby boomers' remaining preretirement period, because the first of the baby-boom-age cohorts will not turn 62 until 2008. The second 25 years can be thought of largely as when the baby boomers will move fully into retirement. By 2043, the youngest baby boomers will be 79. During the third 25 years, the baby boomers will end their retirement, as the youngest will be 104 by 2068.

During the periods when the baby boomers will draw the bulk of their benefits from Social Security, the combined OASDI trust funds are under-funded by roughly 30% to 40% according to these projections. Some may argue that the funding shortfall is really less because the shortfall over the full 75-year projection period is only about 17% of projected income over the period as a whole. However, whatever solution to the funding short-falls is ultimately implemented it is unlikely to be implemented immedi-ately. Much of the program's cost over the next 25 years is already built into benefits being paid to people currently in beneficiary status or about to enter such status. Although we may be able to reduce marginally the lifetime benefits of those currently receiving or about to receive them, it is unlikely we will realize significant savings from such reductions. Fur-thermore, changes in cost estimates over the last dozen years suggest we should be conservative in picking our funding targets. For example, the OASDI programs' estimated 75-year actuarial balance deteriorated by 2.20% of projected payroll between the system's 1983 and 1996 valua-tions. This deterioration resulted largely from changes in assumptions concerning the economy's future performance, valuation methods and periods, and to a lesser extent from a greater number of disability claims than expected.[17]

There are many reasons to believe future projections will be different than the most recent one. Although the projections might in some cases change the funding balance positively, it has changed to the negative in 13 of the last 14 projection periods, suggesting an estimate that Social Security is underfunded by 40% for the baby boomers might prove con-servative. In any event, we are simply looking for a bottom range for analyzing the implications of various approaches to balancing Social Security's financing on workers at different wage levels. Whether we assume the underfunding to be addressed was 20%, 40%, or 60% would make little difference on the relative results; it would affect only their overall magnitude.

The Social Security shortfalls projected for the baby boomers can be eliminated in essentially three ways: lower benefits, higher taxes, or some combination of the two. To assess these options, we consider three scenarios. The funding shortfall is corrected, in the first, entirely by reducing benefits; in the second, entirely by raising taxes; and in the third, half by reducing benefits and half by raising taxes. In the benefit-reduction scenarios, we look at two alternative forms of reduction: first, everyone's benefits are reduced by a comparable percentage; and second, the system moves to a flat benefit, so that everyone receives the same amount from Social Security regardless of their preretirement wage level. In the tax-raising scenarios, we assume that the worker bears the entire increase in the payroll tax, including the employer's share.

Economic theory suggests employers would consider the added payroll tax part of the labor cost—that is, part of the total wage being paid to workers. If employers already pay workers a wage equal to their marginal products, as economic theory suggests, the employer would react to an increase in the payroll tax by reducing the cash wage paid to workers. Because cash wages are generally somewhat sticky or rigid in a downward direction, such a wage reduction would probably take the form of a slowing in the growth in nominal wages. It was easier in our calculation to assign the assumed payroll tax increases to the workers as a work-related expense than to reduce the basic growth trajectory of wages, which we assume throughout the analysis to grow at a constant rate of 5% per year, although the net result is equivalent to slowing cash wage growth.

In the benefit-reduction scenarios, we consider two different approaches to reducing benefits. First, we calculate workers' benefits using calculation formulas implied by current law and reduced the benefit by 40%. Second, we project the average benefits that would be paid to future workers by indexing current average benefits to the assumed growth in real wages. In the scenarios where we consider benefit reductions would account for the full Social Security adjustments, we reduce the projected average benefit by 40%. In those where we consider increases in the payroll tax rate would fully fund the benefits, we assume currently legislated payroll taxes would increase by 40% over the remaining lifetime of the workers for whom we were calculating benefits. In those where we considerd a combination of benefit cuts and tax increases, we assume the projected current benefit amount or the projected average benefit would be reduced by 20% and that workers' remaining lifetime taxes would be raised by 20%. The 40% and 20% tax increases converted to 80% and 40% because of our assumption that workers would bear the employer's tax.

We realize the benefit cuts we suggest here would have a some-what larger financing impact on Social Security's operations than the tax increases we are analyzing if the relative changes did not have any behavioral effects. We suspect, however, that benefit reductions of the magnitude we consider here would tend to increase the claims under the Disability Insurance (DI) program over the levels of claims under current law. We do not specifiy how benefit reductions might be accomplished, but some options might delay the onset of early-retirement benefits. That would definitely imply that more workers would apply for disability prior to qualifying for a Social Security retirement benefit. Even if benefits were reduced by pushing back the normal retirement age while leaving the early retirement age at 62 with reduced benefit levels compared to current law, the prospect of a retirement period with such significantly reduced benefits would increase the incentives to get into the DI program. Although more finely equilibrating the benefit cuts or tax increases might be important for evaluating the implications of various policy options within wage classes, they are not as important in the current context because the primary focus here is the various options' implications on workers across the wage spectrum.

Implications of Social Security Changes for Workers Without Pensions

Presenting detailed results from the various pension coverage scenarios and combinations of Social Security policy changes and employer-sponsored retirement plan benefits would be overwhelming. The impor-tant thing to understand is the various policy alternatives' ramifications for workers' need to save on their own for retirement and the potential effects on their standards of living in retirement. In this section, we show the marginal changes on saving targets and retirement income replacement rates under the various simulated Social Security policy changes. By consid-ering various situations and scenarios, it is possible to draw some general conclusions about policy options we likely will face in the coming years.

Table 9.13 shows the changes in required saving rates and replacement rates for workers not covered by an employer-sponsored retirement or saving plan under various policy change scenarios. The results are shown for workers whose wage level in 1994 at age 32 was $12,500, $40,000, or $80,000 when they began to save at the required rate for their retirement needs beyond what Social Security would provide under current law. Using these three pay levels gives a sense of what the policy changes imply across a fairly broad range of the economic spectrum.

Table 9.13
Percentage point changes in required saving rates and replacement rates under alternative Social Security policy scenarios for workers with no employer pensions or saving plans retiring at age 62

Policy option	Saving rate changes at starting pay level when saving begins			Replacement rate changes at starting pay level when saving begins		
	$12,500	$40,000	$80,000	$12,500	$40,000	$80,000
Current benefit reduced 40%	4.3%	2.8%	1.6%	-4.3%	-2.8%	-1.6%
Flat benefit at 60% of current average	1.9	4.1	2.7	-1.9	-4.1	-2.7
Current benefit with 40% tax increase	-2.4	-2.3	-2.2	-9.7	-9.5	-8.9
Flat benefit at current average with 40% tax increase	-6.5	-0.1	-0.4	-5.7	-11.8	-10.6
Current benefit reduced 20% with 20% tax increase	1.0	0.2	-0.3	-7.0	-6.1	-5.3
Flat benefit at 80% of current average with 20% tax increase	-2.3	2.0	1.2	-3.8	-7.9	-6.7

Source: Watson Wyatt Worldwide. Dollar amounts stated in 1994 dollars.

Focusing first on the replacement rates in the table, all the options considered would reduce the retirement standard of living for virtually all workers considered. This may seem counterintuitive to anyone who believes preserving current benefits will protect the elderly against benefit reductions and we should attempt to do so at all costs. The problem is that the options to preserve benefits do so at the cost of increased payroll taxes, which imply a reduced level of disposable income and possible consumption during the working period. Under the life cycle model theory underlying this analysis, a decline in preretirement disposable income or standard of living will carry through to the retirement period. Indeed, the options that reduce benefits in this case would appear not to have as adverse an effect on the retirement standard of living as those that involve tax increases for middle- and higher-wage workers.

On the saving side, the options that reduce benefits would generally increase the savings required of workers to maintain preretirement standards of living. From a macroeconomic perspective, almost all economists and many other policy analysts as well would look favorably on policies that encourage workers to increase their saving rates. Those favoring such policies generally oppose policies that drive savings below current levels, and so would regard options that rely on increased tax rates less favorably than those that reduce benefits. In the case where the current-law benefit would be maintained and financed by a 40% increase in the payroll tax, saving rates would fall at virtually every wage level. Policymakers should be concerned that significant increases in payroll taxes to maintain current-law benefits may cut workers' current savings by even more than the table implies as they attempt to maintain their standard of living prior to the tax increase.

If it is desirable to find policy solutions to the Social Security financing shortfall for baby boomers that increase savings, benefit reductions should be preferred to tax increases. If the policy concern is that benefit reductions might disproportionately affect lower-wage workers' retirement security, a shift to a flatter benefit would go a long way toward meeting that goal. No matter how far we move toward benefit reductions or tax increases, we need to do a much better job of helping workers understand what their saving rates must be to meet reasonable retirement goals.

In this analysis, we have assumed workers will attempt to maintain the same retirement patterns as postulated under current law. Another alternative for workers facing reduced Social Security benefits, or pension benefits as well, is to work longer rather than adjusting their savings behavior to offset retirement income program reductions. For a worker who begins to save in his or her early 30s and plans to retire some 30 years after beginning to save for retirement, one additional year of work at the end of the career will reduce the saving target over the working period by between 1% and 2% of pay. We have chosen to focus on needed changes in saving rates and retirement income levels rather than working longer because of the half-century record of career workers' tendency to retire at ever earlier ages. Although changes in Social Security benefit levels or reduced pension promises may reverse this historical trend, the record shows a disposition toward early retirement that may be hard for many workers to relinquish. Many workers may consider, extending their work careers only as a last option in the face of potential benefit reductions.

Implications of Social Security Changes for Workers with Pensions

In the case where workers participate only in a defined-benefit plan, we find essentially the same replacement rate effects of the various Social Security policy changes as in the earlier scenarios where workers were not covered by any employer-sponsored retirement plans. Thus, the need for increased saving is generally true, with the possible exception of low-wage long-service workers.

Because current Social Security benefits in combination with a generous defined-benefit plan result in improved standards of living in retirement relative to the working period, a reduction in the Social Security benefit would not require an increase in saving for these low-wage workers to maintain their preretirement standard of living.

Although the absolute changes in saving rates and retirement income levels are considerably similar, the baseline situations of workers represented in the two cases differ significantly. Workers who have no pension coverage have baseline target saving rates significantly higher than those of workers covered by a pension plan. A policy change that requires a $40,000-per-year worker to increase his saving rate say, 2.8%, would require a marginal increase to an existing saving rate prior to any policy changes of 15.5% for a 22-year-old worker with no pension. The same worker covered under the 90th percentile defined-benefit plan would add the marginal increase to a significantly lower existing saving rate of 9.0%. Although Social Security modifications might make the extra saving burden relatively lighter for the noncovered workers, the original level of required saving prior to any policy change would be so high that many workers without employer-plan coverage might simply ignore their additional saving requirements in the belief they would never reach the standard on their own anyway—that is, they would succumb to a philosophy of "live for today and we will deal with the devil of tomorrow when it arrives." The correspondence in effect between this scenario, where workers are covered by pensions, and the earlier one, where they were not, supports the conclusion that tax increases affect required saving rates more negatively than benefit cuts but reduce retirement standards of living by as much as or more than benefit reductions.

Table 9.14 presents the results where workers are covered by both a defined-benefit and defined-contribution plan. The story in this case is distinctly different than in the earlier scenarios in that most workers covered under a defined-benefit plan who participate relatively fully in a defined-contribution plan would not have to change their saving behavior significantly to maintain their preretirement disposable income levels in retirement. The exceptions are the mid- and high-wage workers, whose benefit reductions generally require an increase to their savings and whose significant tax increases would reduce their required savings levels as before. Under assumptions that workers covered by both types of plans participate in them to the extent they maximize employer contributions, most of the cost of the Social Security shifts analyzed come in reduced income for retirees, albeit from a level that looks excessive relative to preretirement disposable income in many cases under the current-law scenarios. As before, across-the-board benefit reductions would generally hit lower-wage workers harder than those at higher wage levels, a phenomenon that moving to a flatter benefit structure could ameliorate.

Table 9.14 focuses on workers covered by employer-sponsored retirement plans during the last 30 years of their careers. Looking at workers with shorter tenures under the plans tends to yield similar results to those shown here. Analyzing the situation for workers with 20 years of tenure under employer plans, for example, tends to shift the results for workers covered under both a defined-benefit and a defined-contribution plan toward those of a worker covered under only a single plan. The results for workers covered under only a single plan would tend to shift toward those covered by no employer plan at all. The results for workers covered by only a defined-contribution plan are practically identical to those for workers covered by only a defined-benefit plan, under the assumptions on which this analysis has been developed.

Table 9.14
Percentage point changes in required saving rates and replacement rates under alternative Social Security policy scenarios for workers in both a defined-benefit and defined-contribution plan

Policy option	Changes in saving rates at starting pay level when saving and pension coverage begin			Changes in replacement rates at starting pay level when saving and pension coverage begin		
	$12,500	$40,000	$80,000	$12,500	$40,000	$80,000
Current benefit reduced 40%						
Pension at the 15th percentile	3.0%	2.8%	1.6%	−3.0%	−2.8%	−1.6%
Pension at the 90th percentile	0.0	2.8	1.6	−13.2	−2.8	−1.6
Flat benefit at 60% of current average						
Pension at the 15th percentile	0.6	4.1	2.7	−0.6	−4.1	−2.7
Pension at the 90th percentile	0.0	4.1	2.7	−5.7	−4.1	−2.7
Current benefit with 40% tax increase						
Pension at the 15th percentile	0.0	−2.3	−2.2	−2.3	−9.5	−8.9
Pension at the 90th percentile	0.0	0.0	−2.2	0.0	−3.5	−8.9
Flat benefit at current average with 40% tax increase						
Pension at the 15th percentile	0.0	−0.1	−0.4	10.1	−11.8	−10.6
Pension at the 90th percentile	0.0	0.0	−0.4	12.4	−11.7	−10.6
Current benefit reduced 20% with 20% tax increase						
Pension at the 15th percentile	0.0	0.2	−0.3	−5.4	−6.1	−5.3
Pension at the 90th percentile	0.0	0.2	−0.3	−6.6	−6.1	−5.3
Flat benefit at 80% of current average with 20% tax increase						
Pension at the 15th percentile	0.0	2.0	1.2	1.1	−7.9	−6.7
Pension at the 90th percentile	0.0	2.0	1.2	3.3	−7.9	−6.7

Source: Watson Wyatt Worldwide. Dollar amounts are stated in 1994 dollars.

Future Retirement Income Prospects in the Face of Pension Changes

Aging workforces mean many employers sponsoring defined-benefit plans today face significantly higher plan costs in the future for a variety of reasons. Today, because of accounting and regulatory requirements, employers tend to fund their defined-benefit plans under the projected unit-credit funding method, whereby the annual contributions to the plan increase as a percentage of payroll as workers age. In addition to the shift to projected unit-credit funding, a series of federal legal requirements adopted in recent years limit the funding of retirement benefits early in a worker's career. Money not contributed to a plan when a worker is young must be made up with interest later. The relative size of the baby boom generation reduced the average age of the workforce during the early part of its working tenure. The shift in the accounting and regulatory environment reduced pension contributions early in the baby boomers' careers But now, as members of the baby boom generation move toward the latter half of their careers, the average age of the workforce is rising and will significantly increase defined-benefit plans' funding requirements, in part to make up for the earlier reduced funding. Chapter 7 suggested that, as a consequence of population aging, private-sector defined-benefit sponsors may have to increase their current contributions to their retirement plans by as much as 60%, on average, if the plans are to deliver the benefits the current benefit structures imply. Finally, changes in Social Security policy could alter the cost of many defined-benefit plans because of various plan features that coordinate the pension benefit with the onset of Social Security eligibility and the structure of Social Security benefits.

Far more varied changes in pensions may result from rising plan costs related to aging workers than those we will see in Social Security. For technical reasons, some employers may feel they have to maintain retirement programs that will allow their workers to continue to retire at ages comparable to current retirement patterns. If Social Security curtails early retirement benefits, these employers may face the prospect of enhancing their plans' early retirement benefits even though the current benefit structure implies rising future costs. Others may conclude the relative shortage of younger workers in the future will require they keep their older workers at their jobs longer than they do today. In this latter case, increasing the ages of eligibility for early- and full-retirement benefits can curtail growth in defined-benefit plans' costs. Some employers may abandon their defined-benefit plans altogether because of the uncertainty created by the demographic pressures the baby boomers will place on all elements of the retirement system. A shift from a defined-benefit to a defined-contribution plan will insulate employers against the demographic pressures somewhat, but as the latter type is more under the worker's control, it may also limit employers' ability to manage workers' orderly retirement to the extent they can with current plans.

To provide a frame of reference to assess potential changes in defined-benefit plans, we develop one benefit reduction scenario in which we reduce the current benefits that plans provide by 30% across the board. In this case we use the same universe of plans that we have used throughout the presentation in the scenarios where we consider the situation of workers participating only in a defined-benefit plan. In many instances, defined-contribution plans supplement these plans, but as in real life, many workers do not take advantage of these supplemental plans. Even when they do, reducing the defined-benefit level for plans coordinated with defined-contribution plans by an amount of similar magnitude to the one we are analyzing here would have the same proportional effect as this analysis suggests. Table 9.15 presents the changes in required saving and replacement rates for the four levels of plans we have been analyzing.

As one might expect, the results presented in the table show a certain balance and symmetry. The saving and replacement rate effects tend to be greater at higher starting pay levels for a plan of a given level of generosity, and they are also greater as we proceed from less generous plans to more generous. For all practical purposes, the replacement rate changes mirror the saving rate changes, which points to an interesting conclusion about potential reductions in pension benefit levels. Suppose an employer, in accordance with our baseline assumptions, is providing annual pay increases that average 5% per year where the basic inflation rate is 4%. Assume that this employer begins to encounter increases in the cost of operating its defined-benefit plan for reasons discussed earlier and decides to curtail the benefits by 30% because of these cost increases. In this case, workers will have to increase their personal saving rates by 2%–5% of pay, depending on the baseline pension's generosity and the worker's earnings level, to restore their retirement income level to its previous equilibrium where it equaled their preretirement disposable income level. Because they will have to save more of their preretirement gross income, however, the curtailment of the pension will reduce both preretirement and postretirement income levels.

Table 9.15
Impact of a 30% reduction in the defined-benefit pensions on required saving and replacement rates for workers participating only in a defined-benefit plan

Salary when saving and pension coverage begin	Change in saving rates for plans at the				Change in replacement rates for plans at the			
	15th percentile	40th percentile	65th percentile	90th percentile	15th percentile	40th percentile	65th percentile	90th percentile
$12,500	1.4%	1.9%	2.3%	3.1%	-1.4%	-1.9%	-2.3%	-3.1%
15,000	1.4	1.9	2.3	3.1	-1.4	-1.9	-2.3	-3.1
20,000	1.4	1.9	2.3	3.1	-1.4	-1.9	-2.3	-3.1
25,000	1.4	2.0	2.4	3.1	-1.4	-2.0	-2.4	-3.1
30,000	1.5	2.0	2.4	3.2	-1.5	-2.0	-2.4	-3.2
40,000	1.5	2.1	2.5	3.2	-1.5	-2.1	-2.5	-3.2
50,000	1.6	2.1	2.5	3.2	-1.6	-2.1	-2.5	-3.2
60,000	1.6	2.2	2.6	3.3	-1.6	-2.2	-2.6	-3.3
70,000	1.7	2.2	2.6	3.3	-1.7	-2.2	-2.6	-3.3
80,000	1.7	2.3	2.7	3.4	-1.7	-2.3	-2.7	-3.4

Source: Watson Wyatt Worldwide. Dollar amounts are stated in 1994 dollars.

Exactly the same outcome would be achieved if the employer reduced one year's pay raise by 2%–5% of pay, again depending on the baseline pension's generosity and the worker's earnings level. A one-year elimination or reduction in a regular pay increase would carry through to all subsequent years because of the compounding nature of recurring pay increases. In this scenario, a worker's disposable wage is explicitly reduced to preserve the pension's generosity, but the pension benefit will continue at the rate that allows the worker to maintain the preretirement standard of living without having to change personal saving levels. The previous scenario, where the cash wage is maintained but the pension curtailed, implicitly reduces the worker's disposable wage because his or her personal saving rate must increase to reestablish the equilibrium between preretirement and postretirement disposable-income levels. If pensions are reduced, workers may not have the fortitude to adjust their saving behavior to account for reductions in their pensions; they may also lack the ability to invest their personal savings as effectively as a professionally managed pension plan; and they may also be unable to handle retirement annuity markets with the same efficiency as an employer operating a pension plan.

The calculus of the pension-wage trade-off seems to imply employers will be in an extremely strong position in the future to negotiate with workers over the relative merits of maintaining their retirement security as opposed to passing on automatic pay increases if they can explain the dynamics of the trade-offs to the workers. If they cannot, the pressure to pass on regular cash wage increases could exact a high price on the retirement income security of many workers currently counting on their pension plan's continuing as it is currently structured until they retire. It is not clear at this juncture how the slowdown in pension funding in recent years will ultimately affect benefits, but it does jeopardize some workers' benefits. If pension benefits are curtailed, the implied increases in personal saving rates and the commensurate reductions in retirement income levels for workers covered by pension plans will accentuate the changes if Social Security is brought into balance.

Conclusions

All the analyses presented here suggest that what is often currently referred to as America's savings crisis has the potential to become a consumption crisis. The baby boom generation will receive Social Security benefits comparable to current-law promises only if future generations of workers are willing to give up a larger share of their wage income to support future retirees than today's workers do. If those workers are not willing to support taxes perhaps as much as 40% higher than current rates, then the baby boomers are going to see their retirement consumption expectations unfulfilled. If we wait until the baby boomers retire and attempt to resolve the financing imbalance through higher taxes, many future workers may find their working-life consumption expectations unfulfilled to satisfy the baby boom generation's consumption appetites.

In addition to the problems involved in resolving the Social Security financing imbalance, many workers covered by a pension plan will also face the difficult prospect of either dampened retirement benefit expectations or reduced preretirement disposable-income levels as they are forced to pay in the future for the slowed pension funding over the last decade. Either way, ERISA will force the issue in the case of private-employer-sponsored defined-benefit plans. Private sponsors can accumulate some unfunded liabilities in their retirement plans, but not nearly to the extent that public-sector plans, including Social Security, can. At some point, private employers must finance the accruing obligations their current plans imply or freeze them in place. If they do the former, following the earlier example, catch-up financing means workers' wages will be retarded, and they will be forced to defer current consumption to their retirement period. If they do the latter, freezing plans merely means that we have delayed the day of reckoning on current consumption levels out of balance with lifetime income expectations.

Finally, the saving rate calculations reported throughout this analysis are target saving rates and are a far cry from the saving rates actually being attained currently by many, if not most, workers. The very simple conceptual framework laid out at the beginning of the analysis of our current retirement system and potential modifications to it should make it painfully clear that preretirement saving and postretirement consumption are inextricably tied in an economy with mature retirement systems. We can ignore the binding logic of that model during the start-up phase of a pay-as-you-go Social Security system, but the mature system's current financing projections clearly demonstrate we cannot ignore its logic forever. We can also ignore the model's binding logic during the early phases of a pension expansion across an economy characterized by a growing workforce and increasing productivity. We cannot ignore it as pension plan sponsors move into phases of operations where they have nearly as many retirees as—or, in some instances, more retirees than—they have workers. If the working-age population in today's society cannot be convinced to give up some of their current consumption levels, they will be left with the prospect of either working much later in their lives than most workers do currently or submitting to retirement standards of living significantly reduced from those they have achieved during their working years.

If we return to the analogy of our retirement income security system as a three-legged stool, we have a stool too short for the retirement table at which we collectively want to sit. Either the legs of the stool have to be lengthened, or we are going to have to sit at a much shorter table. Congress may be able to legislate higher payroll taxes that will deliver current-law benefits to the baby boomers. But after a decade and a half of pursuing low tax rates, the current political environment belies the willingness of contemporary Congresses to deliver the higher payroll taxes necessary to assure these benefits. Employers may be able to convince workers they should forego current pay to assure their pension expectations, but more than a decade of cutbacks driven by public policies that have divested senior management of their interest in tax-qualified retirement plans makes that contingency unlikely. Workers may become convinced they need to make some provision on their own to cover the possibility that their Social Security and employer-sponsored benefits will be inadequate to meet retirement needs, but the trends of falling personal saving rates tracked across the 1980s and into the 1990s do not bode well in this regard.

The bottom line is that America must save more, and it should begin to do so now. If future Social Security benefits must be cut for the current generation of workers, then we should consider lifting the onerous tax burden the current tax system puts on personal saving outside of tax-qualified plans. If the desire to protect the lower-wage worker against the prospect of having the single solid element of his or her retirement portfolio eroded is important, then we should consider Social Security benefit reductions aimed specifically at middle- and higher-wage workers. Such policies will exacerbate a problem that already exists for current workers in these classes in that their rates of return on their "contributions" to Social Security are extremely low or negative. If the only way we can offer reasonable protection at the bottom of the economic spectrum is through a Social Security system more "economically" unfair to the high-wage worker than the current system, we should consider increasing the tax-preferred benefits high-wage workers can receive through the tax-qualified leg of the system as the price for their subsidization of Social Security.

If the more favorable treatment of individual saving for retirement must have special revenue measures to accompany it, one alternative would be to alter the home mortgage interest deduction. Many who would be hurt by such a change in policy would benefit from the ability to save more for their retirement without the punitive taxation on deferred consumption our current tax system applies to regular savings. Furthermore, limiting the home interest deduction would provide a powerful economic reinforcement of the incentives encouraging people to save for their retirement. In the final analysis, the results here show that avoiding the inevitable need to save more today ultimately means a reduction in future consumption levels anyway. We either pay the piper now and soften the blow of consumption reductions in the future, or we wait and ultimately suffer greater unavoidable consequences.

Notes

The author gratefully acknowledges the help of Alexander Miller of Watson Wyatt Worldwide, who estimated the employer-sponsored benefit levels used in the analysis, and Gordon Goodfellw, also of Watson Wyatt Worldwide, who developed the replacement rate and saving computations throughout the paper. The opinions and conclusions expressed in this paper are the author's and do not necessarily reflect those of Watson Wyatt Worldwide or any of its associates.

1. Sylvester J. Schieber and John B. Shoven, "The Consequences of Population Aging on Private Pension Fund Saving and Asset Markets," chapter 7 in this volume.

2. B. Douglas Bernheim, *Is the Baby Boom Generation Preparing Adequately for Retirement? Summary Report* (New York: Merrill Lynch, Pierce, Fenner & Smith, Inc., 1993).

3. Alan J. Auerbach and Laurence J. Kotlikoff, *The United States' Fiscal and Savings Crises and Their Implications for the Baby Boom Generation* (New York: Merrill Lynch, Pierce, Fenner & Smith, Inc., 1994).

4. See Richard P. Hinz and Sylvester J. Schieber, "Baby Boomers in Retirement: The Best of Times or the Worst of Times?" presented at the annual meeting of the Gerontological Society of America (Atlanta, GA, November 19, 1994).

5. Committee on Economic Security, *Social Security in America* (Washington, DC: Government Printing Office, 1937), p. 202.

6. Adam Smith, *The Wealth of Nations* (first Published in 1776, quotation from 1994 Modern Library Edition, New York: Random House, 1994), pp. 938–939.

7. Ibid., p. 939.

8. Gordon M. Fisher, "The Development and History of the Poverty Thresholds," *Social Security Bulletin* 55(4) (Winter 1992), p. 4.

9. Patricia Ruggles, *Drawing the Line: Alternative Poverty Measures and Their Implications for Public Policy* (Washington, DC: The Urban Institute, 1990).

10. Public Law 89–73 (July 14, 1965).

11. Elizabeth L. Meier, Cynthia C. Dittmar, and Barbara Boyle Torrey, *Retirement Income Goals* (Washington, DC: President's Commission on Pension Policy, March 1980), p. 1.

12. President's Commission on Pension Policy, *Coming of Age: Toward A National Retirement Income Policy* (Washington, DC, 1981), p. 42.

13. See Dan M. McGill, Kyle N. Brown, John J. Haley, and Sylvester J. Schieber, *Fundamentals of Private Pensions*, 7th edition, chapters 18 and 19, for a full description of the model, the estimation of preretirement work expenses, special consumption expenditures related to the preretirement and postretirement periods, and analysis of current retirement plans (Philadelphia: University of Pennsylvania Press, 1996).

14. Bureau of Labor Statistics, U.S. Department of Labor, *Employee Benefits in Medium and Large Private Establishments* (Washington DC: U.S. Department of Labor, May 1993), Bulletin 2422, p. 104.

15. Profit Sharing Council of America, *37th Annual Survey of Profit Sharing and 401(k) Plans Reflecting 1993 Plan Year Experience* (Chicago, IL: Profit Sharing Council of America, 1994), p. 8.

16. That typical defined-benefit and defined-contribution plans can yield comparable replacement of final earnings for comparable workers participating under them is consistent with the findings of Andrew Samwick and Jonathan Skinner in "How Will Defined Contribution Plans Affect Retirement Income?" a paper presented at the Western Economic Association Annual Meetings, July 1995, San Diego, California.

17. John C. Hambor, "Outline for Advisory Council Presentation on Trustees' Assumptions," presentation made to the 1994 Social Security Advisory Council (Washington, DC, October 21, 1994).

10   Policy Directions for Pensions

Sylvester J. Schieber and
John B. Shoven

The common thread that joins much of the analysis presented in various chapters of this volume is the need for greater saving. We have seen that virtually every aspect of our retirement income security system is underfunded in some regard. Social Security is facing substantial financial shortfalls as the baby boom generation moves into its retirement years. The employer-based pension system will require substantially higher future contributions to deliver benefits promised currently. Workers themselves have reduced their personal saving rates in recent years. If we continue our current retirement saving policies and behaviors much longer, the only guarantee our retirement income security system will be able to deliver to the baby boomers is disappointment. If we do not change direction soon, baby boomers will have to work much later into their lives than prior generations, or they will live out their retirements at standards of living well below those prior generations have enjoyed. Changing direction requires that we change behavior, and changing behavior can be encouraged and supported through a variety of public policies, employer initiatives, and individually oriented efforts.

Changing Perspectives and Changing Saving Behavior

Economists, using life cycle models of consumption and saving and factoring in programs such as Social Security and employer pensions, have estimated saving paths workers should follow to accumulate sufficient retirement wealth to meet their retirement needs. Actuaries and retirement plan designers have developed earnings replacement models to aid in the design of retirement programs that allow workers to maintain pre-retirement disposable-income levels. Though most workers undoubtedly would like to accumulate sufficient resources during their working lives to assure their standards of living will not decline during their retirement, the majority are unlikely to use the kinds of sophisticated models economists and retirement plan experts have devised to estimate the level of saving required to meet that goal. Yet when we look at retirees today, the majority clearly have been able to provide sufficiently for their retirement needs.

In most cases workers likely plan for their own retirement by observing the effectiveness of the retirement accumulation of people they know and with whom they work. From observing their parents or grandparents they develop a perception of the level of benefits Social Security provides to retirees. Form observing fellow workers who reach retirement and from materials their employers provide, they develop a perception of the level of benefits they can expect from their pension programs. From periodic benefit statements they receive from their employer, they see the accumulating balance in retirement saving plans and can roughly project the savings they can ultimately accumulate by continued participation in them. As they observe the generation of workers in front of them achieve adequate retirement income to meet their needs, they can gauge their own continued participation in the portfolio of retirement programs available to allow them to achieve comparably adequate retirement income levels.

Until now, sophisticated calculations by economists and actuaries have not been necessary for many workers to prepare adequately for retirement because the retirement programs in which they have participated have performed comparably, or in many cases have improved, from one generation to the next. The baby boom generation today faces the problem that various elements of the retirement income security system are unlikely to perform for them in the same fashion they have for the earlier generations of workers they have observed. Taking into consideration their position in the wage spectrum, baby boom workers are likely to face earnings replacement rates from Social Security significantly below those of their parents. In addition, because of the future increased cost of pensions, many workers currently participating in defined-benefit pension plans are likely to receive lower replacement of preretirement wages from their pension than workers currently transitioning into retirement. Also, the gradual shift from noncontributory defined-benefit plans to contributory defined-contribution plans in recent years means that more of today's workers are personally responsible for their own retirement savings than earlier generations of workers were.

Given the relatively low personal saving rates that prevail in our economy today and baby boom workers' prospects of reduced benefits from organized retirement programs, now is the time to begin to alert the boomers that they have some options for controlling their own retirement destinies. To do so, however, they must increase their own personal saving rates immediately and sustain those higher rates until they retire. Expecting them to do so without communicating to them the urgency of increasing their savings will likely result in continuing low levels of personal and national saving, and ultimately in their failure to reach satisfactory retirement goals. Now is an opportune time to undertake a variety of organized communication programs to educate workers about their personal responsibilities in saving for retirement and consequences for not doing so. Such communications programs should be carried out at two levels.

More vigorous communications by employers already sponsoring retirement saving programs, who have already shown a commitment to providing saving opportunities for workers, would potentially enhance those programs' effectiveness. In most cases, the employer sponsors of these saving plans already communicate with workers periodically, urging them to take advantage of the tax incentives supporting these plans and the supplemental subsidies the plans often offer. Expanding such communications to be more specific about saving targets for workers at various points in the wage spectrum would improve workers' understanding of their role in preparing for retirement and increase the probability they would meet their retirement income targets by the age at which they wish to retire. Even if workers did not respond to the more specific saving goals such communications would provide, they would better understand the implications of failing to save than they do now.

In addition to increased and more effective communications at the individual employer plan level, we believe it is time to undertake a broad public information program encouraging personal savings. The United States has a long history of government-developed and government-funded public service information programs aimed at altering personal behaviors. If government advertising campaigns can increase the prevalence of auto seat belt use or reduce smoking, why couldn't a similar campaign begin to encourage more appropriate saving behavior among baby boom workers? Television and radio have proven extremely effective vehicles in influencing behavior in this country. Listeners are urged daily to buy cars, televisions, vacation cruises, beer, athletic equipment, and a wide range of other goods and services. If these media can alter ordinary consumers' behavior, why not direct that power at the extremely important national goal of increasing savings? If the national media gave air time to the importance of personal saving, maybe the daily consumption-saving trade-offs workers make would become more reasonably balanced.

Our retirement saving communications programs should also describe honestly the strain future retirees will potentially put on other aspects of the retirement income security system. Starting in 1995, the Social Security Administration began sending workers periodic statements about the potential benefits they will receive from the program. Initially these statements were targeted to workers over 60, but ultimately the plan is to provide annual statements to all workers over 35. Telling people while they are working what they can expect from retirement programs is extremely desirable because it will allow them to coordinate other elements of their retirement saving in the pursuit of adequate retirement income. Communicating to people that they can expect benefits from Social Security in accordance with the promises embedded in current law, however, seems fraught with the danger of misleading them about the need to save through other elements of their retirement portfolios.

Encouraging Efficient Investment Behavior

The shift toward a greater dependence on defined-contribution plans in the employer-sponsored leg of our retirement system included a move toward greater participant control of investment decisions over retirement assets. In part, sponsors of defined-contribution plans have moved to allow participants to direct the investment of their own plan accumulations and thereby to transfer much of the fiduciary responsibility for managing the assets effectively to the participants themselves. Concern is growing, however, that participants in these plans tend to direct their assets toward overly conservative investment options expected to generate lower yields over time than a more balanced investment portfolio.

Concerns have also been raised that many participants make marginal investment decisions that follow changes in asset prices to the detriment of their long-term accumulations, that is, some investors tend to enter the equity markets well after a period of price increases occurs and then withdraw from the market after a downturn. Buying high and selling low is hardly an appropriate strategy for accumulating retirement assets, but many people being called upon to make financial investment decisions have little appreciation of how financial markets operate over time or how their investment strategies should be structured to meet their retirement income goals.

Retirement plan participants are being increasingly called upon to become retirement asset managers, and additional participant education on wise investment practices could pay significant returns. But some caution is also in order. Turning a large portion of the workforce into sophisticated investment managers of their own retirement savings might be a goal beyond the reach of current knowledge and technology. Some sponsors of defined-contribution plans that have moved toward partic-ipant-directed accounts should reconsider whether this is the most effec-tive way to deliver an optimum level of retirement benefits to broad cross sections of their workforces. Many of these programs might be able to deliver higher levels of retirement benefits over time at lower costs by moving back toward employer-managed asset pools.

Pension Policy as Part of a Prosaving Program

The evidence of this volume, from the Introduction, which illustrated how net national saving has declined in the United States and pension funds were the only strong component in national saving, to chapter 3, which found personal retirement accounts are adding to household total wealth accumulation, all points to the central role pensions can play in dealing with one of the economy's major long-run problems—the anemic national saving rate. Even our own discussion in chapter 7, which warns that the pension system may cease being a source of aggregate saving when the baby boomers start to retire in large numbers, suggests pensions con-stitute an extremely important component of saving. Any discussion of public policy towards pensions needs to emphasize their actual and potential role in raising the country's saving rate.

The first point to recall about national saving is that it is the sum of household saving, business saving, and government saving. If the primary problem for U.S. society is a shortfall in national saving, as we believe it is, then this must be kept in mind when considering alternative ways to reduce the federal government deficit. People instinctively know that large government deficits are bad economic policy, but they probably don't know precisely why. We feel the answer is government deficits absorb private-sector saving and are a large factor in inadequate national saving. Accepting that implies that all ways of reducing government deficits are not equally desirable. Clearly deficit reduction necessarily means raising taxes or reducing expenditures—possibly including reducing the hybrid "tax expenditures." However, reducing government deficits by discourag-ing pension saving seems counterproductive if the real goal is to increase national saving. It does make sense to look for ways to lower the deficit while at the same time encouraging, or at least not discouraging, private saving. Looked at in this light, consumption-oriented tax increases should be examined—such as energy taxes or a value-added tax—and those that further discourage private-sector saving should be avoided.

Changing pension regulations could help in a focused set of initiatives to improve the saving rate in our society. We can discern two motivations for regulating pensions. The first type of regulation attempts to assure the legitimacy of employer promises regarding pension benefits and to protect the interests of workers and the government, which is an interested party because of the PBGC, if for no other reason. This type of regulation and legislation has a long history, perhaps culminating in ERISA's passage in 1974. At least in theory, we endorse this type of government involvement in this market. The second type of legislation and regulation seems intended to ensure firms and people do not save too much in pension vehicles or, at least, do not erode the tax base too much. In this area, we think people have lost sight of the ultimate goal.

If increasing national saving is a top priority for the economy, which we believe it is, then one has to be skeptical about the wisdom of forcing people to save less in the drive to reduce deficits. The switch in the methodology for determining defined-benefit plans' funding status that was part of the 1987 budget package and had the effect of prohibiting 40%–50% of plans from making contributions is an example of this type of misguided policy. We believe few workers likely increased their personal savings to offset OBRA87's net effects, which were to slow down employer contributions to pension plans and possibly jeopardize the long-term security of the promises being held out to workers. If an increase in personal savings did not match the slowdown in savings through the defined-benefit pension system, the slowdown had the net effect of reducing our net saving rate during the younger years of the baby boomers' working career. In this case, we strongly suspect the marginal reductions in the deficit that flowed through the lower deductions of pension contributions by business generated no more than $0.34 in deficit reduction for each $1.00 reduction in national saving. This is no way to increase national saving in the short term.

In the long term, increased pension savings during the latter part of the baby boomers' careers will possibly offset the reductions in pension saving during the early part of their careers. We think it equally likely that many defined-benefit pension plans will be curtailed as higher costs of delayed saving pressure employers to make up for the earlier period when contributions were reduced. If this occurs, and we think it will in many cases, the short-term loss in saving flowing out of OBRA87 might never be made up.

One could also argue the cost of complying with the multitude of pension regulations of both types, particularly for defined-benefit plans, has discouraged such plans and thereby reduced private and national saving. Even the desirable type of regulation, if carried to excess, could have social disadvantages if the net result is a reduction in the number of people participating in the pension system.

We advocate a thorough simplification of pension regulation with the goal of increasing pension coverage and security. Small employers should have access to a streamlined and inexpensive plan to allow them to initiate plans without undue administrative expenses. We also advocate lifting most restrictions on the amounts of participants' and firms' contributions to pension plans. Although some limits on these amounts may be necessary, current restrictions seem excessive and socially counterproductive. In particular, we advocate substantial increases in the dollar ceilings on deductible amounts that can be contributed to 401(k) accounts, IRAs, and ordinary defined-contribution plans. We would once again allow firms to use the present value of projected benefits to determine their plan's funding status, which would allow firms to increase their contribution levels. We would similarly increase the level of pension benefits which could be paid out in retirement without a tax penalty. However, consistent with our prosaving bent, we would seriously consider increasing the restrictions and penalties for withdrawal of pension money before retirement. The goal of public policy in this area should be clear: the encouragement of long-term retirement saving through the pension system.

Expanding Access to Effective Retirement Savings Plans

One problem with current employer-based retirement programs is that many workers do not have access to them. Those employed by firms not sponsoring a retirement plan can make annual tax-deductible contributions of $2,000 to an IRA, but that is not a reasonable substitute for access to an employer-sponsored plan, even a 401(k) where the employer puts no money into the plan at all. For several years, tax regulations have allowed small employers, among whom the lack of retirement plan coverage is concentrated, to set up simplified employer plans (SEPs), but actual progress in expanding coverage in this arena has been extremely limited.

Given that participation rates average more than 50% in 401(k) plans where the employer provides no matching incentive for workers to participate, we believe it is vitally important more workers be given the opportunity to take advantage of these kinds of plans. One reason more employers do not offer 401(k) plans is the complexity of the discrimination test mandated to assure non—highly compensated workers benefit in proportion to those highly compensated. It is time we simplified tests and minimized administrative requirements to make these plans virtually universally available. In the case of owners of businesses and their immediate family members involved in the business, it may make sense to continue some sort of simplified tests, but the dollar contribution limits should keep other employees from taking unfair advantage of these plans. Tax filers who have no business income in a tax year (i.e., their work-related income is all wages) should be able to contribute an amount equal to the 401(k) limit to an IRA if their employer does not sponsor a retirement plan in which they can participate.

Penalizing individual workers under the federal tax code because their employer does not offer a retirement program seems increasingly short-sighted in light of the pressures our retirement income security system will face shortly after the turn of the century. Undoubtedly, some low-wage workers would still not take advantage of an expanded array of tax incentives encouraging private retirement saving. In the long-term, however, saving a share of an inadequate wage will never be a successful retirement income security device, and we ought to worry a great deal less about nonparticipation in employer-sponsored retirement plans at the lowest wage levels than we seem to today. Low wages at any given point merely reflect a temporary situation for many workers. For such workers, access to meaningful retirement saving programs during the successful higher-wage portions of their careers will be as important as it is to individuals currently earning higher wages. Workers who spend a whole career in low-wage positions must be able to rely on other aspects of the retirement system than personal or employer-based saving to provide adequate retirement income. The laws of arithmetic simply will not allow such workers to accrue adequate retirement benefits through employer-based plans, and we ought to quit expecting things from these plans that they cannot possibly deliver to the detriment of what they would be delivering more widely if permitted.

Public Policy toward the PBGC

In chapter 4, Carolyn Weaver was quite explicit about public policy recommendations on guaranteeing pension benefits, and we merely repeat and endorse them here. Recall that the basic problems with the government-run PBGC insurance system are the classic insurance problems of adverse selection and moral hazard. The current program attempts to be self-funded through premiums charged to the providers of defined-benefit pension plans. A major problem is premiums have never been appropriately priced to generate sufficient assets to cover the program's expected liabilities. Premiums have also never been sufficiently differentiated to reflect the widely varying risk of default inherent in different plans. For instance, even today the premium imposed on a sponsor is independent of the type of asset in which the firm invests its reserves. As a result, firms have a strong incentive to invest in the riskiest assets. Similarly, premiums still do not vary sufficiently with the plan's funding status, with the result that healthy, well-funded and safely invested plans and future plans subsidize underfunded plans of weakly capitalized companies whose pension assets are invested in risky securities.

Such cross-subsidization schemes cannot work on a large scale because firms are free to opt out of the system altogether and stop offering defined-benefit pensions. Similarly, firms just starting a pension plan, which can choose to join a pension insurance scheme with a large net liability from past operations or to stay out of the system by offering a traditional defined-contribution plan or a 401(k) plan, naturally have incentives either to offer no plan at all or to select a defined-contribution plan where the workers bear all the investment risk and responsibility. This, of course, is precisely what has happened with the rather sharp change in the popularity of the two main types of pensions. As this shift continues, the pool of remaining defined-benefit plans may get weaker and weaker, requiring higher and higher premium rates, and ultimately a government bailout.

The PBGC situation has no simple and elegant solution. We have let a situation develop where the group insurance plan for defined-benefit providers, and that is what PBGC really is, has a significant negative net worth. Few rational agents will join such a "club." Those who don't benefit from membership, those whose plans are relatively healthy and safely invested, have a strong incentive to get out. Weaver suggests the taxpayers, in the form of the U.S. Treasury, will have to closely regulate and probably directly subsidize the pension insurance of the weakest and most underfunded plans. She suggests an explicit transfer from the taxpayers to these companies' workers and stockholders. Further, she suggests the rest of the defined-benefit providers be allowed out of the system entirely and required instead to purchase benefit insurance from private and regulated providers, who presumably would carefully assess the riskiness of the liabilities they insure. The argument in favor of these policies is pragmatic: The current system, based on firms with sound plans subsidizing those with weak ones, is simply not viable and threatens to drive defined-benefit pensions into extinction. The only way to deal with this system is to allow healthy firms to buy competitively priced insurance, which Weaver suggests the private insurance market can handle, and to have taxpayers finance the transfer to the weak plans. The hope is that gradually the government could get out of the pension insurance business entirely and turn it over to the private sector. Theoretically, her plan would also work with the government providing the fairly priced insurance for the currently healthy plans, but Weaver obviously has more confidence in the private sector's ability to run such an insurance market.

Funding Public Pension Plans

We believe many of the same concerns about funding and security of employer-based retirement programs in the private sector apply as well in the public arena. Students of public pensions sometimes argue that a significant difference between public- and private-sector employers is the former's power to tax whereas the latter must depend on market forces to stay in business. Theoretically, the ability to tax provides a higher level of security that a public sponsor of a retirement program will be around to pay future pension promises than a private sponsor whose future ability to meet unfunded retirement promises depends on consumers' future tastes and other competitive considerations. We find this argument flawed in two regards.

One problem in not funding public pension obligations as they accrue is the cost of government is transferred from one budgeting period to another. This means the people who benefit from the government services when delivered can transfer some of the cost of those services to future generations of taxpayers. Where individuals can move from a jurisdiction between when services are rendered and when paid for, the failure to fund public pensions can also transfer the cost of government services within generations of taxpayers. This becomes a more serious problem the smaller the level of government, as pointed out in the case of the pension funding for the District of Columbia government workers in chapter 1.

The second problem with the failure to fund public pensions relates to the limits on government power to tax. We have seen a number of tax protests by the general electorate in recent years. Indeed, at the federal government level, the public perception that federal income tax claims were too high largely drove the tax reductions during the 1980s that have led to the unprecedented peacetime deficits experienced in recent years. Despite the strong desire to keep federal tax rates low, we believe most people fundamentally understand that general economic forces will require our federal budget be brought into closer fiscal balance than it has been in recent years. The recent debate over the balanced budget amendment and its apparent appeal to so many voters suggests future expenditure levels might be more tightly governed by taxpayers' willingness to support government programs than they have been over the last decade or so. Benefit promises in unfunded public pension systems are vulnerable to reduction in this environment. For those benefit promises to be kept, they will have to compete with other things the public wants to accomplish through government while limiting total government expenditures.

Given that government employers sometimes appear to pay lower cash wages to workers because of the relatively generous retirement programs they sponsor, some public-sector workers could be doubly exposed if their retirement plan is both generous and unfunded. It makes no more sense to us that public-sector workers should be more exposed to the prospect of their employers' unexpectedly failing to pay accrued benefits than private-sector workers are. On this basis we conclude that public-sector plans should all be subject to the same kind of funding, disclosure, and prohibited-transaction investment requirements as private-sector plans. Adopting these policies at all levels of government would make explicit the costs of government operations as they are being undertaken and would also insulate accrued pension promises from retroactive reductions by government administrators and legislators forced to balance current operating budgets against public intolerance of high tax rates.

Social Security in the Future

Historically, Social Security policy attempted to balance the countervailing goals of adequacy and equity through its financing and benefit structure. Balancing these goals was relatively easy to accomplish in the program's early days when almost everyone received more back from the program, in economic terms, than they put into it. We are now at the end of the start-up period where economic returns for all participants will exceed their investment, and the outlook suggests that future returns from the program will be below current-law expectations for many if not most workers. The demographics of the baby boom generation and the comparatively small size of the generation behind it are exacerbating the problem of Social Security's potential inability to provide fair economic returns. Within this context, a natural conflict arises between the adequacy and equity goals of Social Security as it is currently structured. Meeting the adequacy goal requires a certain amount of redistribution within the program because of low-wage workers' inability to accumulate sufficient retirement claims to meet minimal standards of need on the basis of strictly proportional retirement benefit formulas. At the same time, a redistributional program cannot provide a fair economic return to all its participants in an environment where it pays only a fair return on average. The problem becomes more severe where the program cannot provide even a fair return on average, a problem the baby boom generation may face because the generation of workers behind it may be too small to bear the burden of the benefits current law implies.

We believe the concepts of retirement adequacy and equity need to be considered in a larger context than Social Security's current financing and benefit structure. Participants in Social Security also participate in a host of other retirement plan and saving endeavors that need to be considered within this larger context. We believe that this larger context clarifies some general Social Security policy directions.

First of all, higher-wage workers clearly have a greater likelihood of receiving tax-preferred benefits from employer-sponsored retirement programs, and their benefits are much larger than those of low-wage workers. In this regard, the tax benefits that accrue to high-wage workers' pension savings ameliorate their "investment" in Social Security's social adequacy structure and the equity problems that arise because of their potential negative rates of return from the program. From the larger perspective of total federal tax policy, higher-wage workers' low returns on Social Security contributions are not as large a problem as a singular focus on that program alone suggests. Were we to offer workers the opportunity to save even more than currently through tax-preferred retirement plans, we could dampen the negative implications of Social Security benefit reductions, at least for those participating in the expanded saving opportunities afforded them.

The analysis of the implications of potential across-the-board reductions in Social Security benefits on workers at different income levels suggests that lower-wage workers are at much greater risk of experiencing significant reductions in their retirement standard of living than higher-wage workers. This leads us to conclude that policymakers should seriously consider moves to a flatter Social Security benefit structure than the current one. This will exacerbate the problem of low economic returns for higher-wage individuals under the program, and the broad middle class may strenuously resist such a modification unless alternative saving incentives are made available to them as we have recommended.

Some policymakers understandably concerned about the elderly's income security might conclude that the superior track in solving Social Security's financing shortfalls for the baby boom generation is to legislate higher taxes. Our analysis of merely raising taxes, however, suggests that such tax increases will not protect the higher standards of living current Social Security benefit projections for baby boomers would seem to imply. Raising taxes will lower the standard of living of workers who have to pay them, carrying through to their retirement standard of living in a world where workers adjust their saving and consumption behavior in response to the new tax expense. Indeed, one of the disconcerting results of the comparative analyses of policy options is that Social Security solutions that rely heavily on tax increases portend further declines in our national saving rates, especially in relation to options that would use benefit modifications to achieve a renewed balance in the program.

In addition to the goals of adequacy and equity, a challenge for policymakers to balance, we believe two additional goals for Social Security policy will become as important as these traditional ones: assuring the ongoing solvency of the Social Security system and maintaining broad public support for it. The current policy structure and the annual actuarial valuations that show the system is 40% out of balance cannot be expected to build public confidence in the system. The common observation by younger workers today that they do not expect to benefit from Social Security should hardly be surprising in light of the Social Security actuaries' own assessment of the program and the ongoing deterioration of that assessment over the past decade.

If we cannot restore younger workers' belief that they will ultimately receive some benefit from Social Security, they will begin to view their contributions to the program as pure taxation. If that occurs, the willingness to support current tax rates, much less higher ones, could wane quickly. In the long term, support for Social Security has to depend on the widely held belief that it is a viable entity. In rebalancing Social Security's goals for the future, it is crucial we attempt to address the structural issues that have continually driven it out of balance since the early 1970s.

Optimal Timing for Policy Changes

For a while longer we may continue to delude ourselves that we have no retirement saving crisis. In many regards the standards of living we have achieved today exceed those of every generation before us. Poverty rates among the elderly in this country are significantly below those of the period before Social Security matured or ERISA's implications were felt. Yet we know every facet of our retirement system will face unprecedented challenges when the baby boom cohorts begin their transition from work to retirement. We could continue to ignore the warning signs for as much as another decade and still not notice the implications of our relative complacency to the pending challenges to the retirement system. Even in 2010, Social Security's income is expected to exceed its expenditures under current law, according to actuarial projections. The problem is that things are expected to deteriorate very rapidly after that.

None of the baby boom generation, not even its oldest members, can expect to get through retirement without facing fairly significant changes to the income security system. If baby boomers are to be able to adjust their lives in anticipation of the changes they will face, the sooner we present what their realistic expectations are, the more likely their success in meeting their retirement needs. A worker who can adjust his or her saving level 20 years prior to retirement to account for a future reduction in Social Security will have to make only about half the adjustment a worker only 10 years from retirement would have to make. To delay changes we know must be made to our retirement programs will simply magnify the ultimate adjustments workers must make in response to those changes. Such delays would be patently unfair to those affected, in addition to being bad economic policy.

Index